C. R. Boxer

The Dutch
Seaborne Empire
1600–1800

Penguin Books
by arrangement with
Hutchinson of London

PENGUIN BOOKS

Published by the Penguin Group
Penguin Books Ltd, 27 Wrights Lane, London W8 5TZ, England
Penguin Books USA Inc., 375 Hudson Street, New York, New York 10014, USA
Penguin Books Australia Ltd, Ringwood, Victoria, Australia
Penguin Books Canada Ltd, 10 Alcorn Avenue, Toronto, Ontario, Canada M4V 3B2
Penguin Books (NZ) Ltd, 182–190 Wairau Road, Auckland 10, New Zealand

Penguin Books Ltd, Registered Offices: Harmondsworth, Middlesex, England

First published by Hutchinson 1965
Published in Pelican Books 1973
Reprinted in Penguin Books 1990
10 9 8 7 6 5 4 3

Copyright © C. R. Boxer, 1965
Introduction copyright © J. H. Plumb, 1965

Printed in England by Clays Ltd, St Ives plc
Set in Linotype Juliana

Contents

List of Plates

List of plates

List of Maps

Abbreviations

AGN	Algemene Geschiedenis der Nederlanden
BGN	Bijdragen voor de Geschiedenis der Nederlanden
BMHGU	Bijdragen en Mededelingen van het Historisch Genootschap gevestigd te Utrecht
BTLVNI	Bijdragen tot de Taal-land-en Volkenkunde van Nederlandsch Indië
EIC	English East India Company
Knuttel	Catalogus van de pamfletten-verzameling berustende in de Koninklijke Bibliotheek, by W. P. C. Knuttel
LV	Linschoten Vereeniging
MM	The Mariner's Mirror. Journal of the Society for Nautical Research
TG	Tijdschrift voor Geschiedenis
VOC	Dutch East India Company
WIC	Dutch West India Company

Acknowledgements

While this book has been written mainly from the resources of my own library, and I am solely responsible for the opinions expressed, I am indebted to several colleagues and institutions for help in various ways. The late Professor G. J. Renier and his successor in the Chair of Dutch History and Institutions at London University, Professor E. H. Kossmann, whose respective seminars have been so enlightening to all who have had the good fortune to attend them; the librarians of Utrecht University and of the Nederlandsch Historisch Scheepvaart Museum at Amsterdam, for sending me on loan Dutch books which I could not get in this country; Dr Johan de Vries for presenting me with a copy of his indispensable and virtually unprocurable work on the economic decline of the Dutch Republic; Dr Assis Chateaubriand, former Brazilian ambassador at the Court of St James's, Senhor Walter Pretyman, and the Sociedade de Estudos Historicos Dom Pedro II; the Trustees of the British Museum for permission to reproduce the maps, drawings and prints in PLATES 2, 11, 13, 16; the Director of the Rijksmuseum, Amsterdam, for permission to reproduce the paintings and engravings in PLATES 6, 8, 9; the director of the Nederlandsch Historisch Scheepvaart Museum for permission to reproduce the material illustrated in PLATES 1 and 3 (from the original painting in the Kweekschool voor de Zeevaart, Amsterdam); the Director of the Castle Museum, Cape Town, for the photograph of the painting reproduced in PLATE 4; the Director of the Boymans-Van Beuningen Museum for permission to reproduce the portrait in PLATE 5; the Director of the Mauritschuis at The Hague for permission to reproduce the painting illustrated in PLATE 15; Dr J. H. Plumb for his constructive criticism and helpful suggestions. But above all I am indebted to the late Captain J. C. M. Warnsinck and the late Rear-Admiral S. P. L'Honoré Naber, both of the Royal Netherlands Navy, who first guided my course in the wake of the 17th-century Dutch navigators and seamen they knew so well.

C.R.B.

London University, King's College

Introduction

By J. H. Plumb

1

Over the last fifty to a hundred years, man's belief that the historical process proved that he was acquiring a greater mastery over nature has received a brutal buffeting. In his early youth H. G. Wells, a man of vast creative energy, of rich delight in the human spirit, and of all-pervading optimism, viewed the future with confidence; science, born of reason, was to be humanity's panacea. When, in the years of his maturity, he came to write his *Outline of History*, his vision was darker, although still sustained with hope. World War I, with its senseless and stupid slaughter of millions of men, brought the sickening realization that man was capable of provoking human catastrophes on a global scale. The loss of human liberty, the degradations and brutalities imposed by fascism and communism during the 20s and 30s, followed in 1939 by the renewed world struggle, these events finally shattered Wells's eupeptic vision, and in sad and disillusioned old-age he wrote *Mind at the End of its Tether*. His hope of mankind had almost vanished. Almost, but not quite: for Wells's lifetime witnessed what, as a young writer, he had prophesied – technical invention not only on a prodigious scale but in those realms of human activity that affected the very core of society. And this extraordinary capacity of man to probe the complexities of nature and to invent machinery capable of exploiting his knowledge remained for Wells the only basis for hope, no matter how slender that might be.

If the belief of a man of Wells's passionate and intelligent humanism could be so battered and undermined, it is not surprising that lesser men were unable to withstand the climate of despair that engulfed the Western World, between the two World Wars. The disillusion of these years is apparent in painting, in music, in literature – everywhere in the Western World we are brought up sharply by an expression of anguish, by the flight from social and historical reality into a frightened, self-absorbed world of personal feeling and expression. Intellectual life, outside science, has pursued much the same course as artistic life, although it has shown greater ingenuity and a tougher-minded quality. Theology, philosophy and sociology have tended to reduce themselves to technical problems of exceptional professional complexity, but of small social importance. Their practitioners have largely ceased to instruct and enliven, let alone sustain the confidence of ordinary men and women.

In this atmosphere of cultural decay and of professional retreat, history and its philosophy have suffered. As in so many intellectual disciplines its professional workers have resolutely narrowed the focus of their interests to even more specialized fields of inquiry. The majority of historians have withdrawn from general culture in order to maintain, at a high intellectual level, an academic discipline. They have left the meaning and purpose of history to trained philosophers and spent their leisure hours tearing to shreds the scholarship of anyone foolish enough to attempt to give the story of mankind a meaning and a purpose: writers, as diverse as H. G. Wells and Arnold Toynbee, have been butchered with consummate skill. The blunders of scholarship and the errors of interpretation have counted everything; intention nothing. Few academic historians, secure in the cultivation of their minute gardens, have felt any humility towards those who would tame the wilderness. In consequence, an atmosphere of anarchic confusion pervades the attitude of Western man to his past.

A hundred years ago, in the first flood of archaeological discovery, scholars possessed greater confidence: the history of mankind seemed to most to point to an obvious law of human progress. The past was but a stepping-stone to the future. First adumbrated by the philosophers of the late Renaissance – Bodin in France and Bacon in England – the idea of progress became an article of common faith during the Enlightenment. And progress came to mean not only the technical progress that had preoccupied Bacon but also moral progress. By the 19th century the history of man demonstrated for many an improvement in the very nature of man himself as well as in his tools and weapons. Such optimism, such faith in man's capacity for rational behaviour, was shaken both by discoveries in science and in history as well as by events. By the middle of the 20th century man's irrational drives appeared to be stronger than his intellectual capacities. Freud and Marx laid bare the hollow hypocrisy of so-called rational behaviour either in individuals or in society. Also, the rise and fall of civilizations, laid bare by the spade, seemed to point to a cyclical pattern in human destiny which made nonsense of any idea of continuous progress; and this naturally attracted the prophets of Western doom. Yet more persuasive still, and, perhaps, more destructive of confidence in human destiny, was the utter loss of all sense of human control brought about by global wars and violent revolutions. Only those men or societies who felt life was going their way, the revolutionaries and, above all, the Marxists, believed any longer in the laws of historical progress. For the rest, retrogression seemed as tenable a thesis as progress.

This disillusion in the West suited academic historians. It relieved them of their most difficult problems. If they happened to be religious they were content to leave the ultimate meaning of history to God; if they were rationalists, they took refuge either in the need for more historical knowledge or in the philosophic difficulties of a subject that by its very nature was devoid of the same objective treatment that gave such authority to scientific inquiry. In the main they concentrated upon their professional work. And this was an exceptionally important and necessary task. What the common reader rarely recognizes is the inadequacy of the factual material that was at the command of an historian one hundred years ago or even fifty years ago. Scarcely any archives were open to him; most repositories of records were unsorted and uncatalogued; almost every generalization about a man or an event or an historical process was three-quarters guesswork, if not more. Laboriously, millions of facts have been brought to light, ordered and rendered coherent within their own context. Specialization has proliferated like a cancer, making detail livid, but blurring the outlines of the story of mankind, and rendering it almost impossible for a professional historian to venture with confidence beyond his immediate province. And that can be very tiny – the Arkansas and Missouri Railway Strike of 1921; the place-names of Rutland: 17th-century Rouen; the oral history of the Barotse; the philosophy of Hincmar of Rheims. And so it becomes ever more difficult for the professional historian to reach across to ordinary intelligent men and women or make his subject a part of human culture. The historical landscape is blurred by the ceaseless activity of its millions of professional ants. Of course, attempts at synthesis have to be made. The need to train young professional historians, or the need to impart some knowledge of history to students of other disciplines, has brought about competent digests of lengthy periods that summarize both facts and analysis. Occasionally such books have been written with such skill and wisdom that they have become a part of the West's cultural heritage. A few historians, driven by money or fame or creative need, have tried to share their knowledge and understanding of the past with the public at large.

But the gap between professional knowledge and history for the masses gets steadily wider: professional history becomes more accurate, more profound, whilst public history remains tentative and shallow.

This series is an attempt to reverse this process. Each volume will be written by a professional historian of the highest technical competence; but these books will not exist *in vacuo*, for the series is designed to have a unity and a purpose. But, perhaps, first it is best to say what it is not.

It is not a work of reference: there are no potted biographies of the Pharaohs, the Emperors of China or the Popes; no date lists of battles; no brief histories of painting, literature, music. Nor is this series a Universal History. All events that were critical in the history of mankind may not necessarily find a place. Some will; some will not. Works of reference, more or less factually accurate, exist in plenty and need not be repeated. It is not my intention to add yet another large compilation to what exists. Nor is this a 'philosophic' history. It does not pretend to reveal a recurring pattern in history that will unveil its purpose. Fundamentally philosophy, except in the use of language, is as irrelevant to history as it is to science. And lastly this series will not cover all human societies. There will be two volumes devoted to Russia, none to Germany. There will be histories of China and Japan but not of Indonesia. The Jews have a volume to themselves, the Parsees do not. And so on. Yet this series is called *The History of Human Society* for very good reasons. This history has a theme and a position in time.

The theme is the most obvious and the most neglected; obvious because everyone is aware of it from the solitary villagers of Easter Island to the teeming cities of the Western World; neglected because it has been fashionable for professional and Western historians to concern themselves either with detailed professional history that cannot have a broad theme or with the spiritual and metaphysical aspects of man's destiny that are not his proper province. What, therefore, is the theme of *The History of Human Society*? It is this: that the condition of man now is superior to what it was. That two great revolutions – the neolithic and the industrial – have enabled men to establish vast societies of exceptional complexity in which the material wellbeing of generations of mankind has made remarkable advances; that the second, and most important, revolution has been achieved by the Western World; that we are witnessing its most intensive phase now, one in which ancient patterns of living are crumbling before the demands of industrial society; that life in the suburbs of London, Lagos, Jakarta, Rio de Janeiro and Vladivostok will soon have more in common than they have in difference: that this, therefore, is a moment to take stock, to unfold how this came about, to evoke the societies of the past whilst we are still close enough to many of them to feel intuitively the compulsion and needs of their patterns of living. I, however, hope, in these introductions, which it is my intention to write for each book, to provide a sense of unity. The authors themselves will not be so concerned with the over-riding theme. Their aim will be to reconstruct the societies on which they are experts. They will lay bare the structure of their societies – their economic basis, their social organizations, their aspirations, their cultures, their religions and their conflicts. At the same time they will give a sense of what it was like to have lived in them. Each book will be an authoritative statement in its own right, and independent of the rest of the series. Yet each, set alongside the rest, will give a sense of how human society has changed and grown from the time man hunted and gathered his food to this nuclear and electronic age. This could only have been achieved by the most careful selection of authors. They needed, of course, to be established scholars of distinction, possessing the ability to write attractively for the general reader. They needed also to be wise, to possess steady, unflickering compassion for the strange necessities of men; to be quick in understanding, slow in judgement, and to have in them some of that relish for life, as fierce and as instinctive as an animal's, that has upheld ordinary men and women in the worst of times. The authors of these books are heart-wise historians with sensible, level heads.

The range and variety of human societies is almost as great as the range and variety of human temperaments, and the selection for this series is in some ways as personal as an anthology. A Chinaman, a Russian, an Indian or an African would select a different series; but we are Western men writing for Western men. The westernization of the world by industrial technology is one of the main themes of the series. Each society selected has been in the main stream of this development or belongs to that vast primitive ocean from whence all history is derived. Some societies are neglected because they would only illustrate in a duller way societies which appear in the series; some because their history is not well enough known to a sufficient depth of scholarship to be synthesized in this way; some because they are too insignificant.

There are, of course, very important social forces – feudalism, technological change or religion, for example – which have moulded a variety of human societies at the same time. Much can be learnt from the comparative study of their influence. I have, however, rejected this approach, once recorded history is reached. My reason for rejecting this method is because human beings experience these forces in communities, and it is the experience of men in society with which this series is primarily concerned.

Lastly, it need hardly be said that society is not always synonymous with the state. At times, as with the Jews, it lacks even territorial stability; yet the Jews provide a fascinating study of symbiotic social groupings, and to have left them out would be unthinkable, for they represent, in its best known form, a wide human experience – a social group embedded in an alien society.

As well as a theme, which is the growth of man's control over his environment, this series may also fulfil a need. That is to restore a little confidence in man's capacity not only to endure the frequent catastrophes of human existence but also in his intellectual abilities. That many of his habits, both of mind and heart, are bestial, needs scarcely to be said. His continuing capacity for evil need not be stressed. His greed remains almost as strong as it was when he first shuffled on the ground. And yet the miracles created by his cunning are so much a part of our daily lives that we take their wonder for granted. Man's ingenuity – based securely on his capacity to reason — has won astonishing victories over the physical world – and in an amazingly brief span of time. Such triumphs, so frequently overlooked and even more frequently belittled, should breed a cautious optimism. Sooner or later, painfully perhaps and slowly, the same intellectual skill may be directed to the more difficult and intransigent problems of human living – man's social and personal relations – not only directed, but perhaps accepted, as the proper way of ordering human life. The story of man's progress over the centuries, studded with pitfalls and streaked with disaster as it is, ought to strengthen both hope and will.

Yet a note of warning must be sounded. The history of human society, when viewed in detail, is far more often darkened with tragedy than it is lightened with hope. As these books will show, life for the nameless millions of mankind who have already lived and died has been wretched, short, hungry and brutal. Few societies have secured peace; none stability for more than a few centuries; prosperity, until very recent times, was the lucky chance of a small minority. Consolations of gratified desire, the soothing narcotic of ritual, and the hope of future blessedness have often eased but rarely obliterated the misery which has been the lot of all but a handful of men since the beginning of his history. At long last that handful is growing to a significant proportion in a few favoured societies. But throughout human

history most men have derived pitifully little from their existence. A belief in human progress is not incompatible with a sharp
realization of the tragedy not only of the lives of individual men
but also of epochs, cultures and societies. Loss and defeat, too,
are themes of this series, as well as progress and hope.

2

One of the great shifts in world power and economic strength
took place between 1450 and 1700. Before that time Western
Europe had been of little consequence in the affairs of the world:
only during the first two centuries after the birth of Christ did it
seem likely that an empire, commensurate with that in China,
might develop, which would also embrace the Western lands. In
the political chaos that the fall of the Roman Empire brought
about, the future of Western Europe seemed indeed black. True,
its value as a source of primary produce made it of some consequence to the more sophisticated countries of the Mediterranean,
and its social structure, partially organized for war, gave it a
considerable potential for violence and expansion, a fact to which
the Crusades bore witness. A more eloquent testimony, perhaps,
is the long Hundred Years War between Britain and France that
demonstrated with equal clarity the self-destructive tendencies of
medieval Western Europe. Yet this capacity to organize war on a
quasi-national basis, which was such a marked feature of the later
Middle Ages, is a factor of considerable consequence for the rise
of Western Europe to a position of world dominion.

Never before, perhaps, had predominantly agrarian societies
been so highly militarized, and all governments had become
closely involved in the development of armament. At first, of
course, such involvement was tentative and haphazard, but the
momentum increased as wars grew more complex in men and
materials. Artillery and cannon-equipped navies, as well as the
defences they provoked, fortification of ports and strategic cities,
required not only the mobilization of greater financial and
technical resources by the state, which, in itself, bred far more
sophisticated administration than the Western World had previously known, but it also necessitated a closer control of its

human potential, either by vigorously enforced law or by ideological identification. Only when this process had taken place was a huge expansion on an imperial scale possible.

Of course, this is but one strand in the chaos of causes which led to the world revolution of the 16th and 17th centuries, but it is a vital one. European conquest of the world rested ultimately on the sanction of force. In the killing and the slaughter lay the decision. Yet the reasons that led to the combat were complex and varied – greed, religious zeal, curiosity, rivalry, even imitation of others; perhaps the sheer blind biological need of man to colonize the empty spaces, once a geographical barrier had been broken. In the overseas expansion of Spain, France and Great Britain, all of these factors, and many more, were closely entwined. Although not entirely absent from the Dutch empire, its expansion was more reminiscent of that of Venice in the early Middle Ages; for the commercial motive was always obvious and strident. The efficiency of Dutch expansion, however, depended not only on commercial appetite and naval power but also on the nature of Dutch society.

The United Provinces owed their origins to war: war had settled their boundaries, helped to create the social structure of their towns, and gave them much of their impetus to commercial expansion. The Revolt against Spanish rule, begun as much for traditional urban and class 'liberties' which men of the Middle Ages were so willing to fight for, rapidly acquired the air of a religious crusade. The most bitter anti-Spaniards were naturally enough the dedicated Calvinists who rapidly took charge of the northern Netherlands in order to intensify resistance. And they fought skilfully not only by force of arms but also by aggressive commercial expansion. They stopped the Scheldt when they could and monopolized the Baltic. As the war proceeded, they were joined by men of a like dedication from the south, particularly Antwerp, who were attracted by the quickening commercial life of Amsterdam as well as by the freedom to worship and the social opportunities open to men of their religion. So commerce became an instrument of survival, a branch of war, a magnet for men like-minded in religion, profession and social status. The founders of the Dutch West India Company were high Calvinists, bent on the destruction of Spanish power. During the first few decades of the Dutch Republic many of its commercial activities wore the air of a crusade. Indeed Mars was the midwife of the Dutch Republic. Above all it gave a rare opportunity to Amsterdam whose growth – physical, commercial, intellectual – seemed such a miracle to contemporaries. The religion of a minority and the commercial aggression of a few combined, together with intense urban patriotism, to create, through war, a state and a nation for which neither language, race, culture nor geography had made much provision.

Forged on the anvil of war, and a war of great brutality and seemingly endless length, the Dutch proved themselves superb realists. Although the aggressive Calvinist merchants had launched them on a war of conquest to control Brazil, this intransigent attitude quickly faded. Trade, not a crusade, became the Dutch motto, and trade with Roman Catholics became as good as any other. The destruction of Spain, the elimination of Roman Catholicism at home, even the re-conquest of the separated Southern Provinces, ceased to attract even the most ardent spirits. Security, freedom to trade, toleration so long as it led to stability, became the watchwords of the Dutch. Yet for most of the 17th century the Dutch were forced to fight, by their commercial rivals, first the British and then the French; and perhaps more of the gross national product of the Netherlands was consumed by war than in any other European state at that time: in terms of population, its armies and navies were very large; never large enough, however, to withstand its enemies without allies, yet very remarkable indeed for so small a country, and even more remarkable for a country where the state system was designed for inaction and inertia. In spite, however, of constant war and heavy taxes the Dutch never became a prey to mindless xenophobia. The absence of an uncritical passionate hysterical nationalism may have been due to the nature of the Dutch states system where loyalty was most natural to a city or a province rather than to a dynasty or a country.

In essence, as Professor Boxer shows, the United Provinces were a confederation of states and towns, all with jealously guarded rights and liberties, and a confederation in which the

House of Orange, the hereditary Statholders, played an equivocal part. Only because of its immense financial contribution could Amsterdam impose some sort of unified policy on the chaos of individual interests, and time steadily eroded Amsterdam's leadership. The 17th century witnessed an intensification of oligarchy throughout the Seven Provinces in towns great and small, and as soon as external danger passed, with the defeat of Louis XIV in the war of Spanish Succession, Dutch society lapsed contentedly into that inert, *bourgeois* self-enjoyment which had only been prevented in the 17th century by the external dangers which had threatened it. As a state the Netherlands never disentangled themselves from their medieval past. They never forged, as did their great commercial rivals, a highly centralized state system capable of quick, secret and decisive action. This is why so many Dutch historians have come to regard the rapid extension of Dutch power between 1580–1640 as a miracle. The miracle lies in the fact that in spite of intense rivalry between state and cities, and the constant obstacle of entrenched rights and privileges, the Dutch were able to mount great navies and armies and pay for them mainly out of taxation. And this was achieved largely through the dedication of the Calvinist oligarchies who possessed a strong and viable sense of their own destiny as a class and as a nation.

They stamped indelibly the *persona* of their class on Dutch society. Their cautious, prudent, self-satisfied, unostentatious faces stare out of the canvases of Rembrandt or Hals, giving little away of their unconscious drives, but speaking eloquently of the sobriety and dedication of their lives. The comely façades of their great houses along the Keizersgracht and Heerengracht of Amsterdam, dignified, restrained, so unemphatic in their elegance, bespeak the integrity of generations of *bourgeois* endeavour – that amalgam of hard work, calculated risk, guarded self-indulgence, all without panache or ostentation or flamboyance, which became the hallmarks of the Dutch character. Entwined in their guarded, almost secretive, lives was a self-righteous pride which brought them to identify themselves with the cities in which they lived generation after generation and which rewarded them with power and sinecures.

Such a society could easily have become graceless, hypocritical, gross; too lethargic for ambition, too self-indulgent for reform or change. Indeed, towards the end of the 18th century such a fate nearly overtook the Dutch. In the 17th century, these tendencies, although constantly strengthening, never became dominant, for the northern Netherlands lived too near the edge of disaster to succumb to total social paralysis. Time and time again they saved themselves from total defeat by courage and self-sacrifice, opening their dykes, as well as their purses, to withstand the French. As in Europe, so in the East and West Indies, their outposts, except in Java and the Moluccas, rarely possessed more than a tenuous hold. The Dutch grew accustomed to the whirligigs of fortune, and became attuned to the sense that their affluence was poised on the thinnest of ice. They lost their position in Formosa; and were kicked out of Brazil; the British threw them out of New York. And the ocean trade itself was a gamble: either huge profits or severe losses. In Dutch life in the early days of the Republic there is a hectic quality, a touch of fever, that bursts out in strange ways – in the fantastic mania for tulip bulbs, or the similar addiction which swept them for Chinese porcelain, and the frequent bursts of chronic speculation in the Amsterdam Bourse. In their politics, also, there remained a raucous, unresolved element that could and did lead to revolts that shook, even though they never completely toppled, the dominant oligarchies. The serenity of so much of Dutch art, the beauty and order of their cities are in some senses illusory, speaking of a stable world which the United Provinces scarcely knew during the first century of its existence. Uncertainty with its need for speculation – economic, political, religious and intellectual – remained a factor in Dutch life until the 17th century drew to a close : it may have been one which helped to strengthen the wide toleration which the northern Netherlands permitted in religious and political speculation, and so provided a refuge for Descartes, a home for Spinoza, and the vigorous stimulus necessary to make John Locke publish.

Dutch society was deeply involved in reality, more intensively, perhaps, than any other society of its time. Neither its Stadtholders nor its aristocracy projected any delusive images of feudal greatness, nor was it distracted by a panopolistic Church from its daily pursuit of profit and power. In contrast with England, its political problems and social divisions were never caught up in an imaginary sense of the past. The real world was the Dutch world. The precarious nature of its strategic situation as well as the nature of its economic activity bred a sense of actuality. This was intensified by the social problems created by a rapid growth of urban life, and by the concentration of a very large population in a tiny, difficult land, and the effective part of it, the land between the mouth of the Rhine and the southern shore of the Zuider Zee tinier still. By 17th-century standards it pullulated with people, creating problems of social organization – urban growth and welfare, transport and food supply that required an application of intelligence and an acute observation of problems that were quite novel, as indeed were many of the Dutch solutions. The neatness, order, cleanliness of their urban life and its physical sophistication entranced and amazed Europe. It fascinated particularly the English intellectuals Sir William Petty, John Locke and Sir William Temple, who were concerned with the practical problems of social living. Only Venice had achieved a comparable success – the cities of Lombardy and Tuscany which might have produced a *bourgeois* civilization of equal complexity, affluence, and good order had failed to do so. They had been unable to divest themselves of the relics of feudal control and their stability had been constantly threatened by civil war; also, their merchant-oligarchies had never succeeded in securing absolute control of government. Of course, as Professor Boxer points out, there was intolerable poverty in the United Provinces, both urban and rural, yet the standard of social affluence, as expressed in the amenities of civic life, were greater than any yet experienced in Europe. This, combined with their obvious riches, made them the object of both envy and admiration in all other countries of north-western Europe, and particularly of Britain.

The interconnections between art and society remain mysterious, yet there seems a certain inevitability about the fluorescence of Dutch art in the 17th century. The Netherlands possessed a long tradition of artistic achievement, as long almost as that of

Italy, and it was not the northern Netherlands alone that dominated the painting of this period and this region, for Rubens, Van Dyck and their followers brought a distinction to the Spanish Netherlands which their northern neighbours could not match in the early decades of the 17th century. Dutch art was more sombre, more deeply rooted in everyday reality, whether it be the old men and women of Rembrandt, worn by experience and broken by time, or the golden estuarine landscapes of Cuyp, or the mysteriously still yet expectant interiors of Vermeer. Yet by the 1680s Dutch art was hurrying towards a decline, and one should never forget how most Dutch artists were rejected by their own generation : Hals died in a poorhouse; Rembrandt went bankrupt; Steen supported himself as an innkeeper; and Vermeer had to pawn his pictures to get bread. In the 17th century aristocratic societies were far more confident in their artistic taste than the middle-class burghers of Amsterdam and Haarlem, and, as Professor Geyl rightly points out, 'France, whose armies had been arrested by the Water Line, saw its spirit overrun the field of art in the unvanquished land of Holland.'

The reverse was true of the pursuit of knowledge. Intellectual and philosophic speculation, so potentially inimical to absolutist governments, flourished in the freer air of the United Provinces, as they did in Britain. Not only did the Dutch provide refuge for great speculative philosophers and publicists such as Descartes, Peter Bayle, and for a time John Locke, but they also produced native scientists and thinkers – Spinoza, Huygens, Leeuwenhoek – of international stature. Good as Dutch science was, nothing was done to institutionalize it or to promote it. Although Louis XIV deplored many aspects of speculative philosophy he realized the potential value of science and created the *Academie de Sçavans* to promote it. The Dutch created no scientific academies, neither did the House of Orange. In spite of this lack of public support the contribution of the Dutch not only to science and philosophy but to ancillary disciplines – hydraulics, agriculture, geography, law, etc. – was quite staggering, in view of the total population. And science and philosophy were both stimulated by the great extension of human knowledge that the geographical discoveries brought about. The trans-ocean trade brought more than a profit: it made windows into the mind.

Rich and valuable as the trans-ocean trade was for the Dutch, stimulating as it was too to the mind and the imagination as well as to science and technology, nevertheless it would be rash to overvalue the part that it played in the Dutch miracle of the 17th century. And Professor Boxer brings us back time and time again to those other factors which also played their part – the rich Baltic trade which the Dutch dominated, and of course the vigorous European commerce borne on the great rivers that the Dutch controlled. And the very density of population stimulated both agriculture and industrial crafts, creating thereby a buoyant market amongst the thickening middle class. Had all the Netherlands been united the further stages of rapid economic progress, which was to develop in Britain, might have taken place earlier. Belgian steel and coal, the vital water power that was available in the Ardennes, could have provided the essential elements for an industrial revolution, but the Dutch lacked them. As it was, devoid of all heavy industry but shipbuilding, Dutch industry remained craft-based, and, as Dutch commercial expansion slowed, its economic development grew outwards into investment and export of capital, rather than forwards into industrial growth. The consequence was that Dutch society, after 1650, changed very slowly and its structural pattern acquired a remarkable stability. But a stable society proved a prosaic society, and after 1700 the Dutch contributed little to the civilization of Europe; and the startling beauty of its waterborne cities, so modern and so functional in the 17th century, acquired the patina of age. A country without a history began to live in the past.

I

The Eighty Years War and the evolution of a nation

On 10 June 1648, the Portuguese ambassador at The Hague, Francisco de Sousa Coutinho, wrote a dispatch to his royal master announcing that the Dutch had just celebrated the treaty of peace signed at Münster between their envoys and those of King Philip IV of Spain. 'The peace was proclaimed here,' he noted, 'simply by reading the articles of the Treaty in the Supreme Court of Justice at ten o'clock on the morning of the fifth of this month – that day and hour being chosen because on that day and at that time eighty years ago the Counts of Egmont and Hoorn had been executed by the Duke of Alva in Brussels; and the Estates wished their freedom to begin at the same day and time as those two gentlemen had died in defence thereof.' Sousa Coutinho was clearly impressed by the sense of timing displayed by the rulers of the United Provinces of the Free Netherlands on this historic occasion, since he again stressed the deliberation with which they had chosen this date in a dispatch written five days later to his colleague at Paris. As a patriotic Portuguese, he had done his best to prevent the conclusion of this treaty, which now left Portugal's hereditary Spanish enemy with one hand free – the other being still engaged in fighting France – to deal with her; and he reported, correctly enough, that the Treaty of Münster was far from being universally welcomed by the inhabitants of the self-styled United Provinces. He concluded his second dispatch on a philosophical note, observing that 'God has ways to raise up and cast down men which they do not understand, and usually they turn out the opposite of the expected. Anyone who lives will see many changes and in a short time.'[1]

1. Francisco de Sousa Coutinho to the King of Portugal (The Hague, 10 June 1648) and to the Marquis of Niza (15 June 1648), *apud* E. Prestage, *Correspondência diplomática de Francisco de Sousa Coutinho durante a sua embaixada em Holanda, 1643–1650* (3 vols.,

Eighty years was not a short span as far as the expectation of human life went in those days. This was about thirty to thirty-two years in most European countries, and few of the youthful inhabitants of the Netherlands in June 1568 could have lived to see the day described by Sousa Coutinho. But no intelligent Netherlander or Spaniard living in 1648 would have denied that the previous eighty years had been times of unprecedented change and vicissitudes. In 1568 the Netherlands formed a complex congeries of states and towns, Flemish- and/or French-speaking, loosely federated in seventeen provinces under the sceptre of a Spanish Hapsburg king, whose dominions stretched from the Frisian Islands in the North Sea to the Philippines in the China Sea. Admittedly Lutheranism, Anabaptism, Calvinism, and other forms of Protestant heresy had made considerable inroads in the Netherlands, as evidenced by the *beeldenstorm* or iconoclastic riots of 1566, when churches were pillaged, images smashed, and priests maltreated. But the bulk of the population was still Roman Catholic, and the Protestants were scattered in minority groups throughout the whole country, being, if anything, less strongly represented in some of the northern provinces than in the southern. Alva had easily defeated (21 July 1568) the make-shift forces raised by William the Prince of Orange in a first attempt at armed resistance to Spanish rule and religious persecution There seemed to be no great chance that the dispirited and disorganized rebels could challenge Spain again without effective aid from England or France, and of that there was no sign. The Flemish and Walloon nobles who might be expected to provide the leadership of a

---

Coimbra & Lisboa, 1920–55), Vol. III, pp. 13. 23. Another contemporary, Lieuwe van Aitzema, implies that the coincidence was accidental rather than deliberate; *Saken van staet en oorlogh, in ende omtrent de Vereenigde Nederlanden, 1621–1668* (6 vols., The Hague, 1669–72), Vol. III, p. 272. It is perhaps worth pointing out that in either case the calculation did not take into account the ten days gained by the change from the Julian to the Gregorian calendar, which the States of Holland adopted in 1582. For the Treaty and its antecedents cf. J. Poelhekke, *De Vrede van Munster* (The Hague, 1948), and J. H. Kernkamp, *De economische artikelen inzake Europa van het Munsterse vredesverdrag* (Amsterdam, 1951).

successful revolt were either dead, in prison, in flight, or thoroughly cowed. Economically, Antwerp was the undisputed trading and banking centre of Europe north of the Alps and Pyrenees. Amsterdam, the leading city and shipping centre of the northern Netherlands, though increasingly prosperous through its carrying-trade with the Baltic, western France, and the Iberian peninsula, seemed unlikely to rival, let alone replace, Antwerp as the commercial lynch-pin of the Western World.

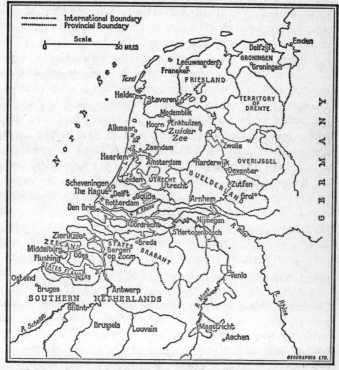

1 - The Dutch Republic in the second half of the 17th century

Eighty years later the picture had changed beyond recognition. The Seven United Provinces of the Free Netherlands were now sharply differentiated from their ten southern neighbours which had remained faithful to – or been reconquered by – the Spanish

Crown and the Roman Church. The seven northern provinces not only had secured complete independence but were the possessors of a maritime and commercial empire which surpassed that of the Portuguese and rivalled that of the Spaniards, extending as it did from the Spice Islands of Indonesia to the shores of the Caribbean. Instead of being ruled by a Hapsburg king, the Free Netherlands were governed by a burgher-oligarchy, whose first servant was a wealthy and influential Prince of Orange, grandson of the hunted fugitive of 1568, and married to an English royal princess. Calvinism had completely disappeared in the southern Netherlands – *Las Provincias Obedientes*, as the Spaniards called them – by 1648, along with all other forms of Protestanism. In the seven northern provinces Calvinism was the official and only fully accepted faith, although its orthodox adherents probably numbered less than one-third of the population. The motley levies whom Alva had crushed so easily in 1568 had been succeeded by a well-paid, well-led, and well-disciplined army which was regarded as second to none in Europe. The Dutch navy, which did not exist in 1568, had achieved the reputation of being the best in the Atlantic world by a series of victories culminating in M. H. Tromp's destruction of a Spanish Armada in The Downs (21 October 1639). Last, but by no means least, Amsterdam had not merely replaced Antwerp as the commercial capital of Europe but had achieved such a pinnacle of prosperity that its name was known in remote regions round the world that had never heard of London, Paris, and Venice. Whatever the inhabitants of some of the other provinces might think of the Treaty of Münster, the burgher-oligarchs of Holland had much to be satisfied with when they surveyed the fireworks, bonfires, and illuminations which they had ordered for the night of 5 June 1648. Nor was their satisfaction noticeably damped by the exceptionally wet summer which followed and which left the hay rotting in the fields. Domestic agriculture did not provide the principal sinews of their wealth.

Religious, military, and geographical factors all played their parts in contributing to the evolution of the Dutch nation during the Eighty Years War with the mightiest empire of the time. This struggle, apparently so unequal at the start, ended with the

Most Catholic King accepting terms virtually dictated by his upstart burgher adversaries. The greatest single reason for the Dutch success was the truly remarkable economic development of the two maritime provinces of Holland and Zeeland, the agricultural wealth of the remaining five provinces being of scant importance by comparison. More particularly, the sudden and dramatic upsurge of Dutch maritime trade from 1590 onwards provided something of a surprise for contemporaries and a puzzle for posterity. 'The prodigious increase of the Netherlands in their domestic and foreign trade, riches and multitude of shipping', wrote Sir Josiah Child in 1669, 'is the envy of the present and may be the wonder of future generations.'[2] How came it that two low-lying and relatively uninviting provinces by the North Sea formed the core of a confederation which became the principal seafaring nation of the world within the lifetime of a single generation?

Surprising as the spectacular rise of the Dutch maritime power seemed to many people both then and later, it grew from solid foundations which existed long before 1568. The basic reasons for the economic development of the two maritime provinces were explained clearly enough in a petition of the States of Holland to the Emperor Charles V, shortly after he had brought all the seventeen provinces of the Netherlands under his rule in 1543 – the culmination of a complicated process involving marriage-policy, accidents of fortune, and the occasional employment of force.

It is noticeably true that the province of Holland is a very small country, small in length and even smaller in breadth, and almost enclosed by the sea on three sides. It must be protected from the sea by reclamation works, which involve a heavy yearly expenditure for dykes, sluices, mill-races, windmills and polders. Moreover, the said province of Holland contains many dunes, bogs, and lakes which grow daily more extensive, as well as other barren districts, unfit for crops or pasture. Wherefore the inhabitants of the said country in order to make a living for their wives, children and families, must maintain themselves by handicrafts and trades, in such wise that

2. J. Child, *A New Discourse of Trade* (4th ed., London, n.d.). First published in 1694, this work was originally drafted in 1669, as Child states in the preface.

they fetch raw materials from foreign lands and re-export the finished products, including diverse sorts of cloth and draperies, to many places, such as the kingdoms of Spain, Portugal, Germany, Scotland, and especially to Denmark, the Baltic, Norway, and other like regions, whence they return with goods and merchandise from those parts, notably wheat and other grains. Consequently, the main business of the country must needs be in shipping and related trades, from which a great many people earn their living, like merchants, skippers, masters, pilots, sailors, shipwrights, and all those connected therewith. These men navigate, import and export all sorts of merchandise, hither and yon, and those goods that they bring here, they sell and vend in the Netherlands, as in Brabant, Flanders, and other neighbouring places.[3]

In other words, the merchants and mariners of Holland and Zeeland had a large, perhaps a preponderant, share of the seaborne carrying-trade between the Baltic and Western Europe by the middle of the 16th century and before the struggle with Spain had begun. The dairy and farming industries of the northern Netherlands were probably more important than the petitioners of 1548 were prepared to admit; but it was none the less true that the 'great fishery' of the North Sea and the carrying-trade with the Baltic, France, and the Iberian peninsula were of far greater importance. One reason for the growth of Dutch foreign trade was obviously the geographical position of the Lowlands by the North Sea, with their easy access to the markets of Germany, France, and England. But the main reason for the lead secured by the Dutch over their principal rivals, the Hanseatic towns, was that the Hollanders and Zeelanders worked their ships more thriftily and so were able to offer lower freight rates and to undersell their competitors.

A characteristic feature of seaborne trade – and of other forms of business for that matter – in the northern Netherlands was known as the *rederij*. This was a highly flexible type of co-operative enterprise by which a group of people would join together to buy, own, build, charter, or freight a ship and its cargo. Down

3. E. Luzac, *Hollands Rijkdom* (2 vols., Leiden, 1780), Vol. I, Bijlage A, pp. 5–6. The Emperor's rescript embodying the original representation is dated Mechelen (Malines), 13 October 1548.

to the second half of the 17th century the skipper or master of a vessel was very often the part-owner and directly interested in the sale of the cargo. The individual *reders* would contribute capital in varying proportions, and they might range from wealthy merchants on shore with substantial quotas to deck-hands with their mites. A writer of 1644 claimed that 'There is hardly a fishing-buss, a hulk, or a boat which is fitted out or put forth from this land without this being done by several persons in conjunction', and he claimed that not one ship in a hundred was operated other than by a *rederij*. In any event, this practice facilitated a widespread investment in shipping and a wide diffusion of ownership, integrating the mercantile and maritime communities to a great extent.

It was only natural that in a community of merchants and mariners, such as that described by their representatives in 1548, the political as well as the economic power would tend to gravitate into the hands of the merchant class, and more particularly the wealthier members thereof. These latter had secured control of the town or municipal councils during the autumn of the Middle Ages; and, so far as Holland and Zeeland were concerned, most of the town councillors were either shipowners themselves or directly interested in some branch or branches of the overseas trade – the grain and timber of the north, the wine, fruits, and salt of the south, or the herring fishery and fish-export industries. So much is obvious from the already quoted petition of the States of Holland to Charles V in 1548; and the growth in the power and influence of the town councils was accelerated rather than retarded by the war with Spain. This war was accompanied, save for relatively short intervals, by a steady increase in Dutch overseas trade, particularly after the year 1590. In turn, this seaborne trade gave the town councillors, and the so-called regent class from which they were drawn, greater economic and (as we shall see) greater political power.

Here again this development was much more marked in the maritime provinces of Holland and Zeeland than in the other provinces, where agriculture was relatively more important and where the rural nobility (as in Guelderland) and the richer farmers (as in Friesland) exercised more influence than the town councils.

In any event, the position of the town councils in all the provinces was much stronger with regard to the first Prince of Orange than it had been *vis-à-vis* the Dukes of Burgundy or the Kings of Spain. Despite three successive marriages with wealthy heiresses, William the Silent was merely a half-successful rebel, increasingly dependent on the towns' financial and moral support. It is true that when Holland and Zeeland recognised him in 1572 as their Stadtholder – a term originally denoting a medieval overlord's *locum tenens* – they thereby gave him a voice in the appointment of the members of the town council, who, in their turn, ultimately appointed him. But several of the towns which adhered to the revolt of the Netherlands after the capture of Den Briel by the semi-piratical Sea-Beggars in 1572 explicitly disclaimed giving him any such authority, though this was one of the Stadtholder's legal attributes.

The division of the low countries into a predominantly Protestant north and a wholly Romanist south was not a foregone conclusion but resulted from the interplay of various factors – geographical, military, religious, and economic – among which the town councils played an important role. William I of Orange fought for the freedom of the United Seventeen Provinces, and he (who had been by turns Lutheran, Romanist, and Calvinist) visualized a State in which Protestants and Roman Catholics could live on terms of mutual respect and equality, or at least of mutual toleration. But the hard core of his Calvinist supporters among the Sea-Beggars regarded such tolerance with contempt. These men were resolved to impose the supremacy of their particular brand of Protestanism by hook or by crook. Most of the towns which surrendered to them in the summer of 1572 did so on condition that the Roman Catholic inhabitants would not be molested and would be allowed the performance of their religion in their own churches. These conditions were systematically disregarded by the victors, who filled the town councils with their own nominees in places where the existing occupants showed any reluctance to forward Protestantism at the expense of Roman Catholicism. Having secured control of the town councils, they then drove out the Romanist clergy, and allowed only liberty of conscience to the Roman Catholic laity insteady of liberty of public worship.

8

The militant Protestant minority was able to act in this way partly because many wealthy Roman Catholic burghers were among the 4,000 or so people who fled from Holland alone during the troubled summer of 1572. Their places could be filled by Protestant burghers and merchants who had previously left the Netherlands when Cardinal Granvelle, the Holy Office of the Inquisition, and the Duke of Alva successively intensified the persecution of religious dissenters, and these exiles now returned with the Sea-Beggars. Although we have insufficient knowledge of the changes that occurred in the composition of all the town councils during the early years of the revolt against Spain, it seems safe to assume that most men of substance and property behaved as their likes have done in other revolutions before and since. That is to say, many of the wealthy burghers who elected the town councillors conformed to the new state of things lest worse befall. In order to retain their privileged position and business interests – to say nothing of the security of their wives and children – they accepted Protestantism with more or less good grace. As time went on and it became evident that the Dutch Republic had come to stay, they conformed more closely, at any rate outwardly, to official Calvinism. But they usually resisted, sometimes actively, more often passively, the efforts of the Calvinist zealots in general and of the *predikanten* or ministers in particular to subordinate the interests of the state – and of trade – to the tenets of the 'True Christian Reformed Religion'.

The problem of how far and how fast the population of the northern Netherlands abandoned the old faith for the new is a complex one, but we may briefly note that different kinds of pressure were brought by the ruling Calvinist minority to bear upon patricians and proletarians to induce them to accept the new order. Since all municipal and government offices were soon reserved for those who professed orthodox Calvinism, this alone was a great inducement for the urban regent class to conform. This tendency was accelerated by the politico-religious crisis of 1618–19, when Prince Maurice's *coup* against Oldenbarnevelt and the proceedings of the synod of Dordrecht combined to strengthen the influence of the Calvinist ministers and their lay sympathizers. By the time the Treaty of Münster was signed in

1648, the great majority of the regent class had become professing – if not always conspicuously active – Calvinists. At the other end of the social scale, all measures concerned with the supervision of charitable foundations and poor-relief were, after a greater or lesser time-lag, taken over by the Calvinist clergy and laymen after the expulsion of the Roman Catholic clergy and the confiscation of their convents, alms-houses and pious foundations. This induced many of the urban proletariat, particularly the unemployed and those who suffered (like sailors and fishermen) from seasonal unemployment, to conform to the new faith if only to get bread for themselves and their families. The teaching and curriculum of the elementary schools, many of which were housed in buildings confiscated from the Roman Catholic Church, were also placed under the supervision of convinced Calvinists. This measure necessarily increased the hold of the Reformed Religion upon successive rising generations among all classes.

The recent researches of Enno van Gelder and A. L. E. Verheyden regarding the social origins of the 12,302 victims condemned by the notorious 'Council of Blood' (*Conseil des Troubles*) in 1567–73, have shown that a remarkable cross-section of the population of the Netherlands was either passively or actively hostile to the Roman Church in the 1560s. Gentry, merchants, surgeons, lawyers, apothecaries, goldsmiths, carpenters, masons, shearmen, and men of many other trades and callings were all involved in large numbers. Although the majority of these were probably not Calvinists, it is likely that many of those who survived exile or imprisonment subsequently became so in the towns where the Sea-Beggars tried to implant the rule of God's Elect. Under the circumstances, the progress of Protestantism was inevitably more rapid in the towns than in the countryside, being particularly slow in the rural districts where the landed gentry remained loyal to the old faith and where the tenantry followed their example. The progress of the new faith in the northern Netherlands was thus a rather patchy affair. By the time of the Treaty of Münster, it is doubtful whether the Protestants of all persuasions had more than a bare majority over those of their countrymen who had remained faithful to or who had been reconciled with Rome.

Since the influence of the urban regent class was only fleetingly shaken by the outbreak of the rebellion against Spain, and since the regents were in fact able to consolidate their position as the ruling class during the Eighty Years War, it may be as well to consider in more detail their function and status, taking the province of Holland as the most important. The towns in this province had been administered, since the latter part of the Middle Ages, by councils composed of from twenty to forty of the 'richest and most honourable' citizens, originally elected from among 'the wise and the rich' burghers of each town. Their tenure of office was for life, or until they went to live elsewhere. Their colleagues then filled the resulting vacancies from among the burghers of their own social status. These town councillors or regents elected yearly from among themselves the burgomaster(s) and aldermen who formed the municipal government or 'magistracy', and whose principal duties were the administration of justice and of local taxation upon their fellow townsmen. Order was maintained by citizen militia companies or civic guards, not unlike the English train-bands, but they were officered, at any rate in the higher ranks, by members of the regent class. The local burgomasters often acted as colonels of the *schutterij*, as these civic guards were called, and their appearance is familiar to us from paintings such as Rembrandt's 'Night Watch' (1641) and Frans Hals's 'Banquet of the Civic Guards at St Adrian' (1627).

When the States of Holland formally renounced their allegiance to King Philip II of Spain in 1581, they also enacted a law forbidding the town councillors to consult with the representatives of the guilds (from whom they had originally sprung in the Middle Ages) or of the civic guards (as such) on any provincial matters. The regents thus took advantage of the struggle with Spain to consolidate their position as a self-perpetuating burgher-oligarchy and to exclude the ordinary citizens from any direct say in either the local or the provincial administration. With variations in such details as the number of burgomasters (from one to four) and of aldermen (from seven to twelve), this system of patrician rule was similar in all the towns of the two maritime provinces. It may also be added that, in the course of the 17th century, most of the land in the provinces of Holland, Zeeland, and Utrecht was bought up by urban capitalists of the regent class. This enabled them to use the town councils for the purpose of fostering the development of trade and industry in the towns at the expense of the home and cottage industries of the countryside.

Each one of the seven provincial States was sovereign. In Holland the States were composed of delegations nominated by the regents of eighteen towns, and one further delegation representing the provincial nobility. Every town could send as large a delegation as it liked, but each delegation had only one vote. In Zeeland likewise the towns had all the votes save one. In Guelderland the nobility, and in Friesland the landowning farmers, exercised much more influence, and there were considerable variations in the other land provinces. But even where the representatives of the urban patriciate were not dominant, as they were in the two maritime provinces, they usually wielded some power by virtue of their economic importance. The urban magistrates were elected by the municipal councils, and the rural and judicial posts were filled through the provincial States. In this way, as Professor G. J. Renier has written, the recognition of the sovereignty of the provincial States meant the domination of the whole of the Dutch Republic between 1581 and 1795 by the upper middle class. Or, as Dr B. M. Vlekke puts it, the Dutch Republic was governed, in effect, by an oligarchy of some 10,000 persons who monopolized nearly all the important provincial and municipal offices.[4]

4. G. J. Renier, *The Dutch Nation. An historical study* (London, 1944), pp. 16–31, and B. M. Vlekke, *Evolution of the Dutch Nation* (New York, 1945), pp. 162–6, provide two admirable syntheses of the complicated system of government in the Dutch Republic, on which I have relied heavily, but not exclusively, for the above and what follows. For a more detailed analysis see S. J. Fockema Andrae, *De Nederlandse Staat onder de Republik* (Amsterdam, 1962). For a contemporary English description cf. also Sir William Temple, *Observations upon the United Provinces of the Netherlands* (ed. London, 1676), pp. 91–144. For the composition of the social classes and the effects of the Eighty Years War, cf. the standard works of P. Geyl, *The Revolt of the Netherlands, 1555–1609* (London, 1962), and *The Netherlands in the 17th Century*, I, 1609–1648 (London, 1961); the chapters by various hands in the *Algemene Geschiedenis der Neder-*

Foreign policy was in the hands of the States-General at The Hague, since by the Union of Utrecht in 1579 the rebellious provinces had agreed to present, in this sphere at least, a united front to the outside world. The States-General were merely an assembly of delegates from the seven sovereign provincial States, closely bound by the instructions which they had received from their respective provinces. Any resolution which concerned the 'Generality', or the Union as a whole, had to be voted unanimously in order to be valid. In the event of disagreement, or whenever a proposal was mooted which was not covered by their instructions, the delegates had to return to their respective provincial assemblies for further consultation and fresh instructions. Often enough the provincial States in their turn had to refer the matter back to the town councils before reaching a decision. No province considered itself obliged to obey an order of the States-General unless its own delegation had given their authorized consent thereto. Each delegation had only one vote, or, rather, a voice that was regarded as single.

Apart from an unimportant Council of State, the States-General were the only national administrative body of the Dutch Republic. It was difficult for them to function effectively when provincial interests conflicted, or sometimes even when these merely failed to coincide. In times of deadlock or crisis, some strong man or influential group had to take the lead and impose a decision by a mixture of authority and persuasion. The two obvious forces for

---

landen (12 vols., Utrecht, 1949–58, hereinafter quoted as AGN), Vol. V, *De tachtigjarige Oorlog, 1567–1609* (Utrecht, 1952). Of the numerous specialist studies, attention may be directed to A. L. E. Verheyden, *Le Conseil des Troubles. Liste des condamnés, 1567–1573* (Brussels, 1961), and the articles of H. A. Enno van Gelder, listed by J. C. H. de Pater, *Bibliografie van de belangrjkste geschriften van Dr H. A. Enno van Gelder* (The Hague, 1960), to which should be added, 'Aanteekening naar aanleiding van drie vragen omtret het vroegste Nederlandse Calvinisme gesteld door Dr J. Roelink', in *Bijdragen voor de Geschiedenis der Nederlanden*, XVI (1961), pp. 58–63. Cf. also J. Craeybeckx, 'Alva's tiende penning een mythe?', in *Bijdragen en Mededelingen van het Historische Genootschap Utrecht*, Vol. LXXI (Groningen, 1962` pp. 10–42.

supplying such leadership were the province of Holland and the House of Orange. The former carried in theory 58 per cent of the Republic's financial burden and in practice far more. The overwhelming economic importance of Amsterdam after about 1585 gave this city as predominant a part in the States of Holland as these exercised in the States-General. Other things being equal, therefore, the province of Holland, which, in effect, often meant the town of Amsterdam, tended to take the leadership. It exercised this leadership through its highest official, commonly termed the *Raadpensionaris*, working in co-operation with a small committee elected by the States-General. The economic preponderance of Holland was the basis of the political power of Johan van Oldenbarnevelt after the death of William I (1584), and of Johan de Witt after the death of William II (1650).

The position of the House of Orange in an oligarchic republic was peculiar, to say the least. As Stadtholder of one or more provinces, and as virtual commander-in-chief of the armed forces, the Prince was the servant of both the provincial States and the States-General; but he had a strong (and in some cases, decisive) voice in the appointment of some of the members of those bodies. The Princes of Orange, owing to their birth, their wealth, their prestige, and their military prowess – whether actual or potential – inevitably became the focus of that monarchist sentiment which was widespread among those of the upper classes who hankered after a court life and a crowned head, and among those of the lower classes who had more respect for a prince of the blood than for a merchant prince. In this connection, it is probable that much of the pro-Orangist feeling among the lower reaches of the working class was due more to dislike of the ruling burgher-oligarchs than to anything else. The Princes of Orange, on their side, although they usually married with foreign royalty after 1644, were much influenced by the outlook and mentality of the burgher-oligarchs with whom they were so closely associated in the work of government, and on whose support their own position so largely depended.

When the Prince of Orange and the highest official of the province of Holland co-operated amicably, as they did in the time of William I and Oldenbarnevelt, and again in the days of William

III and Anthony Heinsius, then both the States-General and the provincial States could usually be induced to follow a predetermined policy. But when there was friction between those two outstanding personages, or when one or the other did not exert an unchallenged supremacy (as did Prince Maurice in 1618–25, Johan de Witt in 1654–68, and William III in 1672–8) then the perennial jealousy between Holland and Zeeland, or between these two maritime provinces and the other five, or else general dislike of Amsterdam's often overweening predominance, was apt to turn the loosely federated United Provinces into what Sir William Temple termed the Disunited Provinces. Even at the best of times they would have been described more accurately as Allied than as United. Moreover, even when the Stadtholders exercised unchallenged political control, they depended on the co-operation of the regent class for the financial and economic means of carrying out their policy. They could infiltrate the burgher-oligarchs in the States-General with their own personal friends among these and the landed aristocracy; but they could not destroy the economic power of the upper middle class which made the wealthy burghers – and not the princely Stadtholders – the ultimate arbiters of the Republic's destiny.

Although the capture of Den Briel and a number of other towns by the Sea-Beggars in the summer of 1572 marked the beginning of successful armed resistance to Spain, it is arguable to what extent the original revolt of the Netherlands can be described as a popular movement. There was certainly wide and (in some regions) deep-rooted dissatisfaction with the Church of Rome among all classes, as shown by the fact that the adherents gained by Lutheranism, Anabaptism, Calvinism and other forms of heresy came from all sections of society. But this dissatisfaction with the Old Religion did not always and everywhere imply the determination to discard the celebration of the Mass, the celibacy of the priesthood, and the suppression of the Religious Orders. Militant Calvinists were always in the minority, as were, for that matter, militant Romanists in many regions. Both burghers and manual workers usually preferred political to religious freedom, though the great majority of both could not stomach the establishment of the Holy Office of the Inquisition. It must also

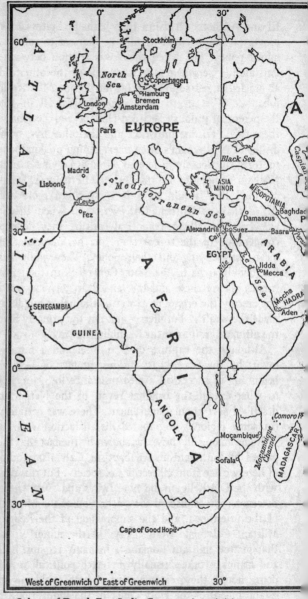

2   Sphere of Dutch East India Company's activities

Mercator's projection

be acknowledged that sufficient nobles and gentry joined the rebel cause to provide it with the necessary leadership. The Sea-Beggars' success in 1572 was largely due to the fact that though this ill-assorted rabble of militant Protestant noblemen, burghers, artisans, peasants, and semi-piratical sailors were unwelcome guests to the upper and middle classes of the towns of Holland and Zeeland which reluctantly admitted them, yet the prospect of Spanish soldiers being billeted on them, and of the Inquisition being established among them, was even more repellent.

The urban working men and the unemployed – these latter inevitably numerous in those years of politico-religious disturbances and high prices – obviously had little to lose by joining the side of the Sea-Beggars. Hunger and unemployment were particularly widespread in the years 1567–72, when economic and social conditions in the Netherlands were adversely affected by the rupture of commercial relations with England, by difficulties of trade in the Baltic, by an outbreak of plague in 1571, and by high grain prices in 1571–2. The last straw was the threatened imposition of a sales-tax called the Tenth Penny, modelled on the Spanish *alcabala*, which Alva began to impose in the spring of 1572, though its collection had not proceeded very far when the revolt broke out. Moreover, when the direction of the revolt was taken over by the town councils, stiffened by militant Calvinists, then the poor and lowly had additional reasons to follow the lead of the only people who could give them work and a livelihood. On the other hand, in the towns that were recaptured by Spanish arms, many people of all classes found little difficulty in readjusting their religious convictions to the teachings of the Roman Church, now renovated and purified by the reforms resulting from the Council of Trent. If the excesses of Alva's Spanish and Italian soldiery forced many who would rather have stayed neutral on to the side of the rebels, the similar atrocities of the Sea-Beggars induced many other waverers to return to the obedience of Church and King.

We noted above that Calvinism had originally found more adherents in the southern Netherlands than in the northern provinces. In fact, the division which ultimately took place seemed at first likely to crystallize along an east–west rather than a north–south axis. Antwerp had a strong Calvinist community at a time when Amsterdam held out for the Romanists. The eastern provinces, including the nowadays strongly Protestant north-east, remained for some time predominantly Roman Catholic. But Parma's reconquest of Flanders, Brabant, and part of the north-east in the 1580s could not be pushed beyond the naturally strong defensive line formed by the rivers Scheldt, Maas, Rhine, and Ijssel, together with the marshes of southern Friesland. After Parma's death in 1592, Prince Maurice was able to complete the conquest of the north-east, and his successor, Frederick Henry, made some precarious gains in the south, including the Roman Catholic stronghold of Maastricht. Nevertheless, the Spanish threat to the heartland of the northern provinces was not finally removed until the recapture of Breda in 1637.

Frederick Henry, like William the Silent, was desirous of granting a reasonable measure of toleration for the public profession of Roman Catholicism in the regions regained from Spanish control, hoping thereby to induce the 'Obedient Provinces' to rejoin the self-styled United Provinces of the Free Netherlands. Unfortunately, the stricter elements among the Calvinists were strong enough to prevent the implementation of this policy to any significant extent. The Roman Catholic inhabitants of the 'lands of the Generality', as the conquered districts were termed, were allowed no political or voting rights, and they could not take an important part in either the economic or the intellectual life of the Dutch Republic. The Spanish rulers of the southern Netherlands on their side were even more resolved to stamp out heresy in the provinces controlled by Church and King; with the result that people of Protestant sympathies emigrated northwards or eastwards, and Calvinism became extinct in the provinces governed from Brussels. These embittered Calvinist refugees from the south greatly strengthened the influence of their militant co-religionists in the north, who were only prepared to accept the reunification of the Seventeen Provinces on the basis of uncontested Calvinist supremacy in Church and State. Thus the Low Countries were split, not along a geographical, a linguistic, or an ethnic boundary, but along a purely artificial one determined by the military vicissitudes of an eighty years war and by the parallel growth of mutual religious intolerance.

When Parma captured Antwerp in 1585, he facilitated the surrender of the town by offering to allow those Calvinists who were resolved to emigrate (rather than to renounce their religion) two years' grace in which to remove their capital and goods. In the course of the 16th century Antwerp had become the greatest commercial entrepôt in Europe, as we have had occasion to observe. Her resident Flemish and Walloon merchants had acquired the book-keeping, banking, and insurance techniques which had hitherto flourished only south of the Alps and the Pyrenees. Calvinism had many adherents among these wealthy merchants, though not all of the rich men who emigrated were Protestants. Their dispersal over the whole of Europe during the last two decades of the 16th century had consequences even more far-reaching than the *diaspora* of the Iberian Jews a century previously, or the exodus of the Huguenots a hundred years later. Flemish merchants frequented many of the trading ports from Danzig to Livorno before 1585, but during the next fifteen years their number and influence were greatly increased by the arrival of the wealthy and enterprising refugees from the southern Netherlands.

Those who emigrated to Holland and Zeeland – and they included many of the wealthiest and most enterprising – had blood relations and business associates spread over Europe from the Baltic to the Levant, since families did not as a rule emigrate *en bloc* to one place but dispersed themselves over different regions. Those who settled in Italy and the Iberian peninsula perforce retained their Roman Catholicism, but they made no difficulty about co-operating with their Calvinist or Lutheran cousins in the northern Netherlands; just as the emigrant Iberian Jews usually retained family and business connections with their 'New Christian' or Marrano relatives who had remained in Spain and Portugal. The capital and the business connections brought by these emigrants to Amsterdam, Middelburg, and other Dutch towns gave a great stimulus to their trade in general and to that of Amsterdam in particular. Of course, the great majority of the thousands who emigrated from the southern provinces were not rich burghers but middle- and working-class people, among whom were many small traders, expert craftsmen, and skilled artisans, as well as casual and unskilled labourers. The textile industry of Leiden, for example, was largely developed by this influx of new capital and labour from the south.

While many Dutch towns benefited from this gain in financial and human resources, the effects were particularly noticeable in Amsterdam. The population of this city increased by some 75,000 souls between 1585 and 1622; and out of a total of 105,000 inhabitants in this last year one-third were immigrants from the southern Netherlands or their first-generation descendants. One of these recent arrivals wrote with pardonable exaggeration in 1594: 'Here is Antwerp itself changed into Amsterdam.' [5] Another factor in the building up of Amsterdam's capital resources has been pointed out by Violet Barbour. She reminds us that in Holland – or in the rest of the northern Netherlands, for that matter – there was little land to be had; and what there was was highly priced for sale or rent and severely taxed into the bargain. Consequently many people of moderate means, who in other countries would have aspired to buy or lease farms or smallholdings, invested their savings in buying shares in ships, in fishing or in short-term trading voyages, in land reclamation schemes, and, later on, in municipal or provincial loans. The rapid growth of Amsterdam as an international commercial emporium was reflected in the publication of weekly commodity price-lists from 1585 onwards – something which London began to do only about eighty years later. We may also note that the Amsterdam Exchange Bank was founded in 1609 and the Lending Bank in 1614.

5. Letter of Jacques della Faille, 23 April 1594, *apud* J. H. Kernkamp, *Johan van der Verken en zijn tijd* (The Hague, 1952), p. 9. For detailed facts and figures concerning the contribution of southern Netherlanders to Amsterdam's growth and Dutch overseas trade cf. *AGN*, V, pp. 220 ff.; W. Brulez, 'De Diaspora der Antwerpse kooplui op het einde van de 16e eeuw' (*Bijdragen voor de Geschiedenis der Nederlanden*, XV, 1960, pp. 273–306). For a concise general survey of the economic growth of Amsterdam see Violet Barbour, *Capitalism in Amsterdam in the 17th Century* (Baltimore, 1950), pp. 11–42.

Thanks partly to the network of Flemish and Walloon merchants in Iberian and Mediterranean ports, the Dutch were able to expand their already prosperous carrying-trade to unprecedented heights in the last decade of the 16th century. Five successive years of bad harvests in southern Europe (1586–90) gave them the chance to seize and retain new markets beyond the Straits of Gibraltar. Whereas their ships had been only occasional visitors to Mediterranean and Levant ports before 1585, twenty years later their trade thither was second only in importance to that with the Baltic, with which, incidentally, the Antwerpers had also been closely connected before the fall of their city. The ties of language, of blood, and of business proved to be stronger, at any rate for a time, than those of religion and politics. At Livorno, for instance, resident Flemish merchants acted as consuls for both The Hague and the Brussels régimes. Cornelis Haga, the first Dutch envoy to the Sublime Porte, stated in 1616 that all the agents of Dutch firms in the Levant were Brabanters by birth, and subjects of the Archdukes who ruled the 'Obedient Provinces' on behalf of the Spanish Crown. Another factor in the accelerated expansion of Dutch seaborne trade in the 1590s was the evolution of a cheaper and more efficient cargo-ship, the *fluit*. This 'flute' or 'fly-boat', as the English called it, was manned by relatively few hands, carried a bulky cargo, mounted few or no guns, and could be built cheaply and in large numbers. In some ways it may be considered as the counterpart of the liberty ships of World War II.

Marine insurance also underwent a notable development at Amsterdam during this period. A chamber of assurance was organized there in 1598, which supervised the registration of policies and settled any disputes about claims arising out of them. In 1628 four wealthy Amsterdam merchants elaborated an ambitious scheme for the compulsory insurance of all Dutch ships sailing in dangerous waters. This plan was rejected, as were subsequent proposals to revive it in various forms; but Amsterdam continued to handle a large and increasing volume of insurance, including much foreign business. Re-insurance was being practised in Amsterdam by the last quarter of the 17th century, and the city retained its primacy in handling marine insurance until well into the 18th century.

The decline of Antwerp as an international entrepôt and the phenomenal growth of Amsterdam; the influx of wealthy entrepreneurs and skilled workers into the northern provinces from the southern; the resulting increase of industrial production and the need for new markets; the confiscatory embargoes which the Crown of Spain (and of Portugal from 1580) laid on north Netherlands shipping in Iberian harbours in 1585, 1595, and 1598; the help and guidance which Hollanders and Zeelanders could often count on receiving from Flemish, Walloon, and Marrano merchants overseas – all these factors soon led to the extension of Dutch maritime enterprise to more distant regions than the Mediterranean and the Levant. Direct Dutch trade with Brazil, for example, which had been negligible prior to 1585, subsequently increased greatly, at first in co-operation with Germans from Hansa ports and then chiefly in collaboration with Portuguese crypto-Jews or New Christians. A Dutch skipper bound for Brazil in 1591 fell into the hands of the Portuguese from São Tomé Island, where he gathered much valuable information about their trade with the Gold Coast. After his return to the Netherlands he made a successful pioneer voyage thither, returning in 1594 with a valuable cargo of gold and ivory. Such were the vigour and persistence with which the Dutch exploited these new markets, that by 1621 they had secured between half and two-thirds of the carrying-trade between Brazil and Europe, while virtually the whole of the United Provinces' gold coinage was minted with gold brought from Guinea. Following for once in the wake of the English, the Dutch also developed the Arctic trade-route to Russia during those years; but the most spectacular outburst of their national energy was directed to the spice-trade of the East Indies.

One of the most peculiar features of the Eighty Years War was the way in which both sides were largely kept going with resources provided by trading with the enemy. Contraband trade and smuggling usually feature to a greater or lesser degree in all wars, but in the years 1572–1648 they were carried by both sides to unprecedented lengths. The authorities in the Dutch Republic, many of whom were shipowners and merchants deeply involved in trade with the Iberian peninsula and with lands dominated by the Spanish and Portuguese crowns, allowed (save for short intervals) this trade to continue on payment of special port-charges by those concerned therein. The receipts from this 'convoy and licence money', as it was called, formed the chief source of income for the five provincial admiralties or navy boards (Rotterdam, Zeeland, Amsterdam, North-Quarter, and Friesland) which maintained the Dutch warships, most of which were hired or converted merchant-men. The Spaniards and Portuguese on their side found that they could not do without the raw and finished materials, particularly grain and naval stores, which the Dutch carriers brought – from the Baltic and northern Europe. The confiscatory embargoes which the Iberian authorities periodically imposed on Dutch shipping turned out to be operations in the nature of cutting off the nose to spite the face, and they could never be maintained effectively for long.

Since the Dutch were rapidly expanding their trade in the Mediterranean, the Levant, and the South Atlantic during the early 1590s, it is hardly surprising that they tried to extend it to the Indian Ocean region about the same time. Dutchmen who had sailed there in the Portuguese service, the best known of whom is Jan Huighen van Linschoten, had returned to their homeland with plenty of information to indicate that the Portuguese claim to be lords of the 'conquest, navigation, and commerce of Ethiopia, India, Arabia and Persia' was not so effective as was implied by this grandiloquent title assumed by King Manuel I in 1501. Memories of the Iberian embargo of 1585, and anticipation of that to come in 1595–6, may well have made the Dutch realize that their use of Lisbon as a spice-mart was becoming increasingly precarious. However that may have been, in March 1594 nine north Netherland merchants found sufficient inducements and funds to organize a 'Company of Far Lands' at Amsterdam, with the object of sending two fleets to Indonesia for spices.

The first fleet had no clear-cut leadership, the voyage was badly mismanaged, and only three ships and eighty-nine men returned to the Texel in August 1597, out of four sail and 249 men which had left that anchorage two years earlier. But the modest cargo of pepper which they brought from Bantam more than covered the cost of the expedition. Since this pioneer voyage showed that even a badly led fleet could reach the East Indies, no fewer than twenty-two ships fitted out by five different – and largely rival – trading companies left Dutch ports for Indonesia in 1598. One, commanded by a seafaring Rotterdam innkeeper, Olivier van Noort, took the South American and Pacific route to make the first Dutch voyage round the world; but the most encouraging result was achieved by the second fleet of the Amsterdam 'Far Lands Company', led by Jacob van Neck. Four of these vessels returned in July 1599, after a fifteen-month absence and with a costly cargo of spices. 'So long as Holland has been Holland,' an anonymous participant observed, 'such richly laden ships have never been seen.' The chief officers and merchants were given a civic reception, while the bells of Amsterdam rang peals of joy. The investors had every reason to be satisfied with a return on their capital of over 100 per cent, even before the four remaining ships arrived with cargoes which brought the total profit up to about 400 per cent. Van Neck stressed that this profit was not obtained by force or fraud, as jealous Portuguese Jews at Amsterdam insinuated, but by free and honest trading with Indonesian merchants, in accordance with the Directors' orders 'not to rob anyone of their property, but to trade uprightly with all foreign nations'.[6]

Commercial companies for trading to the East Indies now sprang up like mushrooms. Admittedly, none of them achieved the enviable success of Van Neck's first voyage; and out of the above-mentioned twenty-two ships which left the Netherlands for the East in 1598, only fourteen returned. Nevertheless, the lure of the spice-trade was such that fourteen fleets totalling sixty-five ships left for the East Indies in 1601. It was by now obvious that these pioneer companies were getting in each other's way, and that their internecine competition tended to increase purchase prices in Asia and threatened to lower sale prices in Europe. These companies were organized on a regional or municipal basis, and rivalry between those of Holland and Zeeland was particularly acute. As early as January 1598, the States-General had suggested that the various companies should amalgamate or co-operate

6. H. Terpstra, *Jacob van Neck. Amsterdams Admiraal en Regent* (Amsterdam, 1950), pp. 31–73, for Van Neck's voyage and the quotations from contemporary sources.

amicably instead of engaging in cut-throat competition. This injunction had little effect at the time; but long and difficult negotiations, ably guided by the leading Dutch statesman, Johan van Oldenbarnevelt, and helped by a push from Prince Maurice at the critical moment, finally brought about the fusion of the competing pioneer companies into one monopolistic corporation (20 March 1602). The negotiations had been prolonged not only by Zeeland's natural jealousy of Holland's stronger economic position but by the ingrained dislike of the free-trading Dutch merchants for anything in the nature of a commercial monopoly. Moreover, some of the leading directors in the pioneer companies, such as the southerners, Isaac le Maire and Baltazar de Moucheron, possessed temperaments like those of 20th-century opera stars. Thus it needed all of Oldenbarnevelt's patient tact and Prince Maurice's powerful influence to achieve the formation of the United Netherlands Chartered East India Company (hereafter usually referred to by its Dutch abbreviation of VOC) with a capital amounting to nearly 6½ million florins. The new corporation was subdivided into six regional boards or chambers (*kamers*) which were established in the former seats of the pioneer companies at Amsterdam, Middelburg, Delft, Rotterdam, Hoorn and Enkhuizen respectively.

Under the charter awarded by the States-General to the VOC in 1602, the Company was given a monopoly of Dutch trade and navigation east of the Cape of Good Hope and west of the straits of Magellan for an initial period of twenty-one years. The governing body or court of seventeen directors (*Heeren* XVII) was empowered to conclude treaties of peace and alliance, to wage defensive war, and to build 'fortresses and strongholds' in that region. They could also enlist civilian, naval, and military personnel who would take an oath of loyalty to the Company and to the States-General. The VOC was thus virtually a state within a state, but the type of warfare envisaged by its founders was merely defensive action against the Portuguese, who claimed a monopoly of European trade in Eastern seas by virtue of a series of papal bulls and briefs of 15th and 16th century origin. Nevertheless, the authorization to wage war was sufficient to frighten away a number of leading investors in the pioneer companies, who sold their shares rather than transfer them to the VOC, 'since they as merchants had themselves organized those companies solely for the purpose of honourably engaging in peaceful and friendly trade, and not to indulge in any hostilities or aggressive actions'. These critics rightly foresaw that the VOC would often be induced to make as much use of the sword as of the pen.[7]

The organization of the West India Company, which received its charter from the States-General on 3 June 1621, was modelled in many ways on that of the VOC, although the offensive role of the Western Company in the war against the Iberian Atlantic empire was emphasized from the start. The WIC, which was given a monopoly of all Dutch trade and navigation with America and West Africa, was likewise authorized to make war and peace with the indigenous powers, to maintain naval and military forces, and to exercise judicial and administrative functions in those regions. It was composed of five regional chambers – Amsterdam, Zeeland (Middelburg), The Maas (Rotterdam), North-Quarter, and Groningen with Friesland. The WIC counterpart to the *Heeren* XVII was the central board or governing body of the *Heeren* XIX. The WIC took much longer to raise its working capital than the VOC had done – two years as against one month – but the sum finally subscribed was substantially larger, being just over seven million florins. The formation of a West India Company was suggested much earlier in the 17th century, but was delayed by the conclusion of the twelve-year truce between Spain and the United Provinces in 1609. This truce was the work of Oldenbarnevelt and his supporters among the regent-oligarchs, and it was concluded against the wishes of Prince Maurice, a powerful section of Amsterdam merchants, and the Calvinist extremists known as the

7. Declaration of 4 December 1608, *apud* K. Glamann, *Dutch-Asiatic Trade, 1620–1740* (Copenhagen, 1958), p. 7. For the pioneer companies and the founding of the VOC. cf. H. Terpstra, 'De Nederlandsch voorcompagniën', in F. W. Stapel (ed.), *Geschiedenis van Nederlandsch Indië* (5 vols., Amsterdam, 1938–40), Vol. II, pp. 275–475; J. A. Van der Chijs, *Geschiedenis der stichting der Ver-eenigde Oost-Indische Compagnie en de matregelen der Nederlandsch regering betrekkend de vaart op Oost-Indië* (Leiden, 1857), still a standard work though published over a century ago.

Counter-Remonstrants. The truce was ill-observed in the colonial world, and the official renewal of the war in 1621 – after the trial and execution of Oldenbarnevelt on a trumped-up charge of high treason – gave both the VOC and the WIC great scope for offensive action.

Although Spain was the *erf-vijand* or hereditary-foe in neighbouring Flanders, where the war became increasingly bogged down in minor sieges and inconclusive manoeuvring, the Dutch attack on the Iberian colonial world was directed far more against Portuguese possessions than against those of Spain. From the time when the men of the VOC passed to the offensive with the capture of Amboina in 1605, they concentrated on Portuguese strongholds and settlements in the tropics, whether in the Moluccas, Malaya, Ceylon, or India. When they did venture to attack the Spaniards in the Philippines, they were almost uniformly unsuccessful. The pertinacious and rewarding Dutch blockades of Malacca (1635–40) and of Goa (1638–44) contrast strongly with the humiliating fiascos of their expeditions to the Philippines in 1610, 1617, and 1647–8. The Dutch could not even drive the Spaniards from their precariously held strongholds on Ternate and Tidore, where the latter remained for over a decade after the Treaty of Münster, and whence they only withdrew when Manila was threatened with invasion by Coxinga, the Chinese conqueror of Dutch Formosa in 1661–2.

On the other side of the world, the WIC, though founded largely with an eye on Spanish America and the silver of Mexico and Peru, actually concentrated on the sugar of Portuguese Brazil, and on the gold, ivory, and slaves of Portuguese West Africa. Piet Heyn's spectacular capture of the Mexican silver-fleet in the Cuban harbour of Matanzas (1628) has tended to overshadow the fact that his contemporaries and successors in the service of the WIC had relatively few other major successes against the Spaniards. Their renown, their victories, and their prizes were mostly achieved at the expense of the Portuguese in the South Atlantic. Johannes de Laet, the contemporary chronicler – and director – of the deeds of the WIC, ends his *Iaerlyck Verhael* (*Annals*) of 1644 on a note of triumph, by listing in detail the ships and booty captured by the arms of the Company 'from the King of Spain' between 1623 and 1636.[8] A careful reading of this list discloses that the overwhelming majority of those losses were inflicted on the possessions and shipping of the Crown of Portugal – the silver-fleet of 1628 excepted. In the years 1636–48, the WIC's attacks against Spanish-America were even less significant, save for Brouwer's expedition to Chile in 1642, and that proved abortive. At one time the Dutch had deprived Portugal of half Brazil and Angola, to say nothing of the Gold Coast and Cape Verde, but their only noteworthy conquest in the Caribbean was the capture of Curaçao in 1634. In comparison with the great efforts it put forth in the South Atlantic, the West India Company's attempts to found a 'New Netherlands' on Manhattan Island and on the banks of the Hudson River made only a modest showing.

It is true that a rebellion by the Portuguese of Pernambuco in 1645, which received more or less clandestine support from the mother-country that had broken loose from Spain five years earlier, forced the Dutch to retire behind the walls of Recife and a few other places along the north-east Brazilian coast. It is also true that a few months after the proclamation of the Treaty of Münster, a Luso–Brazilian expedition – partly supplied with munitions and ship's stores from Amsterdam – recaptured Luanda and expelled the Dutch from Angola, just as they and their negro allies were on the point of annihilating the last remnants of the Portuguese in the interior. Nevertheless, the situation of the Dutch in Brazil did not yet seem lost beyond repair, and by the Treaty of Münster King Philip IV explicitly recognized the right of the Dutch to conquer and retain all the Portuguese colonial territories to which the two great India Companies laid claim.

In many respects the Treaty of Münster forms the high-water mark of the United Provinces' golden age. By 1648 the Dutch were indisputably the greatest trading nation in the world, with commercial outposts and fortified 'factories' scattered from Archangel to Recife and from New Amsterdam to Nagasaki. If some of these places were precariously held, others yielded encouraging profits.

8. J. de Laet, *Iaerlyck Verhael van de verrichtingen der Geoctroyeerde West-Indische Compagnie* (Leiden, 1644). Cf. pp. 280–98 of Vol. V of the 5-vol. edition edited by S. P. L'Honoré-Naber and J. C. M. Warnsinck (The Hague, 1931–7).

Dutch achievements in European waters alone make impressive reading. 'By extraordinary enterprise and efficiency', writes C. Wilson, 'they had managed to capture something like three-quarters of the traffic in Baltic grain, between half and three-quarters of the traffic in timber, and between a third and a half of that in Swedish metals. Three-quarters of the salt from France and Portugal that went to the Baltic was carried in Dutch bottoms. More than half the cloth imported to the Baltic area was made or finished in Holland.'[9] All this in addition to the fact that they were the largest importers and distributors of such varied colonial wares as spices, sugar, porcelain, and trade-wind beads.

This unprecedented achievement was mainly due to the dynamic energy and enterprise generated in the seaports of Holland and Zeeland, which bore the financial brunt of the war against Spain and forged the spearhead of colonial expansion, thanks to the resources derived from their shipping and overseas trade. It was therefore logical that the leading merchants and shipowners of those provincial towns should secure, in effect, the control of the new republic, and that they would use their dominance of the town councils and of the provincial States to forward their own interests. We have already seen (pp. 14–15) that, when the interests of the various provinces conflicted, then those of Holland and Amsterdam tended to prevail, provided they were in agreement. The conclusion of the Treaty of Münster affords an instance of this. Opponents of the Treaty were many and powerful. They included the Orange partisans who were desirous of retaining the French alliance, and of strengthening the Stadtholder's dynastic interests by conquering the southern Netherlands and supporting the failing Stuart cause; the province of Zeeland, in default of adequate state support for the WIC, in its losing fight with the Portuguese in Brazil; the province of Utrecht and the town of Leiden, from a mixture of religious and political motives. Yet the regents of the other towns of Holland, and, above all, those of Amsterdam, were able to drive the Treaty through against the opposition of so many of their fellow-countrymen and without yielding to the Spanish king any of his most insistent demands,

9. C. Wilson, *Profit and Power. A Study of England and the Dutch Wars* (Cambridge, 1957), p. 41.

such as the opening of the Scheldt and the official toleration of Roman Catholicism in the United Provinces. Dutch insistence on the closure of the Scheldt was due not only to Amsterdam's fear that Antwerp might regain much of its importance as an entrepôt if the river was opened but to the fear of some south Holland and Zeeland ports (Rotterdam, Middelburg, Flushing) that their own transit trade would likewise be diminished.

The Treaty of Münster showed that the movement which had begun eighty years before in an explosion of popular wrath had ended with the formation of a loosely federated republic dominated by a group of merchant oligarchs. Before discussing these burghers in more detail, it may be worth asking to what degree a nation had evolved under their leadership. If we accept Renan's criterion of the consciousness of nationality: 'avoir fait de grandes choses ensemble, vouloir en faire encore', then the victors of 1648 measure up to this on both counts. They could recall with pride such martial exploits as the siege and relief of Leiden, the victorious campaigns of Maurice and Frederick Henry, Piet Heyn's capture of the silver-fleet, the destruction of one Spanish armada off Gibraltar (1607) and of another in 'the King of England's chamber' at The Downs (1639). In this last year, the unparalleled expansion of Dutch trade 'to distant and exotic lands, as far as shines the sun', was celebrated by Joost van den Vondel in an ode which reflected the sentiments of many Dutchmen besides the poet and the *Heeren* XVII: 'Wherever profit leads us, to every sea and shore, for love of gain the wide world's harbours we explore.' If Renan's 'grandes choses' are taken to include erudition, literature, and the visual arts, then the names of Grotius, Huyghens, Hooft, Vondel, Hals and Rembrandt suffice to recall the achievements of the young republic. As for the future, the Dutch could and did look forward confidently to further expansion in the East Indies; and though their position in Brazil was clearly precarious, yet the possibility of their creating an empire in the South Atlantic still existed.[10]

10. Renan's remark *apud* P. Geyl, *Studies en strijdschriften* (Groningen, 1958), p. 3. The translation of Vondel's ode to Maria de Medici on the occasion of her state visit to the East India House at Amsterdam in 1639, from the version by Donald Keene, *The Japanese Discovery of Europe* (London, 1952), p. 7.

For these and other reasons, many of the inhabitants of the United Provinces of the Free Netherlands were proudly conscious that they were indeed a free nation in their own right. But there were many others who were still assailed by nagging doubts, or who had no special reason to rejoice at the peace of Münster. The militant Calvinists claimed then – and have often since received – the credit for forging a nation under God's blessing and with His active support; but they regarded their still numerous Roman Catholic fellow-countrymen as second-class citizens and potential traitors. They even looked askance at many of the Protestant dissenters as being weaker and therefore inferior brethren. This scorn of the self-appointed elect for so many of their compatriots must have provoked widespread resentment among the latter. The lack of a king or of a sovereign prince was a cause of mingled embarrassment and regret among some sections of the population, though not necessarily for the same reasons. The fact that the original rebellion had been one against their lawful prince was not easily lived down at home or abroad. Even such a staunch republican as Johan de Witt later expressed his uneasiness on this point. Inter-provincial jealousy had been aggravated in some respects by the very success of Dutch overseas expansion, which made the preponderance of Holland so much the greater. The Brabanters, Flemings, and Walloons who had emigrated from the southern Netherlands in the first decades of the Eighty Years War had mostly been absorbed by 1648, though jealousy of the more successful ones and their descendants still smouldered at Amsterdam. But there were many foreigners and half-assimilated immigrants in the Dutch Republic, and they could be a source of weakness, especially in wartime, with an army composed mainly of foreign mercenaries.

Finally, how did other and older European nations regard the upstart *bourgeois* republic which had first obtained general recognition in 1648? Criticism by crowned heads and by trade rivals must always be heavily discounted, and it is not surprising that James I observed ill-naturedly of the Dutch in 1607, 'Let them leave this vainglorious thirsting for the title of a free state.' It is more significant that a century after the Treaty of Münster, and after Great Britain and the United Provinces had been alternately

allies and enemies, the English envoy at Madrid could write con-
descendingly of his recently arrived Dutch colleague: 'He is indeed young but generous and friendly, and has as much or more
the air of a gentleman than any I ever saw of his nation, if it
deserves that name.' [11]

11. Keene to Castries, Madrid, 14 March 1749, *apud* R. Lodge, *The
Private Correspondence of Sir Benjamin Keene, K.B.* (Cambridge,
1933), p. 106.

2

Burgher-oligarchs
and merchant-adventurers

The urban patricians who triumphed at the Treaty of Münster were in many ways different from their fathers and grandfathers who had sustained the struggle against Spain in the days of Prince Maurice and William the Silent. From being a class primarily concerned with trade and secondarily with local government and administration, the urban patriciate in 1648 was well on the way to becoming a closed oligarchy whose priorities were exactly the reverse. In 1615 a burgomaster of Amsterdam stated that the town regents were either active merchants or those who had recently retired from business. Thirty-seven years later we find the Amsterdam traders complaining that their regents were no longer merchants nor actively engaged in overseas trade, 'but derived their income from houses, lands, and money at interest'.[1] In other words, the merchants had become *rentiers*. This particular complaint was obviously exaggerated, for one has only to think of the influential Bicker brothers, merchants and regents of Amsterdam, who inspired the defence of the town against Prince William II in 1650, and whose commercial connections spanned the greater part of the globe. Moreover, some of the regents in the towns had always lived mainly on their incomes from real estate, and gave only part-time attention to trade and commerce. But the complaint of 1652 did reflect the fact that many members of the regent class were changing over from actively participating in trade to living on their incomes from land, investments and annuities, supplemented by their usually more modest official salaries. This tendency became increasingly obvious as the 17th century progressed, and the descendants of the merchant-oligarchs of the 1630s had become

1. Aitzema, *Saken van staet en oorlogh*, Vol. III, p. 762. Cf. also G. J. Renier, *The Dutch Nation*, pp. 100–107.

burgher-oligarchs by the 1690s. It must, however, be remembered that being a member of the municipal council of Amsterdam was a full-time occupation for those who held office by 1650. Merchants who sat on the council could hardly have given much direct attention to their own business affairs. The separation of office-holding from direct participation in trade was more or less inevitable. However, even when the regents had become a *rentier* and official class in whole or in great part, they were still closely related through investment and marriage ties with the wealthy merchants and bankers of the towns, and thus they remained aware that the prosperity of the Seven Provinces depended mainly on overseas trade. Intermarriage between the regent families and the wealthy merchants who lived on the same footing as themselves became more common as time went on, but it was not a speedy process. A merchant family had to live in style for a good many years, perhaps a generation or two, before one of its members could marry into the urban patriciate and thus gain access first to the lower and eventually to the higher ranks of municipal office.

As indicated in the previous chapter (pp. 7, 12), the differences between the various provinces were in some respects so considerable that generalizations concerning the social structure of the Dutch Republic are apt to be more than usually misleading. But since Holland was by far the most important of the Seven Provinces, and since the present work is mainly concerned with the Dutch Republic as a seaborne empire, we will continue to ignore the gentleman-farmers of Friesland, the hedge-squires of Guelderland, and the tenant-farmers of Overijssel, in order to concentrate our attention on the regents, the merchants, and the mariners of Holland and Zeeland.

The transition from a merchant oligarchy to a *rentier* oligarchy, which occupied the greater part of the 17th century in the province of Holland, is exemplified by three generations of the family of Johan de Witt – 'the perfect Hollander', as Sir William Temple described him, and one of the greatest Netherlanders of all time. His family had been represented on the town council of Dordrecht since the end of the 15th century, and they came into greater prominence after 1572 when they chose the side of William I and Calvinism. Cornelis de Witt, born in 1545, inherited a flourishing timber-business from his father, which he continued to manage personally but which did not take up all of his time. He was repeatedly alderman and burgomaster of Dordrecht in the years 1575–1620, representative of the province of Holland in the Zeeland admiralty 1596–9, and the largest subscriber to the Zeeland chamber of the VOC in 1602. His three sons, Andries, Frans and Jacob, studied law and travelled abroad in their youth, in order to fit themselves later on for official and municipal employment – a practice which was becoming the general rule for regents' sons. Although Jacob continued to carry on his father's business for some years, he was already treasurer of the Synod of Dordt in 1618, and he took his father's place on the town council after the latter's death in 1622. Thenceforward, he concentrated increasingly on his official duties, and disposed of the family business between 1632 and 1651. He served repeatedly as alderman and burgomaster; he represented Dordrecht in the States of Holland and in the States-General; he was a member of many government committees, an envoy to Sweden in 1644, and a prominent opponent of William II in 1650.

Jacob de Witt, though taunted by a political opponent in 1647 with being from an upstart family, certainly felt himself to be a fully fledged member of the regent class, and he is credited with the observation that 'while the burgher is small, he should be kept small'. He was also typical of the pious members of the regent class in that, while remaining a regular church attendant and an assiduous Bible reader who led the family prayers for his household every day, he was resolutely opposed to any interference by the Church on the political plane. His most famous son, Johan de Witt, though not so ostentatiously devout, followed his father's precepts and practice as a life-long defender of the power and privileges of the regent class. 'Unqualified and mean persons' should have nothing to do with government and administration 'which must be reserved for qualified people alone', he stated categorically. Johan de Witt, with his brother, Cornelis, received an excellent education in the classics at Dordrecht's 'Illustrious School' and read law at the University of Leiden, though he took his degree at the Huguenot University of Angers. Nor was his physical education neglected, a fact which helped his naturally strong constitution to withstand the exhausting office hours and paper-work with which he later had to cope for years on end. He was remarkably fluent in French, and acquired some knowledge of English, German and Italian. He was also a mathematician of exceptional ability, and wrote a treatise on life-annuities (1671) which entitles him to be considered as the founder of actuarial science.

In the years 1645–7, the young De Witt brothers made what Johan called 'the grand tour' (*den grooten tour*) through most of France and part of England, after paying a brief visit to their father in Stockholm. On returning home from their travels both brothers qualified to practise as advocates; but whereas Cornelis remained in Dordrecht when he was elected alderman and decided to follow his father's career, Johan, after building up a good legal practice at The Hague, became successively Pensionary of Dordrecht (December 1650) and Grand Pensionary of the States of Holland (July 1653). His marriage to the wealthy Wandela Bicker in 1655 brought him into close and advantageous contact with the leading members of the regent families who controlled the town council of Amsterdam for many years. His further career as a statesman is too well known to need recapitulation here; but it may be mentioned that though this career was exclusively an official one and his money was mostly invested in government bonds, his friends included the Amsterdam merchant-banker, Jean Deutsz, and the Leiden industrialists, the brothers De la Court. Fairly well-to-do at the beginning of his career, he left a fortune of half a million guilders at his death, as a result of his economical way of life and the shrewd investment of his own and his wife's capital.[2]

The De Witt family of Dordrecht were typical in that they had been regents of the town for several generations, but more sudden rises to the seats of municipal power were not altogether unknown before the regents became a closed and self-perpetuating

2. N. Japikse, *Johan de Witt* (Amsterdam, 1928), is my chief authority for the above.

rentier-oligarchy. Francis Banningh Cocq, the central figure of Rembrandt's 'Night Watch', who became a burgomaster of Amsterdam in 1650, was the scion of an upstart family. The erudite Nicholas Tulp, who is likewise familiar to us from another painting by Rembrandt – 'The Anatomy Lesson' – was also a man of humble origins who rose to be a burgomaster of Amsterdam. But such instances became even rarer as the 17th century progressed, and still more so in the 18th. Moreover, while it may be roughly true that the regent class grew out of the merchant class, this was probably not a universal process, particularly as regards the smaller towns. The whole problem of the origins of the regent class and its gradual development into a burgher oligarchy is one which requires a great deal of further investigation and research, as D. J. Roorda has recently shown in a penetrating study of the ruling classes in Holland in the 17th century.

Whatever their origins, the extent to which the burgher-oligarchs had become a well-defined ruling class during the administration of Johan de Witt, the period of 'the true freedom' as its adherents and admirers termed it, is apparent from the classic *Observations upon the United Provinces of the Netherlands* by Sir William Temple, who knew the Republic well in the years immediately preceding the publication of his book (1672).[3]

Those families which live upon their patrimonial estates in all the great cities, are a people differently bred and mannered from the traders, though like them in the modesty of garb and habit, and the parsimony of living. Their youth are generally bred up at schools, and at the Universities of Leiden or Utrecht, in the common studies of humane learning, but chiefly of the civil law, which is that of their country ... Where these families are rich, their youths after the course of their studies at home, travel for some years, as the sons of our gentry use to do; but their journeys are chiefly into England and France, not much into Italy, seldomer into Spain, nor often into the more Northern countries, unless in company or train of their public ministers. The chief end of their breeding, is to make them fit for the service of their country in the magistracy of their towns, their provinces, and their State. And of these kind of men are the civil officers of this government generally composed, being descended

3. My quotations are from pp. 161–4 of the 1676 edition.

of families who have many times been constantly in the magistracy of their native towns for many years, and some for several ages.

Such were most or all of the chief ministers, and the persons that composed their chief councils, in the time of my residence among them, and not men of mean or mechanic trades, as it is commonly received among foreigners, and makes the subject of comical jests upon their government. This does not exclude many merchants, or traders in gross, from being often seen in the offices of their cities, and sometimes deputed to their States; nor several of their States, from turning their stocks in the management of some very beneficial trade by servants and houses maintained to that purpose. But the generality of the States and magistrates are of the other sort; their estates consisting in the pensions of their public charges, in the rents of lands, or interest of money upon the *Cantores*,[4] or in actions of the East-India Company, or in shares upon the adventures of great trading merchants.

Nor do these families, habituated as it were to the magistracy of their towns and provinces, usually arrive at great or excessive riches; the salaries of public employments and interest being low, but the revenue of lands being yet very much lower, and seldom exceeding the profit of two in the hundred. They content themselves with the honour of being useful to the public, with the esteem of their cities or their country, and with the ease of their fortunes; which seldom fails by the frugality of their living, grown universal by being (I suppose) at first necessary, but since honourable among them.

The mighty growth and excess of riches is seen among the merchants and traders, whose application lies wholly that way, and who are the better content to have so little share in the government, desiring only security in what they possess; troubled with no cares but those of their fortunes, and the management of their trades, and turning the rest of their time and thought to the divertisement of their lives. Yet these, when they attain great wealth, choose to breed up their sons in the way, and marry their daughters into the families of those others most generally credited in their towns, and versed in their magistracies; and thereby introduce their families into the way of government and honour, which consists not here in titles, but in public employment.

4. 'And the common revenue of particular men lies much in the Cantores either of the Generality, or the several Provinces, which are the Registries of these public debts' (op. cit., p. 253). Cf. V. Barbour, *Capitalism in Amsterdam in the Seventeenth Century*, pp. 81, 83.

It is worth noting that Sir William Temple rated the scions of the old landed aristocracy and titled nobility far below the regent class in importance. He added that nevertheless 'they value themselves more upon their nobility than men do in other countries where 'tis more common, and would think themselves utterly dishonoured by the marriage of one that were not of their rank, though it were to make up the fortune of a noble family, by the wealth of a plebean'. In other words, the Dutch landed nobility – where it still existed – was more of a closed aristocracy, like that of France, Spain and Portugal, than a relatively open aristocracy like that of England, where intermarriage with recently ennobled families of men who had made their money in trade, political office, or the law, was more common. The Dutch nobility were not large landowners as a general rule, and even the largest estates in Friesland could not be compared to the broad acres held by many other European landed nobles from Poland to Portugal. Sir William Temple deprecated the tendency of the Dutch nobility to ape the manners and dress of the French aristocracy, but admitted that 'they are otherwise an honest, well-natured, friendly and gentlemanly sort of men, and acquit themselves with honour and merit, where their country employs them'. They were naturally mostly Orangist in sympathy, though down to the time of William III's stadtholdership (1672-1702), the regents could always find some nobles, like Jacob van Wassenaer van Obdam, commander-in-chief of the Netherlands Navy in 1655-65, who preferred a *bourgeois* republic to a princely Stadtholderate, either from personal conviction or else from jealousy of the House of Orange. As for the social relations of the old aristocracy and gentry with the ordinary burghers, a visiting Englishman noted in 1685: 'Those that govern themselves with prudence and moderation and make themselves familiar with their inferiors are highly respected and popular, while those that are stiff and haughty are generally hated and despised.' [5]

5. James Monson's unpublished account of his journey through Western Europe in 1685-6 (quoted by kind permission of the late Lord Monson from the original MS. at Burton Hall, Lincolnshire). This particular remark seems to have been copied from Jean Parival,

It was a commonplace with all foreign travellers in the United Provinces during the first seven or eight decades of the 17th century that the regent and merchant classes, and even (though to a lesser extent) the titled aristocracy and the army officers, were all more sober in 'maintaining a port' than their equivalents in other countries. Sir William Temple observed how Michiel de Ruyter and Johan de Witt, 'the one, generally esteemed by foreign nations, as great a seaman, and the other as great a statesman as any of their age', were not to be distinguished in their daily dress and deportment from, respectively, 'the commonest sea-captain' and 'the commonest burgher of the town'. Their households were on the same modest scale, and though both of them amassed great wealth, neither of them was attended by more than one man-servant, whether indoors or out. 'Nor was this manner of life affected,' adds Sir William, 'or used only by these particular men, but [it] was the general fashion or mode among all the magistrates of the State: for I speak not of the military officers, who are reckoned their servants, and live in a different garb, though generally modester than in other countries.' Doubtless the sobering influence of Calvinism was at work here, and we shall see that when the plain burghers of Amsterdam and Middelburg were transplanted to the East and West Indies they could indulge in as much pomp and circumstance as did their Iberian predecessors and their English rivals.

Many contemporaries noticed that during the last quarter of the 17th century the upper middle class began to adopt a more ostentatious and luxurious way of life. For instance, Michiel de Ruyter's bachelor son, Engel, lived on a much more lavish scale than his father ever did. In addition to his well-furnished town house staffed with two menservants, two maids and a coachman, Engel de Ruyter also maintained a sizeable country-house, which he used for week-ends and summer holidays. Similarly, Lieutenant-Admiral Cornelis Tromp, son of the famous

Les Delices de la Hollande (1662), p. 190, an account of the United Provinces which went through many editions and rivalled Sir William Temple's *Observations* in popularity. Cf. also, Temple, *Observations* (ed. 1676), pp. 165–6; W. Carr, *An Accurate Description of the United Provinces* (ed. London, 1691), pp. 23–8.

'Tarpaulin' admiral, M. H. Tromp, had a much higher standard of living than his father, 'who contented himself with a pickled herring for his breakfast'. Cornelis married into an Amsterdam regent family and spent his last years leading the life of a grand-seigneur between his town-house on the Heerengracht at Amsterdam and his luxuriously furnished country-house 'De Trompenburg' in 's-Graveland. William Carr, the English consul at Amsterdam, whose description of the Seven Provinces was first published there in 1688, was much struck by the noticeable increase in high living among the regents and the wealthy burghers which had occurred in the sixteen years since Temple wrote his famous work. 'The old severe and frugal way of living is now almost quite out of date in Holland; there is very little to be seen of that sober modesty in apparel, diet, and habitations as formerly. Instead of convenient dwellings, the Hollanders now build stately palaces, have their delightful gardens, and houses of pleasure, keep coaches, wagons and sleighs, have very rich furniture for their horses, with trappings adorned with silver bells ... yea, so much is the humour of the women altered, and of their children also, that no apparel can now serve them but the best and richest that France and other countries afford; and their sons are so much addicted to play that many families in Amsterdam are quite ruined by it.'[6]

Carr's strictures, and those of other contemporaries who could be quoted to the same effect, apply mainly if not exclusively to the Province of Holland, and above all to the wealthy *bourgeoisie* of Amsterdam and The Hague. The impress of Calvinism on this particular section of Dutch society had never been so marked as it was elsewhere, and the rich young men who made the 'grand tour' were undoubtedly influenced by what they saw in England and (above all) in France. Another factor which may have helped to foster this display of wealth was, perhaps, the return of people who had made their fortunes in the East Indies. These Dutch

6. Temple, *Observations* (ed. 1676), pp. 128–9; W. Carr, *Accurate Description* (ed. 1691), pp. 71–4; N. de Roever, *Uit onzer oude Amstelstad. Schetsen en taferelen betreffende het leven en de zeden harer vroegere bewoners* (3 vols., Amsterdam, 1890–91), Vol. I, p. 77 ff.

equivalents and precursors of the English 18th-century 'Nabobs' had become used to a luxurious way of life in the tropics, and they can hardly have felt inclined to conform to a puritanical existence after their return home. Be this as it may, Dutch art and architecture of the period clearly reflect this change, though the Dutch ruling classes always remained less extravagant than the French and English aristocracies. William Carr summed-up the situation fairly enough when he observed that although the Dutch 'were not addicted to such prodigality and wantonness as the English are ... nevertheless, the grave and sober people of Holland are very sensible of the great alteration that now is in this country'.

One of the 'grave and sober people of Holland' had sounded the alarm even at the time when Sir William Temple was admiring the frugality and modesty of the Dutch ruling class. An anonymous pamphleteer of 1662 complained that small shopkeepers, tailors, cobblers, publicans and their respective wives, now dressed in velvet and silk clothes to an extent which made it difficult to distinguish between these base-born persons and their social superiors. Things had come to such a pass, he averred, that 'Mr Everyman thinks he is entitled to wear what he likes so long as he can pay for it'. Similarly, some small traders and artisans furnished their houses in a manner unbefitting to their lowly station in life. 'Can you bear it,' he asked indignantly, 'when you see that a tailor has a room or a parlour hung with gold leather or tapestry? Or here and there, a mercer or an artisan who decorates his house as if it was a gentleman's or a burgomaster's?' He urged that this unseemly state of affairs should be ended by the promulgation of sumptuary laws, restricting the use of silk and velvet clothes to the upper middle class, and ordering the working class to dress only 'in wool and other stuffs'. The upper middle class he defined as being composed of the regents, magistrates, sheriffs, bailiffs, receivers and other senior officials, as well as merchants and traders who possessed a capital of from forty thousand to fifty thousand guilders, 'and who are taxed accordingly'. He opined that advocates and medical doctors might be considered the social equals of magistrates, but attorneys and notaries were a grade below them and ranked with clerks and sheriff's officers. Shopkeepers, small traders, and minor officials were lumped together in the lower middle class which, in his view, was barely a cut above the artisans. He admitted that military officers formed a class apart; but he was baffled by the social status of artists and actors. Many of these were apt to be 'of a madcap humour' (*dol van geest*), though some of the former were 'divine in artistry and intelligence'. The further proposals of this anonymous pamphleteer do not concern us here, but his work is of interest as reflecting that acute class-consciousness which permeated social life in the Golden Age of the Dutch Republic and which became intensified in the following century.[7]

The grave and sober deportment of the upper middle class – their banquets and drinking-bouts always excepted – during the first half of the 17th century, and their high regard for financial solvency, did not mean that nepotism, bribery, and corruption were unknown. On the contrary, they were an integral part of the social structure, though it may fairly be claimed that they were no worse than elsewhere in Europe, despite the allegations of some foreigners to the contrary. One thing which helped to keep such malpractices in bounds was that they could be exposed with relative ease in that voluminous pamphlet-literature which was such a feature of the Seven Provinces. The authorities could seldom exert a fully effective control over determined pamphleteers, owing to the lengths to which decentralization of the government was carried and to the mutual jealousy of the sovereign provinces. Pamphlets banned in one town could often be reprinted in another.

Outspoken press criticism did not, of course, prevent such scandals as the Amsterdam regents using their official position to make outrageous profits in land sales during the extension of the town in 1615; nor the regents of Hoorn from enriching themselves in the depression year of 1619 at the expense of the poor and lowly; nor the members of the Rotterdam Admiralty from embezzling official funds in 1626. It is also very doubtful if the

7. J. van B. I. C. Tus, *Een onderscheyt Boeckje ofte Tractaetje van de fouten en dwalingen der politie in ons Vaderlant* (Amsterdam, 1662); Knuttel nr. 8670. Cf. also P. Zumthor, *Daily Life in Rembrandt's Holland*, pp. 224–37.

denunciation by the Zeeland delegates to the Grand Assembly of 1650 of bribery and corruption in official circles had more than a passing effect. The delegates were obviously thinking of Cornelis Musch, the late *Griffier*, or confidential clerk to the States-General, whose shameless greed in taking bribes was notorious, and who did not hesitate to supply the Portuguese ambassador with copies of all the secret dispatches and confidential resolutions which the latter needed. A few years later, Sir George Downing, the unscrupulous English envoy at The Hague, affirmed that 'there is scarce any who come in the States-General but get in to make themselves a fortune by it and must be bought'.

The previously quoted Portuguese envoy, Sousa Coutinho, gives us an amusing glimpse of how temptation was placed in the way of a selected individual who was married and had several children. In paying a courtesy call on such a person, and discussing the matter in hand, 'one lets fall, as if by accident, a jewel worth about a thousand *cruzados* more or less (according to that person's relative standing and position) into the hand of one of the children'. The father would not make the child return the jewel, and so 'face' was saved all round. Honourable exceptions were probably more numerous than these unfriendly critics were prepared to admit, and the French ambassador, D'Estrades, was undoubtedly exaggerating when he wrote that 'hors de M. de Witt, il n'y pas un qu'on ne fasse changer d'avis pour de l'argent'. But if the 'perfect Hollander' enjoyed an exceptional reputation for honesty where his country's interests were concerned, he found it more difficult to ignore the ties of kinship and friendship when suitable candidates for office asked him to use his influence on their behalf. Even so, the favours he did his relatives and political friends on such occasions never assumed the dimensions of a major scandal.

The same could not be said of many of his contemporaries, and nepotism was ineradicably and unavoidably ingrained in the oligarchic system of the Dutch Republic. Both the regent supporters of 'the true freedom' and the Stadtholders of the House of Orange were equally wedded to the practice of placing their respective adherents in key positions or in lucrative posts, whenever this could be done without provoking excessive scandal – and sometimes even then. In the long run, nepotism probably did more harm to the body politic than did bribery and corruption. It certainly aroused more opposition, and it increasingly divorced the interests of the ruling oligarchy from those of the middle and lower classes. The most scandalous features of this regent nepotism were reflected in the agreements made between members of a town council to take turns in appointing their relatives and friends to office or public employment. Originally oral, and later written, these 'contracts of correspondence', which were relatively rare in the 17th century, became increasingly common in the 18th. While men of ability were not necessarily kept out of office by this patronage system, the fact remained that a candidate's primary qualification was apt to be not so much his character as his family connections. In other words, public offices in the Dutch Republic – as elsewhere for that matter, though for different reasons – came to be regarded as private, more or less negotiable, family properties. As an Englishman long resident in Holland wrote in 1740: 'Their government is aristocratical; so that the so much boasted liberty of the Dutch is not to be understood in the general and absolute sense, but *cum grano salis*. The Burgomasters and senate compose the sovereignty [of the Towns] ; and, on a vacancy by death, the Burgomaster would be highly offended if any petulant burgher presumed to murmur at his filling it up with one of his own sons, or relations.' [8]

Although the regent oligarchy became increasingly differentiated from the ordinary burghers during the 18th century, it would be wrong to lay too much stress on the gulf that separated

8. Anon., A *Description of Holland: or, the present state of the United Provinces* (London, 1743), p. 73. For contemporary evidence of bribery and corruption in regent circles, cf. Aitzema, *Saken van staet en oorlogh*, Vol. III, pp. 525 ff.; F. de Sousa Coutinho, *Correspondência Diplomática*, 1643–1650, Vol. II, p. 49; *Ibidem*, Vol. III, pp. 163, 165, 174–6, 227–8, 234, 248, 251; Downing's correspondence during 1661 *apud* N. Japikse, *De Verwikkelingen tusschen de Republiek en Engeland* (Leiden, 1900), especially p. 183; D'Estrades' letter of 18 November 1665 *apud* N. Japikse, *Johan de Witt* (1928), p. 106 n.; J. E. Elias, *Geschiedenis van het Amsterdamsche regenten-*

rulers and ruled in an earlier period. Admittedly, many – perhaps most – of the regents in the 'Golden Century' would have agreed with Jacob and Johan de Witt that the small man must be kept small, and that the regents alone were fully qualified to govern their fellow-countrymen. But despite the resentment which this aristocratic hauteur sometimes aroused, and despite the widespread admiration for the House of Orange, the fact remains that for much of the time most people were content to accept the regents as their natural leaders. They only turned to the House of Orange in times of acute danger, such as the French invasions of 1672 and 1748. As several Dutch historians have pointed out, many large groups in the Republic, though not nearly so vocal as the Calvinist extremists or the convinced Orangists, had good reason to prefer the regent oligarchy to its strident opponents. Roman Catholics, Remonstrants, and Protestant dissenters in general, who, in the aggregate, probably formed about two-thirds of the population (*c.* 1662), realized that the regents were their main bulwark against the intolerant *predikanten* of the 'True Reformed Christian Religion'. These zealots would have placed the supremacy of the orthodox Calvinist Church above that of the relatively tolerant state if they had had their way.

Nor was it only the regent class which was distrustful of the dynastic ambitions and the monarchical leanings sometimes displayed by the House of Orange. It is significant that on the occasion of William II's attack on Amsterdam in 1650, the entire population sided unhesitatingly with the oligarchic Bicker brothers. Even in the days of Johan de Witt and 'the true freedom', the regents had to take some account of public opinion, as Sir William Temple observed when he wrote that 'the way to office and authority lies through those qualities which acquire the general esteem of the people'. Though the regents later became an unrepresentative minority, most of their compatriots did not dispute their right to rule during the years when they

---

patriciaat (The Hague, 1923), pp. 194–6, 202–10; D. J. Roorda, 'Een zwakke stee in de Hollandse regentaristocratie: de Hoornse vroedschap in opspraak, 1670–75', in *Bijdragen voor de Geschiedenis der Nederlanden*, Vol. XVI (1961), 89–116.

governed the Dutch Republic at the greatest period of its history.[9]

For contemporaries and for posterity, one of the most spectacular manifestations of Dutch commercial enterprise was supplied by the rise of their East and West India Companies, even though the economic importance of these two great trading corporations was in reality less than that of the more humdrum carrying-trade of Western Europe and the North Sea Fisheries. The grain-trade with the Baltic was, as De Witt observed in 1671, the 'source and root of the most notable commerce and navigation of these lands.' At the beginning of the 17th century some 1,200 Dutch vessels were engaged in this trade, and during the first half of the same century the total of Dutch ships passing the Sound outnumbered the English by roughly thirteen to one. As late as 1666 it was estimated that three-fourths of the capital active on the Amsterdam bourse was engaged in the Baltic trade. The North Sea Fisheries for herring, haddock, cod, and ling were also termed the 'chiefest trade and principal gold-mine' of the United Provinces in 1580–1639. Some forty years later, De la Court claimed that these fisheries were estimated to employ over 1,000 busses or fishing-smacks of 48–60 tons burden. He calculated that the fishing industry with its ancillary trades then employed about 450,000 persons, compared with about 200,000 engaged in agriculture and about 650,000 engaged in other industries. Estimates of the value of the catch vary widely, but De la Court's figure (in 1662) of Fl. 8,000,000, or not far short of f.1,000,000 is probably somewhere near the truth. The fishing industry was closely controlled by guild and government regulations which ensured the high standard of the herrings barrelled in brine for export, and of the fresh and smoked fish which were widely eaten in a country where only the rich ate meat more than once a week. Enkhuizen and Rotterdam were the two chief centres of the herring fishery for most of the 17th century, as Amsterdam was for the Arctic whaling industry. This last was organized as a monopoly of the Northern Company in 1614–42,

9. Temple, *Observations* (ed. 1676), p. 130; P. Geyl, 'Historische appreciaties van het zeventiende-eeuwse Hollands regentenregiem', in *Studies en strijdschriften* (Groningen, 1958), pp. 180–200; C. Wilson, *Profit and Power*, p. 15.

and subsequently – and more successfully – as a free activity when the States-General declined to renew the Company's charter.[10]

The failure of the grandiose plans of the monopolistic Northern Company affords an interesting contrast with the development of the East and West India Companies during the same period, although the WIC later came to a sticky end. Like other institutions in the Dutch Republic, these two India Companies had a strongly oligarchic stamp which became more marked with the passage of time. Their organization and early development also illustrate the interaction of the merchant and the regent classes on each other, and the increasingly preponderant part played by Amsterdam capitalists and investors in overseas trade.

Each of the six regional chambers of the East India Company (p. 26) had a board of directors, originally identical with the local directors of the amalgamating pioneer companies, who retained their positions for life. When a director died or – more rarely – resigned, his fellow-directors submitted a list of three names to the local representatives of the provincial States, who were usually the burgomasters of the town concerned and who chose one to fill the vacancy. The *Heeren* XVII were chosen from among the regional directors who in their turn were drawn from subscribers with a minimum holding of Fl. 6,000 for most of the regional chambers and of Fl. 3,000 in the smaller ones of Hoorn and Enkhuizen. These leading shareholders were termed *hoofd-participanten*. Eight of the *Heeren* XVII represented the Amsterdam chamber, four the Middelburg, with one representative from each of the other chambers. The seventeenth director was provided by rotation among all the chambers save Amsterdam.

10. Pieter de la Court, *Interest van Holland, ofte gronden van Hollands Welvaren* (Amsterdam, 1662), the English version of which, entitled *The True Interest and Political Maxims of the Republic of Holland and West-Friesland* (London, 1702), was wrongly ascribed to Johan de Witt, although he did have a hand in amending De la Court's original draft. Cf. especially pp. 26–30, 40–42 of the 1702 edition, and also V. Barbour, *Capitalism in Amsterdam*, pp. 26–7; C. Wilson, *Profit and Power*, pp. 1–24, 32–47; P. Zumthor, *Daily Life in Rembrandt's Holland* (London, 1962), pp. 306–10.

The self-perpetuating and oligarchic nature of the directorships soon aroused much adverse criticism, both among the ordinary shareholders who exercised no influence whatever on the directors' policy and among the *hoofdparticipanten* who remained outside the small circle of the directors and their friends. When the Company's charter was first renewed in 1623, the States-General made a rather half-hearted effort to meet this criticism by ruling that thenceforth the directors could only be elected for a three-year term of office, and that the list of three names for a vacant directorship should be submitted by a committee which included equal numbers of directors and *hoofdparticipanten*. In the upshot, this made little practical difference. All the retiring directors were eligible for re-election, and those leading shareholders who had a vote did not wish to prejudice their own future chances of election by antagonizing the actual directors. Hence retiring directors were almost invariably re-elected, and vacancies caused by deaths continued to be filled from the same small circle of *hoofdparticipanten* – sometimes by casting lots.

The close connection of the directors with the regent class was cogently expressed by a pamphleteer of 1622, who echoed English and French complaints about the impossibility of obtaining redress for real or alleged wrongs done by the servants of the VOC to those nations in the East. 'For, they say, if we complain to the regents and the magistrates of the towns, there sit the directors, ... if to the admiralties, there are the directors again. If to the States-General, we find that they and the directors are sitting there together at the same time.' This intimate connection of the directors with the regent class was the chief reason why they were able to sidetrack or to ignore criticism of their conduct by disgruntled shareholders, and to consolidate their own position as a self-perpetuating oligarchy accountable to nobody. So sure of themselves did the *Heeren* XVII feel by 1644 that they told the States-General: 'The places and strongholds which they had captured in the East Indies should not be regarded as national conquests but as the property of private merchants, who were entitled to sell those places to whomsoever they wished, even if it was to the King of Spain, or to some other enemy of the United Provinces.' It may be added that criticism of the directors by shareholders in the Company rapidly declined after 1634, when the *Heeren* XVII began to distribute generous annual dividends in cash. These ranged between 15½ per cent and 50 per cent, reaching a climax in 1715–20 with six successive dividends of 40 per cent each.[11]

Subscribers of the original working capital of the VOC were drawn from all classes of society, though naturally the rich and the well-to-do predominated, for reasons explained by a contemporary chronicler relating the success of Van Neck's voyage: 'This profit was for a few rich and powerful people, who could afford to lay out their capital for a long time; whereas the common man cannot afford to lock up his daily earnings for so long, and such people do much better by investing their money in trade with neighbouring nations.' High officials, town councillors, wealthy traders and merchant capitalists contributed the bulk of the capital, subscribing sums ranging from Fl. 10,000 to Fl. 85,000. Prominent among the original large investors were the refugee merchant-bankers from Antwerp and the southern Netherlands, and their financial preponderance was still greater at the end of a decade. As time went on these wealthy immigrants were absorbed into the regent class, and the larger shareholders bought out most of the small investors. At the same time, Amsterdam investors who had originally subscribed more than half the Company's working capital extended their tentacles into the other chambers. By the end of the 17th century, 108 Amsterdammers were holding about three-eighths of the capital stock of the Zeeland chamber, and more than half of the entire capital of the VOC was owned in Amsterdam.[12]

Apart from its financial preponderance in the VOC, Amster-

11. O. Van Rees, *Geschiedenis der staathuishoudkunde in Nederland tot het einde der achttiende eeuw* (2 vols., Utrecht, 1865–8), Vol. II, pp. 156–60, 195.

12. J. G. Van Dillen, *Het oudste aandeelhoudersregister van de kamer Amsterdam der Oost-Indische Compagnie* (The Hague, 1958); W. S. Unger, 'Het inschrijvingsregister van de kamer Zeeland der verenigde Oost-Indische Compagnie', in the *Economisch-Historisch Jaarboek*, Vol. 24 (The Hague, 1950); H. Terpstra, *Jacob van Neck*, pp. 74–5; V. Barbour, *Capitalism in Amsterdam*, pp. 28–9, 79.

dam likewise exercised a great and growing influence on the Company's policy and administration. This influence was consolidated by Mr Pieter van Dam, who filled the post of the Company's advocate at Amsterdam from 1652 until his death in 1706. The resident English consul in 1688 compared the sixty-eight-year-old advocate with the great Johan de Witt 'for parts, though not so in [political] principle. This great minister is a man of indefatigable industry, and labours day and night in the Company's service. He reads over twice the great journal books which come from the Indies, and out of them makes minutes to prepare matters of concern necessary to be considered by the grand council of seventeen, and by the inferior committees of the Company, and prepares the orders to be sent to their chief ministers in the Indies.' That William Carr did not exaggerate is proved by Van Dam's encyclopedic description of the Company and its activities which he compiled for the secret and confidential use of the directors between 1693 and 1701. These bulky manuscript volumes were kept from the knowledge of outsiders and remained the *vade-mecum* of successive generations of directors until the Company's dissolution in 1795.[13]

The extent to which the regent class became in some ways separated from the merchant class was reflected in the directorships of the VOC. Whereas in 1644 the *Heeren* XVII had told the States-General that the Company was the property of private merchants, in 1743 the regents who occupied the chairs of the *Heeren* XVII passed a resolution that merchants might, after all, be allowed to become directors! Out of twenty-four regents who filled the burgomasters' chairs at Amsterdam in the years 1718–48, only two were active merchants – a striking contrast with the composition of that town council a century previously. Admittedly the contrast becomes less striking when we recall (p. 35) that an Amsterdam municipal councillor's job was a full-time one after about 1650. An active merchant could hardly serve as burgomaster and give much attention to his own commercial business at the same time. But here again one must not be too

13. W. Carr, *Accurate Description* (ed. 1691), p. 38; P. Van Dam, *Beschrijvinge van de Oost-Indische Compagnie* (ed. F. W. Stapel, 6 vols., The Hague, 1927–54).

categorical. The Orangist *coup d'état* of 1748, which brought another group of regents to power, resulted in a balance much more favourable to commercial interests. Out of thirty-seven Amsterdam burgomasters in the period 1752–95, thirteen were active or recently retired merchants, and the remainder had close family connections with commercial firms. It is also worth noting that from first to last a burgomaster of Amsterdam was nearly always a director of the VOC.[14]

The West India Company likewise had a marked oligarchic stamp and close connections with the regent class, although one of its earliest promoters, the indefatigable pamphleteer Wilhelm Usselincx, had vainly advocated that 'no magistrate should be a director and that no director should be a magistrate at one and the same time'. In the governing board of the *Heeren* XIX (p. 27), Amsterdam provided eight directors, Zeeland four, and the other three chambers two each, the nineteenth being nominated by the States-General. As with the *Heeren* XVII, the *Heeren* XIX likewise assembled for six successive years at Amsterdam, followed by two at Middelburg. The original directors were chosen by the regents of the five towns where the provincial chambers were seated, from among the leading shareholders with a minimum investment of Fl. 6,000 for Amsterdam and Fl. 4,000 for the remainder. Vacancies were filled in a similar manner to those of the VOC, by consultation and co-optation between the town regents and the directors of the chamber concerned. The small investor was for long a more important factor in the WIC than with the sister company. This was particularly noticeable in Zeeland, where it was alleged in 1648 that over a fifth of the inhabitants of Middelburg, Flushing and Veere were shareholders in the WIC.

As had happened with the older Company, the rules concerning the periodic public audit and inspection of the accounts, and the publication of balance-sheets, were either ignored or evaded by the directors. The result in both cases was the strengthening of the directors' power *vis-à-vis* the shareholders; though in the case of the WIC the *hoofdparticipanten* sometimes held their

14. J. E. Elias. *Geschiedenis van het Amsterdamsche Regentpatriciaat*, pp. 101, 216, 232–8.

own meetings, and may have exercised more influence on their directors. A comparison of the names of the directors of both companies before 1636 shows, as might be expected, that some prominent merchant-oligarchs, such as the Bickers of Amsterdam and the Lampsins of Flushing, were represented on the boards of both corporations. While there was markedly less enthusiasm among the merchants of Amsterdam for the WIC in 1622 than they had displayed for the VOC twenty years earlier, yet the eighty-three leading shareholders of the Amsterdam chamber of the WIC subscribed over a million florins, which was more than a third of that city's total contribution. As with the VOC, the Amsterdammers later extended their influence by buying up shares in the other regional chambers. By 1670 more than half the total capital of the WIC was owned in Amsterdam, and this town had advanced money to the other chambers.

Colonization of suitable regions was specifically envisaged in the WIC's charter of 1621, but this Company was from the first intended as an offensive weapon for striking against the roots of Iberian power in the New World. The WIC soon became involved in efforts to conquer all or part of Brazil; and the resulting naval and military expenditure far exceeded the profits derived from the sugar and other exports of its precariously held South American territory. Piet Heyn's capture of the Mexican silver-fleet in 1628 enabled the *Heeren* XIX to declare a bumper dividend of 75 per cent in 1629–30, but the Company only distributed another one or two before its dissolution in 1674. Down to about 1650, the West African trade, particularly that in Guinea gold, yielded good profits, but these were all sunk in the Brazilian financial morass. On its reorganization in 1674, investors received only 30 per cent of their deposits, but its creditors were repaid in full and the new Company was still able to borrow money at 4 per cent in 1694. By this time it had become primarily a slave-trading concern for the export of negroes from West Africa to the West Indies, where the island of Curaçao was an excellent base for contraband trade with Spanish America.

We have seen (p. 28) that the organization of the WIC was delayed until after the judicial murder of Oldenbarnevelt and the triumph of the militant Calvinist or Contra-Remonstrant party in

which the south Netherland emigrants were powerfully represented. For this and other reasons, the WIC formed a bulwark
of this party in Holland for a few years and in Zeeland for much
longer; but less fervent Protestants – the so-called Arminians and
Libertines – were always represented among both directors and
shareholders. During the 1630s and 1640s these latter elements
gained the upper hand in Holland; although, as late as 1649,
Burgomaster Bicker of Amsterdam, who had sold his WIC
shares many years previously at the top of the market, is alleged
to have said of the semi-bankrupt Company : 'Let the Brabanters
and Walloons see now what baronies they are going to get out of
it !' But the internal stresses and strains which so largely contributed to the ruin of the first West India Company were caused
not so much by lack of co-operation between Calvinists and
Libertines on the boards of directors, as by the provincial jealousy
between Holland – more especially, Amsterdam – and Zeeland.
This is reflected in the pamphlet literature of the time, which is
both voluminous and vituperative where the WIC is concerned,
whereas printed criticism of the *Heeren* XVII virtually ceased
after 1625 for over 150 years.[15]

One criticism which was frequently applied to the employees
of both Companies by their stay-at-home contemporaries was
that those men who served in the East and West Indies were
generally of inferior character. This allegation was not confined
to scurrilous pamphleteers, but forms a recurrent theme in the
correspondence of the directors with their senior representatives
at Batavia and Recife. The great 19th-century Islamic scholar,

15. J. F. Jameson, *Willem Usselincx, Founder of the Dutch and
Swedish West India Companies* (New York, 1887); C. Ligtenberg,
Willem Usselincx (Utrecht, 1915); C. R. Boxer, *The Dutch in Brazil,
1624–1654* (Oxford, 1957); W. J. Hoboken, 'The Dutch West-India
Company : the political background of its rise and decline', in J. S.
Bromley and E. H. Kossmann (eds.), *Britain and the Netherlands.
Papers delivered to the Oxford-Netherlands Historical Conference,
1959* (London, 1960), pp. 41–61; J. G. Van Dillen, 'De West-Indische
Compagnie, het Calvinisme en de politiek', in *Tijdschrift voor
Geschiedenis* (1961), pp. 145–71; V. Barbour, *Capitalism in Amster-
dam*.

Snouck Hurgronje, was writing with a good knowledge of these sources when he characterized the Dutch East India Company's two centuries in the East in the following scathing terms: 'The first act of the Netherlands–Indian tragedy is called "Company", and it begins almost exactly with the 17th century. The chief actors deserve our admiration for their indomitable energy, but the objective for which they worked, and the means they employed to attain it, were of such a kind that we, even with the full application of the rule that we must judge their deeds and doings by the standard of their times, have difficulty in restraining our aversion. The "experiment" began in such wise, that the inhabitants of Asia came into contact with the dregs of the Dutch nation, who treated them with almost unbearable contempt, and whose task it was to devote all their efforts to the enrichment of a group of shareholders in the Fatherland. The servants of this chartered company, kept all too short by their employers but not less greedy for gain than they, displayed a picture of corruption which overshadows the worst of what the Oriental peoples are accused of in this respect.' [16]

I hope to show in subsequent chapters that this sweeping judgement is in some respects unfair, and that it was not only the dregs of the Dutch nation who went out to the East. But it cannot be denied that Snouck Hurgronje's denunciation contains a large element of truth. The VOC, like the Portuguese Crown before it, and like the English and French Companies competing with it, paid all but a few of its servants such small wages that they could not possibly live on their pay and allowances. They were thus compelled to resort to more or less dishonest means in order to earn a livelihood. Moreover the hardships of a six or eight months' voyage, and the dangers of life in tropical countries where little or nothing was known of the prevention and cure of such deadly diseases as malaria, cholera, leprosy and dysentery, naturally deterred the great majority of people who could get any sort of a job at home from taking their chance in the East and West Indies. The reluctance of the average upper- or middle-class Dutchman to serve a monopolistic trading com-

16. Apud E. du Perron, *De Muze van Jan Compagnie* (Bandung, 1948), p. 13.

pany also helps to explain why the directors could seldom afford to pick and choose their subordinates but had to make the best of those they could get. What David Hannay wrote of the servants of the English East India Company in the 17th century is equally applicable to their contemporaries and competitors of the VOC. 'Nothing is more common, or more grotesque, than the contrast between the profuse assurances of the Company that it has every confidence in the virtue of Mr A. who is just appointed to this or that factory, and its furious rebuke of his scandalous dishonesty written perhaps within a year and a day.' [17]

The higher ranks of the VOC and WIC overseas were staffed mainly by men who came from the middle and lower ranks of the burgher class, with a sprinkling from the urban patriciate. Representatives of the landed nobility were conspicuous by their absence; Hendrik Adrian van Reede tot Drakenstein, Lord of Mijdrecht, who was governor of Malabar in 1669–77, was one of the few exceptions. Directors often found jobs for their – mostly poorer – friends and relations who were prepared to seek their fortune in the Indies; but, generally speaking, for the reasons given above, the better class of Dutchmen preferred to seek employment nearer home and only took service with either of the two India Companies as a last resort. This helps to explain why both Companies employed such a high proportion of foreigners. But it also meant that the ladder of promotion could easily be climbed by men of ability and determination; for a career in these two Companies was, despite a good deal of inevitable nepotism, in the main a *carrière ouverte aux talents*. This is proved by the numerous instances of men who entered their service in a lowly or even, in some cases, a menial capacity and rose to the highest ranks. Antonio van Diemen, the undischarged bankrupt who enlisted as a soldier and became Governor-General at Batavia in 1636–45, and François Caron, the ship's cook who became Director-General there in 1647–50, are two examples of men who rose to the top exclusively through their own merits

17. D. Hannay, *The Great Chartered Companies* (London, 1926), pp. 190–92.

and exertions.[18] Two of the most distinguished Governors-General in 18th-century Batavia, Jacob Mossel (1750–61) and Reinier de Klerk (1777–80), both started their respective careers as common seamen in the East India Company's service.

On the other hand, the scandalous career of the Zeeland regent's son, Pieter Nuyts, who avowed that he 'had not come out to Asia to eat hay', and who collected Fl. 18,000 from the Company after having been dishonourably discharged at Batavia for his misconduct in Japan and Formosa (1627–30), showed what those who had influential family connections could get away with. There was probably no important difference between the type of man who enlisted to serve in the East or in the West Indies; though one of the many individuals who served both Companies claimed in 1655 that the senior officials of the WIC were a set of 'drunken fools' who would never have been promoted to high rank by the sister Company in the East.[19]

If the general run of the two Companies' servants left much to be desired, there were always some honourable exceptions. Although the vast majority of Dutchmen, like most of their Portuguese predecessors and of their English and French rivals, went out East (or West) 'to shake the pagoda tree', there were some who were not mainly concerned with making money. I see no reason to doubt the sincerity of Jacob van Neck's avowal that 'all his life long he had a desire to see foreign countries' and that this was the main motive which took him to the East. The same can be said of the ship's surgeon, Nicholas de Graaff, who, although happily married and comfortably installed in his home

18. W. P. Coolhaas, 'Gegevens over Antonio van Diemen' (*BTLVNI*, Vol. 103, 1943–6, pp. 469–546); ibid., 'Een Indisch verslag uit 1631, van de hand van Antonio van Diemen' (*BMHGU*, Vol. 65, 1943–6, pp. 1–237); C. R. Boxer (ed.), *A True Description of the Mighty Kingdoms of Japan and Siam by François Caron and Joost Schouten* (London, 1935).

19. W. P. Coolhaas, 'Een lastig heerschap tegenover een lastig volk' (*BMHGU*, Vol. 69, 1955, pp. 17–43); D. P. de Vries, *Korte Historiael ende Journaels Aenteyckeninge van verscheyden voyagiens in de vier deelen des wereldtsronde, als Europe, Africa, Asia ende America*, Hoorn, 1655 (ed. H. T. Colenbrander, The Hague, 1911, p. 178).

town, could never resist for long the call of the sea and of the tropics.[20] Men of this type may have been relatively rare; but there were others who, having gone out to the East solely to make money, became fascinated by the life or by the people in the tropics, and recorded their impressions for posterity. The foregoing remarks, of course, apply chiefly to the members of the *bourgeoisie*, whose motives are explained in their own writings and books. We have now to consider the more numerous but less literate members of Dutch society who had to earn their daily bread by the sweat of their brow.

20. H. Terpstra, *Jacob van Neck*, p. 185; J. C. M. Warnsinck (ed.), *Reisen van Nicolaus de Graaff gedaan naar alle gewesten des Werelds, 1639–1687* (The Hague, 1930).

3

Sedentary workers and seafaring folk

Although adequate unemployment statistics and other relevant materials are lacking, it is clear from numerous contemporary accounts of the Dutch Republic in its 'Golden Century' that economic expansion and national prosperity were accompanied by great poverty among many groups of workers, as happened later in England during the Industrial Revolution. This was, no doubt, largely due to the price revolution and the resulting increase in food and housing costs, which reached a climax in the northern Netherlands about the middle of the 17th century, while wages, as usual, lagged behind rising prices. Other contributory causes, here as elsewhere, may have been a sharp increase in the population of some towns (particularly of Amsterdam) and periodic dislocations of trade by involvement in foreign wars; even though the period of the Eighty Years War (1568–1648), taken as a whole, was one of great and increasing prosperity for Dutch overseas trade. As early as 1566 a Leeuwarden chronicler noted that, in sharp contrast with the wealthy regents and merchants, stood the mass of the 'humble, distressed, and hungry common people'. Exploitation of child labour was denounced at Amsterdam in 1597, when it was alleged that some employers 'often took in two, four, six, or more working-class children on the pretext of charitably providing for them and teaching them a trade, whereas they retained them for many years and treated them more like slaves than apprentices'. At the height of the Leiden textile-boom in 1638–40, at least 4,000 child workers were brought to that town from Liège; and the Walloon drapers domiciled at Leiden were accused of bringing beggar-boys from as far away as Norwich, Douai and Cleeves. The poor-houses and workhouses also supplied women and children for industrial labour, and here again there is an obvious parallel with England during the Industrial Revolution. It is true that some steps were taken to check these abuses, such as fixing the textile operatives' working day at a maximum of fourteen hours (!) in 1646; but thirteen years later a leading Leiden industrialist noted that many workers were living in overcrowded slums, and that some were forced to burn their beds and furniture to keep themselves warm in winter.[1]

Out of 41,561 households at Amsterdam in 1747, some 19,000 were living in squalid back premises, cellars, and basements. Until the end of the 17th century most houses in the country districts and many in the towns were built of wood and clay. Stone or brick homes were a rarity for all save the rich. Of course, living conditions for the poor in the Dutch Republic were probably no worse than in 18th-century England, where, as J. H. Plumb reminds us: 'The houses of the poor were one or two room hovels, frequently made only of weatherboard with a pitched roof, placed back to back; or they were the houses of the rich, deserted because their owners were seeking more salubrious suburbs – ramshackle warrens of filth, squalor and disease. Most cellars were inhabited, not only by people but also by their pigs and fowls, sometimes even by their horses and cattle.'[2] In the first half of the 17th century, houses in Holland and Zeeland were said to be two or three times better than those of France, but this flattering comparison can hardly have been true of the overcrowded dwellings of the very poor. Still, the fact remains that by all accounts the ordinary Dutch burgher and his wife were more house-proud than their equivalents in any other European nation. Dark and dank their houses might be, but they were well scrubbed and polished when their occupants had any pretensions to self-respect.

Dutch alms-houses, poorhouses and workhouses aroused the unqualified admiration of numerous foreign visitors, and even

1. Save where otherwise stated, my chief source for the facts and figures given in the first half of this chapter is J. de Bosch Kemper, *Geschiedkundig onderzoek naar de armoede in ons Vaderland* (Haarlem, 1851), which has not been superseded in this field. Cf. also *Algemene Geschiedenis der Nederlanden*, VI, pp. 89–146.

2. J. H. Plumb, *England in the Eighteenth Century, 1714–1815* (ed. 1961), p. 12.

lunatics seem to have been better cared for in the Republic than elsewhere in Europe. Amsterdam, in particular, had a deservedly high reputation for its charitable institutions, which were described by James Monson in 1685 with an enthusiasm that was duplicated in many other contemporary accounts. 'There is nothing shows more the charitable inclination of the Hollanders,' he wrote, 'than their great care in relieving, maintaining, and educating their poor, for there are no beggars to be seen anywhere in the streets.' He was much impressed by the Weeshuis, 'or hospital for poor children, particularly orphans, wherein are constantly maintained above 500 poor wretches who are very carefully looked after, taught to read, write and some kind of trade, and have at last money given them to set up'. He also visited the Gasthuis or the hospital for sick people, 'which is fair and large', where he found 'a great number of poor souls who are yet so well looked after and so neatly and cleanly kept that they give little or no offence to one another or those that see them or live with them ... The Mannenhuis or man hospital is neat and convenient, but I think that for the old women exceeds them all, and is perhaps no ways inferior to the best in Italy, though it is built of brick and those at Milan of stone: but I am sure such extraordinary neatness and cleanliness as is to be seen and admired anywhere within in their chambers, jakes and kitchens (which yet is chiefly desirable and commendable in such a society) is not to be met with in any country or town I have yet seen.' This last building contained over 400 poor women when James Monson inspected it, and he concluded his account of Amsterdam's charitable institutions by stating: '... besides the great expense and charges that this city or state is at in maintaining so many hospitals, there are (according to report) above eighteen tons of gold distributed every year to poor families, which proves as well the great riches of the town as the good and charitable disposition of the inhabitants'.[3]

3. James Monson's unpublished MS. account of his visit to the Netherlands in 1685. W. Carr, in his 1688 description of Amsterdam, stated that the charitable institutions of that town catered for 20,000 people daily 'at bed and board'. Cf. Sir William Temple's tribute to 'the many and various hospitals that are in every man's curiosity

The money for the upkeep of these charitable foundations came from a variety of public and private sources, the latter, perhaps, predominating. Some of it was derived from suppressed Roman Catholic Church property (monasteries, chantries), which had been taken over by the towns or by the provincial States, or allotted to the Reformed Church for distribution. Much of it was financed by municipal and local taxation, ranging from a fluctuating poor-rate to such perquisites as 'the right of the best clothes' of a deceased person to belong to the poor, which the heirs of the deceased usually ransomed for a cash payment. In some places the orphanages had the exclusive right of making coffins, and in others the poor received the eightieth penny on all sales of immovable property. The East India Company also paid a poor-rate of the thousandth penny on all its sales, which brought in large sums annually. These public and municipal contributions were supplemented by generous private benefactions and legacies. An English resident at The Hague in 1740 affirmed that 'upwards of 100,000 florins, or £10,000 sterling, are annually collected for the use of the poor, either in the churches, or from door to door, and that over and above the fixed rates, legacies and supplies out of the public treasury'. A century earlier, Louis de Geer, the famous industrialist and entrepreneur, contributed Fl. 200 a year to the poor-box for each of his living children – and he had sixteen. Similarly, Admiral M. A. de Ruyter always gave a contribution to the poor-box each time he came safe home from a sea-voyage, increasing his contribution as he got older and richer. This generous private charity was all the more creditable, as an orthodox Calvinist could not hope for salvation through good works. Wealthy burghers, both men and women, often served on the committees which ran these charit-

---

and talk that travels their country'. (*Observations*, ed. 1676, pp. 170–71). He was particularly impressed by the home for aged seamen at Enkhuizen; but, as Paul Zumthor points out, the beneficiaries of this institution were a small, privileged minority within the great mass of seafaring folk (*Daily Life in Rembrandt's Holland*, p. 244). On hospitals as distinct from alms-houses cf. A. Leuftink, *De Geneeskunde bij's lands oorlogsvloot in de 17e eeuw* (Assen, 1953), p. 57.

able institutions, and it was sometimes remarked that those run by women were better than those run by men. However this may have been, readiness to serve on such committees was not entirely unconnected with prestige reasons, judging by the frequency with which such committees had their group-portraits painted.

While Holland and Zeeland were well provided with such institutions, the same could not be said of the north-eastern provinces in all respects. Poorhouses existed everywhere, but neither Delfzijl, Harlingen, or Groningen, all of them important towns, boasted of a public hospital before the year 1800, whereas even the smallest town in the two maritime provinces possessed one. Moreover, despite the eulogistic accounts of James Monson and other foreign travellers, it remains true that unemployment was often a serious problem in the Dutch Republic's Golden Century, that beggars and vagrants were a perennial problem in town and countryside, and that the industrial proletariat lived a miserable life on the edge of bare subsistence. In 1682 the States of Holland decreed that each locality must be responsible for the maintenance of its own poor, and that vagrants coming in from elsewhere should be returned to the places whence they came. New arrivals who intended to work or settle in a given place were supposed to supply the local authorities with financial or other evidence of their bona fides; but this regulation seems to have been widely ignored, particularly in Amsterdam. It is true that William Carr averred in 1688 that the only beggars to be seen in Amsterdam were Walloons and other foreigners, but this was a palpable exaggeration. Foreign vagabonds and disbanded mercenary soldiers were certainly well represented among the swarms of pauper mendicants against whom the town councils and the provincial Estates legislated in vain throughout the 17th and the 18th centuries; but a large section of the Dutch working-class lived on the brink of penury and were liable to frequent unemployment, owing to their dependence on ill-paid casual labour and the impossibility of saving money.

From the Dutch worker's point of view, the labour situation was worsened by the fact that the obvious prosperity of the United Provinces as a whole acted as a lodestar to the unemployed and the under-employed of neighbouring countries. Not only Flemings and Walloons, but Scandinavians and Germans swarmed into the Republic in the belief that the streets of Amsterdam were paved with gold. As a well-informed pamphleteer wrote in 1623: 'Our land teems with people, and the inhabitants run each other's shoes off in looking for work. Wherever there is a penny to be earned, ten hands are at once extended to get it.' [4]

Admittedly there was at times some movement the other way; not only of Dutch capital and skilled labour to France, England, Sweden, Denmark and Germany, but also, though the evidence on this point is fragmentary, of unskilled labour. In any event, although wages were usually very low and working hours very long, unemployment in the northern Netherlands was never sufficiently severe to induce industrial and agricultural workers to emigrate on an adequate scale to the overseas possessions of the Dutch East and West India Companies. Conditions seemed to have improved somewhat after about 1664, in comparison with those prevailing during the Eighty Years War and during the disastrous struggle with England in 1652–4. Private charity increased and public charity was better administered. The periodical heavy mortality among the poor did not occur so often or so severely as previously. Oscillating grain prices did not have quite such unfavourable effects, as bread was now supplemented by potatoes. Working-class housing also improved slightly, to the extent that wooden houses with thatched roofs were increasingly replaced by brick or stone houses with slate or tiled roofs. But overcrowding and slum living conditions continued to be the general rule for the urban poor in the Dutch Republic for two centuries, and in this respect matters probably deteriorated rather than improved. There seem to have been many more people living on poor-relief in the second half of the 18th century than there were a hundred years earlier.

Dutch agriculture suffered greatly in the early part of the Eighty Years War owing to incidents like the deliberate flooding of the country-side during the siege and relief of Leiden. It was estimated, no doubt with some exaggeration, that two-thirds of

4. *Fin de la guerre*, p. 23 (Knuttel, nr. 3428).

the province of Holland was still under water in 1596. But Dutch agriculture revived rapidly in the 1590s with the additional security gained from Prince Maurice's victories and from the higher prices paid for agricultural products during this phase of the price revolution. The great increase of the overseas trade of the northern Netherlands during the first half of the 17th century was accompanied by a considerable though less spectacular growth in agriculture, as larger amounts of capital became available for investment in land. Pieter van Hoorn, a member of the government Council at Batavia in 1674, in discussing whether the Dutch ought not to think about turning their commercial and maritime empire into a true colonial one, i.e. one based on the settlement of white people in the tropics, pointed out that love of the soil was something deeply implanted in mankind the world over. Even in commercial-minded Holland, he averred, most of the successful merchants sought to buy a bit of landed property and to engage in farming or gardening, if only on a small scale and as a hobby. Certainly, during this period, more land was made available for agriculture through extensive reclamation projects, of which the drainage of the Beemster in 1610 is perhaps the best-known example. The leading authority on the history of husbandry in the Low Countries has stated that 'during the 17th and 18th centuries Dutch farmers excelled in stock-breeding and dairy produce, in the cultivation of commercial crops, in horticulture, and in the invention of simple and cheap tools'.[5] This was, of course, a slow process, and only gathered momentum after the Peace of Westphalia in 1648, nor was it evenly distributed over the whole country. Furthermore, it would be wrong to assume that because Dutch agricultural production flourished in some regions and in some ways which aroused the envious admiration of foreign visitors to the United Provinces, that all the peasants lived in a land of Cockaigne. Dutch agriculture became more intensified not so much because the Seven Provinces became richer but because of the need for a dense rural population to make a living in an age when there

5. B. S. Slicher van Bath, *apud* Bromley & Kossmann (eds.), *Britain and the Netherlands*, pp. 130–53; ibid., *De Agrarische Geschiedenis van West Europa 500–1850* (Utrecht, 1960), pp. 129, 221–4, 234, 264–7.

were limits to what the urban industries could absorb. Moreover, a distinction must be drawn between the peasantry of Holland and Zeeland and those of the eastern provinces. In Guelderland and Overijssel, for example, where the landowners had virtually unfettered control of local justice and administration, the peasantry were less favourably placed than in the two maritime provinces, apart from the fact that the soil was poorer. In Friesland, too, though the soil was rich, the local nobility or wealthy farmers likewise exercised close control over their tenants. The 'ancient Frisian freedom' of which 17th-century Frisians boasted was in reality restricted to the rural landowners who virtually monopolized political, administrative and economic power.

In two respects, the Dutch peasantry and the urban workers were relatively better off than their counterparts in (say) Germany, Flanders, Spain and France. Firstly, they were less subject to the ravages of invading armies. The Spanish-Imperialist raid in the Veluwe in 1629, and the French invasion of several provinces in 1672–3, both involved only a brief occupation. Secondly, the country was so small and communications (especially by river and canal) so good, that a dearth in any part of the United Provinces could easily be relieved at a period when Amsterdam was justly termed the 'corn-bin of Europe'. This was not the case, for instance, in France, where a primitive and expensive transport system meant that famine in one region might not be relieved by a superfluity of grain in a distant province. On the other hand, it must be admitted that the use of the widespread canal network was unnecessarily hindered by the rivalry of the different municipalities which owned, maintained, and operated them. These institutions jealously maintained their medieval privileges which gave them the right to route all traffic along the canals in their respective localities through the chief towns concerned, so as to ensure the imposition of a municipal toll (or tolls). These tolls and routing restrictions were particularly vexatious at Dordrecht, Haarlem and Gouda; but despite these administrative obstacles and the numerous bridges and dikes which compelled frequent trans-shipments, canals still provided a much better and smoother means of communication than most of the roads.

The frugality of the Dutch peasant impressed all foreign visitors, though several observers agreed with Sir William Temple that 'the clowns or boors as they call them' were 'diligent rather than laborious'. Their staple diet was limited to vegetables, milk, and bread and butter or bread and cheese, which Temple thought was the reason that 'neither their strength nor vigour seems answerable to the size or bulk of their bodies'. Even moderately well-to-do people seldom ate meat more than once a week, and many workers were lucky if they got it once a month. The rations in 17th-century alms-houses, which presumably reflected the staple diet of the urban poor, comprised beans, peas, groats and rye-bread. Although the richer burghers and merchants naturally ate more meat than did their social inferiors, their staple diet in the first quarter of the 17th century was described by a contemporary Englishman as being mainly 'buttermilk boiled with apples, stockfish, buttered turnips and carrots, lettuce, salads and red herrings, washed down with small beer'. Englishmen were fond of calling the Dutch 'butter-boxes', as the French called them *'mangeurs de fromage'*; but Temple stated that the frugal Dutch farmers sold their high-quality butter and cheese for export, buying 'the cheapest out of Ireland or the north of England for their own use'.[6]

If the peasants had to be satisfied with what Sir William Temple called 'short and heartless food', at any rate they usually got more to eat than the lowest class of urban workers, the so-called *grauw*, or rabble. This element proliferated in the larger towns, and the strong aversion with which it was regarded by the upper classes comes out very clearly in contemporary literature and correspondence. If the regent-oligarchs were decidedly of the opinion that the middle-class burgher was a small fellow who should be kept small, they were still more scornful of 'the sottish ill-natured rabble, who ever hate and are ready to im-

---

6. Temple, *Observations* (ed. 1676), 158–9, 182, 232; W. Carr, *An Accurate Description* (ed. 1691), p. 72. Cf. also De Laet, *Republyke der Zeven Vrye Nederlanden* (ed. 1652), p. 63; De Bosch Kemper, *Armoede* (ed. 1851), p. 129. For a more detailed discussion of 17th-century Dutch diet see P. Zumthor, *Daily Life in Rembrandt's Holland* (1962), pp. 68–73.

peach the aristocratical rulers of their republic', as the author of the *Interest of Holland* declared in 1662. Nor did this scorn mellow with the passage of time; for over a century later the regents still denounced the 'surly gruffness, bestial stupidity and disgraceful dissoluteness' of the urban proletariat.[7] As may be gathered from these and many other typical denunciations of the *grauw*, the regents were also rather afraid of the rabble, or rather, of what the rabble might do if it got out of hand. The mob could certainly show its teeth on occasion; but the worst example of misguided popular fury, the lynching of the brothers De Witt at The Hague (20 August 1672), was primarily the work of the burgher civic-guards, and was deliberately instigated by Orangist agitators.

The hard core of the *grauw* was composed of day-labourers, vagrants and the local unemployed at any given time, reinforced by other workers whose livelihood depended on casual employment and who were liable to instant dismissal. Sailors were often included in the *grauw* for reasons which will be apparent later. Workers whose employment was more regular, such as the self-employed, skilled labourers and artisans, small shopkeepers, junior clerks and small traders, were grouped together under the terms of the 'small man' (*kleine man*) or the 'common man', among whom petty officials, small farmers, and master-mariners may also be numbered. In other words, the 'common man' comprised the lower middle class and the more respectable sections of the working class. At times the term was extended upwards to include the wealthier shopkeepers and traders, and the senior clerks and officials employed by the provincial and municipal administrations – practically everyone between the *grauw* at the bottom of the social ladder and the regent-oligarchs and wealthy merchants at the top.

There were three kinds of guilds in the 17th-century United Netherlands: the craftsmen's guilds for certain skilled workers;

7. *Interests of Holland* (ed. 1702), p. 394; Betje Wolff and Agje Deken, writing in 1785, *apud* De Haan, *Priangan*, Vol. IV, p. 731. I am obliged to Dr J. W. Smit of the University of Utrecht for tracing the original of this quotation to Wolff & Deken, *Economische Liedjes*, Part III (The Hague, 1781), p. viii.

the traders' guilds for merchants; and the ordinary workers' guilds which included people like corn-porters, beer-carriers, bargees, draymen and herring-packers. In most places the guilds clung stubbornly to their right of regulating the hours, wages and number of apprentices, for which they were roundly criticized by the 17th century Leiden industrialist, Pieter de la Court, in his *Interest van Holland*, and also by several twentieth-century historians. Nevertheless, as Professor Geyl has pointed out, if their narrow-mindedness and routine spirit hindered the rise of independent large-scale capitalists in the spheres where the guilds were strong, they also retarded the growth of a rightless and propertyless rabble – the *grauw* – in some places. This did not apply to certain great industries such as shipping, brewing, soap making and sugar refining, which were wholly or largely outside the guild system. The Leiden textile industry remained subject to effective guild control over the grading and inspection of its cloth, but not over its poorly paid labourers. However, even guild craftsmen often worked from dawn to dusk, and a twelve- or even fourteen-hour day was quite common for the working-man. This contrasted strongly with the office hours of their employers, some of whom only worked between one and four hours a day.[8]

Rather surprisingly, social discontent was only spasmodically translated into action by the sedentary workers, and strikes were relatively infrequent even among the sweated textile workers of Leiden. There was a time in this town when 20,000 people – not all of them unemployed – had to be kept by charity from starving; and the chronic under-nourishment of these workers was doubtless responsible for the high incidence of tuberculosis among them. The brewery workers of Amsterdam petitioned for higher wages in 1578, claiming that their scanty pay was insufficient to keep them and their families from starving at a time when food and housing costs were rising. They only received a fraction of what they asked, and they renewed their requests in 1595 and 1617. The cloth-workers of Amsterdam also evinced

8. De Roever-Dozy (ed. F. H. Fischer), *Het leven van onze voorouders* (3d. ed., 4 vols., Amsterdam, 1938–9), Vol. IV, pp. 122–5; Vol. III, p. 408.

dissatisfaction with their living conditions at times, but not on the scale one would expect from the admitted fact that the contagious diseases which periodically ravaged them early in the 17th century did not afflict the better-fed and better-housed 'burgomasters, regents, ministers of the Church, schoolmasters or town officials'. The lot of the ordinary manual worker was hard; and the infrequency of overt unrest was due rather to the absence or weakness of the workers' organizations (as Violet Barbour points out) than to the 'paternal and enlightened régime of the upper-middle-class dictators', as claimed by Professor G. J. Renier. It is true, however, that class differences in the Dutch Republic, as elsewhere, were usually accepted as an aspect of the eternal scheme of things.[9] Moreover, the urban proletariat were unarmed, and the burgher militia or civic-guards could be relied on to obey the orders of the regents in the event of any conflict with the *grauw*.

Taxation in the Dutch Republic, as in most other countries, was apt to fall more severely on the poor than on the rich, but it was not framed entirely without consideration for 'ability to bear'. A vast net of excise was levied on most consumer goods and on many of the ordinary activities of living. These imposts naturally bore more heavily on the peasant, the sailor and the artisan than on the wealthy burgher, the merchant and the rentier. But many manifestations of good living, which would have escaped taxation in other countries, were taxed in the United Provinces on a sliding-scale according to a man's rank and wealth, or even according to the appearance thereof. The English Consul at Amsterdam in 1688 gave a lengthy list of taxes which the householders had to pay and which included such items as an annual poll-tax for every male and female servant over eight years old; for wine, 'as your quality is'; to the watch, 'as your house is in greatness'; for street lighting, 'as the largeness of your house is'. Coaches, carriages and sleighs were also taxed according to their quality as well as their quantity.

The necessities of life which were taxed included salt, soap,

9. De Bosch Kemper, *Armoede* (ed. 1851), pp. 82–3; V. Barbour, *Capitalism in Amsterdam*, pp. 70–72; G. J. Renier, *The Dutch Nation*, pp. 100–102.

butter, beans, turf (mainly used as fuel), wood, meat and bread. 'Then there are many taxes in trade, as that no man can weigh or measure his own goods in gross, but the States' officers must do it. Then the States have a tax called the *verpounding* on all lands and houses in their dominions. Then they have a tax on sealed paper, and a tax for registering lands or houses; likewise a tax on cows, horses, calves and on all sorts of fruit.' Anyone entering or leaving a walled town after dark had to pay a *stuiver* to pass the gate. Tolls were levied over bridges and at canal crossings for the passage of men, animals and vehicles. 'Milk first pays as milk, and again if it be made butter; yea, the buttermilk and whey pays a tax likewise, for all which a man would think that a people that stand so much upon maintaining of their liberty should mutiny and refuse payment.' William Carr assures us that this very seldom happened, and, when it did, the offenders were punished very severely. He added, fairly enough: 'Should we in England be obliged to pay the taxes that are here imposed, there would be rebellion upon rebellion. And yet after all that is here paid, no man may bake his own bread, nor grind his own corn, or brew his own beer, nor dare any man keep in his house a hand-mill, although it be but to grind mustard or coffee.'

After giving some instances from his own experience of the short shrift given to tax-dodgers, whether they were of high or low estate, the Consul commented: 'So sacred are taxes here, and must so exactly be paid. And were they not here so precise, it were impossible for so small a country to subsist. And therefore you may hear the inhabitants generally say, that what they suffer is for their *Vaderland*. Hence the meanest among them are content to pay what is laid on them, for they say that all that is the *Vaderland*'s is ours.' While it may have been true that the Dutch paid their taxes with relatively less unwillingness than did other peoples, since they could see that there was no question of the money being squandered on the personal extravagances of a king or a court, William Carr's picture of the cheerful Dutch tax-payer is undoubtedly overdrawn for the edification of his own complaining countrymen. Taxes for the Dutch navy, which he implies were voted readily and paid promptly, were often voted reluctantly and stumped up slowly. Of the five provincial admiralties, only the wealthy Amsterdam Admiralty had a consistently good record, as we shall have occasion to observe (p. 119). Pieter de la Court and other industrialists objected strongly to paying taxes on 'all imported rough goods, which our inhabitants are to work up'. Evasion of the convoy duties was widespread by wealthy shippers; and the poorer classes, whom Carr represents as paying up so uncomplainingly, would doubtless have agreed with an Englishman's definition of Excise as 'an infamous tax levied by scoundrels'.[10]

Hard as were the living conditions of the industrial and agricultural workers, the life of the seafaring communities was even harder. The very nature of a sailor's calling, and the long cold winters to which the northern Netherlands were liable, meant that seasonal unemployment among the *varend volk* (seafaring men) was inevitable to some extent. It was frequently aggravated by contrary winds, or by ice, which might close harbours for weeks on end;[11] by wars, or rumours of wars, which might close home or foreign ports; by periodic embargoes on Dutch ships in Iberian harbours before 1648; or by stoppages in the vital Baltic trade through the Sound. Despite the phenomenal growth of Dutch shipping and maritime enterprise between 1585 and 1650, there seems to have been a surplus of sailors for most of this period, and, perhaps, for the next sixty or seventy years. During this time a Dutch skipper could usually count on mustering a crew despite the low wages and the spartan rations which

10. W. Carr, *An Accurate Description* (ed. 1691), pp. 46–50. Cf. Temple, *Observations* (ed. 1676), pp. 250–54. Cf. also C. Wilson, 'Taxation and the decline of empires, an unfashionable theme' (*BMHGU*, Vol. 77, pp. 10–26) for an interesting paper on the incidence of taxation in the United Provinces, received as this work goes to press.

11. '... many times their havens are all shut up for two or three months with ice, when ours are open and free' (Temple, *Observations*, ed. 1676, p. 155). The same perspicacious observer noted that the Dutch 'spring is much shorter, and less agreeable than with us; the winter much colder, and some parts of the summer much hotter' (*op. et loc. cit.*).

were the general rule. Such, at least, was the case with ships trading in European waters; for it was often otherwise with East and West Indiamen bound for distant seas and notoriously unhealthy tropical lands, from which there was not much more than an even chance of returning alive.

The provincial admiralties likewise often found difficulty in manning their warships, particularly the senior but impecunious admiralty of Rotterdam, which was a notoriously bad paymaster. When, however, money was available, there was seldom any lack of recruits for the naval service in the second half of the 17th century, when the Dutch were able to send fleets to sea manned with anything from 16,000 to 24,000 men, virtually all of whom were volunteers. Although the Dutch government did not resort to the naval pressgang, as did the English, the authorities sometimes found it necessary to place a temporary embargo on outward-bound merchant-shipping in wartime, so as to induce sailors to enlist in the navy as the only chance of earning their daily bread. Dutch historians often allege that in normal times the naval rates of pay were deliberately kept below those prevailing in the merchant service, for fear lest a rise in the former would result in an increase in the latter. A rise in the merchant sailors' wages would hamper shipowners in facing foreign competition, since the low wages that Dutch shipowners paid their crews formed a prime reason for their ability to offer lower freight rates. This differential, if it applied at all, certainly did not do so after about the middle of the 17th century, so far as I can ascertain. From 1665 to 1780, the basic rate of pay for a naval able seaman remained unchanged at fifteen guilders a month. But during this period an able seaman in the service of the VOC often received less, ten or eleven guilders a month being the usual rate.

When (in 1629) some leading Amsterdam shipowners claimed, correctly enough, that during the twelve-year truce the Dutch had secured the lion's share of the carrying-trade of Europe thanks to their low freights and superior techniques, they forbore to add that this had been achieved largely by the owners economizing on the number and the rations of their crews. Other contemporaries were franker. Van Meteren, in his chronicle of 1599, observed that the North Sea herring fishery was such a hazardous and uncertain occupation that 'neither the English nor anyone else' would sail in it for the low wages and the poor food which the Dutch fishers accepted. Another chronicler observed a few years later that the Dutch 'skippers and sailors are so skilled in seafaring and fishing and so economical in their feeding, that they save our shipowners at least a third of the expenses in men and rations, which other nations demand in greater quantity and better quality'. A third commentator was even more explicit in his explanation of the success of Holland and Zeeland shipowners in competing with their Scandinavian and German rivals. The former, he wrote in 1645, 'run their ships more economically and give their sailors less rations ... so that it is believed that where a ship of the Easterlings would need more than ten men, a Dutch ship of the same size can be worked with six'. The *Hollandtse Mercurius* of October 1661, referring to the increasingly bitter rivalry between Dutch and English fishermen in the North Sea, observed: 'The brave Hollanders could not endure that the English (who would rather play the Monsieur with gloves on their hands than do any work) should deprive them of the use of the common element, which they have possessed for over a hundred years.'

Portuguese and Spanish contemporaries freely admitted that the Dutch Indiamen were more economically and efficiently managed than their own, an admission sometimes made by the English as well. On the other hand, an experienced English seaman who served in the homeward-bound *Burcht van Leiden* in 1674 considered that the poor quality and quantity of the rations were responsible for the higher mortality on board Dutch ships than in those of their English rivals. The development of the *fluit* or flute-ship, which was such an important factor in the growth of the Dutch carrying-trade (p. 22), had the disadvantage that when this economically manned vessel was first brought into service, many Dutch sailors were thrown out of work, some of whom enlisted with the Barbary Rovers. The frugality of Dutch shipowners engaged in the Norwegian timber-trade was also adversely criticized. The ships concerned were often crazy old vessels that were scarcely seaworthy, the nature of their cargo helping to keep them afloat – or so it was alleged.[12]

In the same year that the Amsterdammers boasted that they had secured the lion's share of the carrying trade of Europe, the seafaring population of Maassluis was described as being 'miserably poor and wretched, ... consisting of fishers who gain their bread in grinding poverty and in great peril'. Of course, a seaman's life was almost invariably a hard one in days of sail, and similar observations about the hardships of (say) British, French or Portuguese mariners are not far to seek.[13] In any event, there is plenty of evidence that Dutch sailors and fishers were living, as often as not, on the edge of bare subsistence, particularly when they were married men with families to support. This was a fact of which their employers, whether directors of the India Companies, members of the provincial admiralties, or merchant-shipowners, took full advantage. The temptation for shipowners and skippers to man their ships with low-paid and frugally fed crews was strengthened by the fact that not only were Dutch seamen usually available in abundance but many of the foreigners who came to seek work in the United Provinces, 'lured by the sweet smell of greater profit', were sailors from Scandinavia and Germany.

As early as 1588 there were reportedly over 2,000 sizeable

12. For the above and what follows cf. De Bosch Kemper, *Armoede* (ed. 1860), p. 103; J. E. Elias, *Schetsen uit de geschiedenis van ons zeewezen, 1568–1654* (6 vols., The Hague, 1916–30), Vol. I, pp. 46, 59–65; R. E. Weber, *De Beveiliging van de zee tegen Europeesche en Barbarijsche zeerovers, 1609–1621* (Amsterdam, pp. 32–7); AGN, V, p. 229; *Barlow's Journal of his Life at Sea, 1659–1703*, Vol. I, pp. 232, 236–7; Anon, *Aenwysinge det men vande Oost ende West-Indische Compagnien een Compagnie dient te maken* (The Hague, 1644), p. 3.

13. The contemporary French fishers of the Dunes de Maisy were 'si chétifs que devant les plus âpres gelées, ils sont presque nuds à la Mer et n'ont qu'un morceau de toille pour les couvrir' (*apud* F. Mauro, *Histoire Générale du Travail*, Paris, 1960, Vol. II, p. 317). William Hickey, calling at Lerwick in the Shetlands in 1780, described it as 'the most wretched town I ever beheld, principally consisting of fishermen's huts with only three or four houses fit for a human creature to inhabit'. (*Memoirs of William Hickey, 1749–1809* (ed. Alfred Spencer, 4 vols., 1925, Vol. II, p. 232).

Dutch merchantmen suitable for service as warships, and the Vice-Admiral of Holland claimed that he could raise 30,000 sailors in a fortnight. In 1608 the directors of the VOC claimed that there were then 40 ships manned by 5,000 men in Asia, 20 ships with 400 men off the coast of Guinea, and 100 ships with 1,800 men in the West Indies, while the number of ships and men in European waters greatly exceeded those employed in the colonial trades. In 1644, an apparently well-informed pamphleteer stated that the Dutch then had over 1,000 vessels which were fit for use as warships, and another 1,000 topsail merchant-ships on the high seas, apart from 6,000 herring-busses and vessels used on the inland waterways. He added with patriotic exaggeration that these ships were manned by over 80,000 of the best and finest seamen in the world, the East India Company alone having 150 ships and 15,000 men in its employ (not all of whom were sailors, obviously). In the last quarter of the 17th century it was confidently asserted that the VOC maintained over 200 capital ships and 30,000 men in pay, about half of whom were sailors.

The Dutch seafaring communities were, on the whole, much less resigned to their hard lot than were the more submissive urban workers and agricultural labourers. Mutiny was far from uncommon, and when sailors felt defrauded of their wages they were apt to riot in ways which frequently worried the regent class in the seaports. In 1629 some sailors of the WIC, dissatisfied with their share of the prize-money after Piet Heyn's capture of the silver-fleet, tried to break into the buildings where the booty was stored and had to be dispersed by the civic guards. More serious was a riotous demonstration at Amsterdam by mutinous sailors from the fleet in September 1652. This was only quelled after the soldiers had fired on the mob and two of the ringleaders had been hanged. On 15 June 1665 an angry crowd of sailors' wives, children and dependents at Den Briel tried to lynch Johan Evertsen, Lieutenant-Admiral of Zeeland, whom they falsely accused of cowardice in the recently fought battle of Lowestoft. The unlucky admiral was rescued by soldiers just in time, but the authorities did not dare to arrest or punish any of the rioters. Seventeenth-century official reports and popular literature repeatedly stress the wild and undisciplined nature of the *varend volk* and the difficulty which their officers and employers had in controlling them. The officers, indeed, were often of the same breed as their men, as the 'Tarpaulin', Lieutenant-Admiral M. H. Tromp, explained when declining an invitation to dine with Admiral Sir John Pennington in The Downs – 'He said that he had a great many of clownish boors amongst his captains, that neither understood civility nor manners'.[14]

Whether they were 'clownish boors', or burghers' sons, the ships' officers usually relied on severe discipline and savage punishments to keep their men in order; treating them 'like men ashore and like donkeys on board' according to a proverbial saying. 'For the sailors on board Indiamen', wrote an experienced voyager in 1751, 'cursing, swearing, whoring, debauchery and murder are mere trifles. There is, therefore, always something brewing among these fellows, and if the officers did not crack down on them so quickly with punishments, their own lives would certainly not be safe for a moment among that unruly rabble.' The East India Company's soldiers and sailors, wrote one of that corporation's more strait-laced employees in 1677, 'behave like wild boars; they rob and steal, drink and go whoring so shamelessly that it seems to be no disgrace with them'. For this reason, he adds, they must be ruled with a rod of iron, 'like untamed beasts; otherwise they are capable of wantonly beating-up anybody'. Nicholas de Graaff, a more sympathetic and experienced voyager, showed greater perception of the sailors' lot and the potential causes of their unruliness when he wrote: 'Jan Maat, the least and lowliest person aboard, must be ready on the slightest nod or command of any superior, to do everything he is told without grumbling. At any show of reluctance, he is threatened and beaten with the rope's end. The sailors must climb and clamber in the shrouds and on the yardarms by day and night, in storm and tempest. They must load and unload the ships, and they must stand like a lot of subservient slaves with

14. Journal of Peter White for 26 September/6 October 1639, *apud* C. R. Boxer, *The Journal of Maarten Harpertszoon Tromp Anno 1639* (Cambridge, 1930), p. 182 n.

hat in hand by the gangway whenever the skipper or another officer leaves or returns to the ship.' [15]

Punishments included the death-sentence for murder, mutiny and homosexuality (usually by being thrown into the sea bound to the body of the victim or the other culprit); keel-hauling; ducking from the yard-arm; and nailing the culprit's hand to the mainmast; flogging with anything from ten to five hundred lashes; and imprisonment in irons on bread and water and in very confined quarters. The thrifty side of the Dutch character appears in the wide-ranging scale of fines which were levied, either *per se* or in conjunction with physical punishments – the Dutch East India Company being particularly exacting in this respect. Insolence to superior officers, blasphemy, drunkenness and fighting with knives (*snicker-snee*) were among the most common offences. Mutiny and insubordination undoubtedly occurred more often aboard East and West Indiamen than in the navy and the ordinary merchant marine. This was, perhaps, partly due to the longer voyages made by Indiamen and to the higher percentage of foreigners in their crews, although opinion was not unanimous on this last point.

The *Heeren* XVII had originally and optimistically enacted that no Norwegians and 'Easterlings' should be engaged as sailors, much less French, English and Scots, but this ruling was a dead letter from the start. The enormous wastage of European lives in the tropics, and the reluctance of many Netherlanders to serve there, or to serve a monopolistic trading company, meant (as we have seen) that both the VOC and the WIC had to take what men they could get. Many people saw no harm in this, agreeing

15. For the above and what follows see the copiously documented articles of J. de Hullu, 'De handhaving der ordre en tucht op de schepen der Oost-Indische Compagnie' (*BTLVNI*, Vol. 67, pp. 516–40), and 'De matrozen en soldaten op de schepen der Oost-Indische Compagnie' (*BTLVNI*, Vol. 69, pp. 318–65); N. de Graaff, *Oost-Indische Spiegel* (Hoorn, 1703). De Graaff's testimony is particularly valuable, as he served in the navy, in whaling ships, and in East and West Indiamen. C. R. Boxer, 'The Dutch East-Indiamen: their sailors, their navigators, and life on board, 1602–1795' (*Mariner's Mirror*, Vol. XLIX, May, 1963, pp. 81–104).

with Nicholas Witsen, who observed in 1671 that the mixture of nationalities on board a ship lessened the chances of a successful mutiny being hatched among the men. Others, however, agreed with Governor-General Jacques Specx, who in 1629 deplored the high percentage of foreigners, reminding the *Heeren* XVII 'how often we have been troubled in Asia with having so many Frenchmen and Englishmen, which we hope that your honours will prevent in future by providing us with good trusty Netherlands' hearts'. Alas even when the Netherlands' hearts were available, they were not always good and trusty, as shown by the shipboard mutinies in which they were often actively involved.

Opinions naturally varied concerning what kind of foreigners were more desirable – or least undesirable – as subordinates. For example, orders were repeatedly promulgated by the two Companies against the employment of Roman Catholics in any capacity, but these orders were usually ignored or evaded when it came to enlisting soldiers and sailors. Even Lutherans were long regarded askance; but though upright and God-fearing Calvinists were officially preferred, there were never enough of them to go round. English and (to a lesser degree) Scots were suspect on account of the long-standing Anglo-Dutch rivalry, but at times they were enlisted in considerable numbers. Governor-General Reynst spoke a good word for those aboard his flagship in 1614, claiming that they were willing and obedient workers 'who usually keep themselves clean'. But for obvious reasons, Scandinavians and Germans were more strongly represented among Dutch ships' complements, alike in the navy, the Indiamen and the ordinary merchant marine.

At the end of the 17th century, the VOC advocate and chronicler, Pieter van Dam, complained that whereas in its early years the Company could easily enlist seamen for 8 or 9 florins a month, it now had difficulty in finding adequate crews, though offering 10 or 11 florins a month as well as the bonus of a month's wages. For reasons which are discussed later (pp. 121–122) the difficulty of manning East Indiamen with a majority of Dutch seamen became more acute during the 18th century. The Swedish traveller, C. P. Thunberg, noted when he visited Nagasaki in 1775, that although by Japanese government regulations

all of the ship's company were supposed to be Dutch-born, yet there were many 'Swedes, Danes, Germans, Portuguese and Spaniards' among them, apart from thirty-four slaves.

If foreigners were relatively numerous among the sailors, there was a still higher proportion of them among the soldiers, as we shall see below. The traditional rivalry between the two groups in all countries and climates was very much in evidence aboard the Dutch Indiamen. They gave each other insulting nicknames, and only the strict discipline which was imposed on both sides prevented them from coming to blows more often than they actually did. As an outgoing colonial governor wrote to the *Heeren* XVII from his flagship in Table Bay in 1630: 'I see that the old passion still persists and that the sailors are deadly enemies of the soldiers.'

Although the ships' officers aboard Indiamen were not authorized to inflict any save minor punishments without the concurrence of a majority of the ship's council – composed of the skipper, mates and senior merchant on board – this rule was very ill-observed. The skippers of the East Indiamen, in particular, were repeatedly criticized for their propensity to play the shipboard tyrant, despite the *Heeren* XVII's order of 8 August 1705 that offenders would be fined six months' wages for the first offence and discharged with ignominy for the second. Apart from their real or alleged brutality, many skippers made themselves still more unpopular by economizing on the crew's rations and selling the surplus on arrival at Batavia. So long as the Indiamen were east of the Cape of Good Hope, there was relatively little chance of the crews manifesting their resentment too strongly, since they feared they might be made to serve longer in Asian seas, or sent to some particularly unhealthy region. But when the homeward-bound Indiamen were nearing their voyage's end, the crew sometimes virtually took over the ship and wreaked their vengeance on those they hated. An eyewitness of such a scene in 1701 reported how the unfortunate ship's cook was dragged out of hiding and so severely beaten with his own kitchen implements 'that he was maimed for a long time and could not even go to the East India House to get his sea-chest and wages'. The skipper of this vessel managed to evade the sailors' wrath at first, but when the ship reached harbour 'they told him to his face in the presence of the directors who were paying us off, that he was a scoundrel, a ration-thief and a bully, and they threatened that they would pay him his due ashore. As indeed they did at Middelburg, where they beat him almost to a jelly.'

As may be gathered from the foregoing, the sailors of the East India Company were apt to become something of a special breed, and Nicholas de Graaff tells us that ordinary merchant skippers were very chary of engaging men who had sailed before the mast in the service of the 'Laudable Company'. But those who enlisted in the navy, or who sailed in the Baltic, Atlantic and Mediterranean trades, were hardly less tough if the evidence of contemporary ships' journals is to be trusted. Jan Snoep, a Calvinist minister who served as chaplain in De Ruyter's fleet in the Mediterranean in 1661–2, paints a picture of his shipmates which can be taken as typical. He was horrified at the roughness of the sailors, their ignorance, their irreligion, their cursing, quarrelling and fighting. The Church afloat, he avered, resembled an 'Ecclesia Porcorum' rather than the Spouse of Christ. He complained bitterly about the numerous Papists, Remonstrants, Lutherans, atheists and mockers to be found among them, particularly on board De Ruyter's flagship, *De Liefde*. They listened to the Word without paying attention; they attended prayers without devotion, and they profaned the Sabbath unnecessarily. When questioned about the tenets of Christianity, they were 'as dumb as fishes'. He naturally found it very difficult to instil the rudiments of the 'true Christian Reformed Religion' in such a crew, whose devotions were paid primarily to Bacchus and Venus.[16]

If such was the spiritual condition of the sailors aboard a ship commanded by Michiel de Ruyter, a genuinely pious and psalm-singing Calvinist, it can be imagined what occurred in other ships whose captains were not exemplars of puritanical virtue. Both de Ruyter and his predecessor, the elder Tromp, were

16. Rev. Jan Snoep's Latin letter to the classis of Walcheren, from aboard the *Vlissingen* in Malaga harbour, 19 April 1662, *apud* N. Kist & W. Moll, *Kerkhistorisch Archief*, Vol. I (Amsterdam, 1857), pp. 345–63.

anxious to have Calvinist ministers as naval chaplains who would be a civilizing influence on their crews, and thus an aid in maintaining discipline. But as can be gathered from Jan Snoep's journal, qualified Calvinist ministers never volunteered in sufficient numbers to make much difference. Discipline continued to be enforced chiefly by flogging and other savage punishments, even in fleets commanded by admirals so popular with their men as those two great seamen, both of whom were called *Bestevaer*, or 'grand-dad', by their crews.

The Rev. Jan Snoep also complained about the inferiority of the rations and the difficulty of keeping provisions fresh in the heat of a Mediterranean summer. In this respect, conditions were naturally much worse aboard an East Indiaman, which might be continuously at sea from six to eight months. Before the scientific and engineering discoveries of the 19th century, the wit of man could hardly have devised thoroughly satisfactory ways of preserving food and drink for months on end in the holds of wooden ships sailing under a tropical sun. The outward-bound Governor-General Gerard Reynst, while accusing the contractors of supplying inferior provisions in the hope that their subsequent deterioration would be ascribed to the tropical heat, admitted that they might have deteriorated anyway. 'The water and the wine which are daily taken from the hold are about as hot as if they were boiling, and this is the reason why much of the victuals go bad', he wrote from his flagship off Sierra Leone in 1614. In truth, the wonder is not that food and water often became rotten and stinking, irrespective of whether the contractors and ship's-chandlers were dishonest, but that supplies sometimes lasted in relatively good condition during a voyage of over six months.

The rations varied at different periods, as can be seen from the typical ration-scales given by Nicolaus de Graaff and O. F. Mentzel. These indicate that seamen got two or three meat-days a week at a period when the Dutch peasants and workers were lucky if they got one; but contemporary evidence varies widely as to whether the sailors' rations were adequate in quantity and quality. In all probability, when the skipper, purser and steward were honest, and the cook(s) efficient, the crew had little or nothing to complain of. But when, as often happened, the skipper or the purser tried to embezzle the crew's rations, or when the provisions became putrid through tropical heat or other causes, then the men suffered accordingly.

The officers admittedly fared better in any event. Those of the rank of boatswain and below received a double drinking-ration, while at the skipper's table in the great cabin few restrictions were imposed on the participants' thirst and appetite. Readers of William Hickey's *Memoirs* will recall how well that gourmand fared aboard the Dutch East Indiaman *De Held Woltemade* from the Cape of Good Hope to the Texel in 1780. Almost exactly a century earlier, Robert Knox, after his escape from the kingdom of Kandy, voyaged to Batavia with the Dutch governor of coastal Ceylon. 'He so far favoured me,' wrote Knox, 'that I was in his own mess, and ate at his own table, where every meal we had ten or twelve dishes of meat with variety of wine.' This sharp contrast in living standards between officers and men was not, of course, peculiar to the Dutch. It was a general feature in the shipping of all nations, not least in the vessels of the Royal Navy and John Company. Readers of Parson Teonge's *Diary* (1675-9) will recall the guzzling and boozing in the captain's cabin at times when the sailors were dying of hunger and malnutrition.[17]

The importance of fresh provisions in combating scurvy had been vaguely realized from the time of the early Portuguese voyages. Oranges, lemons and apples were often carried in Dutch Indiamen, although the superiority of the lemon as an antiscorbutic over all other citrous fruits was not understood. Before the foundation of the settlement at the Cape of Good Hope as a victualling-station for East Indiamen, the commanders of earlier fleets made sporadic efforts to plant fruit-trees and vegetables in

17. J. de Hullu, 'De voeding op de schepen der Oost-Indisch Compagnie' (BTLVNI, Vol. 67, pp. 541-62); N. de Graaff, *Oost-Indisch Spiegel* (Hoorn, 1703), pp. 57-60; O. F. Mentzel, *Life at the Cape in the Mid-18th Century* (Cape Town, 1919), pp. 34-5; *Memoirs of William Hickey*, Vol. II, pp. 228-33; R. Knox, *An Historical Relation of the Island of Ceylon in the East Indies* (London, 1681), p. 173; G. E. Manwaring (ed.), *The Diary of Henry Teonge, chaplain on board H.M. ships Assistance, Bristol, and Royal Oak, 1675-1679* (London, 1927).

such places as Saint Helena and Mauritius, so those coming after them might reap the benefit and plant seeds in their turn. These two islands were exceptionally healthy; but at other places, such as the Cape Verde Islands, Sierra Leone and Madagascar, where the Indiamen sometimes called for fresh fruit and provisions, the scorbutics might be cured by a change of diet but many men might become infected with malaria or other tropical fevers.

Another source of disease was the lack of shipboard hygiene, or rather, the difficulty of enforcing adequate sanitary standards in the cramped and crowded crews' quarters. The Dutch Indiamen of the Golden Century have been rightly compared to the ordinary Dutch houses of the same period, which are equally familiar to us from paintings by the Old Masters. Picturesque and colourful from the outside, they were cold, ill-ventilated and dank inside. The soldiers and sailors lived in the confined space between decks, where they swung their hammocks, kept their sea-chests and messed together. Light and ventilation came through a few hatches and gun-ports, which often had to be closed in wet or stormy weather, thus making the living-quarters insufferably hot when the ship was in the tropics. This stifling atmosphere was frequently aggravated by heat and smoke from the cooking-galley, to say nothing of the exhalations from sopping wet, dead tired and seasick humanity. As the Indiamen were often over-loaded, and in any case had to carry drinking-water and pro-visions for at least nine months, there was seldom sufficient space to isolate the sick from the healthy or to nurse them properly.

Worst of all, perhaps, was the reluctance or the inability of some men to use the 'heads' for their intended purpose, these miscreants relieving themselves behind their sea-chests or in holes and corners. This insanitary behaviour was, of course, strictly forbidden; and it was the exception rather than the rule aboard Dutch ships, at any rate in comparison with those of most other nations. The French sailor, Pyrard de Laval, writing of his voyage in a Portuguese East India carrack in 1610, observed: 'These ships are mighty foul and stink withal; the most men not troubling themselves to go on deck for their necessities, which is in part the cause that so many die. The Spaniards, French and Italians do the same; but the English and Hollanders are exceedingly scrupulous and cleanly.' Nevertheless, the raw recruits supplied by the crimps were often too seasick to make their way to the 'heads' before they got their sea-legs; and even veteran Dutch sailors sometimes drank themselves into such a state of insensibility that they lay wallowing in their own filth. Last but not least were the fleas, lice and other vermin abounding in the men's filthy clothing, which they often had no opportunity of changing for weeks on end, and the rats, cockroaches and other pests which thrived on the rotting provisions in the ship's stores. Under such circumstances, the cleanliness aboard even Dutch ships sometimes left a good deal to be desired. The captain of an outward-bound Indiaman from Zeeland, which arrived at the Cape in 1774, wrote of one of his consorts which landed eighty sick ashore: 'She was between the decks so choked with filth, that some of my officers assured me, they had never seen so much dirt, not even aboard of any French ship.' [18]

Want of adequate clothing was another cause of the high incidence of disease among seamen. The *Heeren* XVII, for example, seem to have shared the crimps' belief that men who went on board ship in the depth of a Dutch winter did not need warm clothes, since they would soon be sailing in tropical seas under the Southern Cross. Yet the directors were closing their eyes to easily ascertainable facts. If Vondel made only a passing reference to the chronic wastage of men through hardship and cold (*het spillen van het volk door ongemack en kou*) in his poem 'In Praise of Navigation', which he dedicated to Dr Laurens Reael,

18. J. S. Stavorinus, *Voyages to the East-Indies, 1768-1778* (3 vols., London, 1798), Vol. II, pp. 90-91. For ship hygiene (or the lack of it) aboard Portuguese East Indiamen see C. R. Boxer, *The Tragic History of the Sea, 1589-1622* (Cambridge, 1959), pp. 15-22; *The Mariner's Mirror*, Vol. XLVI, pp. 41-2. For the conditions in Dutch Indiamen and warships, cf. J. C. M. Warnsinck (ed.), *Reisen van Nicolaus de Graaff, 1639-1687* (Amsterdam, 1930), *passim*; J. de Hullu, 'Ziekten en doktors op de schepen der Oost-Indische Compagnie' (*BTLVNI*, Vol. 67, pp. 245-72); D. Schoute, *De geneeskunde in den dienst der Oost-Indische Compagnie in Nederlandsch-Indië* (Amsterdam, 1929), pp. 40-103; A. E. Leuftink, *De geneeskunde bij's lands oorlogsvloot in de 17e eeuw* (Assen, 1953).

a former Governor-General of the East Indies, the same plaint was made more often and more forcibly by many of the Company's senior officials as a result of their own experience. Reael himself had shared the hardships of a sailor's life in the Atlantic and the Mediterranean, as well as in the Indian Ocean and the South China Sea. Simon van der Stel, Governor of the Cape of Good Hope, 1679–91, indicted long letters to the *Heeren* XVII, explaining that want of adequate food and clothing caused much of the sailors' high mortality rate. 'They lose heart from want of nourishment,' he wrote, 'and all germs of strength failing them they die.' [19] Even in European waters, the death-rate was often disturbingly high. The sailors of the Dutch fleet in the icebound harbour of Copenhagen during the winter of 1659–60, for example, suffered severely from frostbite, spotted typhus and other diseases, in conditions which remind one of the horrors of a Crimean winter in the war of 1854–5. If anything, food and clothing standards worsened during the 18th century, especially in the Dutch navy. This state of affairs was given as one of the principal reasons for the difficulty in securing sufficient sailors in 1780.

When we consider the hazards inseparable from a deep-sea sailor's life in days of sail, it is not surprising that the death-rate often reached catastrophic proportions, especially aboard East Indiamen. The most common and dreaded shipboard diseases may be defined as follows. Scurvy, which was the term used to cover a group of diseases caused by dietary deficiency; ship- (or jail-) fever, i.e. typhus, usually introduced on board by the infected clothing of the contaminated recruits provided by the crimps; dysentery, or the 'bloody flux', as the Dutch and English sailors called it. Colds, pleurisy, pneumonia and suppurative lung conditions also took a heavy toll of lives. Retention of urine was another dreaded disease, often caused by prostatic hypertrophy, especially among elderly sailors in their fifties and sixties. The accident-rate was by no means negligible, and the primitive

19. Apud Alice Trotter, *Old Cape Colony. A chronicle of her men and houses* (Cape Town, 1903), pp. 235–6. Cf. V. de Kock, *Those in Bondage* (London, 1950), p. 30.

surgical methods of the time made every operation a major hazard apart from the risk of gangrene.

It is small wonder that when sailors returned home after five years in the Indies they were apt to squander their hard-earned back pay in brothel and grog-shop binges which earned them the nickname of 'lords of six weeks'. Amsterdam was the Mecca of the great majority of these *heeren varensgasten*, whatever their original place or country of origin. The money they spent in this way was a welcome source of income for many traders and tavern-keepers during two centuries. The English Consul at Amsterdam in 1688 was told that brothels in the guise of music-halls were tolerated because the returning seamen 'were so mad for women, that if they had not such houses to bait in, they would force the very citizens' wives and daughters'. A hundred years later, another eyewitness observed that the 'lords of six weeks' reduced themselves from comparative affluence to being 'as naked as Adamites' in that period, but he added complacently: 'And where does the money which they have squandered remain? In Amsterdam. And who has derived the profit from it? The inhabitants of that town.' [20]

We have seen that if foreigners were numerous among the deep-sea sailors, there was a still higher proportion of them among the soldiery, whether in the armies paid by the States-General or among the mercenaries who served the East and West India Companies. Even during the Eighty Years War the majority of the soldiers who fought under the Princes of Orange were not Dutch but Germans, Walloons and other foreigners. Whole regiments of Scots and English likewise served in the armies of the United Provinces for many years, though Dutch soldiers were not so rare as some modern writers allege. A pamphlet of 1623 reminds us that, even in the Free Netherlands, hunger and unemployment were powerful recruiting sergeants. 'The soldiers' mother gives birth twice a year; once in the summer, to those who are work-shy and cannot stand the smell of their own sweat,

20. W. Carr, *An Accurate Description* (ed. 1691), pp. 70–71; *Plan of Welmeenende voorstelling ter verbetering van Neerlands Zeewezen* (Amsterdam, *c.* 1780), pp. lvi–lvii (Knuttel, nr. 19464).

and again on the approach of winter, when there is a scarcity of firewood, turf, and other winter provisions.' [21] The proportion of Dutchmen was undoubtedly much higher in the officer corps than in the rank and file, but there were also numerous German, French, Swiss, English and Scots officers to be found in the commissioned ranks from ensign to field-marshal. Many of the officers, whether Dutch or foreign, were of noble or gentle blood. This was in contrast to the sea-service, where most of the officers were of middle- or working-class origins before the first half of the 18th century.

Despite the disastrous decline of the Dutch navy and – to a lesser extent – of the merchant marine during the 18th century, it was always easier to recruit sailors than soldiers from among the Dutch working class in the provinces of Holland, Zeeland and Friesland. An eyewitness of 1780 reported that a regiment which had been garrisoning several towns in north Holland for the space of two years, could not enlist more than fifteen men (nine of whom were foreigners) in that time, despite a continuous recruiting drive by the officers. It was admittedly not so hard to recruit soldiers in the land provinces, and even in the garrison towns of The Hague and Utrecht; but as a general rule it can be said that in the days of the Dutch Republic it was easier to recruit 1,000 sailors than 100 soldiers.[22]

In the mercenary forces of the East and West India Companies, the proportion of foreigners among all ranks was likewise high. In January 1622, out of 143 soldiers in the garrison at Batavia, there were 60 Germans, Swiss, English, Scots, Irish, Danes and other foreigners, apart from 17 Flemings and Walloons, and another 9 men whose respective nationalities were uncertain. The muster-rolls of the Moluccan garrisons in 1618–20 show a similar diversity, with soldiers from Bremen, Hamburg, Scotland and the Shetlands. Out of some 60 men sentenced in a series of shipboard courts martial held in the South China Sea between July 1622 and August 1623, at least 18 were foreigners, including Swiss, Scots, Flemings, French and Japanese. The garrison at the

21. Anon. *Fin de la guerre* (Amsterdam, 1623), pp. 11, 23.
22. Knuttel, nr. 19464, pp. 3–6.

Cape of Good Hope contained English, Scots and Irish soldiers in 1660; but here, as elsewhere, Germans were in the majority among the mercenaries who served the VOC. The proportion of Germans who served in the WIC does not seem to have been quite so high, at any rate before 1642. When Count Johan Maurits, the Governor-General of Netherlands Brazil, was ordered by the *Heeren* XIX in that year to discharge all of his soldiers who were not of Dutch, German or Scandinavian origin, he replied that the majority of his men were English, Scots and French. About the same time, the garrison of Paraíba included over 150 English soldiers under the command of their compatriot, John Goodlad, and the WIC had to find an English Calvinist minister to preach to the troops at Recife in their own language.[23]

The German who wrote that the garrison at Batavia in 1710 consisted almost entirely of Germans, Swiss and Poles, 'with hardly more than ten Netherlanders', was exaggerating. But eighty years later, the VOC had enlisted for service in the East two complete units of European mercenaries, the German Württemberg and the Swiss De Meuron regiments. As was the case with the home army, the proportion of Dutchmen was higher in the commissioned ranks than in the rank and file, but key positions were often filled by foreigners. To mention a few typical examples: Batavia had a French Huguenot commandant, Isaac de Saint-Martin, in 1686–96, and the Cape of Good Hope a Berliner, J. T. Rhenius, in 1728–40. On the other side of the world, an Englishman, James Henderson, commanded the Dutch garrison at Luanda in 1641–2, and the Scots officer J. G. Stedman's narrative of his services in Surinam in 1772–7 is deservedly

23. For the above and what follows, cf. J. de Hullu's previously quoted article 'De matrozen en soldaten op de schepen der O.I.C.' (BTLVNI, Vol. 69, pp. 318–65); 'Overzicht van de vonissen door den krijgsraad geslagen, 1622–24', in W. P. Groeneveldt, *De Nederlanders in China, 1601–24* (The Hague, 1898), pp. 584–94; S. P. L'Honoré-Naber (ed.), *Reise-beschreibungen von Deutschen beamten und kriegsleuten im dienst der Niederlandischen West- und Ost-Indischen Kompagnien, 1601–1797* (13 vols., The Hague, 1930–32), passim; C. R. Boxer, *The Dutch in Brazil, 1624–1654* (Oxford, 1957), pp. 87, 128–30, 176–91.

a classic. It may be noted in passing that the social prestige of the military officer, never so high in the Dutch Republic as in most other European countries, declined somewhat in the 18th century, though not so much in the United Provinces as in the East Indies. The officers of the States' army and navy who came out to Batavia with Van Braam's expedition in 1783 were disgusted to find that the civilian officials of the VOC treated their military colleagues with undisguised contempt. At this period none of the respectable burghers in Ceylon would invite any of the officers of the garrison to parties in their houses, with the exception of four or five of the senior officers.

Edward Barlow, who was a prisoner of the Dutch at Batavia in 1672–3, affirmed that 'the Hollanders are stronger in the East Indies than all the other Christian nations, having always in the East India, in one place or another, 150 or 200 sail of ships and 30,000 men or servants always in pay. But they are very sickly and die very fast, some ships bringing out of Holland 300 men, and many times there dying 80 or 100 of them by the time they arrive in East India.'[24] In truth, the wastage from death, disease, and desertion among white men in the tropics was always high. Complaints of recruiting difficulties, and of the poor quality of the men enlisted, date from the first decade of the VOC's existence. These complaints continued with few intermissions for nearly two hundred years, reaching a crescendo in the second half of the 18th century. In order to secure soldiers and sailors for service in the East, a class of crimps nicknamed *zielverkoopers*, or soul-sellers, soon came into existence at Amsterdam and other Dutch ports. These men accosted likely looking lads among the penniless unemployed, chiefly Germans, who swarmed into the northern Netherlands in search of work and riches. The crimp offered to provide a prospective recruit with board and lodging until such time as men were mustered for the next India Fleet, in return for an IOU (*transportbrief*) entitling the crimp to recover the cost of the recruit's accommodation and subsist-

24. *Barlow's Journal of his Life at Sea, 1659–1703.* Vol. I, p. 232. The figure of 30,000 men employed by the VOC is also given in Temple, *Observations* (ed. 1676, p. 228), and W. Carr, *An Accurate Description* (ed. 1691, pp. 34–5).

ence through monthly deductions from the man's pay when it became due.

While awaiting the day when the drum was beaten to announce enlistment for the Company's naval or military service, the recruits were kept in conditions which at times recall those of the barracoons for 'black ivory' in the West African slave-trade. They were closely confined in garrets, attics, or cellars, with little light or ventilation, inferior food, and worse sanitary arrangements. An eyewitness of 1778 reported that he had seen 300 men kept in a very low attic, 'where they must stay day and night, where they perform their natural functions, and where they have no proper place to sleep, but must lie higgeldy-piggeldy with each other'. He added: 'I have seen other instances where a very large number of men were shut up in the cellars of such houses, some of whom had already been there five months, during which time they had to breathe a very foul and sickly air. In some of these houses the death-rate is so alarming that the owners, not daring to report the correct number of deaths, some-times bury two bodies in one coffin.' The rations were on a par with the accommodation, consisting chiefly of badly cured bacon, 'slimy river fish', potatoes and bread. Obviously, men who were confined in such quarters for any length of time came aboard their ships in no condition to resist the onset of infectious or contagious diseases, even if they were lucky enough not to have contracted one already.[25]

In view of the fact that the unscrupulous methods of the Dutch 'soul-sellers' soon became notorious throughout the length and breadth of Germany, it seems astonishing that they were able to secure a continual supply of victims, even if we recall the North American adage that a sucker is born every minute. But so it was. The foregoing eyewitness of 1778 assures us that there

25. J. Veirac & B. Hussem, *Verhandelingen over de besmettelijke rotkoorts op de uitgaande Oost-Indische schepen* (Middelburg, 1778), apud J. de Hullu in *BTLVNI*, Vol. 67 (1913), pp. 249–50. The abuses of the *zielverkoopers* reached a climax in the second half of the 18th century and conditions do not seem to have been so bad previously, if O. F. Mentzel's very detailed account is to be relied on (*Life at the Cape in the Mid-18th Century*, pp. 12–27).

were then twenty, thirty, forty and more of these crimps in provincial towns where they had previously been unknown. In Amsterdam, which had always been the main centre of attraction, there were over two hundred. These 'soul-sellers' worked mainly to supply military and naval personnel for the service of the VOC, but they also provided them on occasion for the WIC. When they could not place their dupes with either of the two India Companies, they tried to dump them on the army, the navy or the ordinary merchant marine. In 1634 the term of enlistment with the VOC was fixed at three years for most of the sailors and at five years for all other employees. Later on the five-year engagement was made obligatory for all sailors earning between six and ten guilders a month. Ships' boys had to sign on for ten years.

It will be apparent from the above, and from the abundant travel-literature of the 17th and 18th centuries, that the life of a Dutch sailor was apt to be nasty, brutish and short – particularly for those who sailed before the mast to the East and West Indies. But this was not, of course, invariably so. If many ships suffered severely on the long voyage between the Texel and Batavia, others made it without the loss of a man and with all on board healthy and fit. If the food was often bad, and the discipline sadistically severe, vocal music seems to have done much to sooth the savage breast of Jan Maat. Many voyagers commented upon the sung or chanted orders which formed such a feature of daily life aboard the Indiamen. Sea-shanties helped to lighten the undeniably heavy work, as Mentzel rather reluctantly admitted when recalling his own voyage to the Cape. William Hickey, as usual, was more enthusiastic about the duets and ditties, 'plaintive, sweet and exactly to my taste', which he enjoyed hearing in the Indiaman *Held Woltemade* and the frigate *Thetis* – 'the greater part of the watch frequently joining in chorus with most correct harmony'. Clearly, these two Dutch vessels were both happy ships, and there must have been many others like them.

4

Mare Liberum *and* Mare Clausum

When Pieter de la Court published his famous *Interest of Holland* in 1662, he entitled one of his shortest and most persuasive chapters: 'Above all things war, and chiefly by sea, is most prejudicial (and peace very beneficial) for Holland.' The monthly periodical, *Hollandtse Mercurius*, observed editorially in February of the same year that 'the United Provinces, being filled with worthy Regents and inhabitants who everywhere have a horror of all wars, piracies, and the use of force', heard with great joy that the King of France was prepared to sign a new treaty with them. As rulers of a trading nation whose merchantmen ploughed the seven seas from Archangel to Cape Town and from New Amsterdam to Nagasaki, the States-General naturally cherished peace in theory; yet for most of the 17th century they found themselves involved in wars in one or another region of the globe. Perhaps with the signing of the Treaty of Münster in 1648, they thought that they could look forward to a lengthy period when the United Provinces of the Free Netherlands would be at peace with all the world, but, if so, they were soon undeceived. 'Our state is greatly hated here,' a correspondent wrote from Mechelen to Johan de Witt in December 1652, not long after the outbreak of the disastrous war with the Commonwealth of England. Nearly three years later, Rijkloff van Goens, just returned to Amsterdam from Batavia, informed the *Heeren* XVII: 'There is nobody who wishes us well in all the Indies, yea we are deadly hated by all nations ... so that, in my opinion, sooner or later war will be the arbiter.' [1]

The Dutch Republic was indeed in a position of rather uneasy diplomatic isolation during the decade after the Treaty of Mün-

1. Letter of Alewijn van Halewijn to Johan de Witt, Mechelen, 2 December 1652, in R. Fruin & N. Japikse, *Brieven aan Johan de Witt* (Amsterdam, 1919), Vol. I, p. 44; Rijkloff van Goens' report of 8 September 1655, in *BTLVNI*, Vol. IV (1856), pp. 177–8.

ster. Denmark was her only European ally, and many nations besides Papist Portugal, Protestant England and Muslim Macassar regarded the dynamic Dutch commercial prosperity and overseas expansion with either jealous or apprehensive eyes. Peace-loving the merchant-oligarchs of Holland and Zeeland might proclaim themselves to be; and De la Court was certainly preaching to the already converted when he advocated the maintenance of peace with powerful nations like England and France at almost any price. 'The English are about to attack a mountain of gold; we are about to attack a mountain of iron,' wrote the Grand Pensionary of Holland with gloomy foreboding at the beginning of the first Anglo-Dutch war. But if the 'cheesemongers', as foreigners contemptuously termed them, reluctantly took up arms in self-defence when attacked by England in 1652 and 1664, and by France and England combined in 1672, they did not scruple to take the offensive at other times and places when it suited them. Moreover, even when the States-General, the Stadt-holders and the directors of the East and West India Companies might be peaceably inclined for reasons of state or of trade, it by no means followed that their servants in the Indies would heed the pacific injunctions of their superiors. Those people who were on the receiving end of their blows would have agreed with the 18th-century Portuguese chronicler who wrote: 'It seems that Mars, after wandering around the globe, had finally fixed his headquarters in Holland.' [2]

An example of how the acquisition of a colonial empire complicated the choice between peace and war for the merchant-oligarchs of the United Provinces is afforded by the vicissitudes of their relations with Portugal during the three decades after that country had severed its connection with the Castilian Crown. When the Duke of Braganza was proclaimed King John IV of Portugal in December 1640, Spain was still the *erf-vijand*

2. Loreto Couto, 'Desaggravos do Brasil e glorias de Pernambuco', in *Anais da Biblioteca Nacional do Rio de Janeiro*, Vol. XXIV (Rio de Janeiro, 1902–4), p. 89. A similar observation had already been made by Parival in 1662: 'on peut dire avec fort bon droit que la Hollande est l'Ecole de la guerre.'

(hereditary enemy) of the Dutch, and the Stadtholder and the States-General were both prepared to co-operate with a new ally who would create a major diversion from the front in Flanders. Some of the Amsterdam merchants also welcomed the prospect of increased trade with Portugal itself, particularly for the coveted salt of Setúbal, so valuable for pickling herrings.[3] Not so the directors of the East and West India Companies, who considered that it would be more profitable to continue their conquests at the expense of the Portuguese in the colonial world, even if a truce had to be made with King John IV in Europe. In a memorial presented by the *Heeren* XVII to the States-General in May 1641, the directors claimed: 'That the Honourable Company had waxed great through fighting the Portuguese, and for this reason they had now secured a monopoly of most of the seaborne trade in Asia; that they expected an average yearly return of between seven and ten millions; and that if they were allowed to continue in the same way, the above return would increase yearly.' They further agreed that if they stopped fighting the Portuguese now, then the latter would soon get their second wind and again become dangerous competitors in the Asian trade. In that event, the resultant decline in the Company's own trade would lead to a great decrease in its shipbuilding and supply services in the Netherlands, thus depriving the United Provinces of 'so many powerful warships'. Thousands of sailors and other workers would lose their livelihood, and a drastic decline would occur in the yield from the imports and taxes paid by the Company. The *Heeren* XVII urged that if the States-General insisted on concluding a truce with the Portuguese Crown in Europe, the East

---

3. 'The herring trade is the cause of the salt trade, and the herring and salt trades are the causes of this country having, in a manner, wholly engrossed the trade of the Baltic Sea for that they have these bulky goods to load their ships with thither' (Downing to Clarendon, The Hague, 8/18 July 1661, *apud* C. Wilson, *Profit and Power*, p. 3). For the importance of the Setúbal salt trade cf. Virginia Rau, *A Exploração e o comércio do sal de Setúbal* (Lisbon, 1951); ibid., 'Os holandeses e a exportação do sal de Setúbal nos fins do século XVII', 64-page reprint from the *Revista Portuguesa de Historia*, Vol. IV (Lisboa, 1950).

Indies should be explicitly or implicitly exempted, as had happened during the Twelve Year Truce of 1609–21.[4]

For similar reasons, Governor-General Antonio van Diemen and his councillors at Batavia showed the greatest reluctance to conclude a truce with the Portuguese in Asia. They rejected the preliminary overtures made by the Viceroy of Goa, and for over three years they managed to evade, on one pretext or another, fully implementing the ten-year truce which had been negotiated at The Hague in June 1641. The attitude of the Dutch East India Company's officials to Portuguese pretensions in Asia, whether these latter were well grounded or otherwise, is reflected in a letter written by an English resident at Colombo concerning the boundary dispute between the two nations in Ceylon after the belated proclamation of the truce in November 1644:

The Vice-King having sent an ambassador to Galle to demand Negumbo, according to the conditions made between the King of Portugal and the States of the Low Countries, Maetsuycker, General in Galle for the Hollands Company, told the ambassador plainly that it was true they had order from the States and Prince of Orange to deliver Negumbo to the Portugals, but they were not servants to the Prince nor States but to the Company, from whom (they said) they had received no such order; nor, when they shall receive such order from their Company, will they surrender it but by force. So that the ambassador returned thence without effecting anything he went for.[5]

The directors of the West India Company, who at first welcomed the news of Portugal's break with Spain in 1640, quickly came into line with the *Heeren* XVII in opposing the conclusion of a Luso-Dutch truce in the tropics. In default of signing a firm

4. Memorandum of the *Heeren* XVII *apud* P. Baldaeus, *Naawkeurge Beschryvinge van Malabar en Choromandel en Ceylon* (Amsterdam, 1672), pp. 81–3.

5. M. Bowman at Colombo to the President and Council at Surat, 26 November 1646, *apud* W. Foster, *The English Factories in India, 1646–1650* (Oxford, 1914), p. 55. Cf. also W. Van Geer, *De Opkomst van het Nederlandsch gezag over Ceilon* (Leiden, 1895), Appendix XIV, pp. 92–4.

peace, which would enable them to consolidate and develop their precariously held colony of Pernambuco, the *Heeren* XIX considered that it would be better for them to continue their aggression against the tottering Portuguese possessions in Brazil and West Africa. When the States-General, under pressure from the Stadtholder and the French ambassador, decided to accept the Portuguese proposal for a ten-year truce 'beyond the Line' as well as in Europe, the *Heeren* XIX had already ordered their Governor-General in Pernambuco to conquer as much Portuguese territory as possible before the projected truce could take effect. They persisted in this attitude despite the remonstrances of the States-General, and thus they enabled Count John Maurice to organize the conquest of Angola, São Tomé and the Maranhão at a time when the Portuguese thought themselves secure from any further aggression by the Dutch.

Blandly oblivious of the provocation they had given the Portuguese – morally if not legally – by their new conquests, the *Heeren* XIX recalled the popular John Maurice and considerably reduced the strength of their Brazilian garrisons after they had belatedly proclaimed the truce there in July 1642. This encouraged the Portuguese of Pernambuco to rise against their heretic overlords in June 1645, a rebellion which was at first secretly and later openly supported by the mother-country. When news of this revolt reached the United Provinces, the *Heeren* XIX naturally urged the States-General and the East India Company to reopen hostilities with Portugal in Europe and Asia, an appeal which they renewed with greater force after the loss of Angola and Benguela in 1648. The States-General were hesitant and divided on the issue, largely because of pressure from their French allies and the opposition of the Amsterdam merchants engaged in the profitable salt-trade with Portugal. The *Heeren* XVII were likewise in two minds for some time· but their zeal for economy eventually proved stronger than their bellicosity, and they allowed the truce in Asia to run its course until its expiry in 1652. Even then they renewed the war reluctantly, informing the States-General that they had done so 'only because of insistence and pressure from the State, and out of deference thereto, and on no account from their own desire or self-interest'.

This volte-face from their position twelve years earlier, when they had violently protested against extending the truce to Asia, is explained by the fact that, contrary to what they had feared in 1641, Portuguese trade in Asia had not revived significantly during the truce years, and so their own commercial supremacy in the Indian Ocean had not been adversely affected.

By the end of 1646 it was obvious that the semi-bankrupt WIC was quite incapable of coping with the Pernambuco rebellion, and that massive help in money, men and ships would have to be forthcoming from the States-General. After tortuous negotiations, Holland and Amsterdam eventually agreed to help the WIC in 1647-8, in return for Zeeland's reluctant consent to peace with Spain; but the inter-provincial crisis was renewed in 1649, when it became clear that further help for the Company would be needed. On this occasion the States-General decided to send a fleet to blockade the Tagus, so as to force King John IV to comply with their demands for the restitution of what the WIC had lost in Brazil and Angola. Zeeland refused to ratify the Redemption Treaty signed with Denmark (October 1649), in which Amsterdam was particularly concerned because of the trade through the Sound, unless Holland agreed to implement the decision of the States-General. Holland, egged on by Amsterdam, refused to provide the ships and money for the projected Portuguese expedition, until Zeeland had first ratified the Danish Treaty. Not until March 1651 did Zeeland reluctantly consent to do so; and then Holland refused to pay its share unless all the other provinces paid up their contributions *and* the arrears which they owed on their sudsidies to the WIC since 1630! This they could not do, and the outbreak of war with England in May 1652 made further drastic action against either Lisbon or Brazil impracticable.

Three years after the loss of Pernambuco in 1654, the States-General at last persuaded Holland to agree to the dispatch of a fleet to blockade the Tagus and bring the Portuguese to heel; but English and French diplomatic intervention on behalf of Portugal soon gave Holland a welcome pretext for renewing its opposition to the war and to insist on the resumption of negotiations with the Portuguese envoy at The Hague in 1658. Disregarding the provisions of the Union of Utrecht that all such matters must be agreed unanimously, the deputies of Holland, led by Johan de Witt, pushed the Portuguese peace-treaty through the States-General despite the bitter opposition of Zeeland and the obstruction of Guelderland and Groningen in 1661–2.[6]

The attitude of Holland, and more especially that of Amsterdam, towards the Luso-Brazilian problem in the years 1641–61, brings out very clearly the accuracy of Sir George Downing's observation to his own government in 1664: 'You have infinite advantages upon the account of the form of the government of this country which is such a shattered and divided thing; and though the rest of the provinces give Holland their votes, yet nothing is more evident and certain than that Holland must expect to bear the burden. Even Zeeland can do very little, for that it is very poor, and for the other provinces they neither can nor will.' Fourteen years earlier the Portuguese envoy at The Hague had expressed the same truth even more pithily, when he informed his government: 'If Holland desires peace, that is more than enough to secure it, and the approval of Amsterdam alone will suffice.'[7] For as long as the Dutch Republic endured, it was Amsterdam that paid the piper, and so her regent-oligarchs felt entitled to call the tune.

6. For the tergiversations of Dutch home and foreign policy with respect to Portugal in 1641–61, cf. W. J. Van Hoboken, *Witte de With in Brazilië, 1648–1649* (Amsterdam, 1955), and his article on the Dutch West India Company in J. S. Bromley & E. H. Kossmann (eds.), *Britain and the Netherlands*, pp. 41–61; C. R. Boxer, *The Dutch in Brazil, 1624–1654* (Oxford, 1957); C. Van de Haar, *De diplomatieke betrekkingen tussen de Republiek en Portugal, 1640–1661* (Groningen, 1961), the last of which replaces (for those who know Dutch) the corresponding section in E. P. Prestage, *The Diplomatic Relations of Portugal with France, England and Holland from 1640 to 1668* (Watford, 1925).

7. '... porque como Hollanda quer paz, sobeja, e só Amsterdam basta', *Correspondência Diplomática de Francisco de Sousa Coutinho*, Vol. III, p. 360; Downing to Bennet, The Hague, 24 January 1664 (O.S.), *apud* N. Japikse, *De Verwikkelingen tusschen de Republiek en Engeland van 1660–1665* (Leiden, 1900), p. liv.

It is obvious that the ruling classes in Holland and Amsterdam were moved more by economic considerations than by purely pacifist principles in their dislike of war, as can be seen from the forceful line which they took whenever they thought that the 'mother-trade' with the Baltic was threatened by one or another of the Northern powers. In strong contrast with its reluctance to send a fleet to blockade the Tagus in the years 1645–61, Amsterdam was the prime mover in the dispatch of several Dutch fleets to the Sound during the same period. This naval might was brought to bear on Denmark and on Sweden alternately, against whichever of these two powers seemed inclined to close the Sound, or to inflict on Dutch ships passing through it higher duties than their owners were willing to pay. As it was the age of Swedish imperialism, this country was usually the actual or potential opponent after 1650. When Charles X of Sweden, in conversation with the Dutch envoy, once threatened to close the Baltic to Dutch shipping, Conrad van Beuningen retorted that he had seen the wooden keys of the Sound lying in the roadstead of Amsterdam. In 1645 the enterprising Amsterdam shipowners supplied both Denmark and Sweden with warships for the war then raging between the two Crowns; but as Sweden grew stronger and Denmark weaker, Dutch naval power was used to support the latter in 1658–60, and again in 1675–8.

As the greatest seaborne carriers of the world for over a century, the Dutch early formulated their claims to the freedom of the seas. On 15 March 1608 the States of Holland passed a secret resolution that they would never 'in whole or in part, directly or indirectly, withdraw, surrender or renounce the freedom of the seas, everywhere and in all regions of the world'. They eventually persuaded the States-General to adopt the same standpoint, and this latter body solemnly affirmed in 1645 that 'the existence, welfare and reputation of the State consists in navigation and maritime trade'. Nothing would be easier than to multiply such instances of public and private awareness that the inhabitants of the Dutch Republic must strive to overcome any restriction on free navigation, must reserve the right to sail on all seas, to fish off all coasts, to trade with all nations, to protect the rights

101

of neutrals in time of war, and to limit the definition of contraband as narrowly as possible.[8]

It is obvious that these requirements did not always coincide with those of other nations, and hence (for example) the disputes with Denmark over the payment of the Sound tolls, and with England over the Great Fishery and English claims to the suzerainty of the Narrow Seas. Where, however, the disputes tended to become most acrimonious was over the rights of neutral shipping and the definition of contraband. The Dutch advocated the principle of 'free ship, free goods', under which the cargoes of neutral ships were exempt from detention or seizure by a belligerent except for contraband weapons and munitions of war. 'Contraband' was obviously a vague term; and in the treaties they made with other maritime nations, from 1646 onwards, the States-General tried to have contraband defined in the narrowest sense and to exclude provisions, metals, ship's-stores and other commodities which might well be considered as at least potential war material. They also strove to restrict the right of search to a perusal of the ship's papers, and to forbid any examination of the cargo if these documents were found to be in order. To protect their merchant shipping from interference by foreign warships in European seas, the Dutch made great use of convoys, particularly in the Mediterranean and Baltic trades. They also sent warships to meet homeward-bound East and West India fleets in the English Channel or off the Shetlands and Fair Isle.

It is, perhaps, hardly necessary to repeat that in advocating freedom of international trade in general and the freedom of the seas in particular, the merchant-oligarchs of Holland and Zeeland were primarily, if not entirely, actuated by self-interest. They were convinced, not altogether unjustly for as long as the 17th century lasted, that they would always be able to secure the lion's share of the seaborne European carrying-trade wherever there was a fair field and no favour. This conviction was shared by many of their competitors, particularly by the English, with

8. O. Van Rees, *Geschiedenis der Staathuishoudkunde in Nederland*, Vol. I, pp. 233–48.

whom it was an article of faith for most of that period that the Dutch would always outbid or undersell them in any place where the two nations traded on equal terms. As Clarendon wrote to Downing during the negotiations at The Hague in 1661 : 'The King our Master must never endure that the Hollanders should enjoy equal privileges with him in point of trade.'

On the other hand the Dutch were not slow to abandon their free-trade principles when it suited them, or when they thought they could maintain a profitable monopoly. As Downing observed truly enough on the eve of the second Anglo-Dutch war : 'It is *mare liberum* in the British seas but *mare clausum* on the coast of Africa and in the East-Indies.' He might have added that the Dutch had a *mare clausum* much nearer home. They had kept the mouth of the Scheldt closed to foreign shipping ever since the Treaty of Münster in 1648, for fear lest Antwerp might regain her ancient seaborne prosperity at the expense of Amsterdam. During the abortive negotiations for an Anglo-Dutch alliance in 1650, the Dutch proposed : 'that all the goods of an enemy found on the ships of a friend should be free, and all the goods of a friend found upon an enemy's ship should be prize... only they would exempt the goods belonging to Portugal that are carried out of Europe into Asia, Africa and America, or è contra, because that trade is used to be driven by English ships.'[9] A typical example of wanting to have their cake and eat it. But where the Dutch abandoned their free-trade principles most readily, and where they showed themselves to be monopolists and engrossers *à l'outrance*, was in the seas controlled by their East India Company 'of laudable and redoubtable name'.

'Controlled' is here the operative word; although the VOC's sphere of activity extended from the Cape of Good Hope to Japan, only in certain regions were the Dutch able to exercise an effective monopoly for any length of time. A good review of their position in the East was provided by the 'General Instructions'

9. Downing to Clarendon, 20 November 1663 (O.S.) *apud* N. Japikse, *Verwikkelingen*, p. 103 n; Secretary Thurloe's memorandum on Anglo-Dutch rivalry was first printed in the *English Historical Review*, Vol. XXI, pp. 319–27.

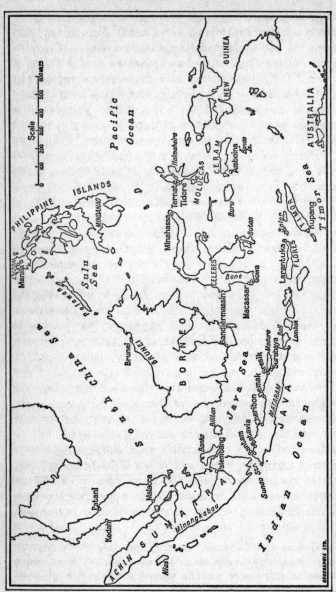

3. The Indonesian archipelago

compiled by the *Heeren* XVII for the guidance of the Governor-General and council at Batavia in the year 1650. These orders replaced the earlier ones of 1609, 1617 and 1632, and they remained in force till the end of the Company's rule, though most of their contents had ceased to have much practical relevance by 1795. Nevertheless, they give us an idea of the motives which animated the directors, and of the distinction which they drew between regions where the Company could use the mailed fist and those where it had to don the velvet glove. The *Heeren* XVII explicitly recognized that the Company's trade in Asia could be divided into three categories. Firstly, trade in regions where the VOC exercised unchallenged territorial control by right of cession or of conquest. In 1650 these places were limited to a few small islands in the Moluccas, and to a sprinkling of fortified trading-settlements such as those established at Batavia (Java), Malacca (Malaya), Pulicat (India) and Zeelandia (Formosa). Secondly, regions where the VOC enjoyed exclusive trading rights by virtue of monopoly-contracts negotiated (usually under duress) with native rulers, such as the Sultan of Ternate and the village headmen of Amboina. Thirdly, trade with other Oriental rulers, 'both on the basis of freely negotiated agreements as well as on the basis of free trade alongside merchants of all other nations'.[10]

It should be noted that although the first two categories were considerably expanded after 1650, by virtue of the Company's conquest of Macassar, coastal Ceylon and Malabar, and by the territorial gains resulting from the Java wars of the 18th century, yet the third category, wherein the Company had no chance of securing a commercial monopoly, was nearly always the most important. Even at the height of its power, the only commodities in which the VOC could exercise an effective monopoly were the cloves, mace and nutmegs of the Moluccas, and the cinnamon of Ceylon. In everything else – pepper, silk, textiles, sugar, coffee and tea – the Company had to face severe

10. 'Punten en artikelen in form van Generale Instructie,' Amsterdam, 26 April 1650, in P. Myer, *Verzameling van instructien, ordonnancien en reglementen voor de regering van Nederlandsch Indië, 1609–1836* (Batavia, 1848), pp. 71–116.

competition, both in the purchase of those commodities in Asia and in their resale in European or in Asian markets. Even in Japan, where the Dutch were the only European traders allowed from 1639 to 1854, they had to compete with a far greater volume of Chinese trade, and they could never manipulate the market at Nagasaki to their own satisfaction. They might monopolize the trade in some spices for a time: but they always had to compete with other nations in purchasing the Indian piece-goods and textiles with which they paid for the spices, in whole or in part. In other words, the Company's trade in a given area was never determined by one commodity alone, but by a plurality of products, some of which were always beyond the grasp of its monopoly.

The *Heeren* XVII stressed the necessity of maintaining their existing monopoly in the Moluccas by force of arms if necessary, but they deprecated the use of force elsewhere, particularly in 'the neutral places belonging to free nations, where we find the laws and do not have to bring them'. They reminded their servants in the East that in such places they had no right 'to appropriate the aforesaid trade according to our own ideas and to constrain such nations thereto by force, just as the Company cannot allow other nations to lay down the law about how trade should be conducted in places under its own jurisdiction'. The instructions of 1650 further stressed the need to treat the inhabitants of Amboina with fairness and consideration, while exacting from them strict obedience to their contracts for clove deliveries. The natives of Formosa, 'having always been a free people, must be kept loyal to the Company by being well treated, without those poor people being too heavily taxed'. The good graces of powerful Asian rulers, such as the Shogun of Japan and the Shah of Persia, were to be cultivated by conciliatory and accommodating behaviour on the part of the Company's servants in those countries. This was particularly so in Japan, where they were enjoined 'to look to the wishes of that bold, haughty and exacting nation, in order to please it in everything'. For this reason, only 'modest, humble, polite and friendly' individuals should be sent to staff the Dutch agency at Deshima. The general tenor of these instructions was reflected in the injunction that 'special attention must be paid to driving a peaceful trade throughout all Asia, which is what keeps the cooking going in the kitchens of the fatherland'.

This emphasis on peaceful trade and on the actual or potential profits therefrom was a constant theme in the correspondence of the *Heeren* XVII, particularly when the wars waged by their servants in the East proved to be costly affairs. In 1644 the directors of the Delft Chamber deprecated the heavy casualties and expenditure incurred in the campaigns of Malacca and Ceylon. They observed that 'a merchant would do better honourably to increase his talent and send rich cargoes from Asia to the Netherlands, instead of carrying out costly territorial conquests, which are more suitable for crowned heads and mighty monarchs than for merchants greedy of gain'. But the men on the spot often had other ideas. Antonio van Diemen and his council, while proclaiming themselves in theoretical agreement with the Delft Chamber's views, added significantly: 'There is a great deal of difference between the general and the particular, and between one kind of trade and another. We are taught by daily experience that the Company's trade in Asia cannot subsist without territorial conquests.' In taking this bellicose line, Van Diemen was echoing the convictions of the founder of Batavia, Jan Pietersz Coen, who had assured the *Heeren* XVII in 1614: 'Your Honours should know by experience that trade in Asia must be driven and maintained under the protection and favour of Your Honours' own weapons, and that the weapons must be paid for by the profits from the trade; so that we cannot carry on trade without war nor war without trade.' [11] Similarly, Rijkloff van Goens, in his report of 1655 (p. 94), averred that 'the Christian maxims' which the directors had inculcated in their instructions of 1650, were being misunderstood or misinterpreted as signs of weakness by hostile Asian powers. These latter, he

11. J. P. Coen to the *Heeren* XVII, Bantam, 27 December 1614, *apud* H. T. Colenbrander, *Jan Pietersz Coen. Levensbeschryving* (The Hague, 1934), p. 64; Van Diemen and Council to the *Heeren* XVII, Batavia, 23 December 1644, *apud* W. Van Geer *Opkomst*, p. 57 of the appendices.

said, were fundamentally jealous of the Company's maritime dominance and sought only its ruin.

When differences over policy occurred between the *Heeren* XVII at home and the Governor-General and his council at Batavia, the latter naturally had an advantage when forceful personalities, such as Coen, Van Diemen, Rijkloff van Goens and Speelman filled the senior posts at the 'Queen of the Eastern Seas'. It took about eighteen months or two years to get an answer from Amsterdam or Middelburg concerning a course of action initiated at Batavia; and under these circumstances it was relatively easy for the Governor-General and council to force the hands of the *Heeren* XVII, if they were so minded. The Rev. François Valentyn found this to his cost in 1706, when he showed the Director-General at Batavia a written order from the *Heeren* XVII, whereat this official cynically observed : 'The Directors in the fatherland decide matters, as it seems best to them there; but we do here, what seems best and most advisable to us.' In other words, a Dutch equivalent of the Spanish *obedezco pero no cumplo* ('I obey but I do not carry out'), with which the viceroys of Mexico and Peru shelved inconvenient orders from Madrid. The Batavian authorities had another advantage in that after about 1650 very few of the directors had ever served in Asia, or indeed showed any great interest in the political situation there. They were thus more dependent on the advice and knowledge of their overseas representatives than were, for instance, the Portuguese and Spanish Crowns, whose India Councils were mainly staffed by ex-Colonial governors and administrators. This helps to explain why the directors, although at times critical of the forceful policies initiated by men with expansionist views, usually ended by accepting the *fait accompli*, or by sending the ships, men and money for which they asked. This was naturally still more so when these policies showed tangible results, as did Coen's conquest of Jakarta (1619), or Speelman's occupation of Bantam (1684). On the other hand, the Directors did sometimes overrule their subordinates. When the Governor-General and Council at Batavia were in favour of allowing the King of Kandy to trade freely from ports on the east coast of Ceylon in the years 1696–1703, the *Heeren* XVII reversed this policy, which was also criticized by the Dutch Governor at Colombo, and ordered the closing of all the King's ports to foreign traders in 1703.[12]

It must be stressed again that the *Heeren* XVII were by no means always and everywhere opposed to the use of force by their subordinates in the East, but only in places where they thought that it would be too expensive or too difficult to secure and maintain a profitable monopoly by this means. As early as 1614 they were fully resolved to take the most drastic steps to secure such a monopoly in the Spice Islands against all-comers, whether Portuguese, Spaniards, English, Chinese or Indonesian traders. They agreed with Coen that in this region at any rate it would be hopeless to try and improve their position merely by 'being virtuous and doing good', and that it was necessary 'to ride the natives with a sharp spur'. Admittedly, they were at first rather horrified by the news of his virtual extirpation of the Banda islanders in 1621, but they soon recovered their complacency and gave him no more than a mild rebuke. They – or rather a majority of them, for the *Heeren* XVII were not always unanimous – ignored the advice of some of Coen's colleagues who disliked his ruthlessness and thought that better results could be achieved by less drastic methods. Laurens Reael and Steven van der Hagen, the leading exponents of this school of thought, both argued that the Company had no right to compel the natives of the Moluccas to sell their spices exclusively to the Dutch, unless the latter could supply them in return with adequate supplies of food and clothing at reasonable prices. 'We ourselves,' wrote Reael (20 August 1618), 'bring insufficient supplies of merchandise to the Moluccas, and prevent others from bringing enough. The inhabitants cannot pick any cloves, because the high cost of importing foodstuffs forces them to cultivate food-crops instead. Sago, which was formerly brought them by the Javanese for a fifth of its present price, now has to be imported from a greater distance by themselves. The [Indian] textiles

12. S. Arasaratnam, 'The Kingdom of Kandy: aspects of its external relations and commerce, 1658–1710' (*The Ceylon Journal of Historical and Social Studies*, Vol. III, 1960, pp. 109–27) gives a well-documented survey of Dutch policy towards Kandy in that period, and the oscillation between force and appeasement.

(which are often of poor quality) have to be brought from us at such high prices that it is not worth their while to go and pluck the cloves (a difficult and dangerous work). Moreover, we are so narrowly grasping over our profits and earnings that we do not allow anyone to earn a farthing or a penny from us.'

Coen and most of the *Heeren* XVII, however, took the view that the Dutch were entitled to monopolize the purchase of cloves and nutmegs at prices fixed by themselves, in return for the 'protection' they had given the islanders against the Portuguese and Spaniards. This attitude ignored the fact that the Dutch spice monopoly speedily became much more burdensome to the islanders than its Spanish and Portuguese counterpart had been; partly because the Dutch paid lower prices, and partly because their monopoly was more ruthlessly and more efficiently enforced. Reael and Van der Hagen also argued that punitive sanctions should not be applied to Indonesian chiefs and headmen who had, under duress, signed contracts disadvantageous to themselves and which they could not fulfil even if they were willing. They urged that it was better, in the long run, for the Dutch to content themselves with large sales and small profits rather than strive for a rigid and oppressive monopoly which aimed at small sales and big profits. Moreover, Reael and Van der Hagen, while prepared in the last extremity to use force against their English competitors in the Moluccas, were reluctant to do so otherwise, for fear of unfavourable repercussions on Anglo-Dutch relations in Europe – a possibility that did not worry Coen. Finally, Reael and Van der Hagen considered that it might be unjust and unwise to exclude Asian traders, whether Chinese, Malay or Javanese, from the Moluccas by force. Unjust, because the existing contracts did not stipulate such an exclusion; and unwise, because such a policy might drive the islanders into the arms of European competitors and increase, instead of destroying, Malay and Javanese trade.

Although the arguments advanced by Reael and Van der Hagen found some support among the directors, the majority of the *Heeren* XVII agreed with the aggressive policy advocated by Coen and Hendrik Brouwer. 'There is nothing in the world,' wrote Coen to the directors, 'that gives one a better right, than power and force added to right.' On receiving the Company's authorization forcibly to prevent Javanese and other Asian merchants from trading in the Moluccas, Coen acknowledged this with satisfaction (10 November 1617), and added: 'The teaching of nature and what has been done by all peoples from age to age has always been sufficient for me.' One reason why the directors were prepared to use force in the Moluccas when they hesitated to do so elsewhere was that the local rulers possessed no warships of any strength, and the spice-growing districts were mostly on the island coasts and exposed to the reach of Dutch sea-power. Dependent as they were on the importation of rice, cotton textiles and other necessities of life from Java, Malaya and India, the inhabitants of the Spice Islands were in no position to take reprisals against the Dutch for real or fancied wrongs; as were, for example, powerful kingdoms on the Asian mainland. Moreover, the spice trade was for long regarded as the principal objective of the Company's activity in the East Indies, and as the actual or potential source of its greatest profits. Hence the *Heeren* XVII enthusiastically supported, when they did not actually initiate, aggressive action in the Moluccas, at times when they deprecated or forbade the waging of offensive warfare elsewhere.

Even so, as Reael and Van der Hagen had foreseen, the struggle to get complete control of the Moluccan spice-crop dragged on for many years and proved extremely costly in men and money. It came to an end only in 1684 when Malacca, Macassar and Bantam had all fallen into the Company's hands, and Indonesian shipping and trade in the Spice Islands had been virtually annihilated, with dire consequences for the economy and living conditions of their inhabitants. In the 1620s the entire indigenous population of the Banda island group was either exterminated or deported to other islands to serve as slaves or soldiers. As a result of the massacre of 160 Netherlanders, including several women and children, in western Ceram in the year 1651, a series of punitive campaigns was carried out by the Dutch, culminating in the forcible transfer of some 12,000 souls from their original villages, and their resettlement in Amboina and Manipa. The spice monopoly was enforced in the Moluccas by the so-called *hongi-tochten*, periodic expeditions of armed outrigger vessels or *cora-coras*, which cut down all unauthorized clove plantations. It is arguable how much this spice monopoly benefited the Company commercially once they had actually achieved it. If they made large profits on the sale of some spices at some places at some times, there were other occasions on which they made little or none – apart from the fact that the cost of enforcing the monopoly with fleets, forts and garrisons may well have swallowed up all the profits on a long-term view. This is something which cannot be ascertained owing to the Company's complicated methods of book-keeping, which prevented the *Heeren* XVII from accurately calculating their real expenses for as long as the Company lasted, but it is at least a plausible supposition.[13]

The relations of the overseas authorities of the West India Company with their superiors in the Netherlands were rather different from those prevailing in the sister corporation, particularly after the recall of Count John Maurice and the outbreak of the Pernambuco revolt in 1644–5. John Maurice was in some ways a virtual law unto himself, but his successors in Brazil and elsewhere were much more under the control of the *Heeren* XIX than he had been by virtue of his princely birth and influence with the Stadtholder's court. After 1645, the *Heeren* XIX, owing to the financial indebtedness of the WIC and its complete dependence on state subsidies, became for over a decade something of a shuttlecock between the rival provinces of Holland and Zeeland. Even after the Company's reorganization in 1670, its overseas activities, whether on the West African coast or in the Caribbean, were more closely controlled from the Netherlands than were those of the VOC; partly because the distances involved were not so great, and partly because the poorer West

13. For details and documentation of the Dutch spice monopoly in the Moluccas and the views of Coen, Reael, and Van der Hagen, see M. A. P. Meilink-Roelofsz, *Asian Trade and European Influence in the Indonesian Archipelago between 1500–1630* (The Hague, 1962), pp. 173–268; P. A. Tiele & J. E. Heeres (eds.), *Bouwstoffen voor de geschiedenis der Nederlanders in den Maleischen Archipel* (3 vols., The Hague, 1886–95); B. Schrieke, *Indonesian Sociological Studies* (2 vols., The Hague, 1955), especially Vol. I, pp. 49–79.

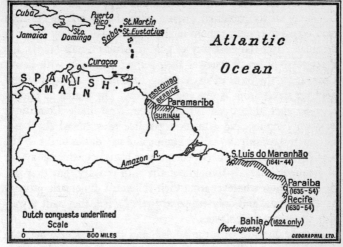

Map labels: Cuba, Puerto Rico, Jamaica, Sta. Domingo, St. Martin, Saba, St. Eustatius, Curaçao, *Atlantic Ocean*, SPANISH MAIN, ESSEQUIBO, BERBICE, Paramaribo, SURINAM, Amazon R., S. Luis do Maranhão (1641-44), Paraiba (1635-54), Recife (1630-54), Bahia (1624 only) (Portuguese), Dutch conquests underlined Scale, 0 — 800 MILES, GEOGRAPHIA LTD.

4 Dutch conquests in the West Indies and Brazil

India Company could not afford to take the stronger and more independent line often taken by its wealthy sister.

On the other hand, if the merchant-oligarchs of the Netherlands, and particularly those of Amsterdam, only gave reluctant support to the WIC in the long-drawn-out crisis of 1644–61, owing to their greater concern with the Baltic and the Setúbal salt-trade, they gave the *Heeren* XIX more positive help on other occasions, when they thought that the national interest as well as the Company's weal was involved. The abortive negotiations for a truce with Spain in 1629–33 largely broke down because of the refusal of the States-General to surrender (or exchange) the West India Company's conquests in Pernambuco, although the Dutch then held only a small part of that region. In 1664, at the instigation of Amsterdam, the States-General authorized the dispatch of Vice-Admiral de Ruyter with his Mediterranean squadron to Guinea, in order to retake the WIC's forts which had been taken by Sir Robert Holmes in time of peace. Not for over a century did they take similar action in the East Indies, when a squadron of States' warships was sent to help the VOC in the Malay archipelago.

113

Nor did the States-General hesitate to support the West India Company in its perennial dispute with the Crown of Portugal over access to certain regions of the Guinea coast during the 18th century. After the discovery of gold in Minas Gerais (1695), the Portuguese of Brazil renewed their former commerce with Lower Guinea, on the basis of exchanging Brazilian tobacco, rum and gold for slaves from Ardra and Dahomey. The Dutch at Elmina claimed that this trade infringed the West India Company's monopoly rights, and whenever possible they forced the Luso-Brazilian slave-ships to call at Elmina and pay duties to the WIC. The Portuguese government complained bitterly of this behaviour at frequent intervals throughout the 18th century, but they got no satisfaction whatever from their reiterated diplomatic protests at The Hague, and only temporary relief when they sent a warship to convoy their slavers.[14]

In their disputes with the English and the Portuguese over the maritime monopolies claimed by the two Dutch India Companies in various regions of the globe, the Dutch were somewhat embarrassed by having Grotius, their foremost champion of the freedom of the seas, constantly quoted against them. In 1612 Grotius himself was sent to England, to explain why the Dutch were entitled to keep the English and all other competitors out of the Spice Islands. His principal argument was that, although the Dutch had originally gone to the Moluccas as peaceful traders, they had been compelled in self-defence to drive out the Portuguese and Spaniards, and to maintain their position against the latter by means of costly garrisons and fleets. Since they were carrying on this struggle single-handed, they were entitled to all the profits derived from the spice trade, apart from the monopoly-contract which they had made with the local rulers. Needless to say, the English did not accept these arguments, any more than

14. Diogo de Mendoça Corte-Real, *Examen et Reponse a un écrit publié par la Compagnie des Indes-Occidentales sous le titre de Refutation des argumens et raisons allegués par Mr Diogo de Mendoça Corte-Real* (The Hague, 1727); A. F. C. Ryder, 'The Re-establishment of Portuguese factories on the Costa da Mina to the mid-eighteenth century', in *Journal of the Historical Society of Nigeria*, Vol. I (Ibadan, 1958), pp. 157–83.

the Portuguese a century later accepted the legality of the West India Company's seizure of their ships off the Guinea coast. In the final analysis however, the Dutch relied less on their rather dubious legal arguments than on their practical preference for

> *The good old rule, the simple plan,*
> *That they should take who have the power,*
> *and they should keep who can,*

which Jan Pietersz Coen, Antonio van Diemen and Cornelis Speelman acted upon so successfully.

It is clear from the foregoing that the picture drawn by Pieter de la Court, and by some modern writers, of the Dutch merchant-oligarchs as invariably peaceful traders who only drew the sword with the greatest reluctance, needs considerable modification. We have seen that, from 1648 onwards, they usually avoided war with a major power whenever they possibly could; but it was a very different story when it came to dealing with weaker or supposedly weaker states, such as Portugal, Denmark, Macassar and Ternate. Then they did not hesitate to enforce the strict observance of treaties and contracts by the other party concerned, even where these agreements had been negotiated under duress, as was often the case. I need hardly add that this attitude was not confined to the Dutch, but was shared to a greater or lesser extent by their rivals. The Portuguese had behaved in the same way to the petty Asian rulers whose coasts were exposed to their superior sea-power; and the Anglo-Portuguese Treaty of 1654, which laid the foundations of English commercial supremacy in Portugal, was a *diktat* if ever there was one.

The contracts and treaties which the VOC made with the minor Indonesian princes during a period of nearly two hundred years followed much the same pattern. From the wording, it is clear that these contracts were usually drawn up by the Dutch, and the Indonesian ruler had to sign on the dotted line. They gave the Dutch extensive monopoly (or preferential) trading-rights in the region concerned, usually to the exclusion of other foreign merchants, whether European or Asian. They permitted the establishment of Dutch forts and garrisons where necessary, and often recognized the right of the VOC representative to intervene as arbitrator or mediator in local disputes. The Dutch nearly always retained jurisdiction over their own nationals who were accused of criminal offences, and usually had the right to try natives involved in disputes with them.

Of course, these conditions could not be negotiated with powerful continental rulers in places where 'it was not so much a matter of the Company tolerating the Indians as of the Indians tolerating the Company', as a critic pointed out in 1624. Even in such places, however, the Company – like the Portuguese and English – often managed to secure what virtually amounted to extra-territorial rights for its representatives, as this was a common practice of Asian rulers towards merchants of all nationalities. One remarkable exception to the normal treaty relationships between European and Asian powers is afforded by the Dutch-Persian treaty of trade and friendship which was signed at The Hague in February 1631. This document stipulated that Persian merchants in the Netherlands would not only be treated on a footing of perfect equality with Dutch citizens but would be given the commercial and judicial privileges enjoyed by the English at Delft and the Scots at Veere. These generous stipulations were probably granted by the States-General because they knew that the Persians had no sea-going shipping. As the land route to Western Europe was barred by hostile Turkey and Russia, the prospects of any Persian merchants establishing themselves in the Netherlands was exceedingly remote. In any event, the VOC took no notice of this treaty, which remained a dead letter.[15]

The territorial expansion of the VOC was limited to Ceylon, South Africa and Java. Elsewhere, in Sumatra and Celebes, for example, the Dutch were content to secure a dominant commercial position by making treaties or contracts with the coastal sultans, many of whom became their satellites or their vassals,

15. J. E. Heeres & F. Stapel, *Corpus Diplomaticum Neerlando-Indicum, 1596–1799* (6 vols., The Hague, 1907–55); L. W. Alders, *Internationale rechtspraak tussen Indonesische rijken en de VOC tot 1700* (Nijmegen, 1956); C. H. Alexandrowicz, *Treaty and Diplomatic Relations between European and South Asian Powers in the 17th and 18th centuries* (Leiden, 1960).

but whose authority did not extend far inland. The Dutch originally intervened in Ceylon (in 1638) to assist Raja Sinha II against the Portuguese, and to conquer all or part of the cinnamon-growing districts in that island. By the time the struggle ended with the expulsion of the Portuguese in 1658, the VOC had become the controlling power in the coastal districts, and the King of Kandy was eventually deprived of an outlet to the sea. The Dutch colonization of South Africa was something *sui generis* in the history of the VOC and is discussed in Chapter 9. As regards the conquest of Java, this started with the reluctant intervention of Governor-General Maetsuyker in a succession-dispute in the empire of Mataram, on behalf of the legitimate but dispossessed Susuhunan in 1677, and it culminated in the establishment of Dutch supremacy over the island a century later. This conquest was not consciously planned by the *Heeren* XVII, who had no desire whatever to transform their commercial and maritime empire into a territorial one. But, like the 'cheese-mongers of Leadenhall Street' in the days of Clive and Warren Hastings, they found themselves committed by their servants at Batavia to a series of interventions in the mutual quarrels of Javanese rulers, which resulted in just this transformation. As Laurens Reael had written in a different connection in 1614 : 'We have begun to pull on a chain and one link drags the other.' [16]

Although during the 18th century both the Dutch Company in Java and the British Company in India ceased to be primarily commercial corporations and became territorial colonial powers there were certain marked differences in their respective transformations. Whereas British seapower accompanied and protected the growth of John Company's power in India, the sea-power of both the VOC and its fatherland declined noticeably during the struggle for Java. The homeward-bound Dutch East Indiamen were as richly laden as ever, though with tea, coffee and porcelain, rather than with spices and textiles; but Dutch domination of Malayan and Indonesian waters was being seriously undermined in many regions by the phenomenal growth of smuggling and piracy. This, in its turn, was largely provoked by

16. Reael's remark *apud* M. A. P. Meilink-Roelofsz, *Asian Trade and European Influence*, p. 219.

the oppressive commercial monopoly which the VOC strove to maintain in the seas which it claimed to control.

Largely but not entirely. For the decline in the Company's maritime strength in the East was in some ways a reflection of the decline in the United Provinces' maritime strength in Europe. The navy which under Michiel de Ruyter had successfully defied the combined fleets of England and France was a shadow of its former self a century later. Despite the losses suffered in the European wars of the second half of the 17th century, Dutch overseas trade in 1699 had again reached the high-water mark attained fifty years earlier at the time of the Treaty of Münster. But in the final struggle against Louis XIV which began in 1702 and ended with the Treaty of Utrecht (1713), the Dutch Republic overreached itself. It sacrificed its naval strength to enable it to support the cost of a disproportionately great military effort in Flanders and in the Iberian peninsula. In particular, the mistaken policy of the English and Dutch statesmen in persuading Portugal to join the Grand Alliance, in order to obtain the use of Lisbon as a naval base, involved the Allies in an unnecessary extension of the war. The strain was enough to make England respond to French overtures for peace after 1710, and it broke the Dutch Republic as a great naval power. In 1709 the English Treasury could still borrow money at 6 per cent, but Holland had to pay 9 per cent, a rate which was higher than any which had been reached since the days of Oldenbarnevelt. The national debt of the Dutch Republic, which amounted to 30,000,000 guilders in 1688, had risen to 148,000,000 by the end of the War of the Spanish Succession.[17]

The four land provinces had paid no contribution whatever towards the upkeep of the navy in the years 1706–7 and 1711–12, and very little in the other years, so that the five provincial admiralties were all deeply indebted by 1713. This indebtedness

17. For the foregoing and what follows, cf. F. Snapper, *Oorlogsinvloeden op de overzeese handel van Holland, 1551–1719* (Amsterdam, 1959), pp. 216–93; J. C. de Jonge, *Geschiedenis van het Nederlandsche Zeewezen* (5 vols., Haarlem, 1858–62), Vol. IV (1861), pp. 1–440, for detailed and documented evidence of the decline of Dutch naval power in the 18th century.

impelled the regent-oligarchs to economize on defence expenditure even after the war was over and Dutch overseas trade began to revive. They became more wedded than before to a peace at any price policy, and they avoided any expense which would involve them in additional taxation, such as the upkeep of an adequate fleet would have necessitated. The provincial admiralties remained so deeply indebted that the Rotterdam admiralty built only seven warships in twenty-eight years (1713–41); the admiralty of the North-Quarter possessed only three sea-going vessels in 1721, two of them between twenty and thirty years old; the admiralty of Friesland had only one warship in 1732; and the admiralty of Zeeland built only four warships in the first half of the 18th century. Only the Amsterdam admiralty managed to find the money to build thirty-three ships between 1723 and 1741, including twelve line-of-battleships of between fifty-two and seventy-four guns.

The fundamental reason for this unsatisfactory situation was one which bedevilled the Dutch Republic for the whole of its existence. With few and fleeting intervals, the land provinces would never pay their full quotas for the upkeep of the navy and the convoying of merchant shipping. Their representatives regarded this as essentially a matter for Holland and Zeeland. They considered that these two provinces, and chiefly Holland, should finance the building and upkeep of the fleet out of the profits of their seaborne trade. Even on the rare occasions when their representatives in the States-General could be persuaded to agree to raise some money for the navy, they made no serious efforts to implement these promises when they returned to their homes. This imbroglio was complicated in the second half of the 18th century, particularly in the decade 1770–80, when even Zeeland refused to vote any money for the upkeep of the navy, and when the Prince of Orange and the land provinces would only agree to the province of Holland's proposals to vote funds for the navy if a still larger amount of money was spent on the army. This, Holland – and more particularly Amsterdam – flatly refused to do, even when the surplus suggested for the army was a relatively small amount. The result of this political deadlock was that nothing effective was done to improve the condition of either the army or the navy, while Holland wrangled with the other provinces over the respective merits of *equipagie* (money for the navy) and *augmentatie* (strengthening the army and the land defences).

The decline in Dutch maritime power was evidenced technically and economically as well as in the purely naval sphere. Whereas in the first half of the 17th century Dutch ships had been more economically manned than those of their competitors, this was no longer so a hundred years later. The Swedish traveller, C. P. Thunberg, wrote from personal experience when he observed: 'The Dutch have also occasion for a greater number of men to work their ships than other nations, as their rigging is made after the old fashion with large blocks and thick cordage, heavy and clumsy in every respect.' Once in the van of the techniques of high-seas navigation and in the production of charts, the Dutch had fallen behind their English and French competitors in these respects even before John Harrison's invention of the chronometer. 'It is really to be lamented,' wrote Rear-Admiral Stavorinus, 'that so powerful a body as the East India Company, and whose prosperity so much depends upon the safe and prosperous voyages of their ships, should trouble themselves so little with the improvement of navigation in general, and the correction of their charts in particular. I could adduce many instances of their faultiness, both with respect to the Indies, and to the coast of Africa. Other nations pursue this subject with indefatigable assiduity, especially the English, whose maps are, in general, infinitely preferable to ours.'

Stavorinus blamed the decline in Dutch navigational skill largely on the bureaucratic routine of the Directors of the East India Company, who insisted that all their ships should follow a fixed course laid down in their printed instructions. Indiamen of other nations, he noted, 'not being bound to follow any particular instruction or sailing-orders with respect to their navigation, generally perform much shorter voyages, both to and from the East-Indies, than the ships of the Company. Hence too, the commanders of Dutch ships, impeded and fettered in their proceedings, cannot possibly make as much progress as others, in the improvement of navigation; and to this it may also, in my opinion, be greatly attributed, that the English, the French and others so far outstrip us in the making of improvements, new discoveries, etc., although our East-India trade might reasonably be supposed to be an excellent nursery for seamen, and a school for the greatest nautical improvements, on account of the number of ships and men it employs, and the distance and diversity of the voyages'. Stavorinus' account of the old-fashioned and time-wasting methods of navigation which were still the rule aboard Dutch East Indiamen in his day and generation is amply confirmed by the comments of William Hickey after his homeward voyage in the *Held Woltemade* from the Cape.[18]

Once the leading shipbuilders of the world, and shipwrights with whom Tsar Peter the Great was still proud to study in 1697, thirty years later the Dutch had to enlist English shipwrights to teach them improved techniques. Whereas in the war of 1672-4 the Dutch warships had fired their broadsides at the rate of three to one compared with their English and French opponents, the exact opposite was the case in 1746, according to the evidence of Dutch naval officers. The Arctic whale fishery, which employed 260 Dutch ships and 14,000 seamen at the end of the 17th century, employed only about fifty ships a hundred years later, the decline being partly due to over-fishing and partly to competition by other nations. The years following the Treaty of Utrecht saw a steady decline in the numbers of Dutch seamen who were available for service in the navy and in ocean voyages, this decline becoming much more noticeable after about 1740. When the States-General decided to fit out a squadron of twenty sail in 1744, recruiting agents had to be sent to Hamburg, Bremen, Copenhagen and other foreign ports, and, since even this recruiting drive and the offer of a higher enlistment bounty did not produce enough men, the ships' complements had to be made up with jail-birds from the Amsterdam prison. The East India Company was equally affected by this decline, as can be seen from

18. C. P. Thunberg, *Travels in Europe, Africa, and Asia, 1770-1779* (4 vols., London, 1795), Vol. I, p. 113; J. S. Stavorinus, *Voyages to the East-Indies, 1768-1778* (3 vols., London, 1798), Vol. II, pp. 111-12; Vol. III, pp. 465-6, 472; *Memoirs of William Hickey*, Vol. II, pp. 230-31.

Governor-General Baron van Imhoff's complaint in the same year: 'I am afraid to say how things are with us, for it is shameful ... everything is lacking, good ships, men, officers; and thus one of the principal props of the Netherlands' power is trembling in the balance.' [19]

I do not mean to infer from the above complaints of contemporaries that Dutch overseas trade was reduced to insignificance, or that the fishing and maritime communities had ceased to exist by the end of the 18th century. On the contrary, the volume of Dutch maritime commerce was still impressive as late as 1780, and the North Sea fishery and the Arctic whaling industries were still nurseries of seamen. But proportionately Dutch shipping and maritime trade *did* decline in comparison with the progress made by the English, French and Baltic competitors of the Dutch. Moreover, the growing scarcity of Dutch seamen seems to have been not merely relative but absolute. Stavorinus may have been exaggerating somewhat when he deplored this decline in the following terms, but he was not exaggerating much: 'Many years ago, a sufficient number of able seamen could be procured, not to be compelled to have recourse to landsmen for filling up a ship's complement; but ever since the year 1740, the many naval wars, the great increase of trade and navigation, particularly in many countries, where formerly these pursuits were little attended to, and the consequent great and continual demands for able seamen, both for ships of war and for merchantmen, have so considerably diminished the supply of them, that, in our own country, where there formerly used to be a great abundance of mariners, it is now, with great difficulty and expense, that any vessel can procure a proper number of able hands to navigate her.' [20]

Although contemporaries were virtually unanimous in deploring the decline of Dutch sea-power and the standards of Dutch seamanship in the second half of the 18th century, they

19. Imhoff's complaint *apud* T. H. Milo, *De invloed van de zeemacht op de geschiedenis der Vereenigde Oost-Indische Compagnie* (The Hague, 1946), p. 16. For detailed evidence of this decline cf. J. C. de Jonge, *Zeewezen*, Vol. IV, pp. 264–81, 433–5, 475–7.

20. J. S. Stavorinus, *Voyages to the East-Indies*, Vol. III, pp. 406–7.

were not so unanimous in the reasons which they gave for it. The Prince of Orange observed concerning the scarcity of seamen when war broke out with England in December 1780: 'In the last century, the wages which the common man could earn were generally lower, the population was greater and poverty was more widespread than at present; and so it was easier to enlist men for the sea service.' All these allegations could have been contested to a greater or lesser degree, but, as De Bosch Kemper points out, it is rather significant that the anti-Orangist weekly periodical *Der Post van den Neder-Rijn*, which so strongly criticized the Prince on other matters, made only a feeble and half-hearted rebuttal of his arguments in this particular instance. This is the more surprising, as it was one of the stock complaints of writers of the decade 1770–80, that unemployment and poverty in the United Provinces were probably more serious and widespread than at any time since the Treaty of Münster.[21]

The growing disinclination – or disability – of Dutch working-class men to seek their livelihood at sea during the 18th century, from whatever causes it sprang, was accompanied by a change in the mentality and outlook of the regent-oligarchs. From being directly concerned with overseas trade in one form or another, as they had been for most of the 17th century, some of them had not only become *rentiers* but *rentiers* who tended to invest much of their capital in foreign funds. It was confidently asserted in the House of Commons in 1737 that the Dutch held about 22·7 per cent of England's public debt; and it was stated with slightly less confidence in 1758 that Dutch investors held a third of the Bank of England, English East India Company and South Sea stocks. There was a widespread (if inaccurate) contemporary belief that the Dutch held a third of the total English debt. In 1762 a well-informed Rotterdam banker told a compatriot that the Dutch held a quarter of the English debt, which then totalled £121 million. Twenty years later the Pensionary Van de Spiegel put Dutch foreign investment at 335 million guilders, of which 280 million guilders (some £30 million in English money) was in England and 55 million in other countries.

21. Cf. J. De Bosch Kemper, *Geschiedkundig onderzoek* (1860), pp. 113–23.

The accuracy of these and other estimates has been disputed; and recent research leaves the impression that only a relatively small number of Dutch capitalists were investing heavily abroad, and that even this group invested more than half its wealth at home. But whether Dutch capital was invested at home or abroad, it was lent to bankers and to brokers of commercial bills, or invested in land or in colonial West Indian mortgages, rather than in developing home industries or in fostering Dutch shipping.[22] Amsterdam was the money-market of the Western World; but many of the regent-oligarchs were wealthy *rentiers* and high financiers who stood apart from the merchant class from which they had sprung. Their changed economic outlook undoubtedly influenced their foreign policy. With a weak navy and a serious shortage of able seamen, neutrality was even more necessary for them than it was for their more enterprising predecessors in the days of Johan de Witt and Pieter de la Court.

It is therefore at first sight somewhat surprising that the Dutch should have blundered into a war with England for which they were totally unprepared, militarily and economically, in December 1780. Their foreign policy since the days of the King-Stadtholder had been based upon alliance with England and dread of French aggression, above all in the southern Netherlands, where they had secured their famous – but useless – barrier of Belgian fortress and garrison towns under the terms of the treaty concluded at Antwerp in 1715. Despite the parlous state of their armed forces, and the numerous grievances they had against England over the Royal Navy's interference with their neutral shipping, the States-General had loyally come to their ally's aid in 1744–5, and had drawn upon themselves a French invasion as a result. English interception and seizure of neutral Dutch shipping during the Seven Years War was particularly resented by all classes in the northern Netherlands as being an ungrateful return for Dutch loyalty to the English alliance twenty years earlier. The difficulties in which England became involved after the outbreak of the American Revolution in 1776, and especially

22. Cf. C. Wilson, *Anglo-Dutch Commerce and Finance in the 18th Century* (London, 1940); Alice Carter, 'Dutch foreign investment, 1738–1800', in *Economica*, November 1953, pp. 322–40.

the formation of the Armed Neutrality early in 1780, provided the Dutch with an apparent chance of increasing their seaborne trade at the expense of the English, which a section of the mercantile community found too tempting to resist.

Partly in the mistaken belief that England would not, in the upshot, involve herself in war with another European power in addition to France and Spain, partly from excessive reliance on the support to be expected from Russia and other neutral powers, but mainly from natural exasperation at English interception and seizure of their shipping, a group of Amsterdam merchants and regents persuaded the States of Holland to vote for a policy of unlimited convoy in March 1779. The Stadtholder and some Orangists, who regarded the English alliance as their sheet-anchor against a French invasion and the triumph of Popery, deprecated this move, which was also deplored by a few far-seeing individuals who realized that England would fight rather than give up her contested right to search Dutch ships for contraband naval stores. The ensuing war was wholly disastrous to the Dutch, and led indirectly to the ruin of the VOC and the collapse of both the Stadtholderate and the regent-oligarchy. But this does not alter the fact that it was not only a group of Amsterdam merchants with their policy of unlimited convoy who were ready to fight but also the self-styled 'Patriots' or pro-French middle-class critics of the existing aristocratic régime, and many of the *grauw*, or pro-Orange proletariat, as well.[23]

23. For the origins and outbreak of the Fourth Anglo-Dutch war, cf. J. C. de Jonge, *Zeewezen*, Vol. IV, pp. 379–440, and *AGN*, Vol. VIII, pp. 118–27. Cf. also Alice Carter, 'The Dutch as neutrals in the Seven Years War' (*The International and Comparative Law Quarterly*, July 1963, pp. 818–34), for a well-documented discussion of the Dutch attitude to neutrality in European Waters in the mid-18th century.

5

Gain and godliness: (a) At home.

When the States-General politely but firmly rejected Oliver Cromwell's suggestion of an Anglo-Dutch offensive alliance against Spain and Portugal with a view to dividing the Iberian colonial empires between the two Protestant powers, the English dictator sourly remarked that the Dutch preferred gain to godliness. This was a reproach which was often levelled at the inhabitants of the United Provinces during their Golden Century, and many of them were far from being ashamed thereat. Typical of these unabashed profiteers was the Amsterdam merchant who, in 1638, told the Stadtholder to his face that not only would he continue to trade with enemy Antwerp but that if he could make a commercial profit by passing through hell, he would risk burning the sails of his ships in doing so.[1] 'For love of gain, the wide world's harbours we explore', Vondel had sung of the Amsterdammers of his day and generation; and it may be relevant briefly to consider in this chapter how the Dutch managed to square the precepts of a religion which denounced this life as a mere nothing (*dit leven is gants niet*) with the practices involved in their possession of a world-wide commercial empire. I also propose briefly to discuss how far Calvinism suffered a sea-change when transplanted from Geneva via Dordrecht to the tropics.

Although Calvinism is often regarded as essentially the religion of capitalism, there is precious little justification for this view. The Dutch Calvinist ministers of the 17th century were mostly of lower-middle-class and working-class origin and they had, as a whole, a deeply ingrained anti-economic bias. They tended to be indifferent when they were not actually hostile to the regents' policy of trade supremacy and to the merchants' desire to secure

1. *Lettres et négotiations du Comte d'Estrades* (ed. London, 1743), Vol. I, p. 28; Secretary Thurloe's memorandum on Cromwell's foreign policy in *The English Historical Review*, Vol. XXI (1906), pp. 319–27; P. J. Blok, *Frederik Hendrik*, pp. 210–11.

new and profitable markets at any cost. This attitude was contested by a prominent Zeeland minister and theologian, the Rev
Godfried Udemans, in his *Spiritual Rudder of the Merchant Ship*,
which was dedicated to the directors of the East and West India
Companies and which went through three editions between 1638
and 1655.[2] It is significant that in this work Udemans finds it
necessary to argue at great length, and with copious quotations
from Holy Writ, that a merchant's calling is not an unlawful or
an ignoble one, but perfectly consistent with the practice of
Christianity, provided that it is exercised honestly and without
making excessive or illicit profits. Udemans also argues that
overseas trade affords an excellent means of spreading the light of
the true Gospel, and should be warmly supported by all pious
believers on that account. He is at pains to justify the creation
of the two India Companies and their expansion in the East and
West Indies, partly on the grounds of self-defence against the
Papistical Iberian world-monarchy, and partly as a vital outlet
for surplus Dutch capital and labour. He maintains that the
Companies' conquests are perfectly lawful and must be held at all
costs, while the divine aid should be invoked by increasing their
support of Calvinist missions to the heathen. Udemans, however,
was an exception. Few Dutch divines evinced any interest in
their country's expansion overseas, devoting their theological and
polemical talents to attacking the Church of Rome, or the Ana-
baptists, or the anti-Orangist attitude of the regent-oligarchs, or
to purely parochial concerns.

Many writers, past and present, have seen Calvinism as the
main driving force in the dynamic Dutch commercial expansion
and cultural flowering which were such marked features of the
17th-century scene. That Calvinism played a great role is indisputable, but its contribution is often exaggerated. Several of
the greatest figures in Dutch art and letters during the Golden

2. Godfried Udemans, *'TGeestelyck Roer van't Coopmans schip.
Dat is: Trouw bericht hoe dat een coopman en coopvaerder, hem
selven dragen moet in syne handelinge in pays ende in oorloge, voor
Godt ende de menschen, te water ende te lande, insonderheyt onder
de heydenen in Oost- ende West-Indien* (Dordrecht, 1638, 1640, 1655).
I have used the definitive edition of 1655.

Century, including Grotius, Rembrandt and Vondel – to name only the most obvious – were not members of the dominant Calvinist Church. Such indubitably Protestant stalwarts as Johan van Oldenbarnevelt and Johan de Witt were often critical of the orthodox *predikanten*, by whom, likewise, they were often criticized. If we turn to the great admirals of the 17th century we find that three of them, Piet Heyn, Martin Tromp and Michiel de Ruyter, were indeed earnest and God-fearing Calvinists whose favourite reading was the Bible, but of how many of their colleagues and subordinates could the same be said? There is no need to accuse Dominie Udemans of more than mild exaggeration when he averred that many Dutch sailors knew as little of the Bible as they did of the Koran. As regards the East India Company, two of the greatest governor-generals at Batavia, Coen and Van Diemen, were devout adherents of the Dutch Reformed Church; but they never ceased to deplore that the overwhelming majority of their countrymen in Asia were anything but ardent or exemplary believers. It was not Calvinism which was the driving force behind Dutch expansion overseas, but a combination of 'love of gain' among the merchants with the threat of unemployment and starvation for many of the seafaring community at home.

'Gold is your god,' said the West African negroes to the Dutch traders in Guinea early in the 17th century, thus anticipating King Charles X of Sweden, who pulled a rix-dollar out of his pocket and said, 'Voilà votre religion', to a Dutch envoy who was making some remark to him about liberty of religion.[3] During the two centuries of the Dutch East India Company's existence, fewer than 1,000 *predikanten* left the United Provinces to serve in the East, and many of them returned home after a few years. This figure compares well with the much smaller number of clergymen supported by the English East India Company in India; but it indicates that the missionary spirit was not very

3. P. de Marees, *Beschryvinghe ende historische verhael van het Gout Koninckrijck van Gunea anders de Gout-custe de Mina genaemt* (Amsterdam, 1602), p. 196 of the Linschoten Vereeniging edition by S. P. L'Honoré-Naber (The Hague, 1912); E. Wrangel, *De Betrekkingen tusschen Zweden en de Nederlanden* (Leiden, 1901), p. 9.

marked in Calvinism, and it forms a striking contrast with the many thousands of missionaries maintained overseas by the Spanish and Portuguese Crowns. For that matter, Protestant religious vocations in the northern Netherlands were not excessively numerous. There were probably never more than about 2,000 *predikanten* at any given time in all the Seven Provinces during a period of over two hundred years.

A distinction must also be drawn between the importance of Calvinism before and after the Synod of Dordrecht in 1618–19, which marks a watershed in the religious history of the United Provinces. Orthodox Calvinism with its stress on undiluted predestination, and on the limitation of salvation to God's Elect, was inevitably the religion of a select minority – of a Gideon band of brothers. But though the militant Calvinists among the Sea-Beggars played such an important part in the revolt of the Netherlands, they were neither the first nor the only group which was determined to break completely with the Church of Rome. Lutherans, Baptists and others who belonged to no dogmatic sect or creed but who were dissatisfied with the Old Religion for one reason or another, were certainly more numerous in the aggregate before about 1580. Marnix van Sint Aldegonde, the Calvinist writer of the scurrilous *Beehive of the Holy Church of Rome* in 1569, was not far wrong when he summarized early Protestant feelings in these terms:

In conclusion, all the holiness of the Catholic Church of Rome began to fall in the ashes: and in place thereof you should hear nothing else, neither in the towns nor without, yea, nothing was read but the Bible, or Saint Paul. The people would pray to none other but to GOD alone, neither would they have any other mediator but Christ Jesus, nor put their trust and confidence in any other things but in his merits: no rejoicings but in his cross, death and passion. They did only esteem for sacraments, Baptism and the Lord's Supper, yea, and did use the same very simply without any stately station or ceremonial bravery, without connivings of the Devil, without spittle, without salt, without greasings, and also without albs, surplices, or copes, without singing of *Per omnia saecula saeculorum*, or *Dominus vobiscum*. They would go no more to shrift under their ghostly father, but to God above, or else before the whole congregation. They did not pass any more for absolution;

they would not pray any more for the silly souls which lie in Purgatory; but every one would ground his prayer upon the holy scripture. They would acknowledge but one supreme head of the Church, namely Jesus Christ the Son of God. They would have Bishops, renouncing the name and office of tyrannical Inquisitors to preach the Gospel, to leave off their trapt [= caparisoned] horses and mules, and go on foot. They did esteem all manner of meats good and lawful, first saying grace in their mother tongues: neither did they much regard the eating of flesh in Lent, no, not even on Good Friday. In sum, they went wholly about to bring in a new reformation of religion and discipline ecclesiastical, the like whereof was never seen in the holy Church of Rome, nor of our forefathers. They took in hand to restore all again to the old and former state of the Apostles and Evangelists.[4]

No mention is made here of predestination, and the emphasis is on the Bible as the sole authority and on the absence of any priestly intermediary between Man and God. Protestants of all denominations and of none would have agreed with this in principle, though they might and did differ widely in their reading and interpretation of the Bible.

The militant Calvinists were only a small minority when the Sea-Beggars overran most of Holland and Zeeland in 1572. They were able to consolidate their power after capturing the towns by force or by fraud, chiefly because they were the only well-armed group among the rebels and the population at large. We have seen that they expelled the Papist priests and Religious as soon as they could, despite the personal inclination of William of Orange and others for a policy of religious toleration; but some time elapsed before the Calvinists could replace the Roman Catholic hierarchy by a ministry of their own. Contrary to what had happened in England, in Scandinavia and in parts of Germany, the Dutch Roman Catholic clergy in the 1570s did not go over to Protestantism after a token resistance and in consider-

4. Marnix van Sint Aldegonde, *The Beehive of the Romishe Church. Translated out of Dutch into English by George Gilpin the Elder* (London, 1579), p. **2 of the preface addressed to Bishop Francis Son of 'sHertogenbosch. The Dutch original is dated 5 January 1569. I have kept the wording of the English translation (reprinted 1580, 1598, 1625) but modernized the spelling.

able numbers. Some authorities estimate the total of those who turned Protestant at between 5 and 10 per cent, and in any case the great majority either fled, were killed or were expelled. Thus the north Netherlands Calvinist Church of 'the True Christian Reformed Religion' had to start, so to speak, from scratch, and could not build upon a foundation of renegade Roman Catholic priests. There were, of course, a fair number of Protestant ministers who had received a theological training at Geneva, Basel, Zürich and elsewhere abroad, but not nearly enough adequately to replace the 'sons of Belial' whom they dispossessed. The University of Leiden was founded (2 June 1575) largely with the object of ensuring a supply of well-educated *predikanten*, but some years elapsed before this result was achieved. Very few (if any) sons of upper-middle-class families were attracted by the Protestant minister's calling, which was badly paid; and the burghers disliked and mistrusted the hedge-preachers sprung from the proletariat, who preached extempore sermons from ill-chosen texts and were inclined to demand social justice for the lower classes. The influx of many well-educated Calvinists from the southern Netherlands, in 1585 and the following years, and the victory of militant Calvinism at the Synod of Dordrecht, helped to improve the social status of the *predikanten*. They were thenceforward treated with marked respect by the political authorities, and took a high place in the order of precedence at official and private functions. It is significant, however, that although the urban regent class took good care to officer the higher ranks of the town militia or *schutterij*, they never bothered to educate their sons for the ministry and never encouraged them to become *predikanten*.[5]

5. In addition to the standard English-language works of Geyl, Renier, and Vlekke, which have been cited previously, I have relied heavily for the above and what follows on the relevant chapters of Vols. V and VI of the *Algemene Geschiedenis der Nederlanden*, covering the religious history of the years 1567–1648. Cf. also Geyl's *Studies en strijdschriften* (Groningen, 1958), and the numerous books and articles on various aspects of the religious and social history of the Netherlands listed in the *Bibliographie van de belangrijkste geschriften van Dr H. A. Enno van Gelder* (The Hague, 1960).

As and when the Calvinists took over from the dispossessed Papists, they established their own Church organization. Each parish had its church council or consistory, composed of Calvinist ministers and laymen with the *predikant* as chairman. Churches were grouped into a *classis* or colloquy, and the *classes* of each of the Seven Provinces formed a synod – there being one each for north and south Holland. These bodies met frequently and were active in bringing pressure to bear on their fellow-townsmen or fellow-parishioners to join the official Church. Understandably enough, they were particularly anxious to convert the younger generation. From 1574 onwards they strove to protestantize the rural and the urban working classes through their control of the village and urban primary schools. Most of the former Roman Catholic convents and other large buildings were converted into schools where elementary religious instruction was given by teachers whose orthodoxy had been tested and approved by the local *predikanten* and church councils. The *predikanten* likewise strove to keep the regent-oligarchs up to the mark in prohibiting the exercise of the Roman Catholic religion and in discouraging all forms of Protestant dissent, whether Arminian, Baptist or Lutheran. This naturally took time. In 1587 the High Court of Holland assured the Earl of Leicester that the majority of the population was 'still inclined towards the Romish religion in their hearts'. The notoriously outspoken liberal Protestant, Dirck Volkertsz Coornhert, termed the Reformed 'by far the smallest band' in one of his pamphlets advocating religious toleration. Some years later Oldenbarnevelt alleged that the richest and best part of the burghers still adhered to the Old Religion. These statements and others like them need not be taken too seriously; but it was certainly no easy task for the zealous *predikanten* and synods to impose on their pleasure-loving and hard-drinking (if also hard-working) compatriots the grim and forbidding tenets of Jean Calvin and Theodore Bèze.

The *predikanten* and their sympathizers among the regents – who, although a minority, were influential at times, even in Amsterdam where God clearly took second place to Mammon – kept hammering away at their self-appointed task, and their pertinacity slowly brought results. They were helped by the fact that since they were the most ardent advocates of the war against Spain, which they regarded in the light of a crusade against Anti-Christ, the more broad-minded regents could not afford to clamp down on them too severely. The conclusion of the Twelve Year Truce in 1609 was regarded by the Calvinist zealots as an act of either despicable weakness or downright treachery. Their resentment was heightened by the support given by Olden-barnevelt and many of the regents to the teaching of Arminius, a theological professor at Leiden, whose views on predestination were somewhat milder than those of strict Calvinists. The division between Remonstrants and Counter-Remonstrants, as the followers of Arminius and his chief opponent, Gomarus, were respectively called, was sharpened by political differences. The Arminians were identified with Oldenbarnevelt and the regent-oligarchs who supported provincial sovereignty in its strictest form. This implied the pre-eminence of the province of Holland and the unchallenged maintenance of the urban patriciate's power, including its supremacy over the Church. The Counter-Remonstrants advocated the untrammelled freedom of the Calvinist Church from any interference or supervision by the civil power. They also wanted the complete elimination of Roman Catholics and of Protestant dissenters from any positions of authority in Church and State.

The pamphlet-war which raged between Remonstrants and Counter-Remonstrants reflected the increasing bitterness with which the dispute became injected on both sides. The Counter-Remonstrants, as the more extreme party, were naturally the more virulent of the two. They were also the more numerous, although the Remonstrants managed to retain a dominant position in the Church down to 1618, thanks to the support of Oldenbarnevelt and those of the regents who agreed with him. *Odium Theologicum* admittedly arouses fiercer passions than almost anything else; but, even so, it is rather surprising to find a respectable Counter-Remonstrant citizen of Rotterdam proclaiming that he would sooner be married by a pig than by a Remonstrant minister, and an Amsterdam burgomaster rejecting a colleague's invitation to attend a Remonstrant service with the observation that he would rather sit in a brothel with seven whores.[6] This doctrinal dispute was settled by the intervention of Prince Maurice on the side of the Counter-Remonstrants, not from any deep-rooted conviction concerning the finer points of predestination but from purely political considerations. Above all, he wished to strengthen his position as Stadtholder and the authority of the States-General (on most of whose delegates he could rely) at the expense of Oldenbarnevelt and the ruling oligarchy of the province of Holland. He was able to do this because the Counter-Remonstrant magistrates of Amsterdam, who were bitterly opposed to Oldenbarnevelt for having concluded the Twelve Year Truce and prevented the formation of the West India Company, happened to be in office during part of those years. Maurice could also count on the support of the land provinces and of their representatives in the States-General who were always jealous of Holland's preponderant influence.

The fall of Oldenbarnevelt coincided with the holding of the Calvinist synod at Dordrecht, which affirmed the orthodoxy of the Counter-Remonstrant doctrines and branded the Arminians as heretics. Henceforward, the Remonstrants, together with Roman Catholics, Lutherans, Baptists, and any others who did not adhere to the tenets of the 'true Christian Reformed Religion', as defined at the Synod of Dordrecht, were excluded (on paper) from holding office in Church and State. But this rule was not always enforced in all of the Seven Provinces in the form of a solemn statutory oath, like the English Test Act of 1673 was. Many regents with Remonstrant sympathies were soon able to secure office on the bare assertion that they adhered to the doctrinal rulings of the Synod of Dordrecht. The banned Remonstrant Church, whose ministers had been dismissed, imprisoned or expelled in 1619, was quickly reconstituted in the form of a more or less private brotherhood, and active persecution of the Remonstrants ceased within a few years. They were organized on the same lines as the official Reformed Church, and they duly accepted the States' Bible of 1637 as the sole repository of

6. *Apud* Busken Huet, *Het land van Rembrand* (3 vols., ed. 1886), Vol. II(1), pp. 79–80; G. H. Betz, *Het Haagsche leven in de tweede helft der zeventiende eeuw* (The Hague, 1900), p. 19.

Protestant doctrine. They differed from the strict Calvinist believers in that they were left free to judge for themselves the value of formulas, confessions and catechisms, instead of being bound by the Heidelberg Catechism and the tenets of the 'true Christian Reformed Religion' as defined at Dordrecht in 1619. The Remonstrants were first allowed their own public church at Amsterdam in 1630, but they continued to be a select and self-contained, if relatively influential, body which never counted more than 12,000 communicants during the 17th century.

One of the resolutions adopted by the Synod of Dordrecht was that an authorized translation of the Bible should be made by a committee of eighteen theologians, linguists and historians, since the existing Dutch version (based on Luther's German Bible) was unsatisfactory. The work was completed in 1627–37, and the States' Bible, so called because the project was financed by the States-General and published by their order, came to occupy in Dutch life and literature a place very similar to that held by the Authorized Version in 17th- and 18th-century England. The parallel is all the closer, as both versions proved that good literature can be written by a committee. The wide dissemination of the States' Bible in the Seven Provinces, and the fervour with which many people read it, undoubtedly strengthened the existing tendency to invoke the name or the help of God Almighty in and out of season, both in official and private correspondence. This vogue for biblical phraseology was not confined to Dutch Calvinists, but they seem to have carried it further and used it longer than elsewhere in Europe, save for Cromwellian England. The most business-like dispatches and the most worldly letters were often heavily interlarded with pious platitudes and invocations.

The triumph of the Counter-Remonstrant Calvinists in 1618–19, though indisputable, was not complete. Some of the results were soon whittled down or pared away by the passive resistance and the uncooperative attitude of many of the regents. The existing regulations against Roman Catholics were tightened up, and the Calvinist churches were purged of any pictures or interior decorations they might still possess, but the regents prevented the *predikanten* from removing the organs as well. The

Calvinist ministers now had a greater say than hitherto, but they were still not allowed to become members of the town councils or of the provincial States, and the ultimate control of the Church still rested to a great extent with the regent-oligarchs who held the purse-strings. As indicated above, throughout the period that the Dutch Republic lasted, most of the *predikanten* came from the middle and lower middle classes – the *gemeene man* so despised by the regents – and they never formed a priestly caste or an ecclesiastical Third Estate, as did their Roman Catholic rivals in countries like France, Spain and Portugal. Though the regents had their representatives at the provincial synods, as we shall see below, they seldom bothered to serve in the consistories and church councils, where the Calvinist elders were drawn from the ranks of the ordinary burghers, as were many of the *predikanten*.

The attitude of the average Dutch Protestant burghers to Church and State was, perhaps, typified by Admiral Michiel de Ruyter, who began life as a ship's boy at Flushing and ended it as a wealthy burgher of Amsterdam. His contemporary biographer, himself a Remonstrant *predikant*, tells us that although the admiral had a great respect for Calvinist ministers and would not tolerate any unfair criticism of them he was equally insistent that they should never interfere in anything outside their proper sphere. He was as convinced an upholder of the supremacy of the State over the Church as were the contemporary regents, who, as Willam Carr noted, had their representatives at all meetings of the provincial synods, 'to hear that they debate nothing relating to or reflecting on the government, or governors: if they do, presently the States cry, *Ho la myn Heeren Predicaten!* (Hold hard, gentlemen preachers!')[7] Nor did the regents tolerate any criticism from the pulpit; but, Carr likewise noted, if the *predikanten* behaved themselves quietly and well, 'they are respected by the common people as gods upon earth'. This may have been so, as a general rule, but there were plenty of exceptions, especially among the rough seafaring communities. The Rev. Godfried Udemans of Zierickzee was not the only Calvinist minister who

7. W. Carr, *An Accurate Description of the United Netherlands* (ed. 1691), p. 28.

contrasted unfavourably the lack of respect shown by many Dutch laymen for their spiritual guides, with the humble deference displayed by Spanish and Portuguese Roman Catholics towards their priests.

It is clear from the foregoing that the Calvinist Church of the 'true Christian Reformed Religion' was not freed completely from control and supervision by the civil power, as the Counter-Remonstrant *predikanten* had hoped in 1618–19. Nor were Roman Catholics and Protestant dissenters persecuted as much as the Synod of Dordrecht had envisaged, even before a reaction set in with the death of Prince Maurice and his replacement of Frederick Henry (1625), and with the overthrow of the Counter-Remonstrant regents at Amsterdam about the same time. We have seen that a Remonstrant church was publicly allowed at Amsterdam in 1630, and next year the town council permitted the erection of a large Lutheran church, a second one being built forty years later. Persecution, however, there was; and inevitably the Roman Catholics bore the brunt of it.[8]

For over a hundred and fifty years after the relative triumph of militant Calvinism at the Synod of Dordrecht, Roman Catholics could not legally worship in public or in private, nor could they be legally christened nor married by a Roman Catholic priest. They were forbidden to give their children a Roman Catholic education, or even to send them abroad for the purpose of receiving one there. The wearing of crucifixes, rosaries or Roman Catholic insignia of any kind, the buying and selling of Roman Catholic religious books, devotional literature, prints and engravings, the saying or reciting of Roman Catholic hymns and songs, the celebration of Roman Catholic feast-days and holidays, were all forbidden by law. No Roman Catholic could hold an official post, whether municipal, university, legal, naval or military. Unmarried Roman Catholic women were not allowed to make a will; and any bequest to a Roman Catholic foundation was automatically held to be null and void in law. In most places, the children of mixed marriages had to be brought up as

8. AGN, Vol. V, pp. 329–47, gives a very useful analytical survey of the position of Roman Catholics in the Dutch Republic, on which I have largely relied for what follows.

Protestants, and there were so many other vexatious legal hindrances in the way of practising the Roman Catholic faith that, if these penal laws had been properly enforced, the liberty of conscience which was grudgingly allowed to Roman Catholics would have been almost valueless by itself. In addition to all these civil disabilities from which the Dutch Roman Catholics suffered, they were for long regarded by many of their Protestant compatriots as being actual or potential traitors – from 1568 to 1648 in the interests of Spain, and from 1648 to 1748 in that of France.

The only thing that made life tolerable for the Roman Catholic citizens of the Dutch Republic was the fact that the penal laws against the practice of their religion were never enforced in full at all times and in all places, and these laws became increasingly easy to evade or to disregard as the 18th century progressed. Fortunately for the Roman Catholics and for the Protestant dissenters, the States-General never accepted the *predikanten* plans for fully implementing Calvinist supremacy. They never insisted that all the inhabitants of the Republic should adhere to the 'true Christian Reformed Religion', and they did not make attendance at Calvinist church services compulsory. Civil marriages were regarded as equally binding as any form of Protestant religious marriage-service, and anybody could choose either form (or both). The Dutch Reformed Church, as defined and established by the Synod of Dordrecht, was the only form of Christian worship accorded full recognition by the State until the bond between Church and State was severed by the revolution of 1795, but it was not a State Church to the extent that, for instance, the Anglican Church was in England.

Though Roman Catholics were legally prohibited from holding any government or official post, and though most of the professions were ostensibly closed to them, yet there were always some practising (or crypto-) Roman Catholics to be found in such positions, save perhaps in the years immediately following the Synod of Dordrecht. Roman Catholic burgomasters and aldermen, though rare, were not unknown; and Roman Catholic officers were relatively numerous in the army. By the second half of the 18th century there were many towns with Roman Catholic families which had furnished lawyers, notaries and doctors for several generations. Disguised Roman Catholic churches and meeting-places functioned in most towns from about 1630 onwards, and everyone, including the local Calvinist ministers, knew what and where they were. Similarly, Roman Catholic priests who took elementary precautions and who avoided flaunting themselves and their cloth, were able to minister to their communities despite the paper prohibitions of their activities.

This systematic flouting of the penal laws against Roman Catholics was partly due to the Erastian and utilitarian views of the majority of the regents which predisposed them in favour of religious toleration, and partly to that 'love of gain' which Vondel celebrated in his Amsterdammers and which the Calvinist ministers never ceased to deplore. The minor officials charged with the enforcement of the penal laws – the deputies of sheriffs, bailiffs, tipstaffs and the like – were regularly bribed to turn a blind eye and a deaf ear to Roman Catholic practices, these payments being termed 'recognition-fees'. They soon became, and they long remained, an unofficial but recognized perquisite of the local authorities concerned, there being no secrecy about them.[9] The Reformed *classes* and synods repeatedly lodged complaints against 'the prevalence of popish practices', and the connivance of the officials involved. The States-General and the provincial States usually responded by publishing hortatory edicts or placards, reiterating the existence of the penal laws, but their enforcement continued to be as regularly evaded by bribery. So regular did the payment of these recognition-fees become, that when they were finally abolished in 1787, as a result of the weakening of Calvinist intolerance due to the spread of the ideas fostered by the Enlightenment, higher salaries had to be paid to the officials who had benefited therefrom.

9. 'In vain are penal laws whilst the city and village bailiffs remain the overseers and prosecutors of criminal affairs; for these will ever dispense with the practices of the priests for a sum of money, which they are always in a condition to furnish upon such an occasion.' Onslow Burrish, *Batavia Illustrata: or, a view of the policy, and commerce, of the United Provinces, particularly of Holland* (London, 1728), p. 149.

The cumulative effect of the legal, social and financial discriminations against the Dutch Roman Catholics did lead to the slow erosion of their numbers in the long run. Whereas Protestants of all persuasions probably had a bare majority (if they had one at all) over the Roman Catholics in 1650, the latter seem to have numbered about 45 per cent of the total population fifty years later, and about 40 per cent in 1795. The allegation of the Reformed Synods that there were some 20,000 Beguines (Roman Catholic lay-sisters) in the United Provinces in 1650 certainly need not be taken too seriously; though even if there were a tenth of that number this is still impressive when we recall that there were probably fewer than 2,000 Calvinist ministers. It is more difficult to gauge how the Roman Catholics were distributed through the class structure, though it is clear that the great majority of the urban regent class, the wealthy merchants and (for want of a better word) the intellectuals had become Protestants by the end of the 17th century. The bulk of the urban proletariat was also Protestant, but many of the lower middle-class traders and the self-employed business-men seem to have remained Roman Catholic. The Roman Catholic lands of the Generality had also stayed faithful to the Church of Rome, despite the pressure brought upon them by their Protestant overlords – or perhaps partly because of this, just as happened with the Roman Catholic Irish under English rule. There were pockets of Roman Catholic villages scattered throughout the Seven Provinces, even in the neighbourhood of such Protestant strongholds as Alkmaar and Leiden. William Carr, writing in 1688, was reflecting a common if erroneous belief when he stated that one-third of the population of Amsterdam belonged to the official Calvinist Church, one-third were Roman Catholics, the remaining third being composed of Protestant dissenters (including Lutherans, Arminians, Brownists, Baptists and Quakers) and Jews. In fact, the baptismal registers indicate that nearly half the population of Amsterdam was Calvinist by 1688: But despite marked local and regional variations, it is perhaps not wildly inaccurate to say that out of a total population of nearly two million, not more than one-third actively adhered to the official Dutch Reformed Church.

Although the Synod of Dordrecht's decisions were never fully implemented and were increasingly evaded or undermined in the course of time, the Calvinist victory of 1618–19 did produce certain lasting results. The alliance between the House of Orange and the *predikanten* which had brought Oldenbarnevelt to the scaffold, persisted for the best part of two centuries, although at times with some misgivings on both sides. Frederick Henry, for example, was Arminian in sympathy if not in practice; and the evident inclination of his son and successor to wine, women and song might have brought him into serious trouble with the Calvinist kill-joys but for his premature death in 1650. William III's patronage of the theatre likewise ran counter to strict Calvinist morality; nor is it surprising to find that some *predikanten* and their wives who attended a party given by Count John Maurice of Nassau after his return from Brazil were 'not at all amused' by a floor-show staged by some stark-naked Amerindians.[10] More serious than these worldly diversions of the princes of the House of Nassau was the support given by the Stadtholders on more than one occasion before 1648 to the Catholic French kings against their rebellious Huguenot subjects. But on the whole it is not an over-simplification to say that after 1618 the *predikanten* mostly regarded successive Princes of Orange as their natural champions against the allegedly free-thinking, 'libertine' or pro-Remonstrant regents of the province of Holland in general, and of Amsterdam in particular. The Calvinist ministers were apt to fan the flame of pro-Orange feeling among the lower middle classes and the masses, from the former of which many of them had sprung. This alliance between the House of Orange and the orthodox Calvinist Church was of special importance in times of national crisis, such as the French invasions of 1672 and 1748, when the lesser burghers and the urban proletariat could be brought out into the streets to bring pressure on the regent-oligarchs in the town halls.

Another lasting result of the crisis of 1618–19 was that people in general, and especially the regents, became more concerned than they had been hitherto to preserve an appearance of ortho-

10. J. A. Worp (ed.), *Briefwisseling van Constantijn Huyghens, 1608–1687* (6 vols., The Hague, 1911–18), Vol. IV, p. 52.

doxy. Even though this attitude was often more apparent than real, it sometimes made the civil authorities more amenable to pressure from the *predikanten*. The exclusion of Roman Catholics and Protestant dissenters from office, though never fully implemented everywhere and at all times, was practised to an extent which induced many upper-class families to turn Calvinist in the course of the next century and a half. The puritanical side of Calvinism was also strengthened by the outcome of the Synod of Dordrecht, where the *predikanten* had deplored the inclination of the Netherlanders 'towards liberty and pleasure'. Calvinist Church members were henceforth subjected to stricter supervision by their consistories, which often interfered in the most intimate concerns. The celebration of 'Popish festivals' such as Christmas and New Year's Eve was constantly denounced; and the theatre and dance were declared to be pernicious in the extreme. But the Calvinists never succeeded in banning these diversions altogether, and in the cosmopolitan centres of The Hague and Amsterdam they hardly affected them at all. On the other hand, in the countryside, in the small towns, and in the other provinces more than in Holland, the *predikanten* were successful in gradually imposing a puritanical cast of thought and conduct on many of the urban middle class and on the peasantry.

The long-lived and zealous *predikant*, Voetius, got the theatre suppressed in Leeuwarden, where he had the support of the staunchly Calvinist Frisian Stadtholder; but the theatre at Amsterdam survived all the denunciations of the *predikanten* down the years. Music-halls and dancing-halls also flourished in Amsterdam to the distress of the *predikanten*; and even the inns which catered for a superior clientele allowed guests to hold parties with wine, women and song in their inner rooms. These inns did not maintain a band of musicians in order to attract custom, as some of the ordinary taverns did, preferring instead to tempt the thirst of prospective clients by offering a wide choice of French, Spanish, Rhenish and even Greek and Italian wines. Some of the music- and dance-halls were more or less thinly disguised brothels, but there were others which provided music without becoming houses of ill-fame. The night-life and variety of diversions at Amsterdam were not equalled elsewhere in the

Seven Provinces, where the general tone was much more sedate. This was particularly the case in Zeeland, where Calvinism had strongly entrenched itself in the 1570s, and where the regents seem to have been more zealous believers than their colleagues elsewhere, and so more ready to co-operate with the *predikanten*. Dutch Roman Catholicism was also strongly influenced by its enforced subjugation to Calvinist puritanism and austerity, as can be seen by comparing its outward manifestations with those of its more exuberant southern and eastern neighbours. Something rather similar happened to Roman Catholicism in England owing to its position *vis-à-vis* a dominant Protestantism.

The Dutch Reformed Church also strove to direct the course of intellectual life through the five provincial universities successively founded between 1575 and 1636. This tendency was likewise strengthened by the events of 1618–19, when the existing universities were purged of all teachers who did not unreservedly subscribe to the decisions of the Synod of Dordrecht. But here again the Counter-Remonstrant triumph was not complete. A doctrinal oath was henceforth exacted – or was supposed to be exacted – from all *predikanten*, professors and schoolmasters; but it was often subscribed to under the reserve of an individual interpretation, and occasionally even a teacher who declined to take it was nevertheless appointed. Remonstrant professors like the famous classical scholar and poet, the Rev. Caspar Barlaeus, who was expelled from Leiden in 1619, were later given chairs at the Amsterdam Academy or 'Illustrious School', and at other colleges where the authorities were more complacent. The Calvinist universities were as firmly rooted in positive dogma and Aristotelian philosophy as were the Roman Catholic universities in other countries; but the Dutch curators lacked the authority – and often the will – to stifle discussion completely, as was shown by the ineffective ban which they promulgated against the dissemination of Cartesian philosophy at Leiden. Even at Utrecht, which became a bastion of Calvinist fundamentalism with the forty-year tenure of the fiery Voetius as senior professor of theology (1636–76), a Remonstrant was admitted to the faculty in 1649, on condition that his appointment should not be regarded as a precedent. Finally, the maintenance of provincial sovereignty by the regent-oligarchs usually ensured that if a well-qualified teacher was not tolerated in one place, he could find another town where the authorities were less exacting.

The orthodox Calvinist attitude to the Lutherans, Baptists, Brownists and other Protestant dissenters, though less hostile than to Roman Catholics, was for long one of rather grudging and piecemeal toleration. After the wild excess of the early Anabaptist movement in Germany and the Netherlands, which were denounced by Luther, Zwingli and other Protestant reformers with a verbal ferocity that matched the sadistic vengeance wreaked by German priests and princes on the followers of Thomas Münzer and John of Leiden, the Baptists in the Netherlands had become a pacifist and ultra-puritanical community. Their most notable sect was that of the Mennonites, so called from their founder, Menno Symonsz, who refused to accept civil office or to bear arms under any circumstances. Active persecution of the Mennonites ceased in 1581, mainly because of the protection afforded them by William the Silent, but they were only accorded full citizenship rights in 1672. The Baptists were originally perhaps the largest Protestant group, but many of them transferred their allegiance to the militant Calvinist *predikanten* in the 1560s and 70s, becoming disillusioned with pacifism and non-resistance in the struggles against Spain and Rome. During the 17th and 18th centuries, Baptists and Mennonites formed two quietly prosperous and self-contained communities, whose ultra-puritanical dress and sobriety sometimes aroused mocking comments from Calvinists and 'libertines' alike. Both these dissenting groups lost ground numerically in the 18th century, but their importance in the social and cultural life of the northern Netherlands has not yet been adequately assessed.

The Jews formed another distinctive group which benefited from the relative tolerance shown to all faiths other than the Roman Catholic by the regent class in the Dutch Republic. The Amsterdam community of Portuguese and Spanish Jews, who had fled from the Iberian peninsula to avoid the Inquisition, numbered about 800 in 1626 and 1,200 in 1655. They were allowed to build their first synagogue in 1597, and a much finer one in 1639. These Sephardim Jews were reinforced by Ashkenazim refugees from Germany and Poland who settled in the eastern provinces as well as at Amsterdam. The Ashkenazim were mostly on a lower cultural and economic level than their precursors and were apt to be despised by Gentile and Sephardim alike. But they were not forced to live in ghettoes, and in 1657 the States-General explicitly recognized all resident Jews as being Dutch nationals, though they did not receive full citizenship rights until 1796.

The Sephardim Jews enjoyed a certain consideration among their Calvinist intellectual contemporaries; men like Grotius, Barlaeus and Vossius consulting learned Rabbis such as Menasseh ben Israel on points of Old Testament textual commentary and Hebrew philosophy. But although Calvinist *predikanten* were always quoting Biblical Jewish precedents in their arguments, and holding up Moses and the Hebrew Prophets as exemplars, the social stigma which was attached to Jewry in Christendom persisted in the northern Netherlands as elsewhere in Europe. The strict Counter-Remonstrant pamphleteer and company-promoter, Willem Usselincx, exhibited a crude anti-semitism in his writings; and a Calvinist *predikant*, who was captured by the Spaniards at Bahia in 1625, assured his captors with evident sincerity that, although Jews were legally tolerated at Amsterdam, they were regarded with contemptuous dislike and aversion by the bulk of the population.[11] The loyalty shown by the Jews in Netherlands Brazil during the Portuguese rebellion, 1645-54, undoubtedly helped to improve the position of the three Jewish congregations at Amsterdam, where the Stadtholder and his wife paid a state visit to the recently built synagogue in 1642.

Jewish merchants of Amsterdam were early active in the sugar and slave-trades, but their golden age came in the 18th century, when they were heavy investors in both the India Companies, and in the Surinam plantations. Jewish army contractors to the King-Stadtholder also made fortunes, and other Jewish financiers enriched themselves by speculation on the Amsterdam stock-exchange in the ways described by Joseph Penso de la Vega's *Confusion de las confusiones* (1688). In the 18th century, Dutch

11. British Museum, Egerton MSS. 592. letter from the Rev. Enoch Startenius to Queixardo de Solorzano, 1625.

Jewish financiers followed the example of their Christian compatriots by heavily investing in English funds. Even at the time of the English war of 1780–4, Dutch buyers of British securities included 'The Parnassim of the Brotherhood of Orphant Boys of the Portuguese Jewish nation, commonly called the Abi Tetonian at Amsterdam', as well as the consistory of the fashionable Amsterdam Walloon Church.[12] Of course, by no means all the Jews in the Seven Provinces were wealthy financiers or even well-to-do burghers. On the contrary, the majority of the local Jewish communities (*kehilloth*) were poor and backward, forming a striking contrast with the wealthy and cultured Sephardim of Amsterdam. The rigid and inward-looking structure of the autonomous *kehilloth* prevented them from developing a vigorous class of workers and artisans, and their *parnassim* or spiritual leaders were averse to any change or new ideas which might affect their authority. By the end of the 18th century over half of the 2,800 Sephardim Jewish members of the chief synagogue at Amsterdam were in receipt of poor-relief, and out of 20,304 Ashkenazim Jews in that city no fewer than 17,500 were classified as beggars.[13]

The oft-quoted lines of Andrew Marvell in his *Character of Holland*:

> *Hence Amsterdam, Turk, Christian, Pagan, Jew,*
> *Staple of sects and mint of schism grew:*
> *That bank of conscience, where not one so strange*
> *Opinion but finds credit and exchange,*

accurately reflect the success of the regent class in preventing Calvinist zealots from sacrificing gain to godliness, despite the partial triumph of the Counter-Remonstrants at the Synod of Dordrecht. The regents' advocacy of (relative) religious toleration

12. C. Wilson, *Anglo-Dutch Commerce and Finance in the 18th Century* (Cambridge, 1941), p. 192.

13. M. E. Bolle, *De opheffing van de autonomie der kehilloth (joodse gemeenten) in Nederland, 1796* (Amsterdam, 1960); J. De Bosch Kemper, *Geschiedkundig onderzoek naar de armoede in ons vaderland* (Haarlem, 1851), table XI f.

was essentially utilitarian and self-interested; but it was none the less genuine and it afforded a favourable contrast to the conditions obtaining elsewhere in Europe. Pieter de la Court, though not a regent himself, reflected the sentiment of many regents when he wrote in his *Interest of Holland*: 'Freedom or toleration in and about the service or worship of God is a powerful means to preserve many inhabitants in Holland and to allure foreigners to dwell among us.' The regent-oligarchs could not, indeed, go as far as De la Court advocated and grant complete freedom of worship to Roman Catholics and to Protestant dissenters alike. Calvinist intolerance and influence were still too powerful for that and they remained so for over another century. But the regents went as far as they could in the prevailing circumstances; and if their attitude was inspired by commercial convenience rather than by religious conviction, they do deserve the credit for making the United Provinces of the Free Netherlands the least intolerant country in Europe over a period of two hundred years.

It is only fair to add that religious conviction among all classes of Dutch society sometimes made itself felt on the side of toleration. In 1662, the States of Friesland, under pressure from the *predikanten*, promulgated an edict forbidding 'some hateful sects' such as Socinians and Quakers, from entering that province and practising their religion there. Offenders were threatened with five years' forced labour in the workhouse followed by expulsion from the province. The printing and circulation of their tracts and books were likewise forbidden under severe penalties. This edict aroused such a storm of criticism that the provincial States were soon compelled to withdraw it. The critics pointed out that apart from the inherent intolerance of this 'inquisitorial' procedure, it was ridiculous to ban Protestant sects, however bizarre, in a country where 'Jews, Turks and Saracens had religious freedom, even to the use of Synagogues'.

In the course of his plea for unrestricted religious toleration, De la Court quoted with approval the recently published *De Jure Ecclesiasticorum* of L. A. Constans, which argued that 'the coercive power is given only to the civil magistrates; all the power and right which the ecclesiastics have, if they have any, must be

derived from them'.[14] The subordination of the Church to the
State which these remarks reflected, and which became increasingly evident in the second half of the 17th century, was still
more clearly evinced by the position of the Calvinist Church in
the spheres of the East and West India Companies, to which we
must now turn our attention.

(b) Abroad

Luther, Calvin, Zwingli and other leading Protestant reformers
seem to have given little or no thought to the possibility of
spreading Protestantism outside Europe, preoccupied as they were
with the bitter religious disputes on their doorstep. It would be
unreasonable to expect the directors of the East and West India
Companies to have concerned themselves closely with an evangelistic problem that was virtually ignored by the founding
fathers of Protestantism, but they soon had to face it in two ways.
Firstly, they had to make some provision for the spiritual needs
of their servants, if only as an aid to the maintenance of their
discipline and morale on the long sea voyages, or during their
stay in tropical lands. Secondly, they had to reckon with the
presence of militant Roman Catholicism in the regions where
their Portuguese predecessors had established themselves. In the
case of the East India Company, they had further to reckon with
the deeply rooted religious and social systems of Islam, Hinduism
and Buddhism.

Although the original charters of the two Companies made no
provision for the maintenance of Calvinist clergy in their respective spheres, or of any obligation to spread the light of the 'true
Christian Reformed Religion' among the benighted Papists and
the blind Heathen, both Companies soon explicitly recognized

14. *The Interest of Holland* (ed. 1702), ch. XIV. For Constans and
his work see D. Nobbs, *Theocracy and Toleration. A study of the
disputes in Dutch Calvinism* (Cambridge, 1938), pp. 245–50. For the
Frisian Provincial edict against Quakers and its subsequent with-
drawal see the *Hollandtse Mercurius*, March 1662.

1 Amsterdam receiving the tribute of four continents

3 Recife, with shipping in the
   roadstead, 1644

2 Amsterdam with shipping in the river Y, 1663

4   *above left*, Batavia, with shipping in the roadstead, 1649
5   *left*, Cape Town, with shipping in the roadstead, 1683
6   Johan de Witt, portrait by A. Hanneman

7 *below*, Pieter de la Court, portrait by A.L. van der Tempel

8 Johan Maetsuyker, Governor-General of Netherlands-India

IOAN MAAT   SUYKER
Gouvernur Generaal v.   *van Nederlands Indien.*

JACOBUS ELISA JOANNES CAPITEIN,
AFRICAANSCHE MOOR.
Beroepen Predikant aan het Kasteel st. George op DElmina.
Aanschoúwer zie dee z`MOOR! zijn vel is zwart: maar wit
zijn ziel, daar JESUS zelf als Priester voor hem bidt.
Hij gaat Geloof, en Hoop, en Liefde aan Mooren leeren,
Op dat zij, witgemaakt, met hem het LAM steeds eeren.

BRANDYN EIGER

t` LEYDEN by ABRAH KALLEWIER

9 *above*, The Negro Predikant, Jacobus Elisa Joannes Capitein,
   from a print of 1742

10 An 18th-century Dutch Governor of Elimina with his Negro
    slave, painting by A. van der Mijn

和蘭人食煙圖

奴隷烏鬼銀盆に唖壺と手爐

とを載て側よたてり

11   An Opperhoofd of Titsingh's time with his Asian servant, from a woodcut by Araki Jogen

食事之間管絃之體

12   A slave orchestra in the Dutch Factory at Deshima,
      Nagasaki, *c.* 1690

13 *below*, The King of Golconda attends service in the Dutch
 Church at Masulipatnam on Christmas Day, 1678
14 (a) Dutch manuscript chart of three of the Banda Islands, *c.* 1660
 (b) Dutch manuscript chart of Hainan Island, *c.* 1660

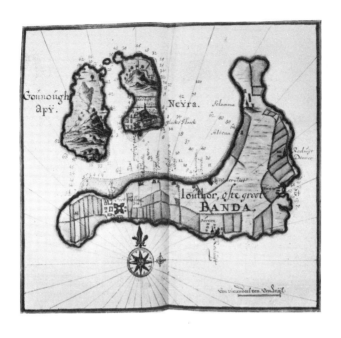

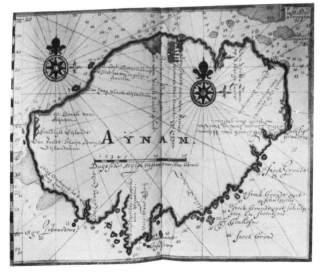

15 *left*, M. A. de Ruyter's flagship, *De Zeven Provincien*, on the
    eve of the Four Days' Fight, 11–14 June 1666, from a grisaille
    by W. Van de Velde the Elder

16 A meeting of the States-General at The Hague, 1651

17 Working-class types in the northern Netherlands at the end of the 17th century, engravings by J. and C. Luiken: Sailor, Bookbinder, Printmaker, Peasant

that they had such obligations, and their official correspondence contains numerous references to these matters. Nor did their performance always fall so far short of their precepts as is often alleged. During the Dutch East India Company's two centuries of existence, the directors sent out to the East and maintained at their own expense a total of nearly 1,000 Calvinist *predikanten* and several thousand lay-readers and schoolmasters. The *Heeren* XVII also provided funds for the building and upkeep of churches and schools and founded several seminaries for the training of candidates for ordination – though these institutions did not always have a long life. They also paid for the printing and distribution of Bibles and devotional literature on quite a considerable scale, both in Dutch and in some of the Asian vernaculars.[15] If their evangelistic efforts were not very impressive when compared with those of the Church of Rome, they were certainly much greater than those made by the directors of the English East India Company during the same period.

15. W. Carr, after visiting the East India House at Amsterdam, wrote admiringly of the directors who 'as good Christians have been at great charge in planting the gospel in many parts there, printing in the Indian Language Bibles and Prayer-Books, and catechisms, for the instruction of the Indians, maintaining ministers and schoolmasters, to inform those that are converted to the Christian Faith ... and on the same gallery or floor, is a chamber where are kept the several books of Divinity, printed in the Indian language, that are sent to the several colonies of the Company' (*An Accurate Description of the United Netherlands*, ed. 1691, pp. 34–9). For a list of some of these devotional works in Malay, Formosan, Tamil, and Sinhalese, cf. C. A. L. Van Troostenburg de Bruyn, *De Hervormde Kerk in Nederlandsch Oost-Indië onder de O.I. Compagnie, 1602–1795* (Arnhem, 1884), pp. 398–503. For the history of the Dutch Reformed Church in Asia, cf. also J. Mooij, *Geschiedenis der Protestansche Kerk in Nederlandsche Indië* (Batavia, 1923); C. W. T. Van Boetzelaer van Dubbeldam, *De Gereformeerde kerken in Nederland en de zending in Oost-Indië in de dagen der Oost-Indische Compagnie* (Utrecht, 1906); ibid., *De Protestansche Kerk in Nederlandsch Indië* (The Hague, 1947); P. Van Dam, *Beschryvinge van de O.I.C., IV Boek* (ed. Boetzelaer van Asperen en Dubbeldam, 1954), and the printed archival sources listed in those works.

If the *Heeren* XVII were sufficiently influenced by their own Calvinist background, and by pressure from the *predikanten* at home, to do something about supporting the 'true Christian Reformed Religion' in the East, they were also firmly resolved to subordinate the overseas Churches to their own authority. They insisted that their governors in Asia should decide where the *predikanten* and the lay-readers were to serve and for how long, instead of leaving such postings and transfers to be arranged by the church councils. The Governor-General and his council at Batavia also exercised their right to read and censor all correspondence addressed to the Church authorities in the Netherlands by *predikanten* and church councils in the East. The *Heeren* XVII likewise insisted that lay officials of the VOC should sit on all the church councils, and the decisions of these bodies could only be carried out with the approval and co-operation of the Company's officials. The *predikanten* and the lay-readers were paid by the Company and not by the Church. They were regarded by the directors as their salaried servants, and their order of precedence in the Company's official hierarchy was regulated accordingly, with the lay-readers at the bottom of the social ladder. Finally, although the *Heeren* XVII acknowledged the need for missionary work by suitably qualified ministers, they closed the missionary training-school (Seminarium Indicum) which they established at Leiden in 1622, after it had functioned for only ten years. They subsequently refused repeated requests by the classes and synods in the Netherlands to reopen this seminary, or to establish a new one, basing their refusal on the grounds of economy, and alleging that sufficient ministers with vocations were forthcoming without it. A more likely reason was that experience had shown them that the graduates of the Seminarium Indicum were apt to be less amenable to the Company's officials than were *predikanten* who had been hand-picked for their docility by the directors of the regional chambers.

In view of this strict subordination of Church to State – and of God to Mammon – it is not surprising that the East India Company experienced great difficulty in finding suitable *predikanten* and lay-readers for service in the East. The Company also found it difficult to keep them there for long, under the often frustrating and sometimes humiliating conditions in which they had to work. The same was true, *mutatis mutandis,* of the *predikanten* and lay-readers employed overseas by the West India Company, and for the same reasons. Apart from anything else, it was a long time before there were sufficient Calvinist ministers in the Seven Provinces to cater adequately for the spiritual needs of their own communities and to prevent them from losing ground to Roman Catholics and to Protestant dissenters. Another factor which made it difficult to recruit suitable ministers and lay-readers for service in the Indies was that they were treated there with a good deal less consideration and respect than they were at home. The servants of the East and West India Companies were notoriously a rough-and-ready lot – we often find them termed 'the dregs of Dutch society', 'louts from the depths of Germany', and so forth – and it is not surprising that friction between them and their ecclesiastical colleagues frequently assumed inflammatory proportions. The *Heeren* XVII repeatedly ordered their subordinates to treat Calvinist ministers and lay-readers with due respect, as was laid down in their *artikul-brief,* or standing orders. But official correspondence and travellers' tales alike are filled with allegations of ecclesiastical arrogance and incompetence on the one side and of secular pride and anti-clerical feeling on the other. Such, at least, were the conditions prevailing in the 17th century. During the 18th century the social prestige of the *predikanten* in the East Indies improved noticeably; partly, perhaps, on account of the frequency with which members of the cloth married wealthy widows.

One of the chief difficulties under which the *predikanten* laboured in the East was that they were not 'called' to serve a parish or a community for a good number of years – as they were in the Netherlands – but were apt to be shifted at short notice from one place to another at the whim of the Governor-General and his council at Batavia. Apart from the personal inconvenience caused by such frequent moves, especially to those ministers who were married, this meant that they usually had insufficient time to learn the local language if they were engaged in missionary work. Alternatively, if they had stayed for (say) four or five years in one place and learnt the language, they might find themselves posted to another region where their painfully acquired linguistic knowledge was useless. This was one of the colonial church councils' most frequent complaints, and some of the Company's senior officials realized this difficulty. Nicholas Verburgh, the governor of Dutch Formosa from 1650 to 1653, who was bitterly critical of the local Calvinist missionaries, suggested that all those who came to the island should bind themselves to stay for a ten-year term, even though this policy might cost the Company more in higher wages. His advice was not taken, and the frequent changes of tenure did undoubtedly hamper the continuity of missionary work.

If complaints of the inferior quality of the *predikanten* were painfully – though often unfairly – frequent, still more devastating criticism was levelled at their lowly assistants, the *Krank-bezoekers* ('sick-visitors') and *Zieken-troosters* ('sick-comforters') as these lay-readers were called. They were recruited almost entirely from the working class, and included ex-soldiers, tailors, cobblers, weavers, cloth-workers and bakers. Few of them had more than the most rudimentary theological training, and they were not allowed to preach extempore sermons or to say spontaneous prayers, but only to read from a few prescribed texts. They often served as substitute chaplains aboard ships, where their duties were described by an experienced traveller in 1703 as follows: 'To read the morning and the evening prayers from a little book, and to sing a verse or two from a psalm. On Sundays, they must read a chapter or a sermon and sing a psalm or a hymn before and after the same. If anyone is sick and like to die, the sick-comforter must encourage him and read some Christian prayers to him [and help him to draw up his will].' These lay-readers were employed ashore as catechists, primary school teachers, hospital visitors and in similar duties under the supervision of a *predikant*.

The complaints of the shortcomings of these lay-readers, which begin in the second decade of the East India Company's (and their own) existence, lasted for as long as they both endured. 'Clownish, uncircumcised idiots', Jan Pieterszoon Coen called them in 1614, and similar abuse was lavished on them for nearly two centuries by high and low alike. The sailors on board ship were particularly resentful of them, largely because of their working-class origin and the fact that they received ship's officers' rank and privileges but did no manual or navigational work. Their title of *krank-bezoeker* ('sick-visitor') was jeeringly transformed into *drank-bezoeker* ('drink-visitor'), and they were often accused of indulging in private trade and loose living. The sort of treatment they had to put up with from ribald officials was exemplified by an incident which occurred at Tamsui in Formosa in 1650. A *krank-bezoeker* was asked by the local governor to come and visit the sick. On his inquiring where they were, he was shown an empty cask of arrack and told to say a prayer for its recovery. Of course, this scurrility was not confined to the Dutch. Readers of Pepys's *Tangier Papers* may remember Admiral Arthur Herbert who always called his ship's chaplain ' "Bollocks", and did talk so bawdy before him and turn his office into sport, that he left his service and would stay no longer.' The lay-readers, even when they were capable men, were often insufficiently supported by their *predikanten*, who were apt to be disdainful of them and jealously guarded their own superior status. Relatively few of the lay-readers became ordained ministers; though this is hardly surprising, as very few possessed a good knowledge of Latin, which was one of the essential qualifications. While the bulk of the available evidence indicates that the standard of the lay-readers was often low, there were always some exceptions, and they did good work as schoolmasters in Formosa and Ceylon.[16]

16. J. P. Coen to the *Heeren* XVII, Bantam, 1 January 1614 ('... plompe onbesneden idioten, ghelijk de voorlesers meestendeel zijn ...'). For the Tamsui incident cf. P. Van Dam, *Beschryvinge*, IV *Boek*, pp. 48, 138, and for Admiral Herbert's abuse of his chaplain, E. Chappell (ed.), *The Tangier Papers of Samuel Pepys* (1935), p. 168. For typical criticisms of *zieken-troosters* and *krank-bezoekers* cf. N. de Graaff, *Oost-Indische Spiegel* (1703), pp. 22, 38; G. Udemans, *'tGheestelycke Roer* (1655), pp. 272 ff.; *Oost-Indische Praetjen* (n.p., 1663); P. S. du Toit, *Onderwijs aan die Kaap onder die Kompanie, 1652–1795* (Cape Town, 1937), p. 134; L. Verwijk, *Verhandeling over de krank-bezoekers in dienst der V.O.C.* (Middelburg, 1790). Cf. also C. A. L. Troostenburg de Bruyn, *Krank-bezoekers in Nederlandsch Oost-Indië* (Amsterdam, 1902) for biographical details.

The extent to which the Dutch Reformed Church in Asia was subordinated to the civil power was strikingly emphasized in 1653. In October of that year the Governor-General and Council ordered a thanksgiving prayer- and fast-day to commemorate Dutch victories against the 'rebels' in the Moluccas and to pray for the further success of Dutch arms. The Batavia church council ventured to criticize this resolution, on the grounds that the war in Amboina was not a just one, having been provoked through the tyrannical misbehaviour of the Dutch themselves – as indeed it had. This remonstrance drew a stinging rebuke from the Governor-General, who accused the church councillors of being highly unpatriotic and of 'giving a bad impression of the Company's righteous trade'. The directors at Amsterdam reacted even more violently, and ordered that any *predikanten* who ventured to make similar criticisms in the future should be dismissed immediately from their posts and embarked for the Netherlands in the first available ship. Before this dispatch reached Batavia, the local church council had come crouchingly to heel at the summons of the Governor-General, and the two *predikanten* who had instigated the critical motion escaped deportation by an abject apology and retraction. So far as I am aware, the Company experienced no further criticism from the ministers of the Dutch Reformed Church concerning its wars, whether just or unjust, for the remainder of its existence.[17]

This incident occurred during the long governor-generalship of Johan Maetsuyker (1653–78), who had been educated at the Roman Catholic University of Louvain, and whose Protestant orthodoxy was notoriously suspect. But even rigidly orthodox Calvinists, such as Jan Pieterszoon Coen, Anthony van Diemen and Rijkloff van Goens the elder, never hesitated to take a strong line when they thought that the *predikanten* were interfering in matters outside their closely circumscribed religious sphere. Moreover, whenever a dispute occurred between the civil and the ecclesiastical authorities, the Governor-General and his council at Batavia and the directors at home almost invariably took

17. J. A. Van der Chijs, *Nederlandsch-Indisch Plakaatboek*, Vol. II, pp. 185–6; P. Van Dam, *Beschryvinge, IV Boek*, p. 60.

the side of the laymen. The *Heeren* XVII might sometimes ask the advice of the synods and classes in the Netherlands on specific points of Church discipline or doctrine, and were usually prepared to receive representations from these bodies. But they made it very clear that the final decision lay with them; where the interests of the Company and those of the Church clashed, the former almost invariably prevailed. As the directors wrote to Maetsuyker and his Council (12 April 1656): 'The nature of government is such that it cannot suffer two equally great controlling powers, any more than a body can endure two heads', for which reason the civil power must always have full and unfettered control over the ecclesiastical.

It is in the light of this strict subordination of Church to State that Calvinist missionary activities in the East and West Indies must be considered. Calvinist orthodoxy in the fatherland was sufficiently strong to ensure that in the East India Company's definitive instructions to the Governor-General and council in 1650, it was enacted that the 'True Christian Reformed Religion', as defined at the Synod of Dordrecht in 1618–19, 'should likewise be followed under Your Honour's government in the East Indies, without the public exercise of any other religion being allowed, and, above all, no toleration of Popery'. In practice, the Company's officials in Asia were not usually so rigid as this injunction implied, though their attitude naturally varied according to time, place and circumstances. In any event, the full rigour of the official policy was seldom insisted on by the directors; and it could only be enforced in places where the Company exercised unchallenged jurisdiction and where it could afford – as in strongly fortified Batavia – to ignore the religious susceptibilities of neighbouring potentates and peoples. Elsewhere the Company was very circumspect. In 1627, for example, missionaries in Formosa were ordered to propagate Christianity as unobtrusively as possible, so as to avoid arousing the antagonism of the powerful rulers of neighbouring China and Japan.

The orthodox Calvinist attitude to Protestant dissenters overseas was even more illiberal than it was in Europe. The Lutherans were only allowed to form their first recognized congregation and to build their first church at Batavia in 1743–9. This was over a century after they had been given these privileges in Amsterdam, but just about the same time as they received belated recognition at Curaçao in the West Indies. The time-lag of toleration in South Africa was even greater, despite the high proportion of German-born Lutherans among the soldiers and settlers at the Cape. Not until 1780 were they allowed to have their own minister in Cape Town. But the private devotions of Protestant dissenters were never interfered with, and these 'weaker brethren' presented a relatively minor problem. From first to last, the Calvinist ministers in the East were mainly concerned with fighting on two fronts, against two creeds as militant as their own – Roman Catholicism and Islam.

The propagation of Calvinism in the East suffered from a threefold disadvantage. Firstly, Roman Catholicism was already firmly established in many regions. Secondly, the colourful cult and gorgeous ceremonial of the Roman Church made a far greater appeal to most Asians than did the harsh words and the white-washed churches of Calvin. Thirdly, the Roman Catholic missionaries were far more numerous, and, as a rule, far more active than their Protestant rivals. To take the last point first, in 1647 there were only twenty-eight Calvinist ministers in the region extending from Ceylon and Coromandel to the Moluccas and Formosa. At Batavia, which had a population of some 20,000 souls in 1670 and some 16,000 in 1768, there were only six *predikanten* in 1669, eight in 1680, twenty-seven in 1725 (several of these awaiting posting elsewhere), and twelve in 1749. By the end of the eighteenth century only one or two were left. These numbers are insignificant when compared with those of the Portuguese, Spanish, French and Italian priests who were working in the Roman Catholic Asian mission-fields. For example, the Roman Catholic communities in 18th-century Ceylon usually had many more priests – even though their presence in Dutch territory was illegal – ministering to them than the Protestant congregations had *predikanten*. Moreover, as indicated above, the *predikanten* were often married men who were frequently transferred from one post to another, whereas the Roman Catholic priest was a celibate who usually stayed in one place for many years – often enough for life.

As regards the greater appeal of Roman Catholicism, the Portuguese Jesuit, Antonio Cardim, when a prisoner at Malacca in 1652, asked a local Dutch *predikant* why the Netherlanders tolerated Muslim mosques and heathen temples but not Roman Catholic churches. The *predikant* replied frankly that, if a Roman Catholic church was allowed, then his own flock would frequent it.[18] This was the simple truth. During all the time that the Dutch East India Company endured, the Calvinist preacher could never contend on equal terms with the Romanist priest. The Eurasian communities of Batavia, Malacca, Coromandel, Ceylon and Malabar, whenever they had the chance, and often at considerable risk to themselves, would leave the *predikant* preaching to empty pews while they heard mass celebrated, or had their children baptized or their marriages conducted, by some passing Roman Catholic priest in disguise. From the Protestant point of view, the circulation of the two faiths was a religious equivalent of Gresham's Law, with 'Papist idolatory' continually gaining ground at the expense of the 'True Christian Reformed Religion'.

Equally well attested was the general superiority of the Roman Catholic missionary personnel and techniques over those of their opponents. Coen and Van Diemen were only two of the many Calvinist laymen in high places who deplored the success of the *papen* ('papists'), as they called the Roman Catholic priests. 'In that matter,' wrote Van Diemen to the *Heeren* XVII in 1631, 'they [=the Spaniards] are too strong for us, and their priests show much more diligence and zeal than do our lay-readers and *predikanten.*' This was said of the missionary situation in Formosa at a time when the outlook really *did* look promising for the Dutch sowers of the gospel seed there. It was a similar story in Ceylon, where, after the conclusion of a truce with the Portuguese in 1644, the church council at Batavia observed that the

18. Cardim's 'Relação', *apud* H. Fitzler, *O cerco de Columbo* (Coimbra, 1928), pp. 98–9; Fernão de Queiroz, s.j., *Conquista Temporal e espiritual de Ceylão* (ed. Colombo, 1916), p. 971. Queiroz added that the Secretary to the Governor-General and Council at Batavia (Jan van Riebeeck?) had admitted to another Jesuit that the *Heeren* XVII and most of the senior officials of the VOC were 'Atheists'. Cf. also J. K. J. de Jonge, *Opkomst*, Vol. VI (1872), pp. xxix–xxxix.

papen would now be able 'to fashion their monstrous half-hatched abortive foetus' right under the walls of the strongholds held by the Dutch.[19] Similar complaints, usually couched in somewhat soberer language, came endlessly from Solor, Malacca and wherever else the two faiths were in contact. Even after the total expulsion of all Portuguese priests from Ceylon in 1658, Roman Catholicism in that island was preserved and revivified by the efforts of the Goan missionary priests of the Oratory, who could work in disguise among both Tamils and Sinhalese.

This state of affairs had its repercussions in Europe, where the exiled Huguenot minister, Pierre Jurieu, tried to controvert the widespread belief that Protestants, in comparison with Roman Catholics, showed little or no zeal for the expansion of Christianity overseas. Oddly enough, he did not mention the relatively successful (if short-lived) story of Dutch missionary success in Formosa, but cited the mass conversions made by John Cotton and John Eliot among the Redskins of New England. This was not a very convincing example, as he seems to have been unaware that the Indian Wars which broke out in 1675 had destroyed all traces of this fleeting success. Jurieu was on safer ground when he admitted that one of the reasons why there were relatively few Protestant missionaries in the East was that there were not enough Calvinist ministers in the United Provinces to cope with the Roman Catholics and the Protestant dissenters at home.

Just as the classes and synods in the Netherlands continually, but for the most part vainly, protested to the civil authorities about the non-observance of the penal laws enacted against the practice of Popery, so did the *predikanten* at Batavia keep fruitlessly protesting about the 'freedom, honour and favour' which they claimed that itinerant Roman Catholic priests received there. These representations received scant support from the *Heeren* XVII, who, while admitting that the anti-Roman Catholic regulations ought to be enforced, observed (in 1654) that it was

19. P. Coolhaas (ed.), 'Een Indisch verslag uit 1631, van de hand van Antonio van Diemen' (*BMHGU*, Vol. 65, p. 41); H. T. Colenbrander, *Jan Pietersz. Coen Levensbeschrijving*, pp. 43, 176; P. Van Dam, *Beschryvinge*, Boek IV, pp. 104, 106, 210–14.

impossible to prevent Roman Catholic priests from going out to the East in disguise. Nor were the governor-generals at Batavia more helpful, especially when they were men of such highly suspect orthodoxy as Maetsuyker and Van der Lijn. Admittedly, events such as the rebellion of the Portuguese settlers in Dutch-held Pernambuco in 1645, and the Revocation of the Edict of Nantes forty years later, naturally caused a tightening-up of the regulations against Roman Catholics when the news reached Batavia. But these reactions proved only temporary and conditions soon reverted to their former laxity. In 1754 the authorities at Batavia allowed a thinly disguised Roman Catholic bishop, of whose identity they were well aware, to baptize and to celebrate mass unostentatiously, despite the vehement protests of the Calvinist church council. By the end of the Company's rule the anti-Roman-Catholic regulations were virtually a dead letter, although the first public Roman Catholic church at Batavia was not built until 1809.

Liever Turck dan Paus, 'Rather the Turk than the Pope', was the motto of the Protestant Sea-Beggars in 1574, but in the eyes of the pioneer Calvinists in the East Indies there was not much to choose between those two forms of Anti-Christ. The derogatory epithets so freely bestowed in Dutch official and private correspondence upon the Roman Catholics were likewise lavished upon the adherents of Islam – even to the extent of calling the Islamic scholars, and more particularly the *Hajjis*, or those who had made the pilgrimage to Mecca, by the incongruous designations of *papen*, or *Moorse papen* ('Moorish papists'). At first the Dutch made common cause with the Muslims of the Moluccas against the Portuguese, but no sooner were the Romanists expelled from the Spice Islands than the Calvinists took over their prejudices against the Muslims in general. Many of the Protestants already possessed such prejudices in full measure, as instanced by the senior Dutch merchant who made a habit of publicly relieving himself against the wall of a mosque at Japara in 1618.[20] The Dutch had to contend with Muslim enemies or

20. F. de Haan, *Priangan*, Vol. IV, p. 698.

trade rivals in Java, in Sumatra, in the Moluccas and in Celebes; and this commercial rivalry strongly influenced their attitude to Muslims elsewhere. They originally legislated against the public performance of Islamic rites just as they did against those of the Church of Rome, wherever they thought they could enforce such legislation. On the other hand, they soon realized – as their Portuguese predecessors had finally done – that they had no chance of converting Muslims to Christianity in any significant numbers. They therefore concentrated their proselytizing efforts on the 'blind heathen' and on the Roman Catholic communities which they had conquered from the Portuguese.

After the final subjugation of Macassar in 1669, the Dutch authorities gradually became more tolerant of Islam and slowly relaxed the rigour with which they had formerly treated Muslims in their Indonesian possessions. The anti-Islamic laws remained on the Batavia Statute-book, but when the Calvinist ministers tried to get these provisions enforced, they met with less and less co-operation from the government. The official attitude was enunciated in 1679 by the *Heeren* XVII, who declared that no pressure must be brought on Indonesians to induce them to change their religion – 'as Paul plants, and Apollos waters, so must God give the increase', they wrote sententiously. Seven years later, Governor-General Camphuis (a convinced Calvinist, incidentally) rejected a representation from the Batavia church council that the local Chinese temples and Muslim mosques, 'which latter are very numerous', should be demolished. Camphuis told the *predikanten* that it would be better to convert Muslims and heathen by kindness and good example, when the temples would gradually fall into disuse. The government at Batavia, which was originally loath to allow Muslim pilgrims to Mecca to embark in its ships trading to the Red Sea, later reversed this attitude and competed for the pilgrim traffic. During the 18th century tolerance of non-Christian religious practices became an increasingly general rule, although it took a century to mature in Ceylon, where the Muslim merchants (called 'Moors') were ineradicable retail and itinerant traders. Here, as elsewhere, the Dutch took severer measures against the adherents of Islam than they did against Hindus and Buddhists. Legally and economically, Muslims were for long discriminated against, being compelled to pay higher dues and taxes than the others were.[21]

Only in three places did the Calvinist missions, supported by the Dutch East India Company, attain a modest degree of success – Formosa, Amboina and Ceylon – and only in Amboina did the success last longer than the Company. Georgius Candidius, the first *predikant* on Formosa (1627–31) rightly foresaw that there was a good chance of planting Christianity in this island, since the aboriginal inhabitants had not been subjected to any outside religious influences, and their own religion was a primitive animism served by priestesses or sorceresses called *Inips*. Between 1627 and 1662 a total of thirty-two *predikanten* laboured in the coastal districts subdued by the Dutch, and they were assisted by a more numerous staff of lay-readers and village school-teachers. Progress at first was inevitably slow, though Candidius reported optimistically that his Formosan school-children could learn in eight days what boys in Holland or in Java would take two weeks to absorb. The Calvinist missionaries relied on the support of the secular authorities to keep their converts up to the mark by making school attendance compulsory, by fining absentees and by prohibiting idolatrous practices. In the early 1640s several hundred of the unconverted Inips were banished from the Dutch-controlled districts, thus creating a spiritual void among the aboriginals which facilitated the work of the *predikanten*.

As the pioneer Portuguese missionaries had discovered elsewhere, there was a far better chance of converting the children than their parents, and the Calvinist ministers likewise increasingly concentrated their efforts on the rising generation. The medium of instruction in the village schools was usually one or another of the local dialects, but from about 1650 increasingly

21. P. van Dam, *Beschryvinge, Boek* IV, pp. 275–6, 288; F. de Haan, *Priangan*, Vol. I, pp. 432*–9*; Vol. III, pp. 12–13, 239, 325; Vol. IV, pp. 698, 741–8; K. W. Gunawardena, 'Some notes on the history of the Muslims in Ceylon before the British Occupation' (*University of Ceylon. Muslim Majlis Magazine*, Colombo, 1960, pp. 82–91); S. Arasaratnam, *Dutch Power in Ceylon, 1658–1687* (Amsterdam, 1958), pp. 204–5, 220–21.

successful efforts were made to use Dutch. Some of the *predikanten* became good linguists and composed devotional works in at least five of the vernaculars, which they reduced to romanization for this purpose. The Dutch governors installed at Castle Zeelandia were not always complimentary about the genuineness or the durability of the numerous conversions claimed by the *predikanten*. For example, Governor Nicholas Verburgh declared in 1654 that the children merely learnt their catechism and doctrine like parrots, without any real understanding of what they glibly repeated. If a single genuine convert could be produced from among the thousands claimed, he wrote, 'I shall with true Christian joy present the church and the schools of Formosa with the sum of one thousand guilders'. Verburgh was notoriously anticlerical and his criticism was certainly unfair. It is true that when the Chinese under Coxinga (Chen Ch'eng Kung) invaded the island in 1661, the great majority of the indigenous inhabitants made common cause with the invaders against their European overlords. But it is also true that they subsequently regretted the substitution of King Log by King Stork. The Jesuit missionary, De Mailla, who visited the island in 1715, found distinct traces of the Protestant Christianity implanted by the Dutch. Several of the aboriginals still had Dutch books which they could read, and the use of the romanized forms of the vernaculars which the Dutch had introduced survived until the second half of the 19th century.

The Calvinist ministers' efforts on Formosa were hampered by the threefold nature of their duties in the island. In addition to their missionary work, they had to attend to the spiritual needs of the Dutch residents and garrison, and also (down to 1651) to act as interpreters, tax-collectors and licensees for the trade in deer-skins, which was one of the mainstays of the island's economy. Apart from this mixture of the sacred and the profane, the continuity of their efforts was hampered by the fact that no *predikant* stayed on the island for more than eleven years, and several for only two or three. If some of the governors were helpful in supporting missionary work, others besides Nicholas Verburgh were openly critical. All things considered, it is to the credit of the *predikanten*, lay-readers and village schoolmasters that they achieved as much as they did. The *predikant* who claimed that he alone had received over 5,000 Formosan adults into the membership of the Reformed Church was clearly nothing if not an optimist; but the evidence of the Jesuit De Mailla in 1715 shows that not all of the aboriginals who accepted Christianity were 'rice-Christians', as Verburgh and other unfriendly critics alleged.[22]

When the Dutch replaced the Portuguese in Amboina in 1605 they found that the Jesuit missionaries had converted about 16,000 of the inhabitants of this island and in the neighbouring Uliasser group, though most of the people were still either Muslim or Animists. Having expelled the Roman Catholic missionaries, the Dutch were able to ensure that they did not return to this region, whether openly or clandestinely – something they never achieved in Ceylon, Malacca, or Batavia. Deprived of their spiritual leaders, the Roman Catholics were gradually converted to Calvinism – or went over to Islam – though many decades elapsed before they became attached to their new creed. Dominie Valentyn, who served off and on in this island-group between 1686 and 1712, testified that at the end of the 17th century very little progress had been made, 'and the Ambonese had no knowledge of the fundamentals of our religion'. He blamed this state of affairs on the Batavian authorities' insistence that High rather than Low Malay should be the medium of instruction, and on the frequent transfers of *predikanten* before they had time to acquire a thorough knowledge of either the language or the people. Stavorinus, who visited Amboina three-quarters of a century later, was even more disparaging. He blamed the local *predikanten* for their 'almost universal negligence and want of zeal', adding that 'the unpleasing result' of the successive changes of religion among the Ambonese had been 'that, from blind idolaters, they have first become bad Roman Catholics, and after-

22. Two well-documented works on the Dutch Reformed Church in Formosa are W. Campbell, *Formosa Under the Dutch Described from Contemporary Records with Explanatory Notes and a Bibliography of the Island* (London, 1903); W. A. Ginsel, *De Gereformeerde Kerk op Formosa of de lotgevallen eener handelskerk onder de Oost-Indische Compagnie, 1627–1662* (Leiden, 1931).

wards worse Protestants'.[23] These criticisms were evidently unfair, or at any rate exaggerated: for it was during the period of the Company's rule that the Christianized Ambonese became firmly attached to Calvinism, a process which was intensified in the 19th century and which widened the gulf between them and their Muslim fellow-islanders. Their increasingly firm adherence to the religion of their white rulers gradually created a bond of sympathy between the Christian Ambonese and the Dutch which has lasted down to the present day, as evidenced by the thousands of Ambonese who took refuge in the Netherlands when Indonesia became independent.

The situation of the Calvinist Church in Ceylon for a time looked more promising than in Formosa and Amboina, but the outcome was very disappointing. When the Dutch finally drove the Portuguese from Ceylon in 1658, they found about a quarter of a million indigenous Roman Catholics in the island, the majority of them in the Tamil kingdom of Jaffna. While a number of these were 'rice-Christians' who accepted Calvinism – or reverted to Buddhism and Hinduism – without difficulty, a surprisingly large number remained loyal to their faith, despite the expulsion of all the Portuguese priests and the legal hindrances placed in the way of the public profession of their religion. This hard core of believers was subsequently strengthened and increased by the devoted labours of Fr. Joseph Vaz and his successors of the Goan Oratorian mission from 1687 onwards. The reasons for the persistence of Roman Catholicism in spite of all the civil and legal disabilities to which its adherents were subjected – though these became increasingly less enforced as the 18th century progressed – are not far to seek. The external observances of the Roman Church were in many ways strikingly like some of those in the Hindu and Buddhist beliefs which it had sought to replace – the use of images, of rosaries, the cult of the saints and so forth. The veneration accorded Hindu Brahmins and Buddhist *Bhikkhus* was paralleled by the respect felt by Roman Catholics for the sacramental

23. F. Valentyn, *Oud en Nieuw Oost-Indien*, Vol. III (1726), pp. 1–152; J. S. Stavorinus, *Voyages to the East-Indies, 1768–1778*, Vol. II (1798), pp. 364–8. Cf. also J. Keuning, 'Ambonnezen, Portugezen en Nederlanders. Ambon's geschiedenis tot het einde van de 17e eeuw' (*Indonesie*, Vol. IX, 1956, pp. 135–68).

and sacerdotal attributes of their own priesthood. It contrasted strongly with the unimpressive status of Calvinist *predikanten* and *krank-bezoekers*. The sacro-magical elements in the three popular religions gave their respective believers a feeling of spiritual security which Calvinism was both unable and unwilling to supply in a similar way.

Dutch proselytizing activity was almost entirely directed against the Roman Catholic community, for the *predikanten* were neither numerous nor knowledgeable enough to work effectively among either Hindus, Buddhists or Muslims. So far as I have been able to ascertain, there were never as many as twenty *predikanten* at any given time in Ceylon, and very few of these had either the ability or the inclination to make a thorough study of the indigenous languages and religions. There were some exceptions, such as the Rev. Philippus Baldaeus, who learnt Tamil, and the Rev. Johannes Ruël, who learnt Sinhalese; but their sporadic efforts could make no impression on two such deeply rooted and well-established faiths as Buddhism and Hinduism. Moreover, the Company's officials, though often quite keen to secure the conversion of Roman Catholics, who were regarded as potential fifth-columnists, were usually very chary of interfering with Buddhist and Hindu religious observances and social practices so long as these did not involve large-scale processions or other manifestations of 'idolatry' near Christian churches.

Since suitable *predikanten* who knew Tamil or Sinhalese were so hard to come by, and so difficult to keep for any length of time in the island, two seminaries for the training of a local clergy were eventually established. The first of these, which functioned at Nallur near Jaffnapatam from 1690 to 1723, was intended to supply the Tamil-speaking area; whereas the second, which functioned intermittently at Colombo for exactly a century (1696-1796), was intended to supply the Sinhalese-speaking region of the island. These seminaries were evidently meant to serve not only for the formation of eventual *predikanten* but also for the training of schoolmasters, catechists, interpreters and clerks for the government service. Dutch, Latin, Greek and even Hebrew were included in the curriculum, and Baron Gustaaf van Imhoff, who was a great supporter of the Colombo seminary during his governorship of Ceylon (1736-40), and who later founded a shorter-lived one at

Batavia (1745–55), was delighted at the ease 'with which the little black fellows chatter in Latin and construe in Greek'. But although some of the graduates of these seminaries were eventually ordained as *predikanten*, several of them afterwards proceeding to the Netherlands and taking a theological degree there, they were not nearly so numerous as the founders had optimistically envisaged. The Batavian seminary, for example, produced only one in its ten years' existence. The two Ceylonese seminaries were certainly more productive, but chiefly in providing catechists, village schoolmasters and government clerks. The few *predikanten* they succeeded in forming were barely enough to minister to the existing Dutch and Burgher communities, and they never supplied any men for missionary work among the unconverted. The Sinhalese and Tamils who adopted Calvinism did so, for the most part, because only adherents of the Reformed faith were eligible for official posts during the period of the Company's rule. The few thousand Tamil and Sinhalese nominal Calvinists at the time of the English conquest of the island abandoned this faith so fast and so completely when the State support of this religion was withdrawn, that it is obvious that Calvinism had made no real or lasting impression on the religions with which it had vainly competed. The Protestant communities in the island today stem from the work of American and European missionaries in the 19th century, and only the merest handful of individuals derive from the 'True Christian Reformed Religion' which held sway in Dutch-dominated Ceylon for a century and a half.[24]

If the role of Calvinism as the helpmate of a great trading company in the East was hardly an inspiring one, the same can equally be said of its presence in the Atlantic sphere of the Dutch West

24. For the vicissitudes of the Dutch Reformed Church in Ceylon and its losing fight with Romanism, Buddhism, and Hinduism, cf. S. Arasaratnam, *Dutch Power in Ceylon, 1658–1687*, pp. 215–36; R. Bouden, *The Catholic Church in Ceylon Under Dutch Rule* (Rome, 1957), and Arasaratnam's review of this work in *The Ceylon Journal of Historical and Social Studies*, Vol. I, pp. 216–22 (Colombo, 1958). For the seminaries at Nallur and Colombo, cf. H. Terpstra, 'Compagniesonderwijs op Ceilon', in *TG*, pp. 26–50.

India Company, which extended from West Africa to the American mainland. In New Holland, or Netherlands Brazil, which led a mostly precarious existence from 1630 to 1654, the *predikanten* had to compete not only with the Roman Catholic Portuguese settlers but also with Jews who emigrated thither in substantial numbers from Europe. In Recife, as in Batavia, the Company's high officials were often lukewarm about enforcing the laws which discriminated against Roman Catholics and (to a lesser extent) against Jews. In particular, Count John Maurice of Nassau-Siegen, who governed Pernambuco with conspicuous success from 1637 to 1644, made a point of ignoring or side-tracking the repeated requests of the local synods that he would strictly prohibit the public practice of 'Popish superstition and idolatry'. In this he had the support of most of the directors at home, who likewise 'preferred gain to godliness', although there were some strait-laced Calvinists among them. In South America, as in Asia, the *predikanten* found that they could not compete on equal terms with the 'Popish priests', wherever these were allowed a measure of toleration by the local government. During the twenty-four years that Netherlands Brazil existed, converts from Romanism to Calvinism were as rare as hens' teeth. What made matters worse from the *predikanten* viewpoint was that many Dutchmen married to local Portuguese women forsook their own religion to embrace that of their wives. The same thing occurred during the short-lived Dutch occupation of Luanda and Benguela in 1641–8.

The *predikanten* achieved more success with their efforts to create Calvinist communities among the unconverted Amerindians, whether these were of the Tupí-speaking tribes or (less often) the cannibal Tapuya. The reason was presumably the same as that which applied to the Formosan headhunters – the absence of any competition from a 'higher' religion. Some of these savage youths were sent to the Netherlands for their education, and in 1641 a Calvinist catechism in Tupí was printed at Enkhuizen for distribution among the Amerindian converts in Brazil. Unfortunately no copies have survived, and a project to translate the Bible into Tupí seems not to have been implemented. Several of the Dutch-educated Tapuya relapsed into savagery after their return to Brazil, but they still retained a strong memory and a certain liking for what they had learnt. A Portuguese Jesuit missionary visiting some Amerindian villages in the interior soon after the final expulsion of the Dutch, was horrified to find that 'many of the inhabitants were as Calvinist and Lutheran as if they had been born in England or in Germany'. Padre Antonio Vieira, S.J., and his colleagues soon eradicated such traces of Protestantism, which otherwise might perhaps have endured in the hinterland of north-east Brazil for as long as they did in Formosa.[25]

The development of the Dutch Reformed Church in New Netherland (1624–64) displayed several of the features which marked its action in the East and West Indies. It was difficult to get *predikanten* to volunteer for service in that remote and in some ways inhospitable land. The *Heeren* XIX likewise ensured that the Church in North America remained strictly subordinated to the civil power, though on balance this had a salutary effect. 'Popery' was no menace in this region, for contacts with the Jesuit missionaries in French Canada were only fleeting. The Calvinist ministers spent more time and energy in combating the presence of Protestant dissenters and (after 1654) of Jews than in the admittedly thankless task of converting the Redskins. 'We can say but little of the conversion of the heathens or Indians here,' wrote two *predikanten* from New Netherland in 1657, 'and see no way to accomplish it, until they are subdued by the numbers and power of our people, and reduced to some sort of civilization, and also unless our people set them a better example than they have done heretofore.' Pieter Stuyvesant, the last Dutch governor of the colony, was a zealous Calvinist, who usually seconded the efforts of the local ministers to banish or completely suppress all forms of religious dissent, but the directors were

25. For the Dutch Reformed Church in Netherlands Brazil, 1630–54, cf. J. A. Gonsalves de Mello, *Tempo dos Flamengos. Influência da ocupação holandesa na vida e cultura do Norte do Brasil* (Rio de Janeiro, 1947), pp. 247–311 *passim*; C. R. Boxer, *The Dutch in Brazil, 1624–1654* (Oxford, 1957), pp. 121–4, 132–6, 140, 177, 299. For the catechism printed in Tupí, see P. van Dam, *Beschryvinge, Boek IV*, p. 115.

more broadminded. They told him (in April 1663) that he must not be too strict with Protestant dissenters, as this would rebound to the colony's disadvantage, discouraging immigration and inducing people already there to leave. He must connive at non-Calvinists celebrating their own forms of worship, provided they did so discreetly and without causing annoyance to their orthodox neighbours. Religious toleration, the *Heeren* XIX reminded their governor, had greatly contributed to the prosperity of Amsterdam, and they opined that it would be equally advantageous to New Netherland. Nor was this an isolated lesson in toleration, for the *Heeren* XIX and the burgomasters of Amsterdam intervened on several occasions to protect the Lutherans, Mennonites, Quakers and Jews against the ultra-orthodox zeal of some of the Calvinist ministers in the colony and their supporters in the synods and classis at home.[26]

About the progress, or rather lack of progress, of Calvinism in Surinam and the Dutch West Indian colonies during the 17th and 18th centuries, perhaps the less said the better. Surinam was undeniably the black spot in the Dutch tropical empire from the humanitarian point of view, and the sadistic cruelty, pig-headed selfishness and short-sighted cupidity of successive generations of its planters and their overseers made the propagation of any form of Christianity extremely difficult. As one of Surinam's 18th-century governors observed: 'The conversion of the so-called Christians in the colony must be undertaken before there is any hope of converting the heathen.' Here, as elsewhere, there were a few individual *predikanten* who did their duty, and the Protestant dissenters known as the Labadists, who practised a form of Christian communism, and the Herrnhutters, a branch of the Moravians, or United Brethren, worked in the colony at various periods; but tropical diseases and the more or less overt hostility of the planters prevented them from achieving results commensurate

26. A. Eekhof, *De Hervormde Kerk in Noord-Amerika, 1624–1664* (2 vols., The Hague, 1913); Mrs Schuyler van Rensselaer, *History of the City of New York in the Seventeenth Century* (2 vols., New York, 1909); J. Franklin Jameson, *Narratives of New Netherland, 1609–1664* (New York, 1909); A. W. Trelease, *Indian Affairs in Colonial New York: The Seventeenth Century* (Ithaca, N.Y., 1960).

with their self-sacrificing efforts. For similar reasons the Roman Catholic missionaries who worked for a few years in Surinam (1683–6) achieved no lasting result before they died of fever, and the mission was not re-established until 1786. It is, however, worth noting that Surinam provided a refuge for an important Sephardic Jewish community, which was established here in the second half of the 17th century and achieved considerable prosperity in the next hundred years.[27]

The role of Calvinism in the African possessions of the West India Company can likewise be dismissed in a few lines. Several *predikanten* were sent out to the Dutch forts and trading-stations on the Gold Coast in the early 17th century, with the dual object of ministering to the spiritual needs of the Dutch traders in black and white ivory and of converting the heathen negroes. Their efforts never amounted to much, and they returned to the Netherlands as soon as they could, discouraged by the deadly climate and the difficult living conditions. From about 1645 onwards no *predikanten* could be found to volunteer for service in West Africa, and the Dutch Reformed Church was henceforth represented by one or two lay-readers (who were sometimes accorded the courtesy title of Dominie) in the three principal forts of Elmina, Nassau and Axim. These men took the regular morning and evening prayers, and gave scripture readings or a sermon to the Dutch residents twice weekly. This was apparently the extent of their duties and they do not seem to have attempted any missionary work.

A noteworthy exception to this general rule was the full-blooded negro *predikant*, the Rev. Jacobus Eliza Joannes Capitein. Born a slave, he had been taken to Holland in 1728, when he was eleven years old, and there he automatically became a freeman. His former master and some influential friends paid for his education, which included a sound theological training at Leiden University. He graduated in 1742 with a Latin dissertation proving the lawfulness of slavery from Holy Writ, which work went through several editions in Latin and Dutch and was widely

27. For the relevant literature on colonial Surinam see J. Meijer, *Sleutels tot Sranam. Wegwijzer in de Surinaamse geschiedenis* (Amsterdam, 1957), especially pp. 19–25.

quoted by apologists for slavery and the slave-trade. In the same year Capitein was sent out by the Directors of the WIC to Elmina, having been ordained as *predikant* by the classis of Amsterdam. He was well received by both the Dutch residents and his countrymen at first, but soon ran into difficulties. He reported that very few Europeans attended his catechism classes, 'as most of those here are Roman Catholics or Lutherans, and the Reformed are always too occupied with their daily business' – an observation which goes far to explain the failure of Calvinism in other regions of the tropical world as well. He also started a school for the negro and half-caste children, and translated the Lord's Prayer and the Twelve Commandments into the local language. Some of the Europeans showed colour-prejudice in their dealings with him, but he was supported by the Governor and was able to marry a Dutch girl from Utrecht, after his abortive romance with an unbaptizèd African girl had threatened to develop into a major scandal. Apparently discouraged by the small result of his labours in the vineyard of the Lord, whether among black or white, he neglected the service of God for that of Mammon, dying insolvent on 1 February 1747 after some unlucky trading ventures. The experiment of training another negro *predikant* was not repeated.[28]

From the foregoing it should be clear to the reader that Calvinism made little or no impression on the inhabitants of the tropical lands where it was preached in the 17th and 18th centuries. Whenever there was an active religious faith, such as Islam in Indonesia, Hinduism in India, Buddhism in Ceylon or Roman Catholicism in the places settled by the Portuguese, Calvinism could make no lasting impression once the state support for this creed was withdrawn. In fact, the principal importance of Calvinism in the East was negative. Like the militant Roman Catholicism which preceded and survived its challenge in Monsoon Asia, the impact of Calvinism served chiefly to strengthen the hold and to extend the influence of Islam in the regions where the Cross and the Crescent met.

28. K. Ratelband, *Vijf Registers van het Kasteel Elmina* (The Hague, 1953), pp. lxi–lxii; A. Eekhof, *De Negerpredikant Jacobus Elisa Joannes Capitein, 1717–1747* (The Hague, 1917).

The penetration of Islam in the Indonesian archipelago had been greatly accelerated during the 16th century by way of reaction to the militant Roman Catholicism propagated by the Portuguese from their bases at Malacca and in the Moluccas, though only in Amboina and Solor did the European intruders achieve any success. To those Indonesians who were already Islamized, the Calvinist Dutch were *kafirs* or 'unbelievers' no less than were the Papist Portuguese. The steady growth of Dutch power after the foundation of Batavia, and the successive conquest of the Moluccas, Macassar, Bantam and finally Mataram, alarmed the Indonesian rulers and many of their subjects much more than the relatively restricted progress of the Portuguese had done. This fear induced them to strengthen their existing ties with the Muslim rulers of India and the Holy Land of Mecca, chiefly by way of Achin, and also of Bantam before the latter was conquered by the Dutch in 1684. Just as the marabouts or holy men of Morocco had inspired, organized and led the Muslim reactions against the Portuguese invaders during the 16th century, so that 'Moorish papists' of Indonesia were behind every effort to resist the expansion of the Dutch Company's power, and they strove to give this resistance the character of a *jihad* or holy war. Many of these Islamic scholars were of Arabian, Indian and Persian origin, but others were Indonesians who had made the pilgrimage to Mecca, or who had been trained in the fanatically Muslim kingdom of Achin, which was a flourishing centre of Islamic studies. Although the naval and military might of the Dutch East India Company, powerfully aided by dissensions among the Indonesian leaders, overcame the principal Muslim rulers in the end – Achin always excepted – Islam continued to expand and strengthen its hold among the Indonesian courts and people.

6

Pallas and Mercury

In August 1785, when Isaac Titsingh, the outgoing chief of the Dutch agency at Nagasaki, recommended that his successors should be chosen from among men who 'as well as possessing commercial ability should also have some knowledge of the arts and sciences', the Governor-General and his council at Batavia observed that 'how gladly soever one admits the salutariness of this proposal, its fulfilment is more to be desired than to be expected, since it is the general rule in these parts to sacrifice to Mercury but never to Pallas'. This forms a striking if not unexpected contrast with the situation in the Seven Provinces during their Golden Century, when a Portuguese envoy at The Hague, contrasting the ignorance of his countrymen with the culture of the Dutch, observed: 'There is not a cobbler in these parts who does not add French and Latin to his own language.' Francisco de Sousa Coutinho was obviously exaggerating but there is plenty of more reliable evidence to indicate that the percentage of literacy in the northern Netherlands was higher than elsewhere in Europe, and that most Dutch people had had some sort of schooling. As Sir George Clark has recently observed: 'So far as it is possible to make a comparison in a field where general impressions cannot be closely tested, the Dutch were a well-educated nation. Literacy seems to have been at a relatively high level, and knowledge of many kinds seems to have been widely spread.' [1] As early as 1525 Erasmus had noted: 'Nowhere else does one find a greater number of people of average education.'

At the bottom of the ladder of education were the village schools, which were nearly always attached to the local Calvinist Church, and where the schoolmaster usually functioned as a

1. Cf. J. A. Van der Chijs, *Nederlandsch – Indisch Plakaatboek*, Vol. X, pp. 803-4; F. de Sousa Coutinho, *Correspondência Diplomática*, Vol. I, p. 245; *The New Cambridge Modern History*, Vol. V, *The Ascendancy of France, 1648-1688* (Cambridge, 1961), p. 193.

parish clerk and precentor. Teaching was limited to reading, writing, simple arithmetic and scripture lessons. Sometimes in the villages and more often in the towns there were also private elementary schools, where French was often taught as well, in addition to the three Rs. The municipal and Calvinist Church authorities kept an eye on these private schools to the extent of ensuring that they were not opened without their permission and that all the teachers were certified members of the 'true Christian Reformed Religion'. Above these elementary schools, whether municipal, church or private, were the Latin schools, and nearly all towns in the United Provinces possessed one of these institutions. They were derived mostly from Roman Catholic foundations which had been confiscated in the early years of the revolt of the Netherlands, and were largely maintained from ex-Roman-Catholic ecclesiastical revenues which had been allotted to the town councils or to the Calvinist church councils for educational purposes. These Latin schools, as their name implies, concentrated on the teaching of Latin but they also aimed at giving their pupils a general knowledge of the classical background of Antiquity. Girls were not admitted, and boys usually attended from the age of nine or ten until that of sixteen or seventeen. After the organization and curriculum of these Latin schools had been rendered more or less uniform by an edict of the States of Holland in 1625, Latin occupied a weekly total of between twenty and thirty hours during the first three years, and between ten and eighteen hours a week during the three final years. Greek and the elements of rhetoric and logic were also taught in the senior classes, but religious instruction did not occupy nearly such a prominent place as might have been expected from the fact that many of these schools had been established in the years 1588–1625, largely at the urging of the Calvinist consistories. Only about 6 per cent of the total number of hours were devoted to studying the Heidelberg catechism, scripture-history, etc., though (after 1619) all newly appointed teachers were supposed to sign a certificate accepting the rulings of the Synod of Dordrecht. In some of these Latin schools it was stipulated that boys whose parents were not members of the Dutch Reformed Church need not attend religious instruction. A similar toleration prevailed in many of the elementary schools, and the Rev. Godfried Udemans alleged (in 1630–55) that some private schoolmasters curried favour with Roman Catholic and other non-Calvinist parents by neglecting orthodox religious instruction almost completely. School hours naturally varied somewhat, but as most pupils went home for the midday meal, morning lessons were from 7 or 8 a.m. to 11 a.m. or noon, afternoon lessons 1–4 p.m. or 2–5 p.m.

Not surprisingly, the standard of the Latin schools during the 17th century was on the average much higher than that of the elementary schools. Dirk Adriaanszoon Valcoogh, author of the *Regel der Duytsche schoolmeesters* (1591), may have been exaggerating when he wrote : 'People who could hardly write their own names, and who could only sing a psalm out of tune, immediately became school-teachers and tried to set themselves up as great masters; but complaints of indifferent housing and gross overcrowding were far from uncommon, 'damp, dark cellars with stone floors' being sometimes used as schools. The elementary school-teacher's pay was low, especially in the country districts, averaging only 150 florins a year in the period 1630–1750, though a teacher often got free housing as well. His salary was raised mostly from school fees paid by the pupils' parents, the exact sum being fixed by the local church council. Owing to the low salary-scale, many teachers took other jobs, and we find them serving as soldiers, barbers, cobblers, bookbinders, sextons and grave-diggers. It was, perhaps, the fact that elementary school-teachers often held such lowly part-time jobs that gave Francisco de Sousa Continho the impression that even cobblers in Holland spoke French and Latin.[2]

Higher education in the Dutch Republic was available at the five provincial universities of Leiden (1575), Franeker (1585), Harderwijk (1648), Groningen (1614), and Utrecht (1636), of which the first- and last-named were by far the most important. In addition there were the so-called 'Illustrious Schools', some of which virtually had university status. The best known of these

2. Cf. E. J. Kuiper, *De Hollandse 'schoolordre' van 1625* (Groningen, 1958); P. S. de Toit, *Onderwys aan die Kaap onder die Kompanjie, 1652–1795* (Cape Town, 1937); P. Zumthor, *Daily Life in Rembrandt's Holland*, pp. 102–19.

was the 'Illustrious School' or Athenaeum of Amsterdam, founded in 1632 by leading Remonstrants and their sympathizers, and the direct ancestor of the present University of Amsterdam. The chief difference between the official universities and the Illustrious Schools was that instruction in the universities was given in the four traditional faculties of 'arts' (letters and sciences), law, medicine and theology, whereas the Illustrious Schools were limited to the first three faculties, and could not confer doctorates. They served not only to prepare young men for entry into the provincial universities between the ages of sixteen and twenty but also gave them the opportunity of acquiring the equivalent of a university education if they did not wish to leave their native towns. The standard at most of the universities and Illustrious Schools in the 17th century was very high, but the latter decayed to the verge of extinction in the eighteenth century, though as late as 1740 a resident Englishman in Holland stated that they provided an admirable alternative to an official university education.

Of the five provincial universities, Leiden was not only the oldest, the best and the most famous, but the one most closely connected with Dutch overseas enterprise, even if the connection was somewhat tenuous and intermittent. Burgomasters and delegates of the provincial states of Holland sat on the governing body of curators, and their Erastian tendencies doubtless prevented the university from becoming mainly an institution for educating aspirants to the Calvinist ministry, which had been the founders' original intention. The traditional medieval faculties of theology, philosophy, law and medicine were soon reinforced at Leiden by an engineering school, a botanical garden, an observatory and an excellent university press. Latin was the usual medium of instruction, though not in the engineering school, and by paying relatively high salaries the curators were able to attract distinguished scholars from the United Provinces and elsewhere to serve on the faculty. The renown of these distinguished professors in turn attracted students from all over Europe, Roman Catholics as well as Protestants, though the latter naturally and overwhelmingly predominated. Of the 2,725 students who registered at Leiden in the university's first twenty-six years, 41 per cent came from outside the United Provinces. In the period 1601–25 the proportion of foreigners enrolled was a little over 43 per cent; and in the next quarter of a century (1626–50) more than 52 per cent of the 11,076 students came from abroad.

In later years Leiden lost something of its lustre, but William Carr noted in 1688 that there were then about 1,000 foreign students 'from all parts, as Hungary, Poland, Germany, yea from the Ottoman Empire itself, who pretend to be Grecians, besides the English, Scots and Irish, who this year were numbered to be above eighty'. The English Consul tells us that he asked one of the curators why such a wealthy province as Holland did not build and endow residential colleges at Leiden, 'after the manner of Oxford and Cambridge'. The curator replied: 'Had we such colleges, our burgomasters and magistrates would fill them with their own and their friends' sons, who by leading a lazy and idle life, would never become capable of serving the commonwealth.' This answer may be taken with a pinch of salt, but there is no reason to question the curator's claim that under the existing system the professors kept the students up to the mark and ensured their attendance at both public lectures and private tutorials.

Biblical studies acted as a sharper spur to the development of Oriental studies at Leiden than they did elsewhere. The French-born Joseph Justus Scaliger, who has been called 'the greatest scholar of modern times', and who was a (non-lecturing) professor at Leiden from 1593 until his death in 1609, stressed the need of going to Chaldean, Arabic and other Near Eastern sources for securing basic materials which would help Calvinist theologians in their controversies with Roman Catholics. Scaliger's literary influence at its peak was perhaps even greater than that of Erasmus had been, and he raised philological and oriental studies at Leiden to an eminence which they retained for a century. His pupil and eventual successor, Golius, became official oriental interpreter to the States-General. The elegant style of the Arabic letters addressed to Muslim potentates which he composed in this capacity is said to have aroused the admiration of the recipients. In 1625, an Oriental press, equipped with Syriac, Chaldean, Ethiopic, Arabic and Hebrew types, was established at

Leiden by the Elseviers as a department of the university press, and it functioned as such until the types were sold to a private printer in 1712.[3]

Elementary schools in the domains of the East and West India Companies followed the same pattern as in the Fatherland, being under a mixture of clerical and lay control. Lay-readers often served as schoolmasters in the absence of better qualified teachers. Colonial school hours were likewise usually from 8–11 a.m. and from 2–5 p.m., with Wednesday and Saturday afternoons free. The curriculum was generally confined to elementary religious instruction in the tenets of the Calvinist faith, reading, writing and simple arithmetic. As in the Netherlands, apart from the East (or West) India Company's own schools, anyone could open an elementary school or a kindergarten, provided he satisfied the local church council as to his Calvinist orthodoxy, and obtained their approval and that of the Company's senior officials. It is worth noting that these colonial schools were often mixed in race as well as in the sexes, the children of slaves and coloured people being educated alongside those of Whites and Eurasians. In 1681, for example, about 200 slaves were being educated at the VOC school in Colombo. Boys usually left school at the age of fifteen or sixteen, but in 17th-century Ceylon the Asian girls were discharged at the age of ten, 'so as to avoid their seduction through the lechery of the boys and others'.

A Latin school was opened at Batavia in 1642, mainly with the object of providing a higher education for the children of the Company's senior officials, who otherwise had to be sent to the Netherlands. Despite the support of the *Heeren* XVII, this institution languished and was abolished by the local authorities in 1656. Reopened ten years later, it expired again after a lapse of four years. A third attempt in the following century lasted rather longer (1743–56), but its demise this time was final. Elsewhere in the VOC's domain no attempt was made to provide higher education for laymen, for the reasons explained by Mentzel in account-

3. W. Carr, *A Description of Holland* (ed. 1701), pp. 14–16; D. W. Davies, *The World of the Elseviers, 1580–1712* (The Hague, 1954), for details about Leiden University, its professoriate, curriculum, and connection with the Elseviers and the book-trade.

ing for the absence of a Latin School at the Cape, where, however, one had functioned between 1714 and 1730. 'Such institutions are not required, for what use could anyone make of learning obtained there in a land where life is still primitive and Company rule is law?' The essential accuracy of Mentzel's observation is attested by the fact that although there were some book-collectors in 18th-century South Africa, and one of them (Von Dessin) bequeathed his collection as a public library to Cape Town in 1761, the evidence indicates that practically none of the residents used it for the next fifty years. Those of the Company's servants who wished to give their boys a good education, and who could afford to do so, therefore continued to send them to Europe, despite the great expense and the long absence that this involved. Higher education for those who wished to enter the Church was also available for much of this period at one or another of the three seminaries briefly described above (p. 165), although, as we have seen, they failed in their main purpose of producing a flow of qualified *predikanten*. The fact remains that, at the time when the rulers of the Dutch Republic left the responsibility for elementary education almost entirely to the Calvinist church councils or to private individuals, the directors of the East India Company, directly or indirectly, subsidized numerous primary schools which, in some places at least, sometimes achieved good results. In 1779 the total number of children attending such schools in the region east of the Cape of Good Hope was 20,936. Of those, the overwhelming majority (19,147) were in Ceylon, but there were 639 at Batavia and the surprisingly high number of 593 in Timor.[4]

The situation in the regions controlled by the West India Company and its successors was basically similar. The schoolmaster who was appointed to take charge of the school at New Amsterdam on Manhattan Island in November 1661 was instructed to see that the children attended daily for classes at 8 a.m. and at 1 p.m. They were to be taught 'the Christian prayers, the Ten Commandments, the meaning of baptism and the Lord's Supper, and questions and answers from the catechism'. Over and above

4. J. A. Van der Chijs, *Nederlandsch-Indisch Plakaatboek*, Vol. X, pp. 327-8, 417-18; O. F. Mentzel, *Description of the Cape*, Vol. II, p. 108; H. Terpstra, 'Companiesonderwijs op Ceilon', *TG*, pp. 26-50.

his annual salary, he received a quarterly allowance ranging from 30 to 60 stuivers for each child who was taught the ABC, reading, writing and arithmetic. Most children who came for further instruction or extra tuition outside school hours would be charged *pro rata* at a fair price, but the poor and needy would be educated free. Before leaving school after the day's work all the pupils had to sing some verses from a psalm. On the other side of the Atlantic, the negro *predikant*, Jacobus Eliza Capitein, ran a kindergarten school for negro, half-caste and white children at Elmina in 1743–4, where the pupils were taught the elements of the 'True Christian Reformed Religion'.[5]

The relatively high percentage of literacy in the northern Netherlands helps to account for the flourishing state of the printing and book trades in the Dutch Republic, particularly in its Golden Century. As elsewhere in Western Europe, sermons were printed in vast quantities and read with avidity by the reading public, which could also absorb a surprising amount of abstruse theological and frankly polemical religious works. The Dutch commercial and maritime expansion was accurately mirrored in an extensive literature of travel and voyages, which quickly flowered in the dynamic decade of 1595–1605, and remained an outstanding feature of Dutch publishing for the next hundred years. The Dutch were not, of course, the first people to cultivate this branch of literature, their Portuguese and Spanish precursors in the tropics having produced epic poems, prose chronicles and narratives of travel and exploration inspired by the Iberian *conquistadores*, navigators and missionaries who pioneered the expansion of Europe. Similarly, the English and French rivals of the Dutch likewise had much to their literary credit, as instanced by the admirable collections of Richard Hakluyt, Samuel Purchas and Melchisadec Thevenot. Nor can the contribution of the Italians be overlooked, for they had in Marco Polo and Ramusio the first great exponents of travel literature, to which German printers, editors and publishers later made outstanding

5. W. H. Kilpatrick, *The Dutch Schools of New Netherland* (Washington, 1912); A. Eekhof, *De Hervormde Kerk in Noord-Amerika, 1624–1664*, Vol. II, pp. 124–5; ibid., *De Negerpredikant Jacobus Elias Capitein, 1717–1747*, pp. 46–50.

contributions, including De Bry's encyclopedic series of *Grands et Petits Voyages*, published at Frankfurt between 1590 and 1634. But when due weight is given to the pamphlets, books and maps which were printed in other countries, the fact remains that those published in the United Provinces of the Free Netherlands set the pace and maintained the lead in both quality and quantity during the whole of the 17th century.

Perhaps the most popular Dutch narrative of travel and adventure published in this period was the story of Skipper Ysbrandtsz. Bontekoe's adventures and misadventures in Eastern Seas (1618–25), which achieved at least fifty editions between 1646 and 1756. Ships' journals kept by officers and passengers aboard Indiamen often found their way into print before 1650, the best of them being grouped into a two-volume collection published at Amsterdam in 1645.[6] These journals are not mere log-books, but describe the ports and places at which the ships touched, the manners and customs of their respective inhabitants and their methods of trading. They are lavishly illustrated – a rarity in Spanish and Portuguese travel literature – and they served the double purpose of imparting practical information for merchants and mariners, and diverting or instructing armchair-travellers at home. One point which emerges very clearly from these journals is the resource and the powers of improvisation displayed by Dutch sailors and castaways in critical conditions, whether among the ice-floes of Nova Zembla or in the hurricanes of the Indian Ocean. Another popular *genre* was formed by travellers' tales and reminiscences, likewise lavishly illustrated with copper-plate engravings or woodcuts.

Since relatively few people outside the Low Countries knew Dutch, many of these books were also published in Latin, French, German or – less often – English editions, with an eye to the foreign market. Two outstanding compilers of such works which

6. *Begin ende Voortgangh van de Vereenighde Nederlantsche geoctroyeerde Oost-Indische Compagnie* (2 vols., Amsterdam, 1645). Edited anonymously by Isaac Commelin, and reprinted in 1646. The standard bibliography of Dutch travel literature for the period 1602–1795 is by P. A. Tiele, *Nederlandsche Bibliographie van Land-en Volkenkunde* (Amsterdam, 1884).

aimed at a European circulation were Johannes de Laet and Olfert Dapper. The former, an Antwerper by birth, was a director of the West India Company who published a number of descriptive works on Europe, Asia and America. Though he never left the Low Countries, he took great pains to get his facts right, and he had an excellent library of his own, as well as access to that of the University of Leiden and to the archives of the West India Company. His best known works deal with America, but the accuracy of his description of the empire of the Great Moghul (*De Imperio Magni Mogolis*, 1631) has been praised by 20th-century Indologists. Dapper was not such a discerning editor as was De Laet, but his bulky folios on Africa, parts of Asia and the Middle East for long remained the standard works on their respective regions, and can still be consulted with profit on some points, as contemporary historians of West Africa have found. These compilations were provided with numerous maps and illustrations, varying from the purely fanciful to the rigorously exact; but irrespective of the quality of these engravings, their quantity was a major factor in establishing the popularity of these works at home and abroad.

The finest examples of Dutch book production in this respect are works by two Calvinist clergymen. The first in point of time was a large folio volume entitled *Rerum per octennium in Brasilia*, edited by the Rev. Caspar Barlaeus and published by Blaeu at Amsterdam in 1647. Barlaeus, a Remonstrant *predikant*, was one of the leading classical scholars of his day and a professor at the Amsterdam Athenaeum. This Latin work was published under the auspices of John Maurice, Count of Nassau-Siegen, whose governorship of Netherlands-Brazil (1637–44) it recounts in a not unreasonably eulogistic style. The text is based primarily on the Count's official papers and dispatches, and the value of the numerous maps and illustrations is enhanced by their having been engraved from the original drawings made in Pernambuco by the Haarlem artist, Frans Post. If this book reflects the high-water mark of the West India Company, that of its Eastern sister is mirrored in the Rev. François Valentyn's *Oud en Nieuw Oost-Indien* ('The Old and New East-Indies'), published at Dordrecht in eight volumes comprising 4,800 pages of text with hundreds of maps and illustrations. Dominie Valentyn's book can fairly be described as encyclopedic in scope; and though he has been convicted of large-scale plagiarism in some sections of this truly monumental work, this only affects its value in a few places where he had misread or misunderstood his original sources. Valentyn did not rely entirely on his own experience of the East Indies, where he had lived for a good many years, chiefly in the Spice Islands and Java, nor did he depend mainly on pilfering the published works of his predecessors with discrimination (if sometimes without due acknowledgement). He also made good use of much unpublished material which was placed at his disposal by senior officials of the Company, including the Deshima diaries of its agents at Nagasaki. Apart from anything else, the publication of this massive work gives the lie to the commonly accepted allegation that the directors of the Dutch East India Company invariably obstructed the dissemination of any information about their Eastern possessions. The *Heeren* XVII and the *Heeren* XIX did, of course, discourage or even forbid the publication of technical information which they thought might be of use to their trade rivals; but otherwise they did not try to interfere with their employees or ex-employees who published descriptive accounts of the East and West Indies.

Apart from travel literature, another branch of publishing in which the Dutch quickly established a supremacy which lasted for about a century was in the production of navigating manuals and atlases. In 1584–5, Lucas Janszoon Wagenaer published his *Spieghel der Zeevaert*, a two-volume folio collection of charts engraved on copper plates, depicting the West European continental coast from the North Cape to Cadiz, accompanied by the relevant sailing-directions. This work, which was translated into English in the Armada-year under the title of *The Mariner's Mirror*, was such a great improvement on the few sailing-directions that had been published previously that it long remained a model for all future productions of this kind, which were called 'Waggoners' in England until far into the 18th century. Wagenaer's *Spieghel* was the first book to print standardized symbols for buoys, sea-marks, safe anchorages, hidden and dangerous rocks. Though the Spaniards had begun to engrave

183

and publish nautical charts a few years before the appearance of those in the *Spieghel der Zeevaert*, these latter were the first popular ones for use at sea. As Commander D. W. Waters has pointed out: 'Their merit was that they eliminated the copyist's errors, their virtue that they standardized hydrographical knowledge and included only the observed facts essential for good pilotage, their achievement that they placed pilotage on a firmer scientific basis than ever before.'[7]

Wagenaer's work was continued by several Dutch publishing houses which specialized in the production of finely engraved maps, charts and books on navigation in various European languages. The most famous firm was the Amsterdam house of Blaeu, which flourished between 1620 and 1673, and whose best-known work is the sumptuous eleven-volume folio world-atlas of 1662. The Dutch kept the lead which they had established in this respect down to about 1675. The English sea-atlas of John Seller, which was published in London that year, and which was regarded as the best work of its kind, was an unblushing 'crib' from the *Zeeatlas ofte water-wereld* ('Sea-atlas or water-world') of Pieter Goos.[8] But after the death of Johan Blaeu in 1673, Dutch map-makers and publishers became less enterprising, and they contented themselves with the more or less mechanical reproduction of the 17th-century masters. Johannes van Keulen, who inherited the nautical and geographical bookseller's stock of Johan Blaeu, and who was the founder of a firm which specialized in the production of globes, maps and charts for nearly two centuries, published in 1682 a world-globe which gave no indication whatever of Tasman's discoveries forty years earlier, though these were already available in, for example, Thevenot's *Voyages*. Maps and charts were also framed and used as pictures in many

7. D. W. Waters, *The Art of Navigation in England in Elizabethan and Early Stuart Times* (London, 1958), pp. 168–75.

8. 'They say that even Seller's new maps are many of them little less than transcripts of the Dutch maps, some of them even with papers pasted over and names scratched. Captain Imman and Captain Saunders do also note that all the titles and words in our English and French Waggoners are in Dutch.' (*Samuel Pepys' Naval Minutes*, ed. J. Tanner, 1926, pp. 135, 345).

burghers' houses, and large wall-maps and globes were often to be found in rich collectors' dwellings and in municipal buildings. Dutch collectors also spent large sums on costly and luxuriously bound atlases, those produced by the firm of Blaeu being the most sought after in the Golden Century and fetching the highest prices on their increasingly rare appearances in the sale-rooms today. Early in the 18th century, both the English and French overhauled and surpassed the Dutch in the production of accurate globes, maps and charts. This lead they maintained, though Dirk van Hogendorp was evidently exaggerating somewhat when he wrote in 1792 : 'There is not a single Dutch chart of the Indies which is even passable; while the French and English have superb charts.'

As regards technical manuals on the science of high-seas navigation, the Dutch for long depended on translations of the classic Spanish work of Pedro de Medina, *Arte de Navegar* (Valladolid, 1545), a Flemish version of which was published at Antwerp in 1580. Not until 1642 did they produce one of their own which rivalled Medina's work in popularity, C. J. Lastman's *Beschrijvinge van de Kunst der Stuerlieden* ('Description of the Navigators' Art'), and this was followed by many other similar works. In all of the great seaports, and particularly in Amsterdam, there were to be found a number of old sailors, more or less well qualified, who taught the science of navigation in their homes to aspiring young mariners, particularly in the winter months when much of the merchant shipping was laid up. Apart from these men with practical experience of the sea, there were others who might never have gone to sea for any length of time, but who regarded themselves as qualified teachers since they had systematically studied mathematics and theoretical navigation. Their counterpart, or perhaps one should say their compeer, in England was William Bourne, the Gravesend inn-keeper and self-taught mathematician, whose *Regiment for the Sea: conteyning most profitable rules, mathematical experiences, and perfect knowledge of navigation for all coasts and countreys* (London, 1574) had a great and well-deserved success at home and abroad, including three Dutch editions between 1594 and 1609.

Competition among the Dutch practitioners of navigational

teaching was very keen and not infrequently degenerated into mutual charges of plagiarism and incompetence. With a view to attracting potential customers, these teachers often advertised their skill by nailing on their doors pieces of paper containing complicated mathematical conundrums with their respective solutions. The two most popular of the many navigating manuals published by these self-appointed teachers were the *Vergulde Licht der Zeevaart* ('Gilded Light of Navigation') by Claes Hendricksz Gietermaker, and the *Schatkamer ofte Konst der Stuerluyden* ('Treasure-chamber or Art of Navigators') by Claes de Vries. The former ran through fourteen editions between 1660 and 1774, and the latter totalled eleven editions between 1702 and 1811, apart from those in other languages. Despite their popularity among many generations of pilots and navigators, Dutch, German and Scandinavian, both these works left a great deal to be desired on the score of clarity and presentation. Their material was badly arranged, their exposition was prolix, obscure and repetitive, and they contained too many cumbersome and complicated rules. Spherical trigonometry was still a mystery to the average Dutch navigator of 1740; but these old-fashioned manuals continued to be widely used at a time when better and up-to-date works, like those of the Amsterdam Admiralty mathematician, Cornelius Douwes (1712–73), were available.[9]

A sphere in which Dutch experts and technicians were the acknowledged masters during the 17th century was in that of hydraulic engineering and land reclamation. This was a favourite field for the investment of Dutch capital (p. 66), and the experience of draining, dyking, canal construction and impoldering which the Dutch had gained in reclaiming marshes, meeres and

9. E. Crone, 'Afgunst en Ruzie tussen leermeesters in de stuurmanskunst', in *Vereeniging Nederlandsch Historisch Scheepvaart Museum, Jaarverslag 1959–61* (Amsterdam, 1962), pp. 37–49. For the foregoing cf. also W. Voorbeijtel Cannenburg, *Het Scheepvaart Museum te Amsterdam* (Leiden, 1947), pp. 72–94, and ibid., *Nederlandsch Historisch Scheepvaart Museum, Catalogus der Bibliotheek* (Amsterdam, 1960), especially pp. 43–103, 661–715; C. Koeman, *Collections of Maps and Atlases in the Netherlands: their history and present state* (Leiden, 1961).

estuaries since the early Middle Ages gave them an unrivalled technical skill. Their foremost hydraulic engineer was Jan Adriaanszoon Leeghwater (1575–1650), who developed the method of pumping with windmills. He drained extensive areas in the province of Holland, though his ambitious scheme for reclaiming the Haarlem Lake in 1641 had to wait for over two centuries before it was implemented. The Zeelander, Cornelis Vermuyden, was invited to England by James I, where he won and lost a fortune with his drainage undertakings in Hatfield Chase and great parts of the Fens.[10] Other Dutch hydraulic engineers were employed in Germany, France, Poland, Russia and Italy. Until well into the 18th century the Dutch remained the acknowledged experts in the Western world for mounting and operating all kinds of windmills. When King John V of Portugal decided to erect a sawmill in the pine-forest of Leiria to saw planks for his warships, he sent to Holland for some Dutch technicians to install and operate this *Engenho do Pinhal*, which lasted until its destruction by fire in 1774. Wherever they went overseas, from Manhattan Island to Formosa, the Dutch dug canals and erected dykes. The surveys which were a necessary corollary of all this engineering activity also encouraged the development of a relatively large group of cartographer-surveyors. Their work often achieved a high degree of artistic merit as well as of cartographical accuracy, recalling in this respect the better-known maps and charts of the navigators.

Since the Dutch were the foremost seafaring nation in the 17th century, it is not surprising that they took the lead in the production of maps, charts, navigational manuals and tales of travel; but, as I have mentioned, these were not the most widely read books in the home market. With the partial exception of Vondel, the great figures of Dutch literature were no more interested in the overseas activities of their countrymen than were, say, Cervantes, Milton and Molière in those of their respective compatriots. As elsewhere in Europe during the first half of the 17th

10. J. Korthals Altes, *Sir Cornelius Vermuyden* (London, 1925); H. C. Darby, *The Draining of the Fens* (Cambridge, 1956). L. E. Harris, *Vermuyden and the Fens. A Study of Sir Cornelius Vermuyden and the Great Level* (London, 1953).

century, religion and theology formed the favourite reading-matter in the United Provinces, followed by the law, politics and classical texts. In the year 1612 the Amsterdam Municipal Library contained only seven books in the Dutch language, and most of the 3,000 books listed in the catalogue of the Utrecht Library in 1608 were theological. During the second half of the century French plays and belles-lettres became increasingly popular with the regent class and wealthy burghers, and the growth of both Dutch and French books at the expense of Latin was evident even in the learned world. The firm of Elsevier, who specialized in the publication of books for scholars, lawyers and theologians, and who had a European reputation and clientele, published over 96 per cent of their titles in Latin between 1594 and 1617. As printers to the University of Leiden from 1626 to 1652, the Elseviers published only about 1 per cent of their titles (in that capacity) in French for the first five years of their contract, but a little over 50 per cent during the last five years of that period. In 1685 the Huguenot philosopher and critic, Pierre Bayle, wrote of the northern Netherlands from his refuge at Rotterdam: 'The French language is so well known in this country that more French books are sold here than all others.'

From about 1650 the number of works published in Dutch also increased noticeably, nearly three times as many being printed in the second half of the century as in the first. But however popular travellers' tales and books of sea-voyages became, they could not vie in popularity with the States' Bible and the doggerel poetry of Jacob Cats. It is no mere figure of speech to say that copies of these works were to be found in virtually every literate Dutch home. The Bible was, of course, the most popular, but an illustrated edition of the poems of Cats, a relatively expensive book, had sold 50,000 copies by 1655, which made it one of the best-sellers of the century. 'Father' Cats's long-winded poems were not for export – save to the southern Netherlands and to South Africa where he was widely read – but the export of English and German bibles printed in Holland was almost a major Dutch industry. One leading Amsterdam printer boasted that 'for several years I myself printed more than a million bibles for England and Scotland. There is no ploughboy or servant girl without one'. This may have been an exaggeration, but in 1672 King Charles II's printer complained that owing to 'the Hollanders continual pouring in vast numbers of bibles' they themselves sold not a tenth part of what they formerly did.[11] By the end of the 17th century there were, in all probability, more books printed in the Dutch Republic than in all other European countries together, and most of these Dutch-printed books were intended for the international market.

In one sense, Dutch literature of the Golden Century is likely to remain what it has been hitherto: a closed book to all but Dutchmen, Flemings and Afrikaners. In contrast to the travel, geographical and nautical works which were quickly translated into other European languages for practical reasons, Dutch literary prose and poetry aroused no interest outside the Netherlands, save to a limited extent in Germany. Joost van den Vondel, by common consent the greatest of all Dutch writers, and one honoured in his own country like Shakespeare in England, Cervantes in Spain and Camões in Portugal, has never found translators or a foreign public, such as these writers have always done. Why this is so is not easy to explain.[12] Admittedly, the French and English neighbours of the Netherlands have tended to be unduly scornful of the Dutch language and critical of what has been called its raucous pronunciation. A Dutch writer of the Golden Century, Pieter Schryver (1576–1660), wrote a poem of praise in favour of his own language, which he termed: 'tongue, unbelievably sweet, princess of all tongues', but contemporary Englishmen termed a croaking frog 'a Dutch nightingale'. Nor has ignorance of the Scandinavian and Russian languages, for example, prevented Kierkegaard, Ibsen, Tolstoy

11. The foregoing is largely derived from D. W. Davies' model monograph, *The World of the Elseviers, 1580–1712* (The Hague, 1954). Cf. also P. Zumthor, *Daily Life in Rembrandt's Holland* (1962), pp. 219–23.

12. Professor Theodoor Weevers, *Poetry of the Netherlands in its European Context, 1170–1930* (London, 1960), argues that the dramatic tension which is so important in Vondel's drama is produced largely by the evocative power of his poetry: 'that is why Vondel cannot be appreciated in translation' (p. 117).

and Dostoyevsky from being widely appreciated in translation. Vondel was a member of the *Muider-kring*, a circle of cultured persons of both sexes who were prose-writers, poets and musicians in their spare time. They met periodically between 1609 and 1647, at the castle of Muiden, where one of their number, the poet, musician and historian P. C. Hooft, was the warden. They included Hugo Grotius, founder with his Spanish forerunner, Francisco de Victoria, of International Law; Laurens Reael, ex-Governor-General of the East Indies, who corresponded with Galileo on scientific questions; J. P. Sweelink, the famous organist; Constantijn Huygens, Secretary to two successive Princes of Orange and a fluent poet in Latin, French and Dutch; and two beautiful and artistic sisters, Anna and Maria Roemers-Visscher. Constantijn Huygens translated some of the poems of John Donne into Dutch, but no contemporary Englishmen returned the compliment; and the members of the Muiden-circle who formed the fine flower of Dutch literature in the Golden Century have been dismissed by a modern English critic as a group of *précieux* who made even their French models appear unaffected.

The wealth which the regent and the merchant classes derived directly or indirectly from overseas trade not only provided a market for the long-winded poetical effusions of 'Father Cats' and for the finely illustrated folio books and atlases published by Plantin, Elsevier and Blaeu, but it contributed to a great flowering of the arts in general and of painting in particular. Nor did only wealthy Dutchmen want paintings to decorate their rooms, but paintings were prized possessions in all save the poorest households. It is probable that, with the one exception of Japan, never in any country has the painter's art – if not the painter himself – been more truly popular than in the land of Rembrandt. 'As for the art of painting and the affection of the people to pictures,' wrote that experienced traveller, Peter Mundy, after his visit to Holland in 1640, 'I think none other go beyond them, there having been in this country many excellent men in that faculty, [and] some at present, as Rembrandt, etc. All in general striving to adorn their houses, especially the outer or street room with costly pieces; butchers and bakers not much inferior in their shops, which are fairly set forth, yea many times blacksmiths, cobblers, etc., will have some pictures or other by their forge and in their stall. Such is the general notion, inclination and delight that these country natives have to paintings.'

John Evelyn, who visited Holland a year after Peter Mundy, was equally impressed. He found the annual fair at Rotterdam 'so furnished with pictures', especially landscapes and low-life, that he was amazed. 'The reason of this store of pictures, and their cheapness,' he observed, 'proceeds from want of land to employ their stock, so that it is an ordinary thing to find a common farmer lay out two or three thousand pounds in this commodity. Their houses are full of them, and they vend them at their fairs to very great gains.' Evelyn's explanation for the popularity of picture-collecting is not very convincing, since it would have been just as easy and more profitable to invest surplus capital in government or municipal bonds. It is more likely that people bought pictures because they liked them, as Peter Mundy observed. Foreign visitors to the Seven Provinces seldom failed to remark on the Dutch love of pictures, and William Carr noted in 1688 that even alms-houses were 'richly adorned' with them.[13]

Dutch painters were appreciated beyond the bounds of the Republic and there was a thriving export-trade in their works. In art, as in commerce and banking, Antwerp lost her primacy to Amsterdam, at any rate after the death of Rubens. The chief centres of patronage – and hence of production – were important towns like Amsterdam, Leiden, Utrecht, Haarlem and Delft, but nearly every town in the northern Netherlands had its painters. The Calvinist Church may have been indifferent to art where it was not actively hostile, but the lack of ecclesiastical patronage was more than offset by the desire of the ordinary town- and country-folk to own some pictures. Many Dutch painters also went to work abroad, apart from those who studied in Italy in their youth. Others emigrated for good, like the celebrated marine artists, the two Van de Veldes, who settled in England at the time of the Third Anglo-Dutch War. Incidentally,

13. R. C. Temple (ed.), *Travels of Peter Mundy, 1600–1657*, Vol. IV (1925), p. 70; *Diary* of John Evelyn, d. 13/23 August 1641; W. Carr, op. cit. (ed. 1691), p. 27.

191

these and other Dutch artists who excelled in depicting ships were not so successful in painting the sea. Ruskin's scornful dismissal of 'the small waves *en papillote* and peruke-like puffs of farinaceous foam which were the delight of Backhuysen and his compeers' may owe something of its force to alliteration; but he is surely right in claiming that Turner was the supreme artist in handling this element in all its moods.

Despite their penchant for collecting paintings, the wealthy regents, merchants and burghers of the Dutch Republic despised artists as a social group. Nearly all the Dutch painters came from the smaller *bourgeoisie* or from the working class. They did not rise above their lowly social origins to attain the status achieved by Rubens, Van Dyck and Velasquez. Rembrandt's wealthy patrons despised him as much for being an undischarged bankrupt as they admired him for being a consummate artist. Painters were commonly regarded as wastrels who spent too much time in taverns, where their pupils would sometimes paint coins on the floor, so as to get a laugh at the expense of their drunken master who tried to pick them up.

The European market was not the only one for Dutch art, and pictures were exported to Asia even before the East India Company was founded. Indonesians and Chinese showed little interest in Western art, but Indian and Persian potentates often asked for Dutch artists to be sent to their respective courts. The Company's officials complied with these requests whenever possible, and, apart from the painters employed by the Company, there were some others who worked on their own account. In 1602 the Dutch presented the King of Kandy with a large painting of the battle of Niewpoort (2 July 1600), which depicted a life-size Prince Maurice on horseback in the foreground. This gigantic picture was preserved for a long time in the throne-room of the Sinhalese ruler's palace. A painting of Amsterdam harbour was presented to the Sultan of Palembang in 1629, and portraits of the Stadtholders to an Indian prince and to the King of Pegu. On the other hand, the Shogun of Japan was not attracted by some oil-paintings presented to him in 1640, and in the same year the Company failed to persuade the Shah of Persia to buy a painting of Heemskerk's naval victory off Gibraltar (1607).

Netherlanders in the East seem to have been as fond of pictures as were their compatriots in the Low Lands by the North Sea. An inventory of the contents of the governor's house at Fort Zeelandia, Formosa, in 1644, listed twenty-two Dutch pictures, fourteen being portraits of the princes of the house of Nassau, and eight biblical subjects. Last wills and testaments filed in the notarial archives at Batavia make frequent mention of pictures, though the artists' names are seldom indicated. But a widow in 1709 bequeathed among other pictures a landscape by Ruysdael and the portrait of a man's head by Rembrandt. Isaac de St Martin, the Huguenot garrison commander at Batavia, left eighty-nine 'large and small pictures' on his death in 1696, besides a portrait of himself. Collections of thirty or forty pictures were quite common among the wealthier inhabitants of Batavia. Some of the Company's officials also collected Oriental art. Governor-General Camphuis bequeathed to his friend, Pieter van Dam, the Company's advocate at Amsterdam, four books with several hundred Chinese, Japanese, Muslim and other Oriental drawings. A century later, Isaac Titsingh brought back from Nagasaki some Japanese prints and two folio volumes of botanical drawings made by the wife of the Shogun's chief physician, Katsuragawa Hoshu, of which a Frenchman who saw them wrote: 'I doubt whether anything more perfect of the kind exists.' Titsingh's contemporary, A. E. Van Braam Houckgeest, who lived for many years at Canton, also amassed a large collection of Chinese drawings, paintings and other 'artificial curiosities', which were sold at Christie's in 1799. We know that Rembrandt owned and copied Mughal miniatures, and it has been suggested that he may have been slightly influenced by Japanese and Chinese drawings.[14]

Although scores of Dutch painters worked in the East during the 17th and 18th centuries, singularly few of the works which they painted there have survived. The only professional artists who worked in the tropics and whose productions have survived

14. Cf. J. de Loos-Haxman, *De Landsverzameling schilderijen in Batavia. Landvoogdsportretten en Compagnieschilders* (Leiden, 1941), especially pp. 17–18, 151–8; C. R. Boxer, *Jan Compagnie in Japan, 1600–1850* (The Hague, 1950), pp. 51, 157 and the sources there quoted.

in any appreciable quantity were Frans Post and Albert Eckhout. They worked not in Monsoon Asia but in Netherlands Brazil during the governorship of Count John Maurice (1637–44), and their paintings and drawings have been the subject of intensive study by art historians within recent years. Whether their artistic value is worth the detailed research bestowed on them, or the astronomical prices now paid for them, are matters on which opinions may vary, but they enjoyed a more modest vogue in their own day. The tropical motifs which permeated much of the work of Post and Eckhout after their return from Brazil were not confined to South America and West African subjects, but were somewhat incongruously blended with East Asian themes in the case of Eckhout. This mixture of East and West is exemplified by some murals painted by this minor master in German castles, but it is best known through the designs of the Gobelin tapestries entitled the 'peintures des Indes'. These were commissioned by Louis XIV – after a good deal of prodding from Count John Maurice – and proved to be so popular in Court circles that they were repeated on the same looms at intervals during the next 120 years.[15]

If Moghul miniatures, Chinese paintings and Japanese prints were collected only by a discerning few of the VOC's servants, and if the aesthetic influence of such specimens of Oriental art as found their way to Europe was nearly negligible, it was quite otherwise with Far Eastern porcelain. Some of this had been brought to Europe by the Portuguese (via Goa) and by the Spaniards (via Mexico) in the 16th century, but most of these consignments were marketed in the Iberian Peninsula or in their American colonies. It was the Dutch who first imported Chinese and Japanese porcelain on a really massive scale into Europe north of the Pyrenees. The impetus was given by their capture of two Portuguese carracks, the *Santiago* off Saint Helena in 1602 and the *Santa Catarina* off Johore a year later. Their cargoes in-

15. T. Thomsen, *Albert Eckhout. Ein Niederländischer Maler und sein Gönner Moritz der Brasilianer. Ein Kulturbild ans dem 17 Jahrhundert* (Copenhagen, 1938); J. de Sousa-Leão *Frans Post* (Rio de Janeiro, 1948); E. Larsen, *Frans Post, 1612–1680, Interprète du Brésil* (Louvain, 1962).

cluded large quantities of Chinese porcelain which fetched high prices when auctioned at Amsterdam, and hence the term *kraak-porcelein* ('carrack-porcelain') was applied to Ming blue-and-white for several decades. These sales revealed a demand which the VOC hastened to supply. As early as 1614 a published description of Amsterdam affirmed that porcelain had come to be 'in daily use with the common people', and twenty-six years later Peter Mundy noted that 'any house of indifferent quality' was well supplied with Chinese porcelain.

This substantial home demand was surpassed by the greater amount that was re-exported to other countries, so that shipments from the Far East to the northern Netherlands increased rapidly. More than three million pieces of Chinese porcelain were shipped to Europe in Dutch East Indiamen between 1602 and 1657, followed by about 190,000 pieces of Japanese porcelain between 1659 and 1682, when China was disturbed by civil strife. Apart from exports to Europe, several millions of pieces (mainly Chinese) were transhipped at Batavia for disposal in the markets of Indonesia, Malaya, India and Persia, etc. As the historian of this export-trade has observed, 'the special qualities of Chinese porcelain, its impermeability and cleanness, its practical beauty and relative cheapness', are sufficient to account for its great and continuing popularity. Nearly all the Far Eastern porcelain imported during the 17th century was of the blue-and-white variety, whether Chinese or Japanese in origin; but during the 18th century the polychrome, monochrome and enamelled wares steadily gained favour in most European markets, though blue-and-white still continued to set the tone in the Dutch Republic itself.

As early as 1614 the Dutch began to imitate the blue-and-white Ming ceramics, and within fifty years the Delft potteries were turning out very passable imitations of Chinese and Japanese porcelain vessels. They continued to produce the famous Delft blue-and-white for the next 150 years, though the first real porcelain made in Europe was that manufactured by Meissen in 1709. Not all of these Dutch wares were servile copies of Far Eastern originals, for some of the Delft pottery painters combined Japanese, Chinese and Indian elements in their decorations. From about 1660 onwards they also produced designs in that exuberant *chinoiserie* style which became so popular in the 18th century. Strange as it may seem, in 1634 the Dutch hoped to create a market for their own pottery in Japan. There was never much chance of this materializing, since what Japanese buyers wanted were pieces suitable for display in the tea-ceremony (*cha-no-yu*), and this taste was inspired by aesthetic conventions which the European producer or importer could hardly hope to understand. In any event, this hope vanished after the great expansion of the Japanese porcelain industry after 1660, though some devotees of *cha-no-yu* continued to collect odd pieces of Delft and Cologne wares. Japanese potters, in their turn, sometimes imitated Delft designs which had originally been copied from or inspired by porcelain imported from the Far East, and in this way the artistic wheel of taste turned full circle.

Two of the characteristics of Far Eastern porcelain, cheapness and washability, help to account for the great and growing demand in Europe for the finer sorts of Indian cotton piece-goods and textiles during the second half of the 17th century. Raw silk and silk fabrics were also imported by the Dutch and English East India Companies, originally – and indirectly – from China, later from Persia and Bengal. Before about 1660 both Dutch and English had exported Indian textiles to Europe, but these were mostly coarse grades intended for re-export to America and West Africa, and the finer fabrics were used for household linen rather than for clothing. The last decades of the 17th century were characterized by the 'Indian craze', forerunner and counterpart of the 'China craze' of the 18th century. The directors of the English East India Company wrote to their factors in Bengal in 1692 : 'You can send us nothing amiss at this time, when everything of India is so much wanted', to which their Dutch rivals at Amsterdam might have said Amen. In the United Provinces as in England, moralists deplored that 'these manufactured goods from India met with such a kind reception that from the greatest

16. T. Volger, *Porcelain and the Dutch East-India Company, as recorded in the Dagh-Registers of Batavia Castle, those of Hirado and Deshima and other contemporary papers, 1602–1682* (Leiden, 1954); ibid., *The Japanese Porcelain Trade of the East-India Company after 1683* (Leiden, 1959).

gallants to the meanest cook-maids nothing was thought so fit to adorn their persons as the fabrics from India'. The designs on these painted and printed textiles were not necessarily of purely Indian inspiration, but often originated with patterns sent out from Europe for copying or adaptation by the Indian workers. We even find Japanese motifs in some Coromandel textiles made for the Dutch market.

In 1697 the Dutch East India Company imported Asian textiles and piece-goods to the value of over five million florins, just under one-third of which originated in Bengal. At this period the Dutch Company was still leading its English competitor but the latter took the lead early in the 18th century, and by 1731-5 the EIC was obtaining double the quantity of silk purchased by its Dutch rival. The success of the English Company is the more remarkable since the importation of Indian piece-goods and textiles did not meet with such strong or effective opposition from textile-workers and industrialists in the United Provinces as it did in England. Whereas English restrictive legislation on such imports culminated in the total prohibition of Indian calicoes in 1720, thirty years later Indian piece-goods imported in Dutch East Indiamen were still treated on a virtually equal footing with home 'fabrics, manufactures and national products' in Dutch customs tariffs. In both countries the value of Asian goods re-exported greatly exceeded the amount consumed by their respective home markets; but whereas the EIC was under constant pressure from wool-producers, clothiers and politicians, to try and sell English cloth in Asian markets, the directors of the VOC never had to make special efforts to dispose of Dutch manufactured goods in the same way.[17]

Another means whereby the rival Dutch and English East India Companies contributed to effect great and lasting changes in European social habits from about 1660 onwards, was in pushing the sales and encouraging the consumption of tea and coffee.

17. Cf. K. Glamann, *Dutch-Asiatic Trade, 1620-1740* (Copenhagen, 1958), pp. 132-51; J. Irwin's articles on 'The Indian textile trade in the 17th century' in the *Journal of Indian Textile History*, nos. 1-4, Ahmedabad, 1955-9); D. K. Bassett, 'Dutch trade in Asia' (*Journal of the South Seas Society*, Vol. XIV, Singapore, 1958, pp. 110-18).

The famous Amsterdam physician, Dr Nicholas Tulp, recommended tea as the sovereign remedy for virtually all ills. Even his enthusiasm for the allegedly medicinal virtues of this beverage was surpassed by that of his colleague, Dr Cornelis Decker, alias Bontekoe, who made his unfortunate patients drink anything from 50 to 200 cups of tea daily. Dr Bontekoe also published a *Treatise of the Excellent Herb Tea* ('Tractaat van het excellente cruyt thee') in 1679, which is said to have been heavily subsidized by the *Heeren* XVII. For some years tea remained a fashionable drink for the rich, since it was served with the best sugar, in Japanese porcelain cups on inlaid tables, and with golden teaspoons, but by the end of the century it was being sold with milk on the streets. Despite fierce competition from the English, French, Scandinavian and Ostend East India Companies, the Dutch continued to import tea on an ever-growing scale to satisfy both their own and the general European demand. The great boom in the Dutch tea-trade occurred between 1734 and 1785, when the total imports rose to 3,500,000 lb. a year in the course of a fourfold increase, tea having become the most valuable single commodity in the return cargoes of the Dutch East Indiamen since 1739.

Coffee was a later innovation in the European market than tea, but it was likewise touted as an unrivalled remedy for all ills by the egregious Dr Bontekoe. He prescribed its use as an infallible cure for 'scurvy, sore throat, colic, gout, billiousness, stinking breath, inflamed eyes' and goodness knows what else. This drink soon became very popular, despite the fact that in the Netherlands, as elsewhere, several physicians denounced both tea and coffee as harmful drugs. This viewpoint was shared by Dominie François Valentyn, who complained in 1724 that 'its use has become so common in our country that unless the maids and seamstresses have their coffee every morning, the thread will not go through the eye of the needle'. It is interesting to note that he blamed the English for introducing this pernicious habit of 'elevenses'. The increasing popularity of tea and coffee helped to curb drunkenness in the United Provinces to some extent, although 'brandy with sugar' remained the Dutch working-man's favourite drink when he could afford it. A century after

Tulp and Bontekoe propagated the virtues of tea and coffee, another Amsterdam physician wrote: 'The common man does drink a great deal of brandy and believes that he is strengthening his stomach thereby, but he is wrong, and would not be able to stand it for long if no tea were to be had.' [18]

It is perhaps unfair to couple doctors Tulp and Bontekoe together, for the former was certainly a more serious and competent physician; but their uncritical advocacy of tea as a panacea serves to remind us that medicine was still far from being an exact science in the Golden Century of the Dutch Republic – or in its 'Periwig Period' either, for that matter. In the 17th and 18th centuries the germ theory of disease and the cellular structure of the body were still unknown. Despite the importance of such scientific landmarks as the discovery of the circulation of the blood by William Harvey and that of red blood corpuscules and spermatozoa by the Dutch microscopist, Anthony van Leeuwenhoek, medical diagnosis and treatment was still largely influenced by the traditional Graeco–Roman humoral pathology, which considered all disease as an imbalance or an impurity of the four bodily 'humours', or fluids. Treatment aimed at readjusting the balance, predominantly by the use of enemas, purging, bleeding and dieting, but also by the employment of stimulants, tonics and drugs. Rigorously scientific biology was only made possible through the great development of the microscope in the 19th century, and effective pharmaceutical drugs date only from about 1880. Admittedly, religious prejudices against the dissection of human corpses for medical and anatomical lessons were not so strong in the Dutch Republic as they were in most other countries, and this helped the progress of both medicine and surgery. Anatomical lessons were often given in public, and Rembrandt was not the only one of the Old Masters

18. For the foregoing quotations cf. G. H. Betz, *Het Haagsche Leven in de tweede helft der Zeventiende eeuw* (The Hague, 1900), pp. 112–14; W. Ukers, *All About Tea* (2 vols., New York, 1935), Vol. I, pp. 28–35; Vol. II, pp. 108–9; O. F. Mentzel, *Description of the Cape*, Vol. III, pp. 256–7. For the coffee and tea trade of the VOC in general, cf. K. Glamann, *Dutch-Asiatic Trade, 1620–1740* (1958), pp. 183–243.

who painted such an occasion. Nevertheless, medical pharmacopoeiae contained so many useless or even noxious compounds, and surgery was still such a primitive science, that most of the startling cures which physicians and surgeons effected must have been due more to their patients' implicit trust in them than to anything else. Such was almost certainly the case with the celebrated Hermann Boerhaave (1669–1738), who held the chairs of medicine, botany and chemistry at Leiden, and whose reputation extended as far as China.

Here it may be noted that apart from Boerhaave, none of the great figures in the natural sciences and in philosophy during the time of the Dutch Republic were teachers in the universities. Simon Stevin, the mathematician and engineer who advocated the adoption of the decimal system; René Descartes, the French-born and bred philosopher who spent most of his working life in the United Provinces; Baruch Spinoza, the Amsterdam lens-grinder and metaphysical philosopher; Christian Huygens, the inventor of the pendulum clock and developer of the wave theory of light; Jan Swammerdam, the pioneer entomologist with the magnifying glass, and Anthony van Leeuwenhoek, the previously mentioned pioneer microscopist; all these men, and others who could be mentioned, did their scientific work outside the academic world, although naturally they had connections with it.

The importance of Descartes and Spinoza in the intellectual achievements of 17th-century philosophy is too well known to need more than a passing mention here. Apart from anything else, their writings helped gradually to undermine blind belief in religious orthodoxy and to foster the spirit of critical discussion, though not, perhaps, so much in the United Provinces where their works were published as outside them. The same may be said of the writings of the Huguenot refugee at Rotterdam, Pierre Bayle, whose widely read *Historical and Critical Dictionary* (1695–7) was infused with a spirit of shrewdly sceptical criticism which must have shaken the rigid religious convictions of many of his readers, whether they were Protestants or Roman Catholics. Bayle was also an outstanding advocate of tolerance, and he effectively contrasted the bigotry of Louis XIV in revoking the Edict of Nantes with K'ang-hsi's edict permitting the preaching of

Christianity in the Chinese Empire. Pierre Bayle lived and died as a Protestant Christian, but his work was largely responsible for the growth of scepticism and rationalism in the 18th century.

In the realm of science, Christian Huygens was undoubtedly the greatest genius produced by the Dutch Republic. His achievements have been admirably summarized by his English biographer, A. E. Bell: 'A man who transformed the telescope from being a toy into a powerful instrument of investigation, and this as a consequence of profound optical researches; who discovered Saturn's ring and the satellite Titan; who drew attention to the Nebula in Orion; who studied the problem of gravity in a quantitative manner, arriving at correct ideas about the effects of centrifugal force and the shape of the earth; who, in the great work *Horologium Oscillatorum*, founded the dynamics of systems and cleared up the whole subject of the compound pendulum and the tautochrom; who solved the outstanding problems concerned with collision of elastic bodies and out of much intractable work developed the general notion of energy and work; who is rightly regarded as the founder of the wave theory in light, and thus of physical optics – such a man deserves memory with the names of Galileo and Newton.'

Huygens started his scientific career as a warm admirer of Descartes, whose *Principia Philosophiae* of 1644 deeply impressed him in his adolescence. 'It seemed to me that when I read this book for the first time', he wrote many years later, 'that everything in the world became clearer, and I was sure that when I found some difficulty, that it was my fault that I did not understand his thought. I was then only fifteen or sixteen years old. But having discovered from time to time some things clearly false and others very improbable, I came back strongly to the preoccupation I was in, and at the present time I find scarcely anything I can accept as true in all the physics, metaphysics and meteors.' But he always acknowledged the imaginative stimulus given himself and others by Descartes, remarking in 1691: 'We owe much to Descartes because he revealed new paths in the study of Physics and started the idea that everything must be reduced to mechanical laws.' Nevertheless, as Bell points out, Huygens became convinced that Descartes had repeated the errors of Scholasticism in trying to found a demonstrative and deductive system which would replace it, and he himself, therefore, returned to the outlook of Galileo. Through Huygens, in fact, 'the main stream of scientific thought may be said to have been diverted from following Descartes and instead directed into the channel which Newton's work deepened into a river.'

It may be added that much of Huygens' best work was done at Paris between 1666 and 1681, under the patronage of Louis XIV, and that after his final return to Holland he lamented the absence of anyone there with whom he could discuss scientific topics. He was probably being unduly derogatory to his companions, for after all there were not many people in Western Europe besides Newton and Leibniz with whom he could have conversed on equal terms in this respect. But it is rather significant that his father Constantine, the poet and *bel esprit*, has always been more celebrated in the United Provinces than the son, despite the outstanding scientific achievements of the latter, which brought him lasting international renown.

The most famous scientist to work in the tropical possessions of the Dutch Republic, George Rumphius, 'the blind seer of Amboina', was a German who enlisted as a soldier in the service of the Dutch East India Company and worked as an official and administrator at Amboina in the Moluccas from 1653 until his death in 1702. He became fascinated by the fauna and flora of this island and devoted his life to collecting all the material he could about them, embodying the result of his experience and researches in massive folio manuscript volumes illustrated with drawings. He became blind; he lost his wife and youngest daughter in an earthquake; and a fire destroyed all the drawings of his work when it was nearly finished, but none of these disasters daunted him. He had new drawings made to replace those lost in the fire, and sent six volumes of the *Amboinese Herbal* to Holland in 1692. The ship was sunk by the French, but luckily his patron, the Governor-General at Batavia, Johannes Camphuis, had previously made a copy, which finally reached Holland four years later. It was published posthumously in six folio volumes in 1741–50, having been preceded by another posthumous work on the sea-shells, molluscs and crustaceans of the Moluccas in

1705. Rumphius's manuscript work on the fauna of Amboina has disappeared, but his published botanical and zoological works, together with what he wrote on Moluccan minerology, geology and palaeontology, are still of actual scientific importance and are consulted by specialists in those fields.

The title of Rumphius's *Amboinse Rariteitenkamer* ('Amboinese Cabinet of Curiosities') of 1705 reflected a fashion for collecting natural history specimens and other 'rarities' in 'curiosity cabinets' or private museums which many wealthy regents and merchants had attached to their town or country-houses. Minerals, sea-shells, stuffed birds, beasts and fishes, coins, medals and exotic bric-à-brac of all kinds found ardent if not always very discriminating devotees among those who had money to spend. Partly as a result of Rumphius's publication, Moluccan sea-shells were in high favour in the first half of the 18th century. Dominie Valentyn after his return to Holland founded a conchologists' club at Dordrecht, where he and several other repatriates from the East Indies spent pleasant winter evenings handling and discussing each other's collections. Rare plants and herbs were also much sought after, the most famous instance being the mania for tulip collecting which culminated in the great crash of 1637 – the collectors' equivalent of the South Sea Bubble.

Rumphius's botanical work in the Moluccas was paralleled by that of Baron van Reede tot Drakenstyn on the west coast of India. One of the very few patricians in the service of the East India Company, this Utrecht nobleman was an enthusiastic amateur botanist. He came out as an ensign to the East in 1657, and from 1661 to 1676 spent most of his time in Malabar, of which he was governor for seven years. Just as energetic as Rumphius, and with far more official authority and social prestige behind him, Van Rheede persuaded the Rajah of Cochin and other South Indian potentates to help him secure botanical specimens. He also organized an advisory committee of fifteen or sixteen learned Brahmins, and he made botanizing expeditions into the countryside accompanied by hundreds of coolies. The result of these field researches was published at his own expense in the lavishly illustrated *Hortus Malabaricus*, completed in twelve folio volumes between 1678 and 1703.

On the other side of the world, Count John Maurice of Nassau-Siegen, Governor-General of Netherlands Brazil in 1637–44, patronized and subsidized the work of two Leiden graduates, the German George Marcgraf and the Hollander Willem Piso, whose medical, botanical, zoological and astronomical researches were embodied in the folio *Historia Naturalis Brasiliae* (Leiden, 1648), and *De Indiae utriusque re naturali et medica* (Leiden, 1658). These books contained, *inter alia*, the first truly scientific study of the fauna and flora of Brazil, a description of the geography and meteorology of Pernambuco, including daily wind and rainfall records, astronomical observations in the southern hemisphere, and an ethnological survey of the local Amerindian races. The illustrations included 200 woodcuts of plants and 222 of animals, birds, insects and fishes, many of which had never been described before. These two works remained the most authoritative studies on the natural history of Brazil until they were replaced by the scientific publications of Maximilian Prince of Wied-Neuwied in the years 1820–50. Mention has already been made of the books on America compiled by the scholarly director of the Amsterdam Chamber of the West India Company, Johannes de Laet, between 1625 and 1644 (p. 182). De Laet was more of an editor and a compiler than an original author; but original scientific work comparable with that of Rumphius in Amboina was done in Surinam by a pious Dutch blue-stocking, Maria Sibylla Merian, whose beautifully illustrated *Metamorphosis insectorum Surinamensium* (1705) is one of the finest books that has ever come from a printing-press.[19]

Many other instances could be given to show that the Governor-General and Council at Batavia in 1785 were exaggerating when they wrote that their countrymen in the East invariably preferred to sacrifice to Mercury rather than to Pallas. No doubt most of them did so, as was to be expected of the

19. For a succinct survey of Dutch scientific achievements in the seventeenth century, see D. J. Struik, *Het Land van Stevin en Huygens* (Amsterdam, 1958). The quotations from and about Christian Huygens are taken from A. E. Bell, *Christian Huygens and the Development of Science in the Seventeenth Century* (London, 1947), pp. 5, 205, 210.

employees of any commercial company in the circumstances, and as was equally true of their French and English competitors. But there were always some exceptions; and just as we find the historian Orme, the philologist Marsden, and the Sanskritist Sir William Jones among the jolly topers of John Company, so we find Rumphius, Valentyn and Isaac Titsingh sacrificing to Pallas while not forgetting Mercury – or, for that matter, Bacchus. It is true that Nicholas Witsen, the erudite Amsterdam burgo-master and director of the VOC, who wrote a standard work on ship-building and another (*Noord en Oost Tartarye*, 1692), on Siberia, frequently complained in his correspondence that his countrymen in Asia were interested in money-making to the exclusion of everything else.[20] Yet Witsen was writing these com-plaints at a period when there were more of the Company's em-ployees (or ex-employees) who were taking an intelligent interest in the Asian cultural scene than at any other time. Daniel Havart was publishing his account of the *Rise and Fall of Coromandel* (1693), and his prose translation (1688) of a Persian epic poem, the *Bustán* of Sheikh Sa'di; Herbert de Jager was discovering the relationship between Old Javanese, Sanskrit and Tamil; Engelbert Kaempfer was compiling his classic account of Japan, which re-mained the best European description of the island-empire down to the publication of Von Siebold's *Nippon* (1832–52); Rumphius and Van Rheede were writing or publishing their previously mentioned zoological and botanical works; Valentyn was com-piling his encyclopedic *Old and New East-India*; and there was even a small literary society, the self-styled 'Knightly Order of the Suum Cuique', existing for a few years (1706–12?) at Bat-avia.[21]

If we turn to those Dutchmen who stayed in the Low Lands by the North Sea during the Golden Century, it is a similar story. Typical of those foreigners who denounced the Dutch as dollar-grinders pure and simple, was René Descartes, who should

20. J. F. Gebhard, *Leven van Mr Nicholas Witsen* (2 vols., Utrecht, 1882), Vol. I, pp. 480–81.

21. For the poetical effusions of the 'Ridder-Orde van Suum Cuique' see E. Du Perron, *De Muze van Jan Companjie, 1600–1780* (Bandoeng, 1948), pp. 136–44.

have known better but who wrote from Amsterdam: 'In this great town, where apart from myself there dwells no one who is not engaged in trade, everyone is so much out for his own advantage that I should be able to live my whole life here without ever meeting a mortal being.' The absurdity of this sweeping judgement is apparent when we recall that among Descartes' contemporaries in Amsterdam were the painter Rembrandt, the poet Vondel and the classical scholar Caspar Barlaeus. Descartes' Huguenot contemporary, Jean Parival, who had lived for thirty-six years in the United Provinces when he published his *Les Delices de la Hollande* (Leiden, 1662), was more charitable and more accurate when he quoted 'ce grand Poëte Barlaeus' and the richly stocked libraries of Amsterdam as proof that the wealthy merchants and burghers of that town had not neglected to foster learning and letters in their ardent pursuit of trade and commerce. John Locke was first induced to publish some of his works by the sympathetic and appreciative reception he met with in scholarly circles when a political refugee at Amsterdam in 1683–8. Nevertheless, many foreign visitors continued to stigmatize the Dutch regent class as exclusively composed of profit-seeking merchants at a time when, as Sir William Temple pointed out, most of them were well educated gentlemen who had been trained for public office from their youth up, and were no longer 'men of mean or mechanical trades, as is commonly received among foreigners, and makes the subject of comical jests upon their government'. Far from being entirely a nation of Philistines, the land of Rembrandt, Vondel and Huygens contained votaries of Pallas as well as of Mercury; and if the former were a relatively small minority, this was equally true of any other age or nation.

A more relevant criticism of the regent oligarchs who formed the ruling class is that as they became a more exclusive class – one might almost term them a caste in some respects – they became more saturated with French culture, often to the virtual exclusion of their own. French cultural influences had always been strong, and the Stadtholder's court at The Hague was a gallicized one in the days of Prince Frederick Henry. Nevertheless, the culture and civilization of the Land of Rembrandt were essentially Dutch. Painting, literature, music and architecture all bear witness to this down to the last quarter of the 17th century. Thereafter, foreign influences, especially French, gain ground among the regent oligarchs and the wealthy burghers at the expense of the Dutch. By the second half of the 18th century the gallicization of the 'ruling few' and those who imitated their way of life was almost complete. Parents corresponded with their children in French, and many people made a point of never reading Dutch literature. The Utrecht blue-stocking who was Boswell's *amorata*, Elisabeth van Tuyll van Serooskerken, alias Belle de Zuylen, of whom he wrote that 'she has nothing Dutch about her but the name', forms a typical and striking contrast with the blue-stockings of the Muiden-circle, Anna and Maria Roemers Visscher, who knew no French.

During the 18th century the northern Netherlands became the chief publishing centre for the European 'Enlightenment'. Bayle, Locke, Hume, Montesquieu, Voltaire, Rousseau and Raynal were all published in numerous editions printed in the United Provinces, often to avoid the French censorship – though not all of the works which bore a Dutch imprint were printed there, since some were clandestinely published in France. But if the works of the rationalist philosophers were widely read and circulated in the Dutch Republic, it did not follow that their ideas were gladly accepted by the 'libertine' regent-oligarchs, still less by the fundamentalist *predikanten*. Both Rousseau's *Contrat Social* and Voltaire's *Essai sur la Tolérance* were officially banned at the request of the Dutch Reformed Church, though this ban was admittedly ineffectual. The new ideas found greater acceptance among the members of the upper middle class who were disgruntled by their exclusion from municipal office, and among the middling classes who read the Dutch *Spectator*-type periodicals. Many of these magazines, though intended exclusively for Dutch readers, were published in French. Yet these ideas had not gained sufficient currency to be an important factor in the pro-American attitude of many Dutchmen in 1780, which was due far more to their long-standing commercial rivalry with England. Thereafter the intellectual ferment increased rapidly, partly as a result of the traumatic shock of this disastrous war

(1780–84), as it did over a century later among Spanish intellectuals of the 'generation of '98' after the Spanish–American War. The cultural gallicization of the regent-oligarchs may also have helped to widen the gap between them and the lower orders whom they so heartily despised, and thus contributed to the ignominious collapse of the ruling class in 1795

English writings and ideas in philosophy, theology and natural science likewise made considerable headway among the better educated classes in the Dutch Republic, mainly through the medium of French translations printed there and through the extensive reviews and notices of English books published in the periodical press. A leading figure in the dissemination of English cultural influences was Justus van Effen (1684–1735), who was a great admirer of Addison and Steele, and whose *Hollandsche Spectator* of 1731–5 was confessedly modelled on its English forerunner and namesake. During the second half of the eighteenth century the works of Samuel Richardson and Laurence Sterne became very popular with Dutch readers, and at one time there were even 'Sterne Clubs', whose members called each other by the names of characters in Sterne's writings. But English literary influences always remained secondary to French. So ardent an Anglophile as Justus van Effen published the greater part of his work in French-language periodicals, and not in his native tongue, despite his declared intention of weaning his educated compatriots from their excessive gallicization and fostering the development of a pure Dutch prose style.[23]

23. C. Serrurier, *Pierre Bayle en Hollande. Étude historique et critique* (Lausanne, 1912); W. J. B. Pienaar, *English Influences in Dutch Literature and Justus van Effen as Intermediary. An aspect of 18th century achievement* (Cambridge, 1929); C. Wilson, *Holland and Britain*, pp. 58–66.

7
Fort and factory

In an article published forty years ago, stressing the importance of Dutch sources for 17th-century Indian history, W. H. Moreland observed: 'We see that the facts of the 17th century lead us from the region of commerce to that of politics. The earlier stages in this journey are the trading voyage, the factory, the fort and the beginnings of territorial acquisition; to understand any one of these stages, we must understand those which went before, and it so happens that both Fort and Factory were due to Dutch initiative. To understand the genesis of factories, it is necessary to study the early Dutch voyages, and ... the Fort, like the Factory, is definitely Dutch.'[1]

This is a surprising instance of Homer nodding, for the European fort and factory in Asia were both of Portuguese origin, as they were, for that matter, in Africa. Their purpose was succinctly explained by a Portuguese Governor who told the Queen of Quilon, in 1519, that the King of Portugal did not build fortresses in India to conquer territory, but merely to protect his merchandise on the sea-shore. The Dutch *factorijen* and the English 'factories', whether fortified or not, were directly descended from the Portuguese trading agencies, or *feitorias*, which were scattered along the African and Asian shores, beginning with the castle erected at Arguim on the Moroccan coast (1445) and ending with the *feitoria* established at Nagasaki (1570). These Portuguese *feitorias*, in their turn, stemmed from and had much in common with the medieval *fondachi*, the residential quarters of Genoese, Venetian and other Italian merchants in the Muslim sea-ports of North Africa and in Ottoman harbours.

The unfortified European 'factory' in Asia – whether Portuguese, Dutch or English – was not, of course, a novelty or an

1. W. H. Moreland, 'Dutch sources for Indian History from 1590 to 1650', *Journal of Indian History*, Vol. II, part 2, May 1923, pp. 223–4.

innovation in so far as Asian rulers and potentates were concerned. Since time out of mind, in many Oriental trading-ports
from the Persian Gulf to the South China Sea, the foreign traders
lived in separate residential districts, each under the administration and to some extent the jurisdiction of its own headman,
and enjoying a greater or lesser degree of what is nowadays
known as extra-territoriality. Such, for example, was the case
with the Arab trading-communities in Canton and Zaiton
(Ch'uan-chou) in Marco Polo's day; with the Tamils, the Gujer-
atis and the Javanese traders in medieval Malacca; with the
Indians, Arabs and Chinese at Bantam, when the Dutch first
arrived there. Nevertheless, though the merchants and officials
of these more or less autonomous residential quarters often
attained great wealth and influence locally, they were still completely at the mercy of the ruler (or of the governors), who could
take their daughters for his harem and seize a foreign merchant's
estate and household on his death. They were also sometimes
exposed to the unreasonable exactions of local high officials, and
to the malice of native trade rivals or even of the mob. Though
the system worked well enough in most countries over the
centuries, and though the Europeans accommodated themselves
to it in powerful empires like China and Japan where they had
no alternative, elsewhere the Portuguese introduced the precedents of the fortified factory and the fortified town for the
greater security of their persons and their merchandise in an
actual or potential hostile environment.[2]

The Dutch very quickly followed the Portuguese precedents
and for the same reasons. Not only were they apt to feel insecure
in an Asian environment which they did not understand, and
among peoples whose languages few of them could speak and
whose religions they regarded with horror or contempt, but they
needed – or thought they needed – some ports where their
persons and their goods would not be liable to arbitrary seizure,
and where they could provision and repair their ships in com-

2. Cf. M. A. P. Meilink-Roelofsz, *Asian Trade and European Influence in the Indonesian Archipelago, 1500–1630* (The Hague, 1962),
passim; C. R. Boxer, *Four Centuries of Portuguese Expansion, 1415–
1825: A succinct survey* (Johannesburg, 1961).

plete security. From about 1605 onwards they were determined to enforce a spice-monopoly in the Moluccas – and later a pepper-monopoly elsewhere – and this alone involved the possession of naval and military bases. Furthermore, they soon felt the need of a 'general rendezvous' where their homeward- and outward-bound fleets could load and unload their cargoes, and where goods from the interport trade of Asia could be collected, stored or transhipped. The forts which they had taken from the Portuguese in the Spice Islands were too remotely situated for this purpose, and they realized that their 'general rendezvous' would have to be found somewhere in the region of the Straits of Malacca or the Straits of Sunda, where the trade-routes and the monsoon-winds converged. Having narrowly failed to wrest Malacca from the Portuguese in 1606, they cast their eyes upon the little Javanese port of Jakarta. Jan Pieterszoon Coen forcibly seized it on 30 May 1619, in direct defiance both of the Sultan of Bantam, who regarded the place as a feudal benefice, and of the *Heeren* XVII at home, who had emphasized that the projected 'general rendezvous' should be secured by peaceful negotiations and not by force of arms.

Coen wrote of his conquest in exultant and enthusiastic terms, reminiscent of those used by Affonso de Albuquerque more than a century earlier after his conquest of Goa and Malacca. 'All the kings of these lands know full well what the planting of our colony at Jakarta signifies, and what may follow from it, as well as the cleverest and most far-seeing politician in Europe might do.' They did indeed. It was precisely for this reason that the old ruler of Cheribon gave the name of 'New Malacca' to the castle and fortified town of Batavia which the Dutch built on the ruins of Jakarta. Not only the Sultan of Bantam but all the other Javanese rulers had hitherto refused to let the Dutch build a stone castle or fortified factory in any of their ports, for fear lest the Netherlanders should follow the Portuguese precedent of gradually absorbing the territory which surrounded their fortified towns. Their fears were fully justified. Within a year of the seizure of Jakarta, Coen laid claim to the 'kingdom' of that name, whose boundaries he thus described in defiance of historical truth and the actual situation: Bantam on the west; Cheribon on the east; the offshore islands on the north; and the Indian Ocean on the south. This claim remained a paper one for a long time, since the highland districts of Preanger were effectively administered only in the 18th century; but in the eyes of contemporary Asian rulers and peoples the occupation of Jakarta gave the Dutch in Indonesia a position comparable to that of the Portuguese at Goa. As Albuquerque had written to his king after the final conquest of Goa: 'The peoples of India now realize that we have come to settle permanently in this land, for they see us planting trees, building houses of stone and lime and breeding sons and daughters.' [3]

Admittedly, Coen was a conscious empire-builder, like Albuquerque, Dupleix and Clive; and neither his masters, the *Heeren* XVII – though they gave their belated approval to his conquest of Jakarta – nor many of his successors had any intention of transforming the Dutch East India Company from a purely commercial concern into a largely territorial power. But such a transformation was sooner or later inevitable. The Dutch had become involved in Javanese power politics at a time when the inland kingdom of Mataram was striving to obtain not merely the hegemony of Java but the acknowledgement of its paramountcy over the whole of the Indonesian archipelago, just as its Hindu predecessor of Majapahit had claimed several centuries previously. Moreover, we have already seen (p. 108) that, although the *Heeren* XVII at Amsterdam and Middelburg gave only reluctant and belated approval – when they gave it at all – to any interference in purely Javanese affairs by their governor-general at Batavia, Coen (like Rijkloff van Goens and Speelman after him) was perfectly prepared to present the directors with a *fait accompli*.

One reason why the Dutch made no effort for a long time to follow up Coen's paper annexation of the whole 'kingdom' of Jakarta and to extend their rule far inland was that they greatly

3. *Cartas de Affonso de Albuquerque* (ed. Bulhão Pato, 7 vols., Lisboa, 1884–1935), Vol. I, p. 338. For Coen's report on the capture of Jakarta and his claims to that 'kingdom', cf. J. A. Van der Chijs, *De Nederlanders te Jakarta* (Amsterdam, 1860), and F. de Haan, *Oud Batavia* (2 vols., Batavia, 1922), Vol. I, pp. 19–45.

overestimated the internal strength and cohesion of the empire of Mataram. This agrarian realm, which had achieved the over-lordship of East and Central Java by 1645, was important to the Company as a principal source of supply for the rice consumed in Batavia and the Moluccas. In Mataram, as in the other Javanese sultanates, society could be divided into four main categories. Most numerous were the dark-skinned peasantry who tilled the land, and who were treated very haughtily by the lighter-coloured aristocracy and officialdom which lived on the fruit of their labour. This aristocracy was a numerous one, ranging as it did from petty officials to princes of the blood, with polygamous households as the general rule. Aside and apart from the peasantry and aristocracy were the Muslim spiritual leaders, scribes, scholars and holy men, who were apt to be stigmatized by the Dutch as *papen ende ander gespuys* ('popes and other scum'). They were scattered throughout the island and en-deavoured to strengthen the hold of Islam on the still largely superficially Islamized mass of the people. The fourth class or group of Javanese society was represented by the merchants, craftsmen and artisans, about whom we have very little infor-mation, but who must have been fairly numerous in the harbour-towns, and much less so in the villages of the agrarian interior.[4]

The empire of Mataram was an Oriental despotism of the traditional kind, where the Sultan or Susuhunan (as he was usually titled) was an absolute monarch in theory and in prac-tice. He was not interested in trade and commerce, nor in the economic welfare of his subjects, but in maintaining his own position at home and in securing acknowledgement of his para-mountcy over other regions of Indonesia. The peasantry lived on the products of the soil, and the aristocracy on the taxes levied in kind and on the forced labour of their subordinates. The

4. For 17th-century Mataram and its relations with the Dutch cf. H. J. de Graaf (ed.), *De vijf gezantschapsreizen van Rijkloff van Goens naar het hof van Mataram 1648-1654* (The Hague, 1956); Ibidem, *De regering van Sultan Agung Vorst van Mataram en die van zijn voorganger, 1601-1645* (The Hague, 1958); B. Schrieke, *Indonesian sociological studies* (2 vols., The Hague, 1955-7), especially Vol I, pp. 1-82, Vol. II, pp. 97-283.

monarch's income was likewise derived from taxation in kind and from labour-service, supplemented by the receipts from toll-stations established at road and river crossings, and by tributary presents from foreign envoys. There was no mint in Mataram,

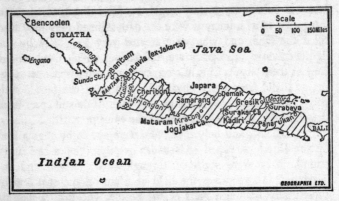

5 Java and the Empire of Mataram, *c.* 1650

and the economy was almost entirely a barter one. The coinage in circulation (mainly Chinese copper cash and Spanish rials) was used for the purchase of weapons, jewellery and the more costly foreign goods such as fine Indian textiles and Chinese porcelain. When Rijkloff van Goens, who was four times envoy to the Susuhunan's court between 1648 and 1654, once suggested that His Majesty might encourage the overseas trade of his vassals in the coastal regions so that they could become richer and able to pay higher taxes, Amangkurat I replied: 'My people, unlike yours, have nothing which they can call their own, but everything of theirs belongs to me; and if I did not rule them harshly, I would not be king for a day longer.'

Though an absolute monarch, the Susuhunan usually exercised his power through a small number of senior officials of varying influence, now one group and then another coming to the fore, depending on their respective personalities and the arbitrary whims of the ruler. The most important regions were originally placed under the closest relatives of the royal family, but Amangkurat I in the last years of his reign became a half-insane tyrant like Ivan the Terrible, and systematically exterminated most of the old nobility. He replaced them with officials whose posts he changed frequently in order to prevent continuous plotting against him. He gave public audience in the courtyard of his *kraton* or palace twice weekly, when he dispensed justice with great pomp and ceremony, ordering the summary execution of anyone who had incurred his wrath. Military service in Mataram was soccage service, the armies consisting almost entirely of able-bodied villagers called to arms for any given expedition, though there was a permanent royal bodyguard at the *kraton*. Rijkloff van Goens alleged in 1656 that the Susuhunan had nearly a million fighting men on the regional muster-rolls. This was certainly a great exaggeration, though the army of 17th-century Mataram was larger than any of the European armies which fought in the Thirty Years War. Spears, pikes, swords and *krisses* were their principal weapons; for although the Javanese had some cannon and firearms, they were not skilled in the use of them.

Sultan Agung had extended the hegemony of Mataram over the whole of Java by the time of his death in 1645, with the exception of the immediate hinterland of Batavia and the Sultanate of Bantam in the western corner of the island. The power of Mataram naturally impressed the relatively few Dutch envoys who visited the royal *kraton*, or those Dutchmen who were detained there as prisoners between 1632 and 1651; but the seeds of decay were inherent in the character of this Muslim empire, as they had been in that of its Hindu predecessor, Majapahit. The system of communications was very bad, the roads being remarkably few, and unusable during the rainy season. The rivers in the heartland of Mataram all flowed southwards into the Indian Ocean, where there were no harbours and where the frail indigenous *praus* seldom navigated at this period. There was an active riverborne traffic along those other Javanese rivers which flowed northward into the Java Sea, but most of these could be used only at certain seasons of the year, and even then the small craft might take as many weeks to go upstream as days to go down. The main regions were geographically isolated from each other by mountain ranges, and until the 19th century there were no technological developments to overcome these natural obstacles. The coastal sultanates of the north and east, which had been conquered by Mataram between 1613 and 1645, were largely devastated in the process, and their peoples were actually or potentially disaffected. Finally, despite the Susuhunan's readiness to kill, banish or remove any of the regional governors whom he suspected of disaffection, those in the outlying districts inevitably tried to obtain or to regain their independence, as Rijkloff van Goens noted in 1680: 'The Javanese regents, especially those far away and in the highlands, appear to wish to be independent rulers, each pretending he can carry on and maintain himself.'

The attempt of Amangkurat I to prevent the inevitable process of disintegration by a policy of 'frightfulness' applied indiscriminately to princes of the blood, landed nobility and government officials, only sharpened discontent with his rule. When a Madurese prince named Trunajaya raised the standard of rebellion against the Susuhunan, he received widespread support. Amangkurat I was forced to flee from his *kraton* and died on his way to the coast, after appealing to the Dutch East India Company to intervene on his behalf in 1677. Thanks to the forceful intervention of Speelman and Van Goens, the Dutch did restore the late Susuhunan's heir to the throne of Mataram, after considerable fighting and against much opposition. But they exacted a stiff price in territorial concessions and commercial privileges for their armed support, and henceforth the relations between the Dutch and Mataram were on an entirely different footing. Whereas in the period 1646–77 the Dutch had acknowledged the Susuhunan's claim to the overlordship of Java to the extent that they periodically sent embassies laden with costly presents to his *kraton* – much as they did to the Shogun of Tokugawa Japan at Yedo – from 1677 onwards the Susuhunan addressed the Governor-General at Batavia as 'protector', 'father' and eventually 'grandfather'. Moreover, the Dutch intervention of 1677 only postponed the inevitable disintegration of the loosely knit empire of Mataram. The jealousy of various pretenders to the throne, and revolts of vassals against the weakened central authority in the 18th century, led to a renewal of the succession disputes, which culminated in the partitioning of the realm and the creation of the two states of Surakarta and Jogjakarta in 1755. By this time the Company had extended its hegemony over the whole island and reduced all the Javanese sultanates to the position of client or vassal states.[5]

It must be emphasized that although the Dutch East India Company became a territorial power in Java, Ceylon and the Moluccas, it always remained an alien body on the fringe of Asian society, even in the regions which it administered directly. This was, of course, still more so in countries like China and Japan, where the Dutch only had simple trading-agencies, and even in southern India, where they at one time exercised jurisdiction over some of the districts and peoples in the immediate vicinity of their forts and factories. Asian society, whether Indonesian, Chinese, Japanese, Indian, Persian or Malay, had no wish whatever to be changed by European contacts in the 17th and 18th centuries, but wished only to retain its traditional and static forms. Some changes did, of course, take place through European pressure and influence, such as the conversion of most of the inhabitants of the Philippines to Christianity as a result of the Spanish conquest of those islands. But the basic social, economic and religious factors which determined the structure of Asian society remained unchanged until the 19th and in many instances until the 20th century, when the repercussions of the Industrial, the French and the Russian Revolutions successively made themselves felt.

If the structure of Asian society was basically unaffected by the activities of the Dutch East India Company and its European contemporaries and competitors, the impact of 17th-century European merchant-capitalism and high-seas navigation did modify the patterns of Asian trade and industry in some instances. The Portuguese had discovered and exploited the sea-route from Europe round the Cape of Good Hope; but on reaching south-east

5. B. Vlekke, *Nusantara. A History of the East Indian Archipelago* (Cambridge, Mass., 1945), pp. 146–63, 201–13, provides an excellent account of the downfall of the Indonesian states and the Dutch conquest of Java.

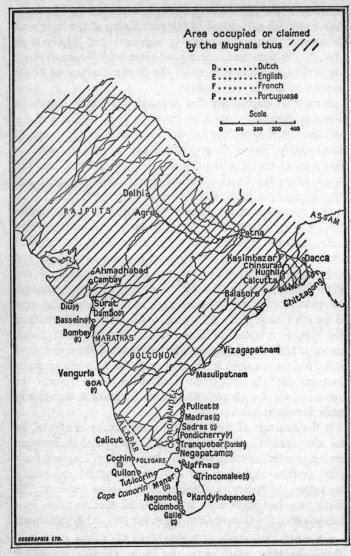

Area occupied or claimed
by the Mughals thus ⁄⁄⁄

D........Dutch
E........English
F........French
P........Portuguese

Scale

0   100   200   300   400

RAJPUTS

Delhi

Agra

ASSAM

Patna

Kasimbazar   Dacca
Chinsura
Hughli
Ahmadhabad   Calcutta
Cambay   Balasore   Chittagong

Diu(P)   Surat
Damão(P)
Bassein(P)
Bombay
(E)   MARATHAS

GOLCONDA   Vizagapatnam

Vengurla   Masulipatnam

GOA
(P)

Pulicat(D)
Madras(E)
Sadras(D)
Pondicherry(F)
Calicut   Tranquebar(Danish)
Negapatam(D)
Cochin POLYGARS   Jaffna(D)
Quilon
Tuticorin   Trincomalee(D)
Cape Comorin Manar
(D)
Negombo   Kandy(Independent)
Colombo
Galle
(D)

MALABAR

COROMANDEL

6   The Mughal Empire and European forts and factories in India
and Ceylon, c. 1700

Africa they followed the old-established maritime and monsoon trade routes frequented by their Muslim predecessors from Sofala to Canton. The regular trans-Pacific route of the Spanish Manila Galleon between Mexico and the Philippines, inaugurated in 1564–5, was something quite new; and this led to the exchange of American silver for Chinese silks for a period of nearly three centuries. The rigid enforcement of the Moluccan spice-monopoly by the Dutch, which was an accomplished fact by the end of the 17th century, was an innovation which adversely affected the inhabitants of those islands and the seafaring communities of Indonesia as a whole. The prosperity of the Javanese coastal states was likewise undermined through their conquest by Mataram, an agrarian Sultanate which had no inclination to foster overseas trade after the fall of its ally, Portuguese Malacca, to the Dutch in 1641. Whereas the Javanese had at one period voyaged as far as Madagascar, which they had partly colonized in the Middle Ages, and whereas their fleets had seriously threatened Malacca at intervals during the 16th century, Javanese sea-power was a thing of the past by 1700. Speelman had already noted in 1677 that 'the eastern Javanese of Mataram, besides their great ignorance at sea, were now completely lacking in vessels of their own, even for necessary use'. Bantam was trying with considerable success to develop an indigenous ocean-going merchant marine at this period, but the Dutch conquest of that Sultanate in 1682–4 put an end to the development.[6]

Outside Indonesian waters the Dutch could not establish a monopoly of seaborne trade in any region, nor did they seriously attempt to do so after the failure of Coen's policy of 'frightfulness' against Chinese junks trading with Spanish Manila. They did try occasionally to bring pressure to bear on Indian rulers with whom they had trade disputes, by seizing their shipping or otherwise interfering with their seaborne trade, as the Portuguese had done in the 16th century. These efforts achieved no lasting success, since the Dutch had no strong base in India, such as the Portu-

6. Cf. B. Schrieke, *Indonesian Sociological Studies*, Vol. I, pp. 49–79; M. A. P. Meilink-Roelofszoon, *Asian Trade and European Influence in the Indonesian Archipelago, 1500–1630*, pp. 269–94.

guese possessed in Goa. The Dutch factories on the coasts of Malabar and Coromandel, whether fortified or not, were liable to the risk of reprisals by powerful Indian rulers whose inland capitals were not exposed to Dutch sea-power as were those of the coastal sultanates in Indonesia. Only in Ceylon did their policy of blockading the coast achieve a high degree of success, since they were here able to cut off the highland kingdom of Kandy from access to the sea. In Coromandel, the flow of Dutch capital into the country, for the purchase of textiles needed in Indonesia, actually stimulated some of the richer Indian merchants (and officials who acted as merchants) to participate in the overseas trade themselves. Indian shipping, which about the year 1600 was confined to the region of the Bay of Bengal and the Malay peninsula, had extended its operations to Java, Borneo, the Celebes and the Philippines by the end of the 17th century. The Dutch, in competition with the English, also provided the impetus for a great increase in the manufacture and production of Indian textiles, which now found a market not only in Asia and East Africa but in West Africa, Europe and even America. The increased volume of production was not, however, accompanied by any significant changes in the techniques of manufacture.[7]

One innovation which the Dutch introduced in the navigation of the Indian Ocean was the use of the 'roaring forties' route by their outward-bound East Indiamen. This ocean passage was discovered by Hendrik Brouwer in 1611 and officially authorized by the *Heeren* XVII six years later. After passing (or leaving) the Cape of Good Hope, the Indiamen steered due east between 36° and 42° southern latitude until they reached the region of the south-east trade winds, when they set a northerly course for the straits of Sunda. Once the Dutch position in the East had been firmly established by their capture of Jakarta and its transformation into a shipping entrepôt and general headquarters under the name of Batavia, the outward-bound Indiamen usually left their

7. T. Raychaudhuri, *Jan Company in Coromandel, 1605–1690. A study in the interrelations of European commerce and traditional economies* (The Hague, 1962).

home-ports in three successive fleets. The *Kermis* (fun-fair) fleet, which sailed in September; the Christmas fleet, which left in December or January; and the Easter fleet, which sailed in April or May. Of these three fleets, the *Kermis* fleet was the most important, as if it reached Batavia in March or April there was time to tranship the cargoes for the most valuable Asian markets – Japan, China, the Bay of Bengal region and the Persian Gulf – without having to wait for the next south-west monsoon. Homeward-bound Indiamen usually left Batavia in two fleets. The first cleared the straights of Sunda just about the year's end; and the second followed a month or two later, after the cargoes from the Bay of Bengal, China and Japan had arrived with the north-east monsoon. After 1652 both outward- and homeward-bound fleets usually called at the Cape. The duration of the voyage in either direction was normally something between five and a half and seven months, longer voyages being by no means uncommon, but shorter ones very unusual.

Nicholas de Graaff, writing at the high tide of the Dutch East India Company's power and prosperity, tells us that the voyages from Batavia to Japan, China, Bengal, Coromandel and Surat were the most profitable and popular among merchants and mariners alike. A little money went a long way in those favoured regions, where everything was plentiful and cheap, and where contraband or 'private' trade flourished exceedingly. This contrasted strongly with conditions in the Moluccas, where the profits of the spice-trade were strictly reserved to the Company and where provisions were few and dear. Mortality was high in the forts and factories of the Moluccas, and consequently service there was unpopular. All the more so, since the authorities preferred to leave there indefinitely those men who had become acclimatized, rather than relieve them by newcomers who would probably soon die.

We have seen that the Company was able to enforce its spice-monopoly in the Moluccas and in Ceylon only with great difficulty, and that elsewhere it had to reckon with active European and/or Asian competition. For example, even after the capture of the chief pepper-producing regions of Malabar from the Portuguese in 1661–3, and after the subjugation of the pepper-trading sultanate of Bantam in 1684, the Dutch still met with keen English competition on the west coast of India and in Sumatra. The plans periodically made by the *Heeren* XVII to monopolize the pepper-market in Europe could never be implemented; and in 1736 the EIC was importing as much pepper to London as the VOC at Batavia was receiving from the entire Malay–Indonesian archipelago. Chinese merchants were likewise very active in the Sumatran pepper-trade throughout the 17th century, and it was a Chinese 'interloper' who prevented the Dutch from achieving a pepper-monopoly in Borneo during the 1730s.[8]

Although the *Heeren* XVII certainly tried to buy cheap and to sell dear where and when they could, this was not always possible or desirable, even with their Moluccan spice-monopoly. As the Court of directors wrote to Batavia in 1673, cloves 'were [formerly] used by the Company for annual dividend payments in place of money, and they have therefore dropped to a low price, but consumption has thereby increased and their use spread throughout the whole of Europe'. Four years later, the *Heeren* XVII were able to fix the European selling-price of cloves at 75 stuivers per lb., and nutmegs were fixed at the same level from the beginning of the 18th century. The directors were able to maintain these prices till 1744, and though prices subsequently fluctuated slightly, the Company succeeded in maintaining an effective monopoly of the Moluccan spices down to the eve of its dissolution. When the warehouses in the Netherlands became full to overflowing, 1,250,000 lb. of surplus nutmegs were destroyed in 1735, just as surplus coffee was burnt in Brazil two centuries later.

The Dutch East India Company, like its English rival, was founded primarily to trade in pepper and spices, and these two commodities formed by far the most valuable part of its homeward cargoes for the first half of the 17th century. But the European demand for Indian textiles and cotton piece-goods, as also

8. K. Glamann, *Dutch-Asiatic Trade, 1620–1740* (Copenhagen, 1958); J. Bastin, *The Changing Balance of the Early Southeast Asian Pepper Trade* (Kuala Lumpur, 1960); D. K. Bassett, 'Dutch trade in Asia' in *The Journal of the South Seas Society*, Vol. XIV (Singapore, 1958), pp. 110–18.

for Chinese, Bengal and Persian silks and silk-stuffs, led to these goods taking priority over pepper and spices, both in purchases and sales, by the year 1700. The 18th century saw the phenomenal growth of the tea and coffee trades, these stimulants becoming more important than the textile group, while the relative value of pepper and spices declined still further. The *Heeren* XVII entered the China tea trade rather late, and the bid they made to dominate this trade by instituting direct sailings between the Netherlands and Canton in the years 1729–34 failed of its purpose. They then reverted to their former practice of shipping the tea *via* Batavia, but they long retained their position as runners-up to the English. The large-scale cultivation of coffee and sugar in Java became increasingly important during the 18th century. In 1721, 90 per cent of the coffee imported into Europe by the V O C still came from Mocha, and only 10 per cent from Java; but five years later the ratio was the exact opposite. By 1780, Javanese sugar and coffee were almost as important for the Dutch East India Company as these products became for the Kingdom of the Netherlands in the next century under the 'culture system' of Van den Bosch.

The requirements of the European market had to be balanced against those of the interport trade in Asia, and this naturally caused a good deal of fluctuation in supply and demand. On a very rough calculation, about two-thirds of the spice production was shipped to Europe, and one-third was marketed east of Suez, where Surat was for a long time the most important factory for the disposal of cloves. Coen's dream of financing the whole of the Company's export trade with Europe from the profits of his projected monopoly of the interport-trade in Asia was never realized; but the *Heeren* XVII always tried to secure as much bullion as they could from Asian countries, so as to reduce their shipments of precious metals from Europe. Down to 1668 the supply of silver from Japan gave the Dutch a great advantage over their English competitors, since they were not so dependent as the latter on supplies of European and Spanish–American silver. When the Japanese government prohibited the export of silver in that year, the V O C turned its attention to Japanese gold, which could be profitably disposed of on the Coromandel coast. The Japanese gold-boom did not last long, being replaced in the 1670s by copper as 'the bride for whom we dance' in Governor-General Van Imhoff's metaphor of 1745. Japanese copper continued to be the mainstay of the Batavia–Nagasaki trade for almost a century, until Swedish copper began to infiltrate increasingly into the Asian market after 1770.

The *Heeren* XVII toyed at intervals with various impracticable plans for securing a monopoly of Chinese and Persian silks, but they never succeeded in cornering the market in either. In 1636, the third great silk-producing area, Bengal, comes into the picture, and by the end of the century the Bengal silk-trade surpassed that of Persia and China. English competition became steadily more dangerous to the VOC in this region, and by 1740 the English in Bengal had quite out-distanced their rivals. It was a similar story with the Indian textile trade in Coromandel. Cotton piece-goods from this region and from Gujerat were rightly described in 1612 as being the 'left arm' of the Dutch Company's trade in the Moluccas for the spices which formed its 'right arm'. Apart from their sale in Europe, different ranges of Indian textiles from coarse 'arse-clouts' destined for negro slaves to the finest 'light fabrics for light women' were readily saleable over most of Monsoon Asia and the littoral of tropical Africa. They were thus as vital as gold and silver for the development of the Asian inter-port trade, and the Dutch and English were as anxious to secure them as their Portuguese predecessors had been. The VOC got a good start over the EIC on the Coromandel coast, but its hold there was seriously shaken by the internecine wars in and around Golconda during the last quarter of the 17th century, at a period when the English surpassed the Dutch in their capital resources. The VOC's left arm withered, and here as elsewhere in India the Dutch Company's former commercial supremacy had passed to the English Company by 1740.[9]

In addition to pepper, spices, textiles, tea, coffee and porcelain, there were, of course, many other Asian commodities which were

9. K. Glamann, *Dutch-Asiatic Trade, 1620–1740*, and T. Raychaudhuri, *Jan Company in Coromandel, 1605–1690*, and the sources there quoted.

handled by the Dutch East India Company. Indigo and saltpetre from India; lacquered goods from Japan; elephants from Ceylon; slaves from Arakan, Buton and Bali; these were only a few of the many which might be mentioned. We have no space to consider all the ramifications of the Company's trade, but there is one aspect which is often insufficiently stressed – the ubiquity of the so-called 'private trade' alongside the Company's lawful business. The directors either could not or would not pay adequate salaries to the great majority of their employees. Moreover, a substantial portion of their meagre pay was retained in the home offices until the expiry of their time in the tropics, partly as a precaution against desertion. From 1658 onwards the *Heeren* XVII also manipulated the rate of exchange against their employees, calcu- lating the rix-dollar (worth 60 stuivers in the Netherlands) at 64 stuivers when debiting a man's pay-book. Virtually nobody was able to live on their official pay, let alone save anything for eventual retirement, and pensions were only awarded under very exceptional circumstances before about 1753. The result was that everyone from Governor-General to cabin-boy traded on the side and everyone else knew it.

Following the precedent of their Portuguese predecessors, the *Heeren* XVII allowed each man to bring home in his sea-chest a small amount of Oriental goods of trifling value, but this privilege was easily and invariably abused. Complaints of the prevalence of private trade began in August 1603, when the Company was little more than a year old. Six years later the directors noted bitterly that 'the senior merchants, junior merchants, skippers, officers, assistants and all other persons in the service of the Company' were buying up and bringing or sending home 'the best and finest porcelain, lacquer-work, and other Indian rarities, contrary to their oath of engagement'. This complaint runs through the Company's official correspondence to the end of its days. The directors periodically revised the quality and the quantity of goods which could be taken home in the sea-chests duty-free (or partly free), but they always reserved the most valuable commodities for the Company alone. As David Hannay wrote of the English East India Company's similar regulations: 'What came of this egregious arrangement might have been forseen by the intellect of a moderate-sized rabbit.' [10] Men who risked their lives to serve for a nominal salary in the tropics were not going to content themselves with 'catching flies' or 'eating hay', but were determined to get rich as quickly as possible. Their superiors in the East normally had no inclination to give their subordinates away, as they themselves were almost invariably more deeply implicated.

The facilities for fraud and embezzlement were endless. Apart from straightforward bribery and 'squeeze', both of which were very common, the Company's accounts in the remoter factories could be 'cooked' with relative ease. Purchased goods could be entered at fictitiously high prices in the ledgers; stolen or damaged merchandise could be heavily over-valued; subsistence and travelling claims could be swollen like modern expense-accounts; building materials and workmen's wages could be charged at higher rates than were actually paid. Some VOC employees lent money to Chinese and other Asian merchants on interest, even when this meant that the price of pepper (for example) might be driven higher by competitive bidding and the Company would have to pay more for it in the open market. Other employees traded in the name of Asian merchants, or in association with them, though both practices were strictly prohibited. As early as 1652 the VOC had forbidden its servants to remit their private fortunes to Europe through bills of exchange on the EIC, but the employees of both Companies continued to use the services of the other for the remittance of their ill-gotten gains in this way. This practice became a major scandal in the second half of the 18th century. Johan Ross, the Dutch Company's agent in Bengal, made at least half a million rupees from

10. D. Hannay, *The Great Chartered Companies* (London, 1926), pp. 190–92. For denunciations of private trade and some examples of the futile legislation against it in the VOC cf. J. A. Van der Chijs, *Nederlandsch–Indisch Plakaatboek*, Vol. I, pp. 11–12; ibid., Vol. II, pp. 442–3, 514–16; Vol. IV, pp. 28–9; Vol. VII, pp. 560–61; *Oost Indische Praetjen* (1663); N. de Graaff, *Oost-Indische Spiegel* (ed. 1703), pp. 18–32; F. de Haan, *Priangan*, Vol. IV, pp. 214–17, 275; Ibidem, *Oud Batavia*, Vol. II, pp. 9–17; J. de Hullu, *Matrozen en Soldaten*, pp. 351–60.

commissions he took on funds which the servants of our John Company sent secretly to England by way of Jan Compagnie and the Amsterdam banking-houses.[11]

There was very little secrecy about the private trade which flourished among Europeans in the East from the time of Vasco da Gama to the early 19th century. Numerous employees of the VOC who published their reminiscences after their return to Europe explained just how and when they had diddled (or bribed) the Company's Fiscal at Batavia – or how they had smuggled the contraband goods in their sea-chests through the regional India Houses in the Netherlands under the noses of the inspecting directors. It must be admitted in extenuation that the *Heeren* XVII, though denouncing the practice of private trade in the strongest terms and repeatedly fulminating orders against it, often turned a blind eye to what was going on. The attitude of the inspecting officials also varied a good deal in accordance with their individual characters and prevailing moods, 'being some times stricter and more rigorous than at other times', as the Company's Advocate, Pieter van Dam, admitted in his confidential *Beschryvinge*. He also tells us that the directors periodically considered whether the canker of private trade could not be removed by paying their employees higher salaries and insisting on a stricter compliance with their standing-orders. But, he adds, they invariably came to the conclusion that even higher wages 'would not lessen the covetousness of their servants nor induce them to do their bounden duty any better'.

Sometimes the *Heeren* XVII at home, or the senior authorities at Batavia, did punish the more outrageous infractions of the Company's rules against private trade, but such displays of zeal invariably proved to be of short duration. Japan and Bengal were the two regions where the greatest illicit profits were obtained and where the scandal was most notorious. Since neither of these countries was controlled by the Company, it was all the more difficult to check smuggling and embezzling by the VOC's em-

11. J. Holden Furber, *John Company at Work, 1783–93* (Cambridge, 1958), pp. 78–109. For the 1652 ban by the *Heeren* XVII on their servants in the East remitting money home through the EIC, cf. Van der Chijs, *Nederlandsch Indisch Plakaatboek*, Vol. II, pp. 180–81.

ployees, particularly as these activities often involved the connivance or co-operation of the local officials, interpreters and merchants. The ships laden at Batavia for Japan were sometimes so 'pestered' with private goods that the Company's own cargoes could not all be taken on board. Hendrik Cansius, the chief of the Deshima factory in 1681–2, boasted on his return to Batavia that more private trade than Company's trade had been driven in Japan in his time. A few years later, there was a tremendous scandal when the Japanese authorities cracked down on this contraband trade at Nagasaki, executing thirty-eight of their com·patriots and deporting the *Opperhoofd*, Andreas Cleijer, to Batavia with orders that he was not to return to Japan on pain of death. A similar sensation was caused in Bengal in the same year, when the inspecting Commissary-General, Van Reede tot Drakenstyn, dishonourably discharged the chief of the Hughli factory and several of his subordinates on account of their private trade and embezzlement of the Company's funds. Opium was a favourite commodity in the private trade of Bengal, since it could be purchased there for 70 or 75 rupees and sold for 220 or 225 at Batavia. In 1722, Governor-General Zwardecroon had twenty-six persons, including eleven European storekeepers, executed at Batavia for contraband trade; and in 1731 the *Heeren* XVII recalled in disgrace the Governor-General and a number of high officials who were deeply implicated in a smuggling-ring. But the exposure of these and other notorious scandals had no lasting effect, and contraband trade continued to flourish throughout the Company's fort and factory system.

Nicholas de Graaff, and others who could speak with authority on this point, alleged that the lay-preachers and *predikanten* frequently defrauded the Company in this way. Some of these allegations may be discounted as smacking of anti-clericalism; but when all the malicious gossip has been duly discounted, it is clear that private trade flourished in the ecclesiastical branch of the Company's hierarchy as it did in the others. Among the worst offenders were the very officials who were charged with its extirpation, from the European Fiscals at Batavia and elsewhere to the Asian peons who manned the guard-boats that watched the loading and unloading of shipping. Nearly all of these people could be bribed with impunity, and Nicholas de Graff's description of how Japanese gold coins were slipped into the hand of the Batavia Fiscal, not as a bribe but as a memento, bears a close and amusing resemblance to Francisco de Sousa Coutinho's description of the technique of bribery in Holland: 'Excuse me, Sir, for troubling you. I know well that Your Honour is not the sort of man to accept any present; this is nothing but a little remembrance for Your Honour's wife and children.' [12]

Private trade and the abuse of office which was its inevitable concomitant were recognized to be among the chief reasons for the collapse of the VOC at the end of the 18th century, when cynics spelt out these initials to read *Vergaan Onder Corruptie*, 'collapsed through corruption'. It is uncertain how much the Company actually lost in this way, and its latest historian is inclined to think that displacements in the requirements of the European market, changed conditions in Asia, and an increasing number of competing foreign companies were more responsible for undermining the commercial position of the VOC than were bribery and corruption among its allegedly 'fraudulent, lazy and incompetent officials'.[13] Statements that the contraband goods in homeward-bound Dutch Indiamen often exceeded in value the regular cargoes of the Company should certainly be treated with reserve; but as early as 1639 the *Heeren* XVII complained that the shops in the United Provinces were so well stocked with contraband East Indian commodities that the regional chambers were handicapped in selling their own official quotas. It was also freely alleged by critics of the VOC in the late 18th century that private trade and corruption among its servants in the East were more damaging than the similar practices which prevailed in the EIC; but this again is something which is hardly susceptible of proof in the absence of accurate estimates of the sums involved in both Companies. It is also worth noting, as Professor Coolhaas points out, that corruption in the English East India

12. N. de Graaff, *Oost-Indische Spiegel* (ed. 1703), pp. 25–6. For Sousa Coutinho's description of the technique of bribery in the northern Netherlands, cf. p. 45 above.

13. K. Glamann, *Dutch-Asiatic Trade, 1620–1740*, pp. 261–5.

Company probably reached its greatest extent during the (real or apparently) most prosperous period of that corporation, the second half of the 18th century.

It is scarcely necessary to add that private trade flourished among the servants of the Dutch West India Company just as it did among those of the East, and for the same basic reasons: the absolute inadequacy of the monthly pay; the uncertainty of life in the tropics; the temptingly easy opportunities of enriching oneself quickly by dishonest methods; and the general conviction that 'there were no Ten Commandments south of the Equator'. The directors of the West India Company, like their colleagues of the VOC, promulgated elaborate rules to check contraband trade, and they threatened offenders with dire penalties if they were caught; but these sanctions proved as ineffective on the shores of the Atlantic Ocean as they did on those of the Indian Ocean and the China Sea. Just as with the sister Company, the fiscals and other officials of the WIC who were charged with enforcing the anti-smuggling regulations were precisely those who were most easily bribed and 'who let themselves be suborned by any and every means'.[14]

The division of duties among the personnel of any given factory naturally varied according to the size of the staff and the importance of the place concerned. Some of the smaller agencies in the Moluccas, for example, were manned by only one or two Europeans, whereas in a fortified harbour and garrison-town there might be several hundreds. The particulars given by Daniel Havart for the Dutch factories on the Coromandel coast about 1680 may be taken as fairly typical and can be summarized as follows. The chief merchant or factor (*Opperhoofd*) dealt with the Indian merchants, ordered the textiles, kept the money-chest, received incoming cash and authorized the cashier to make payments. The *Tweede*, or second in seniority, kept the trading-ledgers, supervised the storehouses or godowns, helped to inspect the quality of the textiles and invoiced them for export. Out-

14. Correspondence between the *Heeren* XIX and the Governor and Council at Recife, 1638–9, summarized in H. Wätjen, *Das holländische Kolonialreich in Brasilien. Ein kapital aus der kolonialgeschichte des 17. Jahrhunderts* (The Hague, 1921), pp. 298–303.

going correspondence had to be signed by both the chief and the second merchant. The third merchant, if there was one, was available for any necessary duty, and was often employed on buying goods in the interior. The assistants, clerks and writers functioned as such under the supervision of their superiors. The principle of civilian control was a corner-stone of the service in both India Companies. The senior post was invariably held by a merchant, usually with the rank of *Opperkoopman* (Senior Merchant), even in heavily fortified and strongly garrisoned settlements, such as Castle Zeelandia in Formosa, Fort Belgica in the Banda Islands, Pulicat on the Coromandel Coast and the Castle of Elmina in Guinea.[15]

The Dutch in the East were not, on the whole, such great builders of castles and fortifications as were their Portuguese predecessors, whose strongholds they usually reduced in size once they had captured them, with a view to economizing on the garrison and cannon necessary to defend their walls. This they did, for example, at Cochin and Colombo, although they built some impressive fortifications in Formosa and the Banda islands, whose ruins could be admired until sixty or seventy years ago. The most costly – and in the event the most useless – of their castles was that of Naarden at Negapatam (Coromandel), which cost the Company about a million and a half guilders and was nicknamed 'the castle with the golden walls'. More original than their castles and their forts was the architectural impress of the Low Lands by the North Sea, which they left on many places where they settled in the tropics. Batavia and Recife were two outstanding examples, but they dug canals and laid out tree-lined streets in front of gabled houses in many other places as well. 'The town itself,' wrote Daniel Havart of the factory at Pulicat in 1693, 'is not unpleasing. There are many streets in which none but Hollanders live, including several with houses all built in a special way after the Dutch fashion, with three rows of trees in

15. D. Havart, *Op-en ondergang van Cormandel* (Amsterdam, 1693), Pt. II, p. 26, Pt. III, p. 57. For the corresponding distribution of duties on the Guinea Coast cf. W. Bosman, *A New and Accurate Description of the Coast of Guinea, 1704* (ed. London, 1721), pp. 81–9; K. Ratelband, *Vijf Daghregisters van Elmina, 1645–7*, pp. lviii–lxiii.

front of them; and there one can enjoy a pleasant stroll both in the daytime and in the evening.'

Throughout the tropics the nature of the trade was mainly seasonal, particularly so in Asia, where seaborne traffic ran in the age-old routes dictated by the alternating monsoon winds. This meant that most factories would be very busy during the trading season, but that once the ships had been loaded and dispatched, there would not be so much to do until the next season arrived. Naturally, the merchants were not necessarily idle during the so-called dead or off-season. They had to dispose of unsold goods as opportunity offered, and they tried to assemble merchandise for export before the arrival of the next season's ships, in so far as this was practicable. In a busy entrepôt such as Batavia, the office hours were from 6 to 11 a.m., and from 1 to 6 p.m., from the year 1620 to 1740. In this year, the hours for senior personnel were fixed at from 7 to 11 a.m., and from 2 to 5 p.m., though many such employees were lax in their attendance despite repeated admonitions from the government. But life in some of the remoter factories and out-stations, which had little or no communication with the outer world once the trading season was finished, could only be described as the dullest and dreariest of routines. Thunberg's description of the daily round in Deshima after the departure of the Dutch ships for Batavia in November 1775 is applicable, *mutatis mutandis*, to life in many of the smaller agencies, where not more than about a dozen Europeans resided.

An European, that remains here, is in a manner dead and buried in an obscure corner of the globe. He hears no news of any kind; nothing relative to war, or other misfortunes and evils that plague and infest mankind; and neither the rumours of inland or foreign concerns delight or molest his ear. The soul possesses here one faculty only, which is the judgement (if, indeed, it be at all times in possession of this faculty). The European way of living is in other respects the same as in other parts of India [= Asia], luxurious and irregular. Here, just as at Batavia, we pay a visit every evening to the Chief, after having walked several times up and down the two streets. These evening visits generally last from six o'clock to ten, and sometimes eleven or twelve at night, and constitute a very disagreeable way of life, fit only for such as have no other way of spending their time than droning over a pipe of tobacco.

Twenty years later, Captain Robert Perceval wrote of the Dutchmen in Ceylon that they began their day with gin and tobacco, and ended it with tobacco and gin. In the interval they fed grossly, lounged about, indulged in the essential siesta, and transacted a little business.[16] Nor was their way of life essentially different in the forts on the Gold Coast and in the houses of the plantation overseers of Surinam during the last quarter of the 18th century.

As a counterpart to Thunberg's description of the dreary daily round on Deshima, may be cited the very similar description of the daily life at Mina on the Gold Coast, penned by the Dutch comic-poet, Willem Godschalk van Focquenbroch (?1633–75), and published posthumously in his *Afrikaënse Thalia* (1682):

... Think, furthermore, that if you look around you for about two miles, you see nothing but a bare and barren waste, whereon neither foliage nor sprout under which you can shelter from the rays of the sun, which is here so frightfully steep in the zenith overhead, that one could not find a finger's breadth of shadow at high noon even near the highest tower in the world. Think, moreover, whether I have not good reason to stay in my cell in the castle for sometimes three weeks on end, where you would see me sitting together with my two black boys, smoking away, rolling their eyes, and that they both of them have their work cut out with slicing and filling tobacco for my pipe. This is the daily routine while writing or reading something amusing, or entertaining one or two honourable souls with the aid of a glass, in order to sharpen the spirit and to drive away melancholy ... But never mind, patience! If the land is bad, the gold is good; and it is this alone which enables me to stomach the many disgusts which I suffer here. For there is no cordial in the world which is so powerful as that; and this is the reason why I am resolved to bear everything patiently, and to jog along quietly while I am here, in so far as I can, and to forget the

16. C. P. Thunberg, *Travels in Europe, Africa and Asia, 1770–1779,* Vol. III, pp. 63–4; Perceval's account *apud* P. E. Pieris, *Ceylon and the Hollanders* (Telippalai, 1918), pp. 166–7.

pleasures of the world for a few years, just as if I was dead. For there is no pleasure whatsoever here, save only in the inner resources of your own mind.

The pipe and the bottle were the inseparable companions of the Dutch overseas, as they were in the United Provinces. 'Our nation must drink or die', wrote Jan Pieterszoon Coen in 1620, and he was not referring to water. His words were echoed by Rijkloff van Goens, Governor of Dutch Ceylon, who regretfully noted in 1661: 'We find, God help us, that our men cannot be made to avoid drink.' In 1674, out of 340 gainfully employed free-burghers at Batavia, fifty-three were tavern-keepers and vintners: in other words one out of every six or seven of the male citizens not directly employed by the Company were directly concerned with the sale of drink. The *Heeren* XVII wrote to the Governor-General and council at Batavia in 1647 that the average Dutchman would spend his last remaining penny for a mug of beer. They were informed that the English had sold beer to the value of 14,000 pieces-of-eight at Batavia, and though they could hardly credit this information, 'if it is true, it only goes to show that our people cannot forget the air of the Fatherland'. In 1648 the 170 Calvinist church members of New Amsterdam [Manhattan] were described as being 'mostly very ignorant in matters of religion and very inclined to drunkenness, an inclination greatly facilitated by the 17 ale-houses which exist here'. In 1631 Jan Claeszoon van Campen, the Dutch commander of the island of St Martin in the West Indies, was described by a visiting Englishman as being 'the only sober Dutchman' that he had ever met. This was, obviously, an instance of the pot calling the kettle black, since there is overwhelming contemporary evidence to show that the English were as earnest devotees of Bacchus as were the Dutch. Daniel Havart, who served for thirteen years in the Dutch factories in Coromandel (1672–85), indignantly denied that his compatriots were more addicted to the bottle than were the English in India. Willem Bosman, Havart's friend and correspondent on the Guinea coast, assured him that the high mortality rate of the English in West Africa was mainly due to their 'excessive tippling' of a 'damnable liquor' called Punch. But Bosman also admitted that among the Dutch Factors in Guinea excessive drinking was 'here too much in vogue; and the larger their salary is, the greater their thirst appears to be'.[17]

Nothing would be easier than to multiply such quotations from official and private correspondence and from books dealing with European life in the tropics during the 17th and 18th centuries, quite apart from some revealing statistics concerning the colossal consumption of wine, brandy, arrack and gin. I think it no exaggeration to say that most of the Dutch and English males who died in the tropics died of drink, even making due allowance for the heavy toll taken by malaria and dysentery. Two lines on a 17th-century tombstone in Coromandel indicate this fact, and they make no invidious distinction between the two hard-drinking nations:

> *The Dutch and the English were here*
> *And they drank Toddy for want of beer.*

Another feature of life in the tropical forts and factories of the East and West India Companies was the excessive preoccupation of the senior employees with official rank and social status. Class-consciousness was highly developed among the Dutch in their home country, and until very recent times a married woman was addressed as *Mevrouw*, *Juffrouw* or *Vrouw*, according as to whether her husband was (say) a doctor, a grocer or a labourer. But in the overseas possessions of the two Dutch India

17. The *Heeren* XVII to the Governor-General and Council at Batavia, 5 October 1647, in *Tijdschrift Bat. Gen.*, Vol. XXII (1875), pp. 539–41; D. Havart, *Op-en ondergang van Cormandel*, Pt. I, pp. 134–5; A. Eekhof, *De Hervormde Kerk in Noord-Amerika*, 1624–1664, Vol. I, pp. 84, 115; W. Bosman, *A New and Accurate Description of Guinea* (ed. 1721), pp. 43–4, 92–3; F. de Haan, *Oud Batavia*, Vol. II, pp. 132–5. C. N. Parkinson, *Trade in the Eastern Seas*, 1793–1813, p. 74, shows that in 1805 over three million bottles of Madeira were imported into India for the consumption of a few thousand English residents, quite apart from vast quantities of claret, brandy and Hodgson's pale ale. Readers of William Hickey's *Memoirs* will agree that an apparently insatiable thirst for strong drink was as well developed a feature of English life in the East as it was in that of the Dutch.

Companies in general, and at Batavia in particular, class distinctions and social gradations were carried to grotesque lengths, more especially during the second half of the 18th century. The Dutch East India Company's official hierarchy was as strictly regulated and minutely graded as was that of the Roman Catholic Church, and rank and precedence were the breath of life to the European citizens at Batavia. 'Every individual is as stiff and formal, and is as feelingly alive to every infraction of his privileges, in this respect, as if his happiness or misery depended wholly upon the due observance of them,' Stavorinus observed in 1768, and virtually every other visitor to late 18th-century Batavia made similar disparaging comments. The dress of the Company's servants (and that of their wives); the number of coaches or vehicles which they could have, and the degree of decoration they were allowed; these and a hundred other personal matters were all regulated in the greatest detail, as were the lengthy toast-lists at official and private parties. The order of precedence at receptions, dinners and funerals was laid down with the minutest exactitude, giving rise to bitter personal quarrels and lawsuits whenever some real or fancied breach of the regulations occurred.

If numerous unkind critics are to be trusted on this point, it was the ladies who were most prone to insist upon each and every prerogative attached to the rank of their respective husbands. 'It not infrequently happens,' wrote Stavorinus, 'that two ladies, of equal rank, meeting each other in their carriages, one will not give way to the other, though they may be forced to remain for hours in the street. Not long before I left Batavia, this happened between two clergymen's wives, who chancing to meet in their carriages, in a narrow place, neither would give way, but stopped the passage for full a quarter of an hour, during which time, they abused each other in the most virulent manner, making use of the most reproachful epithets, and "whore" and "slave's brat" were bandied about without mercy: the mother of one of these ladies, it seems, had been a slave, and the other, as I was told, was not a little suspected of richly deserving the first appellation: they, at last, rode by one another, continuing their railing till they were out of sight; but this occurrence was the occasion of an action, which was brought before the council and carried on with the greatest virulence and perseverance.[18]

Another feature of life at Batavia, and, for that matter, in all the principal European settlements in the tropics to a greater or lesser degree, was the importance attached to a display of pomp and circumstance, largely with the idea of impressing the indigenous population with the White Man's wealth and power.

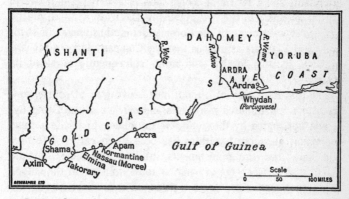

7 Principal Dutch forts and factories in Guinea.

The Portuguese had early adopted such an attitude in 'Golden Goa', where the Viceroy held court in a manner that some European monarchs might have envied. The Lusitanian example was consciously followed by the Dutch at Batavia, and in due course by the English at Calcutta. All trace of Calvinist simplicity quickly disappeared in these surroundings, and an ostensibly pious Governor-General such as Petrus Albertus van der Parra (1761–75) lived with an ostentatious display of luxury.

18. J. S. Stavorinus, *Voyages to the East Indies, 1768–1778*, Vol. I, pp. 301–3; for some typical sumptuary edicts and regulations concerning social status and official precedence cf. *Nederlandsch-Indisch Plakaatboek*, Vol. II, p. 111; Vol. III, pp. 47–8; 536–8; Vol. IV, pp. 75, 127–9, 149, 239–44; Vol. VI, pp. 773–98; Vol. VII, pp. 740–51. For the situation in the Northern Netherlands, cf. G. J. Renier, *The Dutch Nation*, p. 85.

Whenever the Governor-General rode out in his carriage, he was attended by a train of richly dressed outriders and guards, and all those whom he passed had to alight from their own carriages and bow deeply (or curtsey if they were ladies) with bared heads as he went by. The chiefs of even secondary factories, such as Tegenapatnam in Coromandel, appeared in public with a suite of Indian standard-bearers, trumpeters, musicians, twenty armed attendants and a swarm of coolies, besides a bodyguard of twelve Dutch soldiers. On the instructions of the *Heeren* XVII, drastic economies were made in the Coromandel establishments in 1678; and Daniel Havart assures us that the Company lost a great deal of 'face' by this locally, and never subsequently regained its prestige.

The luxurious way of life outlined above was, of course, confined to a few hundred merchants and officials of the Company. It was not shared by the junior clerks, soldiers and sailors, some indication of whose hardships has been given earlier. We may add here that the punishments inflicted on soldiers in the Company's service were as harsh as those inflicted on the sailors. It was not uncommon for a man to be injured for life by the 'wooden horse' and other savage punishments in vogue. In 1706 the Governor-General and council resolved that the 'wooden horse' and flogging should be used more sparingly in future; and it was later enacted that soldiers should not be subjected to ignominious punishments such as the chain-gang in front of the natives, 'in order to maintain the prestige of Europeans'. But the lot of the mercenary soldiers in the service of the VOC, and, for that matter, of those in the service of the WIC, continued to be a hard one, and several travellers commented that the soldiers were treated almost as badly as negro slaves. Thunberg's testimony on this point is sufficiently explicit to be quoted here: 'I now also perceived the reason why the Europeans, both sailors and soldiers, are in many respects treated worse and with less compassion, than the very slaves themselves. With respect to the latter, the owner not only takes care that they are clothed and fed, but likewise, when they are sick, that they are well nursed and have proper medical attendance. The former go as they can, viz, naked, or dressed in tattered clothes, which perhaps, after all, do not fit them; and when one of them dies, it is a common saying that the Company gets another for nine guilders.' [19]

While not a few of the Company's soldiers published their reminiscences of military life in the East, and we are well informed about the lives of its merchants, officials and sailors from the travel literature of the times and from private and official correspondence, we have singularly little information about another group of the Company's servants, the so-called *ambachtslieden*, skilled craftsmen and manual workers. The Dutch seem to have made more use of skilled European artisans in the East Indies than did either the Portuguese or the English. Originally, these men were mostly ship's-carpenters, caulkers, riggers and what would nowadays be called 'dockyard-mateys'; but almost every industrial craft was represented among the hundreds of European artisans who worked in the 'Craftsman's quarter' (*Ambachtskwartier*) at Batavia from 1682 onwards. Carpenters, wood-workers, furniture-makers, blacksmiths, locksmiths, armourers, gunsmiths, gun-founders, type-founders and cutters, masons, bricklayers, glaziers, cobblers, tailors, dyers and jewellers, all these and many more craftsmen were to be found there. Each craft lived, worked and messed together under its own foreman or overseer, who supervised the European workmen and the Company's slaves, who were trained by them and lived alongside them. Many of these latter became highly skilled craftsmen, and the baroque ebony furniture carved by the Company's Indian and Indonesian slaves often achieved a very high standard artistically and technically. In course of time these slaves, who were better clothed, fed and housed than the ordinary

19. C. P. Thunberg, *Travels in Europe, Africa and Asia, 1770–1779*, Vol. I, p. 277. For 17th–18th century court-martial sentences and for the severity of the discipline and the punishments in the military service of the VOC cf. H. T. Colenbrander, *Jan Pieterszoon Coen, Levensbeschrijving*, pp. 216–30; W. P. Groeneveldt, *De Nederlanders in China, 1601–1624* (The Hague, 1898), pp. 584–94; Troostenburg de Bruyn, *De Hervormde Kerk in Nederlandsch Oost-Indië, 1602–1795*, pp. 613, 618; J. de Hullu, 'De handhaving der orde en tucht' (*BTLVNI*, Vol. 67, pp. 516–40). For the soldiery of the WIC cf. C. R. Boxer, *The Dutch in Brazil, 1624–1654*, pp. 128–31.

coolies, became more numerous than the European workmen, but as late as 1759 there were still about 400 of the latter in Batavia alone. Several of the larger Dutch settlements, particularly the factories in Coromandel and Ceylon, also had their own *Ambachtskwartier*, where European and Asian artisans worked together under the supervision of Dutch foremen. There were also European workmen and artisans in the tropical forts and factories of the Dutch West India Company, but they were never so numerous as they were in the East, and the range of their skills was not nearly so wide.

In addition to the craftsmen employed by the East India Company, there were a number who worked for their own account. These comprised European workmen who had come out to the East in the Company's service, but had retired on the expiration of their period of engagement to 'set up shop' on their own. They likewise employed skilled slave-labour, and in the course of the 18th century this form of private enterprise, which was fostered by many of the senior officials in defiance of the wishes of the *Heeren* XVII, competed increasingly successfully with the Company's own craftsmen. Chinese artisans were also active, especially at Batavia, where they had a good reputation as cabinet-makers. The best work in this respect, however, was done by free Sinhalese and Tamil craftsmen in Ceylon and on the Coromandel coast, where the finely carved Indo-Dutch baroque furniture which they produced was superior to the best that the Company's slave-labour could offer.[20] The problem of free white traders and skilled labourers competing with the Company's own commercial and industrial system was a long-standing one; but it is best considered in connection with the abortive schemes for white colonization in the tropics which are discussed in the next chapter.

20. V. I. Van de Wall, *Het Hollandsche koloniale Barokmeubel* (The Hague, 1939), pp. 160–66; F. de Haan, *Oud Batavia*, Vol. I, pp. 351–60; Vol. II, pp. 21–4.

8

Assimilation and apartheid

David Hannay, in an admiring reference to the Dutch novelist Couperus's *De Stille Kracht*, calls this book 'a convincing study of that "hidden force" of the East which permeates and disintegrates the European, who cannot, or will not, stand apart from and above races which, be their natural merits what they may, can never combine with his, but only poison and corrupt.'[1] This definition and defence of *apartheid*, made long before its official application in South Africa, reflects a school of thought which can be traced back to the pioneer days of European settlement in the tropics, but which seems to have been stronger among the Dutch and the English than among their Portuguese and Spanish precursors. The belief that the white man, whether merchant, mariner or settler, should stand 'above and apart' from the coloured races among whom he lived, moved and had his being, naturally implied that white women should emigrate to the tropics in adequate numbers with their menfolk. This, however, was something which most of them were reluctant to do; nor were the great chartered companies, whether Dutch, English or French, organized to foster female emigration. Moreover, there were always plenty of people who argued that white women seldom became acclimatized in the tropics. These people therefore believed that the only hope of founding stable and loyal communities in those regions was to foster intermarriage with the indigenous women, always provided that these latter were converted to Christianity – in other words, a policy of assimilation as opposed to one of *apartheid*.

Although the original directors of the Dutch East and West India Companies had a century of Iberian experience to guide them in this matter, they do not seem to have given the subject any thought when framing their respective *octroys* or charters.

1. D. Hannay, *The Great Chartered Companies* (1926), p. 177.

The directors' attitude to emigration remained a vacillating one until experience taught them that it was hopeless to expect respectable Dutch women to emigrate in sufficient numbers to tropical countries which were rightly regarded as lands where life was short for those bred in northern climes. The acute discomforts of shipboard life on long voyages formed another powerful deterrent, though this was of greater weight in the long haul round the Cape of Good Hope than in the shorter Atlantic crossing. Finally, it is obvious that the conditions which deterred many respectable upper- and middle-class Dutchmen from enlisting in the service of the VOC and the WIC formed a still greater obstacle to the emigration of their womenfolk. Just as the bulk of the two Companies' employees were apt to be men who had no other resource, so many of the women who went to the tropics were apt to be more conspicuous for their adventurousness than for their morals.

As early as 1612 Pieter Both, the first Governor-General of the East Indies, advised the *Heeren* XVII not to allow any more 'light women' to emigrate from the Fatherland, 'since there are far too many of them here already'. These females led scandalous and unedifying lives, 'to the great shame of our nation', and Both advocated intermarriage with indigenous women, after the Roman and the Portuguese precedents, as a much better alternative. He qualified this suggestion by adding that Muslim women would not make suitable brides, since they deliberately aborted any babies they conceived by Christian men, but he urged intermarriage with 'heathen' women or with the Christian converts of Amboina. Similar suggestions were made by other officials of the VOC, and in 1612–13 the *Heeren* XVII authorized the Governor-General and his council to allow the settlement of time-expired married men in the East. They were permitted to trade in certain commodities such as rice, sago and livestock, which did not affect the Company's monopoly of profitable merchandise, such as spices. It was hoped in this way to form a free-burgher class who would be the equivalent of the Portuguese *casados* (married men) or *moradores* (settlers) in the Portuguese colonial empire, and who could supplement the Company's local garrisons in time of war. These so-called free-burghers were to remain strictly subordinated to the Company's officials, rules and regulations; and their presence was envisaged only in the Moluccas. Subsequently, they were allowed at Batavia and at some other places, principally Malacca and Ceylon.

In 1617, the *Heeren* XVII enacted that the free-burghers could not marry without the consent of the Company's local officials; that they could only marry Asian or Eurasian women on condition that these were baptized Christians or Christian converts; and that their children, 'and their slaves in so far as possible', were brought up as Christians. It was later enacted that these potential brides must have a good knowledge of Dutch and not merely of Portuguese, which was the *lingua franca* of coastal Asia for three centuries. Severe restrictions were placed on their acquisition of gold, or of precious stones, and on the remittance of their capital to Europe. Free-burghers who married Asian women were not allowed to return to Europe; and even those who married white women could only take a single chest of clothing and personal effects with them when embarking in a homeward-bound Indiaman. The ban on coloured wives going to Europe, though renewed in 1650 and again in 1713, was eventually relaxed in a few individual cases. But so many restrictions were placed on the residence, means of livelihood and behaviour of the free-burghers, that the term 'free' was and remained a singularly inappropriate one throughout the Company's rule. These burghers were in every respect less advantageously placed than were the Company's officials, not excepting indulgence in smuggling and private trade.[2]

2. For the above and what follows cf. W. P. Coolhaas (ed.), *Generale Missiven van G. G. en raden aan Heeren XVII*, Vol. I (The Hague, 1960), *passim*; Ibid., *Verloren Kansen* (Groningen, 1955), pp. 11–16; H. T. Colenbrander, *Jan Pieterszoon Coen. Levensbeschrijving* (The Hague, 1934), *passim*; J. A. Van der Chijs, *Nederlandsch-Indisch Plakaatboek*, Vol. I, pp. 46–9, 69, 82, 89, 238–9, 254–6, 460; ibid., IV, 151; M. A. P. Meilink-Roelofsz, *Asian Trade and European Influence, 1500–1630*, pp. 227–38; S. Arasaratnam, *Dutch Power in Ceylon, 1658–1687*, pp. 194–214; N. P. Van den Berg, *Uit de dagen der Compagnie* (Haarlem, 1904), pp. 30–63, 350–85; J. K. J. de Jonge, *Opkomst*, Vol. VI (1872), *passim*.

The free-burghers were mostly recruited from time-expired merchants, clerks, soldiers and sailors, whose often irregular course of life does not seem to have been noticeably improved by matrimony, if the reiterated complaints of successive governors are anything to go by. Governor-General Reynst alleged in 1615 that 'the scum of our land' were marrying with 'the scum of the East Indies'. A little later, Laurens Reael and Steven van der Hagen alleged that most of the free-burghers were dissolute drunkards, to whom no respectable Asian father would give his daughter in marriage – as they had done in the Moluccas to the sober Portuguese predecessors of the Dutch. The free-burghers were also accused of indulging in piracy, of trading with the English and with other competitors of the Company, and of smuggling spices and other forbidden commodities.

The real or alleged shortcomings of these free-burghers induced several high officials periodically to advocate the emigration of married couples or families from the Netherlands, as the only means of establishing a reliable settled Dutch community in the East. Coen showed himself an ardent supporter of this policy in 1623. Like many of his contemporaries, he thought that the United Provinces were dangerously over-populated, and that it would be relatively easy to organize large-scale emigration to the East and West Indies. There was room in West Java for 'many hundred thousand people', he optimistically declared; adding that 'the soil was exceptionally fruitful, the water very good, the air healthy and temperate, the sea rich in fish, and the land suitable for all kinds of cattle'. Coen shared his predecessors' dislike and contempt for the inferior quality of the contemporary free-burghers, and he stressed the need for encouraging good, substantial burgher-families to emigrate from the Netherlands with their capital. His enthusiasm communicated itself temporarily to the *Heeren* XVII, who tried to recruit suitable families for emigration to the East, but the response was negligible.

The siege of Batavia by the Susuhunan of Mataram in 1628, and the high death-rate of the Dutch from malaria, dysentery and other tropical diseases, must subsequently have convinced Coen that his optimism about West Java as a suitable region for European colonization was completely misplaced. Moreover, it was already apparent that European free-burghers were no match for their Chinese trade rivals wherever conditions approached a fair field and no favour. Nor did rich or well-to-do heads of families in the United Provinces have any incentive to emigrate to the tropics, when they could make money from Eastern trade by investing in the VOC (or even in foreign East India Companies) at home. As for the 'labouring poor', most of those who could not find work in the Netherlands preferred to seek their fortune in countries nearer home rather than embark on the daunting voyage to the straits of Sunda. Prospective emigrants were thus limited to those who took service with the Company, whether as merchants, soldiers or sailors. The great majority of these men had no intention of spending the rest of their lives in the Indies, but were resolved to return home as soon as possible. In this respect, the Dutch formed a strong contrast to their Portuguese precursors and contemporaries who had struck deeper roots as colonists. Corporal Johann Saar, after some years' service against the Portuguese in Ceylon, wrote of them in 1662: 'Wherever they once come, there they mean to settle for the rest of their lives, and they never think of returning to Portugal again. But a Hollander, when he arrives in Asia, thinks: "when my six years of service are up, then I will go home to Europe again".'[3] Last, but not least, the *Heeren* XVII were nervous about allowing the interport trade of Asia to be thrown open on any adequate scale to the free-burghers, as some of the advocates of colonization had advised. The hampering restrictions which they placed on the commercial activities of the burghers were enough to prevent the development of a prosperous community.

Schemes to foster the settlement and growth of Dutch agricultural communities in the tropics proved equally abortive. Peasant families were understandably reluctant to emigrate from the Netherlands to such unfamiliar and unhealthy surroundings; and time-expired soldiers, sailors and clerks were obviously unfitted to till the tropical soil. They could not hope to compete with the Chinese truck- and market-gardeners who soon established

3. *Reisbeschryving van J. J. Saar* (Amsterdam, 1671), p. 72. Cf. also Gerard Demmer's remarks in the same sense, *apud* J. K. J. de Jonge, *Opkomst*, Vol. VI, pp. ix–x.

themselves at Batavia and elsewhere, any more than they could compete effectively with the skilled Asian labour, whether bond or free, which was available for many trades and handcrafts. Most advocates of European agricultural development in the tropics did not, it is true, envisage that the European peasant emigrant should till the soil himself, but only that he should instruct and supervise Chinese or slave-labourers who would work under his direction. But schemes to implement this suggestion never came to anything in practice east of the Cape of Good Hope. In fact, the only occupation which the free-burghers undertook with any noticeable enthusiasm was that of tavern-keeping, as the senior officials of both the East and West India Companies continually complained. Tippling-houses were a prominent feature of Dutch colonial life from Manhattan to the Moluccas.[4]

Despite the abortion of Coen's ambitious schemes, the idea of large-scale Dutch settlement in the tropics was mooted again from time to time, both in the Netherlands and in the Indies, but these suggestions were never effectively implemented. Pieter de la Court, writing in 1662, declared that 'the ingenious, frugal and industrious Hollanders, by those virtues which are most peculiar to them, are more fit than any other nation in the world to erect colonies and to live on them, when they have the liberty given them to manure them for their own livelihood'. He refuted the widespread opinion that 'our nation is naturally averse to husbandry, and utterly unfitted to plant colonies, and ever inclining to merchandizing'. He argued that not only was there a surplus labouring population, both of Dutch nationals and foreign (chiefly German) immigrants, who would be glad to emigrate if they were assisted to do so, but that many of the regent class who were excluded from a share in the oligarchic government would willingly emigrate with their capital to colonies where they could invest it according to their own inclination. What prevented respectable Dutchmen, whether burghers, artisans or peasants, from emigrating to regions ruled by the East and West India Com-

4. Cf. H. T. Colenbrander, *Jan Pieterszoon Coen. Levensbeschrijving*, p. 408; E. Reimers (ed.), *Selections from the Dutch Records of the Ceylon Government*, III, *Memoirs of Rijkloff van Goens, 1663–1675* (Colombo, 1932), pp. 24, 34, 54.

panies was the restrictive policy of the directors. 'Certain it is that the Directors [=Governors?] of the said Companies, their mariners and soldiers, and likewise their other servants are hired on such strait-laid and severe terms, and they require of them such multitudes of oaths, importing the penalty of the loss of all their wages and estate, that very few inhabitants of Holland, unless out of mere necessity, or some poor ignorant slavish-minded and debauched foreigners, will offer themselves to that hard servitude.' Only the senior employees, he alleged, had the opportunity of making great fortunes through mutual connivance in each other's illicit financial transactions and through private trade.[5]

The *Heeren* XVII were not, however, always so averse from fostering colonization as De la Court alleged. If their support for Coen's ambitious plans of 1623 proved short-lived, they later gave sympathetic consideration and (for a time) active support to Johan Maetsuyker's more modest scheme for Dutch colonization at Batavia and in Ceylon. Maetsuyker, at an early stage of his colonial career, was a professed admirer of the Portuguese system of promoting colonization by encouraging white men to marry Asian or Eurasian women and settle down in the East. The children of these mixed marriages, he averred, were better acclimatized than those born of pure European parentage, and, after the second or third generation, they differed little if at all from pure Netherlanders in complexion. He admitted that many of these half-caste offsprings at present were apt to turn out rather badly; but this he ascribed to their lax upbringing in households where slavery was the general rule, and not to any inherent racial defect. The remedy for this state of affairs, he added, lay in the provision of good schools and in proper supervision by the parents. Maetsuyker maintained that with suitable encouragement by the Company's high officials – which so far had been conspicuously lacking – the free-burghers could establish themselves as cobblers, tailors, smiths, armourers, jewellers, carpenters, masons and surgeons. He even claimed that they could compete with the Chinese in agricultural pursuits. He further alleged that the Company's senior officials were the worst enemies of the

5. *The Interest of Holland* (ed. 1702), pp. 139–55.

free-burghers, since they favoured their Chinese and Asian competitors on account of the 'squeeze' and bribes which they received from the latter.

Maetsuyker endeavoured to put his colonization theory into practice during his governorship of Ceylon (1646–50), but he found that the free-burghers could not compete on anything approaching equal terms with the local 'Moors' or Muslim merchants. His advocacy of colonization through mixed marriages was actively supported by the *Heeren* XVII at this period, but, even so, there were only sixty-eight married free-burghers in the island when he relinquished office in February 1650. His successor, Van Kittensteyn, belonged to the rival and much larger school of thought, which maintained that Dutch settlers would never do any hard work in Asia, and that their indigenous or half-caste wives were inherently vicious and immoral. After the capture of Colombo and Jaffna from the Portuguese in 1656–8, about 200 Dutchmen married some of the Indo-Portuguese women who stayed (voluntarily or otherwise) in the island. The conqueror of Jaffna, Rijkloff van Goens, who subsequently governed coastal Ceylon for many years, was another enthusiastic advocate of Dutch colonization. In default of white wives for the free-burghers, he was prepared to tolerate intermarriage with Sinhalese, Tamil and Eurasian women. But he stipulated that the daughters of such unions should be married to Netherlanders, 'so that our race may degenerate as little as possible'.

Despite the efforts of such powerful personalities as Maetsuyker and Rijkloff van Goens, and even though the *Heeren* XVII authorized a 'moderate bonus' of two or three months' pay to any Dutch soldier or sailor who would marry a 'native woman' in Ceylon, the results achieved by the end of the 17th century were most disappointing. They showed quite clearly that Dutch colonization in the East on the Portuguese model was a failure. The majority of the free-burghers failed to make an adequate living, or to develop into a prosperous and substantial middle class. In Ceylon, as elsewhere, tavern-keeping was the only occupation for which they showed any great enthusiasm, as Rijkloff van Goens gloomily observed. In all other branches of trade and commerce, they proved no match for their Asian competitors; and in their own homes they could not or would not overcome the strong Indo-Portuguese and Asian influences derived from and perpetuated by their womenfolk. In other words, the free-burghers failed to evolve as an essentially *Dutch* colony and to form the nucleus of a 'New Netherlands' in Java, Ceylon or Formosa.[6]

Critics of these abortive colonization schemes were apt to ascribe their failure entirely to the drunken and dissolute (or lazy and improvident) habits of the Dutchmen concerned, but this was not entirely fair. In the first place, the economic interests of the colonists often clashed with those of the Company, and where this happened the latter naturally prevailed. Although the *Heeren* XVII intermittently favoured the free-burghers in various minor ways, they could never bring themselves to offer the settlers any really attractive inducements, such as participation in the spice trade or in the more profitable shipping routes to Japan, Bengal, Surat and Persia. Secondly, the free-burghers could hardly be expected to compete effectively with Asian merchants and itinerant traders, who were far more familiar with their own compatriots' religions, languages, prejudices and environment. The authorities at Batavia and in Ceylon sometimes enacted discriminatory legislation against indigenous traders in an endeavour to help the commerce of free-burghers; but they could not go too far in this direction, since they themselves depended on the co-operation and the services of Chinese and Muslim merchants to some extent. Moreover, such regulations could easily be evaded by judicious bribery, as Stavorinus found when he brought a complaint against the Chinese owner of a gambling-house to an official at Batavia. 'I can do nothing in the business,' replied the latter, 'the Chinese, you hear, denies it.' And this, added the disgruntled Stavorinus, 'is the only answer, and the only satisfaction that can, in such cases, be obtained from the executor of the law, as I have myself experienced'. As

6. K. W. Gunawardena, 'A New Netherlands in Ceylon. Dutch attempts to found a colony during the first quarter century of their power in Ceylon' (*Ceylon Journal of Historical and Social Studies*, Vol. II (1959), pp. 203-44); S. Arasaratnam, *op. et loc. cit.*; J. K. J. de Jonge, *De opkomst van het Nederlandsch gezag in Oost-Indië*, Vol. VI (1872), pp. vi-xxx, especially xiv-xv.

for agricultural pursuits, the chances of European ex-soldiers competing successfully with Chinese, Javanese, Tamils, Sinhalese and Malays in the back-breaking toil of paddy-fields under a tropical sun, were slim indeed. It is not surprising that Governor-General Baron van Imhoff's efforts to settle German peasants in the hinterland of Batavia achieved no lasting result. Those of the free-burghers who became wealthy – and some of them amassed fortunes, especially at Batavia – were ex-employees of the Company who had retired after making a fortune, and increased or maintained it by lending money at usury, or in private trade.[7]

The failure of the Dutch free-burghers, or of the Company's own servants for that matter, to induce their Asian and Eurasian womenfolk to forgo their Indo-Portuguese cultural *mores* and to adopt the Dutch way of life, was most marked. Presumably warned by previous Portuguese experience in inter-racial marriages, the *Heeren* XVII strongly urged (in 1641) that Dutchmen who wished to marry Asian women should choose them from among those of high caste or good social standing. This was easier said than done. Such women, whether Hindu, Muslim or Buddhist, lived in societies which permitted marriage only within certain clearly defined groups. With the possible exception of some Japanese and Chinese Buddhists, any Asian woman who married outside her race, her caste or her religion, forfeited all claim to the respect and consideration of her family and compatriots – as indeed a European woman would have done by voluntarily marrying (say) a Turk, an Indian or an Indonesian. Inevitably, therefore, the Dutch in the East were forced to take their wives, their concubines or their bed-fellows from among women of either Eurasian, low class or slave origins, just as the Portuguese had done before them. Moreover, the *Heeren* XVII had ordained that their servants could only marry with Calvinist believers (p. 243), and this restriction automatically excluded upper-class Asian women, who very seldom became Christian converts.

7. J. S. Stavorinus, *Voyages to the East Indies, 1768–1778*, Vol. III, pp. 393–4; J. A. Van der Chijs, *Nederlandsch-Indisch Plakaatboek*, Vol. VI, p. 44; F. de Haan, *Priangan*, Vol. IV, pp. 93–9; J. K. J. De Jonge, *Opkomst*, Vol. VI (1872), pp. 125–6.

The wives – or consorts – of the Dutchmen who married in Asia were thus mostly of Indo-Portuguese descent. Even those who were not had been brought up under Indo-Portuguese cultural influences, for reasons described by Governor-General Maetsuyker and his council in 1659: 'The Portuguese language is an easy language to speak and easy to learn. That is the reason why we cannot prevent the slaves brought here from Arakan who have never heard a word of Portuguese (and indeed even our own children) from taking to that language in preference to all other languages and making it their own.' In 1674 Maetsuyker and his councillors still maintained this defeatist attitude. Nicholas de Graaff, Johan Splinter Stavorinus and many other visitors to Batavia in the 17th and 18th centuries all comment on the extent to which Portuguese remained the *lingua franca* of the Dutch settlements, despite periodic efforts by the government to displace it in favour of Dutch. Not a few Dutch women, born and bred of European parents at Batavia, spoke a creole form of Portuguese in preference to their mother-tongue, in which they could express themselves but haltingly.

One would have expected their husbands or fathers to have insisted on the use of Dutch in the house, but this obviously was not so. One reason was that (as the Batavian authorities noted in 1674) most Netherlanders 'foolishly' considered it 'a great honour to be able to speak a foreign language' – unlike their Portuguese predecessors, and their English and French successors as empire-builders. Another, and perhaps even more valid reason, for this state of affairs was that given by Stavorinus in 1778: 'Married men neither give themselves much concern about their wives, nor show them much regard. They seldom converse with them, at least not on any useful subjects, or such as concern society. After having been married for years, the ladies are often, therefore, as ignorant of the world and of manners as upon their wedding day. It is not that they have no capacity to learn, but the men have no inclination to teach.' [8]

8. J. S. Stavorinus, *Voyages to the East Indies, 1768–1778*, Vol. I, pp. 313–14; K. Gunawardena, 'A New Netherlands in Ceylon', pp. 203–44; C. R. Boxer, 'Portuguese and Dutch colonial rivalry, 1641–61'

Batavia, and in varying degrees the other Dutch settlements in Asia, thus presented the curious spectacle of a Dutch Calvinist male society wedded uneasily with a largely Indo-Portuguese female society. The girls born of these mixed marriages naturally took after their mothers – or after the slave-nurses who brought them up – rather than after their fathers. In this way, the elements of an Indo-Portuguese colonial culture which the first women had brought with them were perpetuated and handed down to successive generations for nearly two centuries. The Asian elements of this Indo-Portuguese culture, in such matters as food, dress and the harem- or zenana-like seclusion of the women, do not seem to have become much weaker with the passage of time. This peculiar home atmosphere inevitably affected the husbands to some extent in the long run; and so the Dutch settlements in Asia, far from forming a 'New Netherlands' in the tropics, became increasingly removed from the cultural influences of the homeland.

Nicholas de Graaff waxes almost hysterical in his denunciations of the pride, luxury, and lasciviousness of the wedded women of Batavia, whether Europeans, Eurasians or Asians, during the last quarter of the 17th century. With large slave households at their beck and call, they gave themselves the airs of princesses, and would not even pick up a handkerchief from the floor. They relied entirely on their slaves, whom they punished most cruelly for the slightest misdemeanour and often for no fault at all. They adopted – or retained – such Oriental habits as squatting on their hams on the floor, instead of sitting on chairs, and they ate their curry with their fingers instead of with spoon and fork. They spoke little or no Dutch among themselves, but only a bastard form of creole Portuguese. Their sole topics of conversation were the misdemeanours of their slaves and the savoury dishes they perpetually consumed. Whenever they went to church or appeared in public, they were decked out with silks, satins and jewels, and were followed by a train of slaves; but at home they

---

(*Studia*, Vol. II, Lisboa, 1958, pp. 1–42). Cf. also Maetsuyker's observation on the popularity of Portuguese at Batavia in J. K. J. de Jonge, *Opkomst*, Vol. VI, p. 125, and B. Vlekke, *Nusantara*, p. 169.

squatted around in their shifts or in the most transparent of underclothes. Their pride and arrogance were unendurable, and only exceeded by their ignorance of polite society. De Graaff may have been laying on the colours a bit thick in his *East India Mirror*, but a century later Dirk van Hogendorp, who had himself married a Batavian girl, wrote from Patna in Bengal: 'A Batavian education is worse than Hell, and I will rather break the neck of my new born infant than suffer it to be brought to Batavia.'[9]

Obviously these outbursts must not be taken too literally, but there is plenty of other contemporary evidence to show that the morals and behaviour of many of the Dutch–Eurasian women usually left something to be desired. Exactly the same was true of the Indo-Portuguese women of Goa, whose similar defects were chronicled with horrified fascination by Linschoten, Pyrard de Laval, Jean Mocquet and many other visitors to 'India Portuguesa'. The basic reasons were evidently the same in both instances. The women concerned had either been brought up in slave households, or else they had broken away from the forms of social control in the indigenous societies from which they had come. Their resultant demoralization could only be changed by time and favourable circumstances; but their daily environment and way of life were anything but propitious in these respects. To make matters worse, the children of these mixed marriages were generally believed to inherit the vices of both races and the virtues of neither, their defects being ascribed to their Eurasian blood rather than to their unsatisfactory upbringing. The result was that they were usually regarded with a good deal of contempt by European born and bred Netherlanders, thus perpetuating a vicious circle. 'Piebald gentry', 'unbleached dungarees', 'crows' and even 'cockroaches' were some of the injurious epithets bestowed by home-bred Netherlanders on their 'Indo' cousins.

Nicholas de Graaff tells us – and this we can well believe – that the married women of Batavia who went (or returned) to Europe with their husbands could seldom adapt themselves to the simpler

9. N. de Graaff, *Oost-Indische Spiegel* (1703), pp. 11–17; E. Du Perron-De Roos *Correspondentie van Dirk van Hogendorp met zijn broeder Gijsbert Karel, 1783–1797*, p. 152.

way of life in the United Provinces. They were speedily dis-comfited when they tried to bully the Dutch servant-girls as they had done their slaves; and they found that they had either to mend their manners or else do without a maid. Most of them soon regretted that they had ever left their luxurious life in the East, and this regret was often shared by their husbands. In October 1656 the *Heeren* XVII wrote in an admonitory tone to Maetsuyker and his council at Batavia: 'We have observed to our great displeasure that a large number of families have arrived here in the last homeward-bound fleet. Many of them will bitterly repent it; for no sooner have most of them stepped ashore than they wish they were back in the Indies again, and there is not always an opportunity for their return. It is strange that they do not learn from the experience of their predecessors of former years, whether officials, great and small, or free-burghers, who have come here in succession, but who now strain every nerve to go back their again ... Everything here is dear and expensive, and there is little or nothing for them to earn – not to mention the glittering luxury to which they have been accustomed in the Indies but which is not available for them here.' This was a state of affairs which continued for as long as the East India Company endured.[10]

On the other hand, the knowledge that white women of lowly origin had a good chance of making a rich marriage in the East acted as a strong inducement for many enterprising working-class wenches to try and go there, sometimes disguised as sailors or in other masculine garb. It was to this type of adventurous but un-desirable female emigrant that Governor-General Jacques Specx was referring when he wrote to the *Heeren* XVII from The Downs (1 February 1629) a week after leaving the Texel: 'The crew are all fit and well, and we lack nothing save so many honest girls and housewives, in place of so many filthy strumpets and street-walkers who have been found (may God amend it) in all the ships. They are so numerous and so awful that I am ashamed to say anything more about it.' The directors later strictly limited

10. The *Heeren* XVII to Governor-General and Council, 13 October 1656, *apud* N. P. Van den Berg, *Uit de dagen der Compagnie* (Haarlem, 1904), pp. 55–6.

the number of women who were allowed to embark for Batavia, and De Graaff assures us that if they had not done so, there would have been more women than men aboard the ships. This was an evident exaggeration; but it does seem that, relatively speaking, many more Dutch women embarked (or tried to embark) in outward-bound Indiamen than was the case with their Portuguese, English and French sisters. Nor is it surprising that women aboard Dutch East Indiamen were apt to be regarded either as an infernal nuisance or else an irresistible temptation.[11]

The lack of respectable Dutch women as wives for the soldiers, merchants, officials and settlers in Netherlands Brazil was likewise a reason why the ephemeral colony of 'New Holland' in Pernambuco failed to justify its official name. As in the East, many Netherlanders in Brazil and Angola married local Portuguese women, who often had a strain of Amerindian or of negro blood, in default of North European women. These unions were generally regarded askance by the *predikanten* and the high officials, who rightly considered that the husbands were much more liable to become (or to revert to being) Roman Catholics than were their wives to become staunch Calvinists. Count John Maurice of Nassau-Siegen, who governed Netherlands Brazil from 1637 to 1644, never ceased to warn his superiors at The Hague and Amsterdam that unless they would send out Protestant Dutch, German or Scandinavian emigrant families in sufficient numbers to replace (or to mix with) the local Portuguese settlers, the latter would always remain Portuguese at heart and would revolt at the first opportunity – as indeed they did in June 1645. In the Luso-Dutch war which followed, several Dutch officers and merchants holding key positions in Pernambuco, Luanda and Benguela, and married to Portuguese women, chose the side and the religion of their wives when faced with the choice of acknowledging the suzerainty of King John IV or remaining

11. P. Van Dam, *Beschryvinge der O.I.C.*, Vol. I (1), p. 160; J. de Hullu, *De handhaving der ordre en tucht*, pp. 536–8; R. A. M. Immelman, 'Hollandse matroosliedere op die Kaapvaart in die 17e en 18e eeu', in *Quarterly Bulletin of the South African Library*, No. 15 (Cape Town, 1960), p. 14, 'Vroue als Matrose'; N. de Graaff, *Oost-Indische Spiegel* (1703), pp. 16–17.

loyal to the States-General. The existing families of Wanderley in Pernambuco and Van Dune in Luanda owe their origins to their ancestors' change of allegiance.[12]

If 'New Holland', largely for lack of sufficient Protestant immigrants, was unable in the long run to hold out against the military, social and religious pressures exercised by the fervently Roman Catholic population of Pernambuco, it would seem that 'New Netherland' on the banks of the Hudson River and the shores of Manhattan Island stood a better chance. Here, at any rate, Dutch colonists did not have to contend with a tropical soil and climate, or with a preponderately Roman Catholic population, but with natural conditions which resembled those of their own country in some ways. Here, if anywhere, a Dutch colony could be founded where men could live, work and worship in much the same way as they had done at home. Despite the vacillating policy of the *Heeren* XIX regarding the colonization schemes that were periodically suggested to them, and despite the reluctance of some of the colonial governors to allow the settlers that measure of self-government in local affairs to which they were entitled, the colony was alleged to contain 10,000 souls at the time of its seizure by the English in 1664. This was certainly a gross exaggeration, and in reality New Netherland was a sparsely populated enclave in the far more populous, dynamic and expanding settlements of New England. Few people on either side of the Atlantic thought that the States-General had made a bad bargain when they renounced their claims to New Netherland in return for possession of the tropical colony of Surinam, by the Treaties of Breda (1667) and Westminster (1674). Yet with more whole-hearted support from the *Heeren* XIX and the home government, New Netherland might have ultimately justified its name in the – admittedly unlikely – event of the English having left it alone. The Walloons and other non-Dutch

12. For the Van der Ley, or Wanderley (as it is spelt nowadays) family in Brazil, cf. J. A. Gonsalves de Mello, *Tempo dos Flamengos* (Rio de Janeiro, 1947), pp. 163–4, and the sources there quoted. The archives of the Municipal Council at Luanda, examined by me in 1955 and 1961, contain numerous references to the Van Dune family from 1650 onwards.

settlers who were numerous among the original colonists had adopted the Dutch language, the Dutch Reformed Church and Dutch manners and customs, in so far as they did not already possess or share them. Many of their descendants spoke Dutch until far into the 18th century, and the 'Reformed Church in America' only dropped the antecedent word 'Dutch' in 1867.[13]

In view of the temperate climate of New Netherland, sufficient European women could be found to emigrate thither, though in the early days of the colony there was certainly some racial mixture, as evidenced by the name of 'Whores' channel' (*Hoerenkill*) given to a locality where 'the Indians were generous enough to give their young women and daughters to our Netherlanders there'. But it was principally in the tropics, where white women were in such short supply, that Dutchmen had to find bedfellows from among the indigenous women. Some of them did so reluctantly, as indicated by the proverb in our own John Company's India : 'Necessity is the mother of invention and the father of the Eurasian.' But although the Netherlanders in the East seldom married any of the Asian (as distinct from the Eurasian) women with whom they lived, they seldom objected to concubinage, even though they did not indulge in this practice quite so uninhibitedly as did their Portuguese precursors. During the 18th century Buginese female slaves from Celebes were preferred as concubines for reasons which Stavorinus expresses in his inimitable way :

The Bouginese women are, in general, much handsomer than those of any other Indian [= Asian] nation. There are some among them, who, for the contour of their faces, would be esteemed beauties even in Europe; and did they but possess the lilies and roses of our northern fair, they would be equal to the handsomest of the sex. They are all most ardently addicted to the sensual pleasures of love; and, goaded on by the hottest fires of lust, are ingenious in every refinement of amorous enjoyment; on this account the Bouginese girls are preferred throughout the east, for concubines, both by Europeans and by Indians. Mr Van Pleuren, who had resided here

13. A. Eekhof, *De Hervormde Kerk in Noord Amerika, 1624–1664* (2 vols., The Hague, 1913); J. F. Jameson (ed. and trans.), *Narratives of New Netherland, 1609–1664* (New York, 1909; reprinted, 1959).

for eight years, and several other credible people, informed me, that among these women, and those of Macassar, were many who, in common with some of the Portuguese women at Batavia, possessed the secret of being able, by certain herbs and other means, to disqualify their inconstant lovers from repeating the affront to them, insomuch that the offending part shrunk entirely away; with other circumstances, which decency requires that I should suppress.[14]

The concubinage of female slaves with their European masters naturally resulted in a considerable number of illegitimate Eurasian births. In 1716 the Governor-General and council at Batavia expressed great concern at this state of affairs, and they ordained that henceforth the white fathers of such children would not be allowed to return to Europe but must remain in the East. From 1644 onwards the *Heeren* XVII legislated against slaves and coloured people being brought to Europe in homeward-bound Indiamen, and this ban apparently included the half-caste children of white fathers. It was not very strictly enforced, and in 1672 the authorities at Batavia forbade the employment of Asian office-clerks, save with special permission, on the grounds that 'India [= Asia] is full enough of the children of our own nation'. Whether half-castes were included among these children is not clear; but in 1715–17 their employment in the Company's service was categorically forbidden, save only when no suitable Europeans were available. In 1718 this ban was extended to the children born of white parents in Asia; and nine years later the *Heeren* XVII decreed that preference should always be given to the employment of European-born individuals as against Asian-born, whatever the racial origins of the latter. It may be doubted whether this last enactment was ever rigidly enforced, and as early as 1729 the Governor-General and council at Batavia authorized the employment of some Asian clerks, 'in view of the great shortage of competent scribes'. In 1756 the *Heeren* XVII ordered the government at Batavia to send no more European workmen and artisans to the forts and factories outside Java,

14. J. S. Stavorinus, *Voyages to the East Indies, 1768–1778*, Vol. II, pp. 183–4.

where skilled workmen should henceforth be trained from among the local native and Eurasian children.[15]

If the attitude of the Netherlanders to their Eurasian kinsmen was often condescending or openly contemptuous, this was still more so in their dealings with Asians as a whole. It is true that the *Heeren* XVII occasionally stressed the need to treat Asian peoples kindly and fairly, and it is equally certain that the government at Batavia sometimes promulgated instructions in this sense; but their subordinates seldom showed much regard for the indigenous peoples or revealed any sympathetic understanding for their viewpoint. The edicts collected in the Batavia *Plakaatboek* frequently refer to Indonesians, Chinese and Muslims with derogatory epithets such as 'vile' and 'mean'. Even a man like Cornelis Speelman, who spoke fluent Malay and who made a point of studying Asian manners, beliefs and customs, whether he was stationed in India or in Indonesia, sneeringly referred to the 'yellow-brown' Javanese beauties, who, however, he frequently took as bedfellows. Of course there were always some more broad-minded individuals, such as Steven van der Hagen and Laurens Reael in the Moluccas, or Dr Jacob Bontius at Batavia, who protested against the European dismissal of Asians as 'blind heathen', 'treacherous Moors', and 'feckless barbarians'. A remarkably forceful plea 'to see ourselves as others see us' can be ascribed in all probability to the great Admiral Piet Heyn, who had served with distinction in both the East and the West Indies and who had no illusions about the reasons for the hostility to the Dutch which was often displayed by the inhabitants of the tropics:

They feel very deeply the wrong that is done them, and this is why they become even wilder and more savage than they already are. When a worm is trodden on, it turns and wriggles; is it surprising, then, that an Indian who is wronged revenges himself upon someone or other? ... Friendship must begin from our side, for we have sought out these people, and not they us. It could be, and undoubtedly it must be, that in several places the Indians, from

15. J. A. Van der Chijs, *Nederlandsch-Indisch Plakaatboek,* Vol. II, p. 558; Vol. IV, pp. 65, 89, 102, 223; Vol. VII, p. 106.

misunderstanding, will show us more enmity than friendship at first. But this is no reason why we should indulge in hostilities against them, or pay them back in the same coin ... If we treat the Indians harshly and savagely, we will give them cause to hate us. And that hate will quickly strike deep roots and turn their hearts away from us ... Let us make sure that we do not offend God through any unfair dealings, and instead of our serving Him as a rod for others [the Spaniards and Portuguese], incite Him to lay a rod on our own backs.[16]

But such clear-sighted Calvinists as Piet Heyn were always in a small minority. The more general viewpoint was expressed by the Dutch *predikant* in Ceylon, who saved Corporal Saar from being court-martialled after the accidental killing of a Sinhalese by telling his commanding officer that this was nothing to worry about as 'the life of an Indian was worth little enough'. The matter was settled by a small cash payment to the widow from Saar's meagre pay; but he frankly admitted that, if a European had been the victim, he could hardly have escaped the death-penalty. Johan Maetsuyker, on vacating the governorship of coastal Ceylon in 1650, impressed upon his successor the need to treat the Sinhalese chiefs and headmen with due consideration, 'as they are very sensitive regarding their dignity. Your Honour should pay all the more attention to this point as there are many among us who regard them with prejudice, maintaining that

16. D. Spranckhuysen, *Triumphe van weghen de gheluckighe victorie teghen de Silver-vlote* (Delft, 1629), pp. 64–6, cited in abridged form by K. Ratelband *De Westafrikaanse reis van Piet Heyn, 1624–1625* (The Hague, 1959), pp. xxxiii–xxxix, who points out that these words are much more likely to be those of the widely travelled Piet Heyn than of the stay-at-home Rev. Spranckhuysen. For typical derogatory epithets affixed to Indonesians, Chinese and Muslims in the edicts of the Batavian statute-book, cf. J. A. Van den Chijs, *Nederlandsch-Indisch Plakaatboek*, Vol. II, p. 510; Vol. IV, p. 363; Vol. V, pp. 96–7; Vol. VI, p. 545, which it would be easy to multiply from this work and from the *Dagh-Register van't Casteel Batavia, 1624–1682* (23 vols., Batavia, 1887–1938). Cf. also the documented discussion of this problem by F. de Haan, *Priangan*, Vol. IV, pp. 730–39.

these "black dogs", as they insultingly and no less unchristianly call them, should not be allowed to enjoy such honour and favour'. An exceptionally well-educated and cultured man such as Dominie François Valentyn, who prided himself on the excellence of his spoken Malay, and who displayed a deep and genuine interest in many aspects of Asian civilizations, could describe the sadistically cruel and treacherous murder of the Ternaten prince, Kachil Saidi, by the Dutch in 1656 as 'an all too soft end' for 'one who had deserved to live longer, in order that he might have had a still more painful death'.[17] This repellent mixture of Calvinism and sadism was far from uncommon. It was exemplified by Jan Pieterszoon Coen in his extermination of the Bandanese and in his cruel mistreatment of the thirteen-year-old Eurasian girl, Sara Specx, who had allowed herself to be seduced by the young man to whom she was betrothed, and who was executed by Coen's orders.

The Dutch in the East possessed in full measure that innate conviction of white superiority which animated both the Portuguese *conquistadores* of Affonso de Albuquerque and the fictitious but life-like Scotsman in George Orwell's *Burmese Days*: 'Remember, laddie, always remember, we are *sahiblog* and they are *dirrt*.' Portuguese, Spaniards, Dutch, English and French were nearly all convinced that a Christian European was, *ipso facto*, superior to the members of any other race – Christian converts not excepted in practice, whatever they might be in theory. If this was the general conviction among Christians of all denominations, it was inevitably strongest among Calvinists, who, consciously or subconsciously, were bound to believe that they were the Elect of the Lord and the salt of the earth. Obviously this

17. *Reisbeschrijving van J. J. Saar* (Amsterdam, 1671), pp. 56–7. E. Reimers (ed.), *Memoir of Johan Maetsuyker delivered to his successor Jacob van Kittensteyn on 27 February, 1650* (Colombo, 1927), pp. 8, 30. For the cruel and treacherous murder of Kachil Saidi, and the singularly unpleasant reactions of contemporary and contemporaneous Dutchmen thereto, cf. L. Bor, *Amboinse Oorlogen* (Delft, 1663), pp. 297–300; F. Valentyn, *Oud en Nieuw Oost-Indien*, Vol. I (2), pp. 319–20; E. Du Perron, *De Muze van Jan Companjie* (Bandœng, 1948), pp. 126–9.

attitude could not always be openly expressed in countries which had strong governments that stood no nonsense from European traders on their coastal fringes. For instance, we can see from Daniel Havart's *Rise and Fall of Coromandel* (1693) that the social relations of the Dutch Factors with the Indian merchants, officials and courtiers of Golconda, whether Muslim or Hindu, were generally friendly and relatively unconstrained.[18] Nor could the Dutch display any strong feelings of racial superiority in such isolated factories as that of Deshima in Japan or Canton in China. But such manifestations frequently occur in the diaries and the confidential correspondence that were intended for European eyes alone. Exceptions to this general conviction of European superiority there were, but they remained exceptions then and for long afterwards.

We are not so well documented regarding the Asian peoples' opinion of Europeans in general and of the Dutch in particular, save for nations like the Chinese and Japanese, whose historical records are comparable in volume and scope with those of the West. How abstemious Muslims regarded the bibulous and quarrelsome Europeans who dominated the Moluccas can be inferred from the following observation by a Dutch *predikant* at Amboina in 1615: 'This black nation, such as they are, are pretty civil, upright, regular and orderly in their daily life and conduct. They do not come home drunk, staggering, raging, bawling, overturning everything, making an uproar, beating the wife and pushing her out of doors, as our own men often do; and this is the reason why none of them want to give their daughters in marriage to us, and why the girls themselves are afraid to do so.' In the regions of Indonesia where the Dutch established and maintained themselves by force of arms, the population was fundamentally hostile to their rule, though the subjugated peoples could not do much about it. Rijkloff van Goens's admission in 1655 that 'we are deadly hated by all nations in Asia' (p. 94) can be confirmed from many other con-

18. D. Havart, *Op-en ondergang van Cormandel* (Amsterdam, 1693); T. Raychaudhuri, *Jan Company in Coromandel, 1605–1690* (The Hague, 1962), pp. 203–8.

temporary sources, such as the evidence of Edward Barlow, who was a prisoner-of-war at Batavia in 1673 and so had a worm's-eye view of its Dutch occupants which was similar to that of the conquered Indonesians: 'The Javaes, the island people, hate them exceedingly, yet the Dutch keep them so under that they dare not do anything, for they know that if they should rise and overcome them, they would have no mercy on them, and it [Batavia] is so strong, both within and without, that no small force could do them any harm.' The Javanese chronicles also reflect the mistrust and incomprehension with which most of the Javanese regarded the Dutch and their doings. As regards Ceylon, the feelings of the inhabitants in the coastal regions subjected to Dutch rule after the expulsion of the Portuguese in 1658, were epitomized, as Robert Knox noted, in the Sinhalese proverb concerning a man who makes a bad exchange: 'I have given pepper and got ginger.' [19]

Religious differences widened the gulf between Europeans and Asians. If the 17th-century Calvinist Dutch fully shared the contemporary Romanist Portuguese belief in the unquestionable right of European Christians to exploit all lesser breeds beyond the pale of Christendom, the Islamized peoples of Indonesia disliked and despised the Dutch as 'Kaffirs' (unbelievers), just as they did the Papist Portuguese, the Hindu inhabitants of Bali or the pagan Dyaks of Borneo. In Ceylon, where the caste system was almost as deeply rooted among the Buddhist Sinhalese as it was among the Hindu Tamils, the Dutch found that people of the higher castes tended to be more 'disloyal' to them and more open to influences from the independent kingdom of Kandy than were people of the lower castes. Moreover, it was inevitable that Asians should, as a rule, prefer to be oppressed by rulers of their own race and religion rather than by the seaborne intruders from Europe, whose patterns of thought and behaviour were so alien to them. Yet, equally naturally, this was something the Dutch

19. Letter of the Rev. Caspar Willtens *apud* F. de Haan, *Priangan*, Vol. IV, p. 729; *Barlow's Journal of his Life at Sea*, Vol. I, pp. 236–7; R. Knox, *Historical Relation of the Island of Ceylon* (London, 1681), Pt. III, Ch. 9, p. 171.

did not always understand. When Rijkloff van Goens, a true paternal imperialist, was governor of Ceylon, he was very upset to find that a large majority of the Sinhalese preferred the 'tyrannical and oppressive rule' of Raja Sinha to his own 'righteous and Christian' administration. This paternal outlook was seldom evinced by the directors at home. In 1675 they censured the Governor-General and council at Batavia for sending ships with supplies of food to relieve a famine in Ceylon. 'Feeding people is really no concern of ours,' wrote the *Heeren* XVII on this occasion.[20]

The great gulf fixed between Europeans and Indonesians, whether religious, social, linguistic or political, did not mean that the latter opposed a united front to the aggression of the former. Far from it. The inhabitants of Ceram, who were the worst sufferers from the annual *hongi* expeditions which extirpated all unauthorized spice-trees, were so torn by age-old feuds between different chiefs, clans and villages that the Dutch could always rely on informers from one district to give them full intelligence of any smuggling activities in another. The pagan Alfurese head-hunters in the interior of the island were also bribed by the Dutch to act as auxiliary troops against rebellious or dissident coastal Muslim villages in both Ceram and Amboina on more than one occasion. The conquest of Macassar was only made possible, or was at any rate greatly facilitated, by the co-operation of the Buginese prince, Aru Palakka, and his warriors from Boni; in much the same way as Cortes' conquest of the Aztecs was powerfully aided by his alliance with their bitter enemies, the Tlaxcalans. In the Javanese wars from 1674 onwards, the Company also made use of Ambonese, Balinese and (at times) Madurese auxiliary troops; Captain Jonker, a full-blooded Ambonese despite his Dutch name, was the commander who eventually forced the usurper, Trunajaya, to surrender. The Company has often been accused of a Machiavellian policy of 'divide and rule', but in point of fact it seldom did more than

20. S. Arasaratnam, *Dutch Power in Ceylon, 1658–1687*, pp. 231–2; J. K. de Jonge *De Opkomst van het Nederlandsch gezag in Oost-Indië*, Vol. VI, p. lxxxvi.

exploit the deep-rooted antagonisms which already existed between various groups in so many of the Indonesian islands.[21]

The Chinese impression of the Dutch during the 17th century was naturally strongly influenced by the piratical attacks of the Netherlanders against the Fukienese junks trading with Manila, and by the forcible kidnapping of Chinese to help populate Batavia after Coen's capture of Jakarta. 'The people that we call Red-hairs or Red Barbarians,' wrote a contemporary Chinese chronicler, 'are identical with the Hollanders and they live in the Western Ocean. They are covetous and cunning, are very knowledgeable concerning valuable merchandise, and are very clever in the pursuit of gain. They will risk their lives in search of profit, and no place is too remote for them to frequent. Their ships are very large, strong and well-built, and they are called in China double-planked ships. These people are also very resourceful and inventive. They make sails like spiders'-webs, which can be set at any angle to catch the wind. If one falls in with them at sea, one is certain to be robbed by them.' After the Manchu conquest of Formosa and the admittance of the Dutch to the strictly regulated trade at Canton on the same footing as the English, French, Danes, Ostenders, etc., the Netherlanders were regarded by the Chinese in much the same light as these other 'foreign devils', and contacts were virtually limited to commercial relations.

The large Chinese community, which had developed at Batavia and in other places ruled by the Dutch in Indonesia, was procreated through the marriage (or concubinage) of Chinese men with Indonesian women, since very few Chinese women ever left the Middle Flowery Kingdom at this period. The Chinese in Indonesia were regarded as social outcasts by successive Chinese governments, whether Ming or Manchu, since these emigrants had left their birthplace and neglected the proper upkeep of their ancestral family tombs. When the Dutch massacred most of the

21. J. Keuning, *Ambonnezen, Portugezen en Nederlanders*, pp. 135–68; H. R. C. Wright, *The Moluccan Spice Monopoly, 1770–1824* (Kuala Lumpur, 1961); B. Vlekke, *Nusantara* (ed. 1945), pp. 191–213, especially pp. 202–3.

Chinese community at Batavia in 1740, under the mistaken impression that the Chinese were about to rise in rebellion against them, they were at first very nervous of reprisals being enforced against their trade with Canton, but in point of fact they suffered no inconvenience whatsoever. The Manchu Court at Peking showed itself as completely indifferent to the fate of the overseas Chinese as the Ming emperors had been when the Spaniards periodically massacred the Chinese settled at Manila.[22]

A Chinese chronicle of Batavia was compiled in 1793 from the records kept by successive secretaries of the Chinese community there. This gives us a worm's-eye view of the Dutch high officials, which it is interesting to compare with the character-sketches of the governor-generals by Valentyn and by modern Dutch historians. Johan Maetsuyker (1653–78) is described by the Chinese as 'a man of cantankerous and unpleasant character, so that low-class people did not dare to pass by his door. If any of them did so inadvertently, he was apt to arrest and punish them. The Company made no effort to stop this.' Johannes Camphuis (1684–91) is criticized for inaugurating new monopolies, 'so that the Company became rich and the people poor'. On the other hand, this governor-general is praised for allowing the erection of a Chinese school, whereby the Dutch showed that 'they were willing to adapt themselves to the wishes of the people, and to treat foreigners indulgently and generously'. It is interesting to note that Governor-General Valckenier (1737–41) does not receive the chief blame for the appalling massacre of the Chinese at Batavia in 1740, but his critic and successor, Gustaaf Baron van Imhoff, who is stigmatized as 'a disgrace to mankind in his life and death'. The self-righteous Petrus Albertus van der Parra (1761–75) is characterized as being outwardly friendly but secretly mistreating people.

22. For Dutch relations with the Chinese cf. W. P. Groeneveldt, *De Nederlanders in China, 1601–1624* (The Hague, 1898); J. T. Vermeulen, *De Chineezen te Batavia en de troebelen van 1740* (Leiden, 1938). W. H. Medhurst (trans.), 'Chronologische Geschiedenis van Batavia geschreven door een Chinees', in *Tijdschrift voor Neêrlands Indië*, Vol. III, Part 2 (Batavia, 1840), pp. 1–145.

The attitude of the Japanese towards the Dutch was more ambivalent. On the one hand, as we know from the factory records at Hirado and Deshima, both peoples had in common a fondness for strong drink and could indulge in convivial carousels, which the more abstemious Portuguese and Spaniards had found distasteful during the period of the 'Christian Century' in Japan (1543–1640). During the two centuries of seclusion enforced by the Tokugawa military dictatorship (1640–1854), the Dutch also fulfilled the function of 'merchants of light' at Deshima. This Dutch factory was the only channel through which the Japanese authorities kept themselves informed (in so far as they wished to do so) of events in Europe, and through which they received the Dutch books that a small number of the Nagasaki interpreters could read. In the course of the 18th century a few scholars, officials and even *daimyo* began to take an intelligent interest in this *Rangaku*, or 'Dutch-learning'. One or two eccentrics, such as Shiba Kokan (1738–1818) and Honda Toshiaki (1744–1821), even rated European civilization as superior to that of China and Japan in some ways; and the study of Western medicine, astronomy and mathematics made surprising progress in the small circles to which it was necessarily confined.

The Japanese also admired the skills of the Dutch as navigators, shipbuilders and gunners. When the chiefs of the Deshima factory, or the resident physicians there, were men who took an intelligent interest in their surroundings and made an effort to understand the Japanese viewpoint, they were usually respectfully and considerately treated by the officials and *diamyo* with whom they came into contact. Such a man was Isaac Titsingh, who, after a stay of some years in Japan (1780–83), maintained a friendly correspondence from Bengal with a few of the Nagasaki interpreters and with two of the *daimyo* who had learnt to read and write Dutch. But only too often the Dutch on Deshima were of the type criticized by Thunberg in 1775. The Swedish traveller animadverted on: 'the pride which some of the weaker-minded officers in the Dutch service very imprudently exhibit to the Japanese, by ill-timed contradiction, contemptuous behaviour, scornful looks and laughter, which occasions the Japanese in their turn to hate and despise them; a hatred which is greatly increased upon observing in how unfriendly and unmannerly a style they usually behave to each other, and the brutal treatment which the sailors under their command frequently experience from them, together with the oaths, curses and blows with which the poor fellows are assailed by them'.[23]

If the Dutch sailors were frequently assailed with oaths, curses and blows by their officers, it can easily be imagined what sort of treatment was meted out to erring slaves by their owners. Though the Dutch did not originally depend on slave-labour to quite the same extent as did their Portuguese predecessors in three continents, they quickly found that they could not do without it, whatever qualms their Calvinist consciences once had about this trade in human flesh. The early Dutch trade with West Africa was, as we have seen (pp. 23, 54), primarily for gold and ivory, but the conquest of north-east Brazil in 1634–8 brought a great demand for slaves in 'New Holland', apart from those who could be sold to the Spaniards in the Caribbean and the English in Virginia. John Maurice of Nassau-Siegen at first toyed with the idea of using free white labour in the sugar-mills of Pernambuco, but he soon came round to the prevailing view of both Portuguese and Dutch planters in the tropics: 'It is not possible to effect anything in Brazil without slaves ... and they cannot be dispensed with upon any occasion whatsoever: if anyone feels that this is wrong, it is a futile scruple.' [24] In default of colonists from the Netherlands, Batavia was largely populated

---

23. C. P. Thunberg, *Travels*, Vol. III, p. 29. The 'recklessness and thoughtlessness' of many Dutch sea officers in Japan had been denounced by the government at Batavia over a century earlier, in 1670 (*Nederlandsch-Indisch Plakaatboek*, Vol. II, pp. 509–12). For Dutch-Japanese relations in the Tokugawa period cf. J. Feenstra Kuiper, *Japan en de Buitenwereld in de achttiende eeuw* (The Hague, 1921); C. R. Boxer, *Jan Compagnie in Japan 1600–1850* (The Hague, 1950); C. Krieger, *The Infiltration of European Civilization in Japan during the 18th Century* (Leiden, 1940); D. Keene, *The Japanese Discovery of Europe. Honda Toshiaki and other discoverers* (London, 1952).

24. C. R. Boxer, *The Dutch in Brazil, 1624–1654*, p. 83.

by slaves imported from the regions round the Bay of Bengal, young couples with children being sought for this purpose. The Dutch nutmeg-plantations in the Banda Islands were also mainly populated by imported slaves and Chinese convicts, after the removal or extermination of the original inhabitants. Even in places like the coast of Coromandel, where cheap free labour was readily available, the Dutch often made use of slaves; and the search for slave-markets took their East Indiamen as far afield as Madagascar and Mindanao.

If the Dutch entered the slave-trade, whether East or West, with some hesitation and reluctance in the early 17th century, they soon stifled their scruples and made up for their late start. Some of the Dutch pioneer voyagers had professed horror at the Portuguese mistreatment of their slaves, but the Netherlanders were soon guilty of similar atrocities themselves, as is clear from the accounts of 17th–18th-century travellers, and from the draconic severity of their own colonial legislation in this respect.[25] As had happened with the Portuguese, many eyewitnesses noted that the women slave-owners inflicted the worst cruelties on their slaves, especially on young and pretty females whom they suspected of being their husbands' paramours. It should be noted, however, that for different reasons the enslavement of Amerindians, Hottentots and Javanese was strictly forbidden by the directors of the West and East India Companies, respectively.

25. B. Vlekke (*Nusantara*, ed. 1945, p. 142) claims that 'the atrocities that were permitted and did occur under the laws that regulated slavery in the Caribbean islands were absolutely excluded by the laws enforced among both Indonesians and Dutch in the Indies'. This is an over-sanguine view. Although arbitrary violence by owners to their slaves was deprecated by the Statutes of Batavia (1642), it is crystal clear from the accounts of numerous eyewitnesses that there was plenty of it in practice. Apart from this, the laws *did* sanction the most savage and cruel punishments when these were inflicted by the properly constituted authorities. The most that can be said in extenuation is that such sadistic punishments were sometimes inflicted on European criminals as well as on slaves. Cf. V. de Kock, *Those in Bondage* (London, 1950), pp. 145–97, for a documented discussion of this problem.

The majority of Indonesian slaves came from Celebes, Bali, Buton and Timor. The importation of slaves from Macassar and Bali to Batavia was often legally prohibited or severely restricted owing to the propensity of those islanders to run amuck or to take violent revenge if they were ill-treated; but these periodic prohibitions seem to have been largely ignored in practice.[26]

Dutch slave households were often unnecessarily large, and were maintained for ostentation and status-seeking, just as they were in Portuguese Goa, Luanda and Bahia. A newly wed bride, writing from Batavia to her great-aunt in Holland in 1689, described the duties of her fifty-nine household slaves as follows: 'Three or four youths, and as many maids, accompanied herself and her husband whenever they left the house. Another five or six serving men and maids stood behind their respective chairs at meals. They had a slave orchestra which played on the harp, viol and bassoon at mealtimes. Three or four slaves attended constantly on each of them indoors, and one slave always sat at the entrance ready to receive messages or to run errands. The remaining slaves were employed in various household, cellar and buttery duties, and as grooms, cooks, gardeners and sempstresses.' [27]

With the Dutch, as with other colonial powers, plantation slavery was generally more inhuman and unfeeling than the domestic variety. 18th-century Surinam undoubtedly had a particularly bad record in this respect. Slave revolts were endemic throughout that period, and the Surinam planters or their over-

26. J. A. Van der Chijs, *Nederlandsch-Indisch Plakaatboek*, Vol. II, p. 405; Vol. III, pp. 147, 168, 229, 514–15; Vol. IV, pp. 62, 64, 140, 149; Vol. V, pp. 139, 617–18; Vol. VI, pp. 281–9, 443, for some of the varying restrictions or prohibitions on the sale, import and export of slaves from Celebes and Bali.

27. Letter of Cornelia van Beek to Maria Sweers de Weerd, d. Batavia, 14 December 1689, printed in G. D. J. Schotel, *Het Oud-Hollandsch huisgezin der zeventiende eeuw* (Haarlem, 1868), pp. 307–10. For slave-households at Batavia cf. also V. I. Van de Wall, *Figuren en feiten uit den Compagniestijd* (Bandung, 1932), pp. 161–83.

seers never seem to have drawn the obvious conclusion that, as one of the rebel slave leaders observed in 1760: 'The Whites were cutting their noses to spite their faces by so mistreating their valuable field-hands that they forced them to seek refuge in the forest.' The runaway slaves, or 'Bush-Negroes' as they were called, formed settlements in jungle clearings, which were periodically attacked by Dutch punitive columns or commandos of burghers and soldiers – usually with no lasting results. One of the most redoubtable negro leaders, named Baron, on capturing a white army officer who had only been a short time in Surinam, released him with the words: 'Go away, for you have not been long enough in the colony to have been guilty of mistreating slaves.'

Society in 18th-century Surinam was similar in structure to the plantation and slave society which characterized the sugar-colonies of the other European powers in the West Indies. At the top were the white planters who indulged in the same seignorial way of life as did their equivalents in the Antilles and in Brazil. Then came what might be termed an embryo middle class composed of white overseers, clerks and merchants. Next came a group of coloured freedmen, the offspring of white fathers and coloured mothers, and a smaller number of free negroes. At the bottom were the negro slaves, the new arrivals from West Africa being termed 'salt water negroes' in contra-distinction to the old hands who were called Creoles. As in all slave-holding societies, the social distance between these groups was conspicuous, and the most direct contact between the highest and the lowest groups came through the concubinage of negresses and white men. Masters and slaves in Surinam had even less in common than they had in the French and English West Indies, since the *lingua franca* of Surinam was not Dutch, nor even Portuguese, but a curious language called Negro-English, partly a relic of the English origins of the colony in 1650–60. African cultural elements imported by the negro slaves were, perhaps, more strongly entrenched in Surinam than anywhere else in the New World. This was partly because, as we have seen, the planters systematically obstructed the propagation of any form of Christianity among their slaves. By and large, man's inhumanity to man just about reached its limits in Surinam, and it is a relief to turn to a region with a less sordid history.[28]

28. R. A. J. Van Lier, *The Development and Nature of Society in the West Indies* (Amsterdam, 1950); L. L. E. Reus, *The Historical and Social Background of Surinam's Negro-English* (Amsterdam, 1953). C. Douglas, *Een blik in het verleden van Suriname, 1630–1863* (Paramaribo, 1930), gives a chronological survey of slave revolts and their causes, derived from J. J. Hartsinck, *Beschryving van Guiana, of de Wilde Kust* (2 vols., Amsterdam, 1770), J. G. Stedman, *A Narrative of a Five Years Expedition Against the Revolted Negroes in Surinam* (2 vols., London, 1796), and other classic 18th-century sources.

9
The tavern of two seas

I am not sure who first called the Cape of Good Hope the 'Tavern of the Indian Ocean' – *de Indische Zeeherberg* – but Commissioner Uytenhage de Mist, who employed the phrase in his celebrated *Memorandum* of 1802, and to whom it is often ascribed, was certainly not the originator of the nickname. Thunberg, who first visited the Cape in 1772, wrote that it 'may with propriety be stiled an inn for travellers to and from the East Indies, who, after several months' sail may here get refreshments of all kinds, and are then about half way to the place of their destination, whether homeward or outward bound'.[1] I suspect that the phrase is of 17th-century origin, but however that may be, from the time that Jan van Riebeeck planted the Dutch flag there in 1652 until the opening of the Suez Canal over two centuries later, the Cape was the half-way house between Europe and Asia, and the denizens of Cape Town were the hosts of the Tavern situated at the junction of the Indian and the Atlantic Oceans.

Although the Portuguese had discovered and named the Cape before the end of the 15th century, their East Indiamen, whether outward or homeward bound, usually gave it a wide berth and made the picturesque but unhealthy little coral island of Moçambique their main port of call. When the directors of the Dutch East India Company decided to challenge the Portuguese claim to the monopoly of the Indian Ocean, they tried to wrest this stronghold from their enemies in 1607-8. Had they succeeded, they might never have decided to found a refreshment station at the Cape of Good Hope, and the whole course of South African history would have been profoundly different. After the Dutch failure to take Moçambique, both the Portuguese and the English

1. C. P. Thunberg, *Travels in Europe, Africa, and Asia, 1770-79*, Vol. I, p. 228. For J. A. Uytenhage de Mist and his *Memorandum* cf. the bilingual edition by K. M. Jeffreys (Vol. III of the publications of the Van Riebeeck Society, Cape Town, 1920).

occasionally toyed with the idea of founding a settlement of their own at the Cape, in order to forestall a possible Dutch occupation. In July 1620 the commander of a passing English East India Fleet planted the cross of St George on The Lion's Rump and took formal possession of the Cape peninsula in the name of King James. But the 'wisest fool in Christendom' ignored this proclamation, and the Cape remained a no-man's-land until Van Riebeeck implemented the decision of the *Heeren* XVII to found a refreshment and a victualling station for Indiamen there thirty-two years later.

It must be admitted that the Cape of Good Hope did not altogether fulfil the directors' hopes that the crews of Dutch Indiamen calling there would suffer much less from scurvy and other shipboard diseases. Complete mortality returns for these Indiamen are lacking for some periods, but from those which we have we get the impression that the shipboard death-rate was much less in the fifty years before Cape Town was founded than it was in the last fifty years of the Company's existence. At any rate, it can be said with a fair degree of certainty that the mortality rates began to increase in the last decade of the 17th century and grew progressively worse (with considerable fluctuations) in the 18th century, the years 1760-95 being the worst of all. Stavorinus instanced as a typical example: 'Of the crews of twenty-seven ships that sailed from Europe in 1768-9, which altogether amounted, by their muster rolls, to 5,971 hands, the number of dead was 959, which is very near to one in six.' In 1782 ten East Indiamen left the Netherlands, carrying 2,653 men, of whom 1,095, or 43 per cent, died before reaching the Cape of Good Hope, where 915 survivors were admitted to hospital. This institution, incidentally, seldom enjoyed a good reputation, being sometimes dubbed a cemetery rather than a hospital. Mentzel was no doubt correct when he wrote of the sick soldiers and sailors landed from Indiamen at Cape Town: 'The pure air and fresh meat have often contributed more to their recovery than the doctor with all his medicines.' Probably the increasing mortality rates aboard Dutch East Indiamen in the second half of the 18th century were due to the chronic unfitness of so many of the men who embarked in them – those in Dutch ports with their health undermined by the appalling conditions of the crimps' houses where they were quartered (pp. 91–93), and those at Batavia racked by the endemic malarial fever which had turned the 'Queen of the Eastern Seas' into a charnel-house. But bad as the overall mortality figures were for the years 1652–1795, they would presumably have been even worse without the welcome change afforded by a call at the Cape.[2]

Another respect in which the Cape did not, perhaps, entirely fulfil the original expectations of its founders, was that Table Bay proved to be a much less secure roadstead than they had expected. During the (Cape) winter months, and particularly in May and June, there was no safe anchorage in the bay, which was frequently lashed by violent northerly and north-westerly gales. The tale of shipping disasters during a hundred and fifty years is too long to unfold here, but passing mention may be made of the spectacular tragedies of 1697, 1722, 1728, 1737 and 1790, when many richly laden homeward-bound Indiamen were lost, several of them with all hands.[3] In 1753 the *Heeren* XVII ruled that during the winter season from April to September, Indiamen calling at The Cape should anchor in False Bay, which was better protected against north-west gales. This order was not always strictly observed, and still less attention was paid to reiterated orders by the *Heeren* XVII limiting the stay of India-

2. For discussions of the death-rate aboard Dutch East Indiamen in the light of the available statistics cf. D. Schoute, *De Geneeskunde in den dienst der Oost-Indische Compagnie* (Amsterdam, 1929), pp. 40–103; E. H. Burrows, *A History of Medicine in South Africa up to the end of the 19th Century* (Cape Town, 1958), pp. 18–26; C. R. Boxer, 'The Dutch East-Indiamen: their sailors, their navigators, and life on board, 1602–1795' (in *Mariner's Mirror*, Vol. XLIX, May 1963, pp. 81–104), and the sources there quoted.

3. R. F. Kennedy, *Shipwrecks on and off the Coasts of Southern Africa. A Catalogue and Index* (Johannesburg Public Library, 1955), gives the most detailed and documented list of wrecks, but, so far as I know, this cyclostated work in the Johannesburg Public Library has not yet been published. Cf. A. J. Boeseken, *Die Nederlandse Kommissarisse en die 18de eeuse samelewing aan die Kaap* (Cape Town, 1944), pp. 15–17.

men at the Cape to periods ranging from ten to twenty days. The directors at one time considered the possibility of prohibiting Indiamen from calling at the Cape 'save only if unavoidably compelled to do so, for the preservation of the ship and crew'; but in the upshot they decided (in 1766) that ships leaving Batavia after 1 December should not call at the Cape if they could avoid doing so. These injunctions against a long stay by shipping in the roadstead were not motivated only by the desire to avoid shipwrecks but also to lessen the expense involved and, above all, to reduce the extent of smuggling and private trade.

Here, as elsewhere, the authorities fought a losing battle against this perennial 'canker'. Reiterated edicts against smuggling activities, and repeated denunciations of the misbehaviour of sailors and soldiers from passing Indiamen, show how generally these prohibitions were disregarded. The preamble to one of these decrees, promulgated at Cape Town in 1719, plaintively acknowledged that despite the severity of the punishments inflicted for breach of the anti-smuggling and disciplinary regulations, 'the lawlessness of the sailors instead of diminishing through fear of punishment seems, on the contrary, obstinately to increase'. The situation was aggravated at the Cape because foreign Indiamen soon began to call regularly at Table Bay; and in the 18th century there were often more foreign sail anchored in the roadstead than there were Dutch. The *Heeren* XVII at first tried to discourage foreign Indiamen from calling at the Cape by directing that they should be given only the bare minimum of essential supplies; but they later adopted a more liberal policy when they realized that both the Company and the inhabitants of Cape Town could make a profit by selling local produce and services to foreign Indiamen after the colony had become self-supporting in foodstuffs in about 1684.[4]

The extent to which the Tavern of Two Seas became increas-

4. *Kaapse Argiefstukke. Kaapse Plakaatboek*, I, 1652–1707 (Cape Town, 1944), pp. 80, 180–81; ibid., II, 1707–1753 (Cape Town, 1948), pp. 5–7, 32–5, 73–9; A. J. Boeseken, *Nederlandsche Commissarissen aan de Kaap, 1657–1700* (The Hague, 1938), pp. 86–7; ibid., *Die Nederlandse Kommissarisse en die 18de eeuse samelewing*, pp. 13–24.

ingly dependent on foreign shipping for its prosperity is evidenced by the comments of an English lady visitor in 1764–5:

Nothing can be more agreeable to the people of this place, than the arrival of an English ship, as it causes a circulation of money, and indeed it is chiefly by the English that most people in town are supported; not only by taking the captains, passengers, etc., to board at their houses, but by furnishing the ships with provisions. A great many French ships likewise stop here, and all the Dutch passing to and from India; but for the last they are obliged to provide according to certain prices, stipulated by the Dutch Company, and as neither the Dutch nor the French spend their money so freely as the English, of course they are not so desirable guests. The custom is to pay a rix-dollar daily for each person's board and lodging, for which they are provided with everything; the tables are plentiful, the houses are clean, and the people obliging, and what makes it extremely comfortable, is, that most of them speak English. French is likewise spoken by many; so that foreigners find themselves more at home in this port than can be imagined.

A few years later, Stavorinus and Thunberg made similar observations, the Dutchman remarking that visiting Englishmen 'care not for their money and spend it freely upon the ladies', while the Swede noted: 'A French officer, though dressed to the best advantage, and frequently wearing a star on his breast, as a mark of his merit and his king's favour, had but little respect paid him; whereas an English mate of a ship, with his hair about his ears, was much esteemed on account of his being flush of money.'[5]

Apart from its importance as a port of call for East Indiamen of all nationalities, the Cape developed into a colony which was something unique – save for short-lived New Netherland – in the possessions of the Dutch East and West India Companies. It had a healthy, subtropical and partly fertile hinterland, which was virtually unoccupied save for wandering Bushmen and Hottentots who presented no serious menace. White colonization was as feasible here as it had been in New Netherland, with

5. *Letters from the Island of Teneriffe, Brazil, the Cape of Good Hope and the East Indies by Mrs Kindersley* (London, 1777), letter d. February 1765 from Cape Town; J. S. Stavorinus, *Voyages to the East-Indies, 1768–1778*, Vol. I, p. 565; C. P. Thunberg, *Travels, 1770–1779*, Vol. I, pp. 229–30.

the additional advantage that there was no rival European nation close at hand. Admittedly, conditions for Van Riebeeck's pioneers were very rigorous, since everything had to be built from scratch and there was no cheap labour force available as there was in the VOC's Asian forts and factories. Building timber was in such short supply that much of it was imported from Scandinavia via Holland until the discovery of the forests in the Eastern Cape district in the 1760s. The *Heeren* XVII did not envisage any extensive white settlement when they authorized the foundation of the new colony, and for a long time they were anxious to keep it as small as possible in order to save costs. There was even a plan sponsored by Rijkloff van Goens (in 1655–7) to dig a canal between False and Table Bays, so as to transform the Cape peninsula into an easily defended island. But circumstances forced the local government (or 'Commanders' as they were entitled down to 1691) and through them the *Heeren* XVII to permit, however grudgingly, the expansion of the original settlement to an extent undreamt of by its founders.[6]

Van Riebeeck soon realized that ex-soldiers, sailors, clerks and artificers were not the most suitable material for the agricultural workers who were necessary if the settlement was to provide East Indiamen with adequate supplies of fresh meat, vegetables, fruits and other provisions. He and his successor, Zacharias Wagenaer, advocated the introduction of Chinese labourers, since they had both served in the Far East and been impressed with the results achieved by Chinese market-gardeners in Formosa and Java. But the authorities at Batavia could not induce Chinese to emigrate to this remote outpost about which they knew nothing; and though Van Riebeeck pressed for slaves to be sent him as an alternative, these did not begin to arrive in adequate numbers until the slave-trade with Madagascar was developed in the 1670s. Enslavement of the local aborigines had been expressly forbidden by the *Heeren* XVII, and, in any event, experience soon showed

6. G. McCall Theal, *Chronicles of the Cape Commanders, 1652–1691* (Cape Town, 1882); D. B. Bosman & H. B. Thom (eds.), *Daghregister gehouden by den oppercoopman Jan Anthonisz van Riebeeck, 1651–1662* (3 vols., Cape Town, 1952–7); and the two previously quoted works of A. J. Boeseken, for the above and what follows.

that pure-bred Hottentots and Bushmen were useless as hired agricultural labourers, although Hottentot men made good herdsmen, grooms and drivers, and Hottentot women and girls sometimes became domestic servants.

In default of slaves and Chinese, Van Riebeeck necessarily had recourse to the system of free-burghers which had failed so signally in the East Indies. He induced some of the local employees who showed – or apparently showed – an aptitude for agricultural work to leave the Company's service and take up grants of land for farming, on condition that the produce was sold to the Company at prices fixed by the latter. The farmers and burghers were later allowed to charge higher prices for provisions supplied to foreign shipping, save in times of scarcity when they were supposed to sell to the Company alone. Progress was slow for several decades. On the one hand, the authorities complained that the free-burghers tended to abandon work on the land in favour of tavern-keeping in Cape Town. On the other hand, the free-burghers complained that they could not plough fields and grow wheat without the help of draught oxen and of slaves, and that the Company paid too little for their produce. The nadir was reached in 1660, when forty-two out of a total of seventy-odd free-burghers succeeded in embarking clandestinely for the Netherlands aboard a homeward-bound India Fleet with the active help of the sailors. Twelve years later the white population still totalled less than 600 souls, of whom only sixty-four were adult male free-burghers, thirty-nine of them married.

The turning-point came in the 1680s when the directors finally decided that the advantages of modestly encouraging white colonization at the Cape outweighed the disadvantages. They were able to send out assisted emigrant groups of Huguenot exiles from France after the Revocation of the Edict of Nantes (1685), as well as some Dutch families and small parties of marriageable girls from the orphanages in the United Provinces. In 1695 there were still only about 340 free-burghers at the Cape, but thanks mainly to the energetic leadership and pioneering spirit of Governor Simon van der Stel (1679–99), farms and orchards now spread out beyond the limits of the Cape peninsula. The Huguenot immigrants had wanted to live together and preserve their national identity, but Simon van der Stel, who was uncommonly nationalistic for a Dutchman, insisted on splitting them up among the Dutch farmers, and they were completely absorbed after two or three generations. A constant trickle of the Company's military and civil employees left its service at the Cape and became burghers or farmers, and during the 18th century a large number of Germans settled in the colony in this way. The great majority of these men did not bring their womenfolk with them, but married at the Cape with girls of Dutch (or Franco–Dutch) descent. By 1780 there were between 11,000 and 12,000 free-burghers in the colony, of whom at least 3,000 lived in Cape Town. A few years earlier, Stavorinus had noted: 'Although the first colonists here were composed of various nations, they are, by the operation of time, now so thoroughly blended together, that they are not to be distinguished from each other; even most of such as have been born in Europe, and who have resided here for some years, have, in a manner, changed their national character, for that of this country.'[7] In other words, the formation of the Afrikaner people had begun.

The economic development of the colony was handicapped by the numerous restrictions placed by the Company on the commercial and (to a lesser extent) the agricultural activities of the free-burghers, as they constantly complained. Van Reede tot Drakenstyn reported in 1685 that all the free-burghers were discontented with the rule of the Company. Those living near the Castle, because they were not allowed to trade freely; those engaged in arable farming, because they could not charge high prices for their produce; those engaged in stock raising, because they were not allowed to barter with the Hottentots. It would be unreasonable to expect 17th-century Dutch directors to subscribe to free-trade views which only became commonplace in the Victorian England of Sir John Bowring ('Free Trade is Jesus

7. J. S. Stavorinus, *Voyages, 1768–1778*, Vol. III, p. 435. Cf. O. F. Mentzel, *A Geographical-Topographical Description of the Cape of Good Hope* (ed. Van Riebeeck Society, Cape Town, 1924), Vol. II, p. 100, for an almost identical observation. Cf. also J. C. de Haan & P. J. Van Winter (eds.), *Nederlanders over de Zeeën* (Utrecht, 1940), pp. 306 ff.

Christ, and Jesus Christ is Free Trade'); but a few of the visiting commissioners to the Cape in the years 1655–1795 did criticize the irksome restrictions laid on its inhabitants and recommended lightening the burden in various minor ways. One of them, Daniel Nolthenius, went so far as to advise (in 1748), that the Colony could not achieve real prosperity unless free trade and navigation were granted 'not only to the inhabitants of this promontory, but likewise to all who should wish to participate therein, whether they live in Europe or in Asia'.[8] Such a revolutionary view could hardly be expected to commend itself to the directors of a chartered Company which confessedly had 'trade as its compass and profit as its lodestar' for its own shareholders to the exclusion of all others. The desire of the directors to keep the cost of maintaining the colony down to the minimum, and to provide their ships with fresh provisions as cheaply as possible, clashed with the wish of the colonists to get the prices to which they thought they were entitled and which they could usually obtain from the passengers and crews of foreign shipping. This was a conflict of interests which was never resolved to the satisfaction of either party during the period of the Company's rule. A glance at the development of the wheat, the wine and the wool farms of the colony may help to make this clear.

For the reasons indicated above, the settlement at the Cape took longer to become self-supporting in foodstuffs than the directors had originally expected. The vegetable garden planted by Van Riebeeck soon produced enough fresh greens for the crews of the Indiamen, and fresh meat could usually be obtained by barter from the Hottentots. But for almost exactly thirty years the Cape was dependent on the importation of wheat and rice from Batavia and elsewhere, and a small export surplus of corn was first achieved in 1684. As the colony expanded the situation improved. The natural fertility of the soil varied a good deal but, as Mentzel noted, there were very few farms which did not have stretches of good soil together with patches of sandy and stony ground. Farmers usually reaped three annual crops, and left the field lying fallow in the fourth year. Ox-drawn ploughs with six, eight or ten oxen and a team of three men were used; wheat, rye

8. A. J. Boeseken, *Die Nederlandse Kommissarisse* (1944), p. 175.

and barley were the principal crops. The harvest season was at Christmas-time, when all hands, including children and slaves, worked in the fields from dawn till dusk, with a break for breakfast at 7 a.m. and a rest from 10 a.m. to 4 p.m., when it was too hot to work.

When the Cape first produced an exportable surplus of wheat, the suggestion was made that this cereal should be grown for export to the Netherlands, but the *Heeren* XVII rejected this idea as impracticable, since the cost price of wheat at the Cape was just about double that in the fatherland. The directors subsequently tried to encourage the export of Cape wheat to Batavia, but the authorities there pointed out that they could get better and cheaper corn from Bengal and Surat, while they had the Java 'rice-bowl' at their door. The Javanese Succession Wars which accompanied the disintegration of Mataram (1704–55) and laid waste much cultivated land brought a change in this situation. By 1750 the Cape was exporting annually about 2,000 tons of wheat to Batavia, apart from smaller quantities to Ceylon. After 1772 the Cape farmers were able to supply all the Dutch settlements in Asia with this cereal, and the exports of wheat from the Cape to the Netherlands also became practicable owing to a sharp rise in the price of corn in the home market after 1769. The disastrous Anglo–Dutch War of 1780–4 put an end to this as to so many other sources of Dutch colonial prosperity. The problem of what to do with the exportable surplus of Cape wheat was still unsolved when the Company's rule collapsed in 1795. Throughout this period the Company would never pay the Cape farmer as high a price for his corn as the passengers and crews of Indiamen, or even the inhabitants of Cape Town, were usually prepared to do. The free-burghers therefore preferred to sell their corn to foreigners despite the regulations and orders which were periodically promulgated to restrict this practice and to give preference to the Company's needs.[9]

9. A. J. Boeseken, *Die Nederlandse Kommissarisse* (1944), pp. 155–69; O. F. Mentzel, *Description of the Cape*, Vol. III, pp. 162–73, for a good description of farming at the Cape in the 18th century. The varying nature of the soil on even small farms was stressed by J. G.

The production and export of wine was another problem about which the growers and the Company did not always see eye to eye. Viniculture had been introduced by Van Riebeeck, and several of the Huguenot immigrants in the 1680s were selected for their knowledge of vine dressing, but it was a long time before the Cape wines found ready acceptance elsewhere. As with so much else, viniculture owed a great deal to the precept and example of Simon van der Stel, whose lovingly tended vineyards at Groot Constantia gave this name to a wine which became world famous in the course of the 18th century. Despite the improvement in quality, and the fact that production increased steadily and even doubled between 1776 and 1786, exports did not increase correspondingly. Most visitors to the Cape were polite enough about its wines after their long sea-voyage; but once they settled down at Batavia, Pondicherry or Calcutta, they reverted to their preference for French claret, burgundy and champagne. De la Caille, Mentzel and other foreign observers were all agreed that the quality of the more common Cape wines could be improved if greater care was taken with their cultivation. The majority of the wine-growers 'did not know how to treat their wines properly'. Those that did, like the growers of Constantia, kept their secrets to themselves, so as to obtain higher prices if not from the Company then on the 'black market'. The wine-growers had to sell their wine to the Company at fixed prices, and the Company farmed out the licences for selling the wine retail. Although Mentzel maintained that the monopoly was not vexatious, the wine-growers complained that the sale-prices of their wine depended largely on the decisions of a few senior Company officials and privileged persons.[10]

One of the difficulties that retarded the development of wheat farms during the 17th century was that many farmers preferred to engage in stock-raising because this required fewer hands and labour was so scarce. The Company originally relied on barter-

Grevenbroek in 1695 (I. Schapera, *The Early Cape Hottentots*, Cape Town, 1933, p. 271).

10. For wine-growing and the wine monopoly cf. O. F. Mentzel, *Description of the Cape*, Vol. III, pp. 174–82; Vol. I, p. 66; A. J. Boeseken, *Die Nederlandse Kommissarisse* (1944), pp. 169–70.

trade with the Hottentots to obtain sufficient sheep and cattle for supplying the colonists and the Indiamen with fresh meat. Periodic difficulties – though these never amounted to lengthy wars – with the Hottentots, and the decimation of their clans through the ravages of smallpox, brought about a shift of policy. The authorities, though giving preference to the establishment of arable farms, no longer placed any obstacles in the way of stock-breeding by the burghers. Cattle- and sheep-stations were pushed ever further into the interior as the farmers sought new pastures in a land where water was often scarce and where the soil could not support too much grazing. The Cape sheep were bred mainly for their mutton, which formed the staple food of the inhabitants of Cape Town, and visitors from Indiamen who stayed any length of time ashore were apt to complain of the monotony of this daily dish and the greasy way in which it was served. The skins of the sheep were used for shoe-leather, but the wool was virtually useless, 'indeed it is rather hair than wool', as Mentzel noted.

From time to time, efforts were made to improve the breed by importing Persian and Merino rams, but not until near the end of the Company's rule did these produce an appreciable result in the form of wool that could be exported. In 1782 some burghers and officials petitioned to be allowed 'to try and introduce the manufacture of woollen stuffs', but the Company's Fiscal rejected their request with the forthright observation that 'the establishment and fomenting of such manufactures was diametrically opposed to the true welfare and to the sound political system of this government', since it would adversely affect the efforts being made to revive the textile industry in the Netherlands. Nevertheless, sheep-farming for the sake of mutton was both profitable and productive. Flocks of 1,000 sheep were regarded as quite small, and Thunberg stayed with a farmer in the Bokkeveld who possessed 3,000 head of cattle and 12,000 sheep. By the end of the 18th century there were over 1,250,000 head of sheep in the colony, though only about 7,000 of these were wooled sheep.[11]

11. O. F. Mentzel, *Description of the Cape*, Vol. III, pp. 210–12, for sheep-farming at the Cape. Cf. A. J. Boeseken, *Die Nederlandse Kommissarisse* (1944), pp. 191–3.

The Company's attitude to the development of farming at the Cape, while chiefly influenced by its desire to keep prices down and so secure provisions for its Indiamen as cheaply as possible, was not wholly a restrictive one. In 1706, as a result of the complaints of many of the burghers against the energetic but autocratic governors, Simon and W. A. van der Stel, who had allegedly secured much of the best land for their own farms (1685–1705), the *Heeren* XVII forbade their officials and employees to own land on any considerable scale, or to engage in farming. This rule was not always very strictly observed, since it could be evaded to some extent by a judicious marriage; but it did ensure that the free-burghers who engaged in farming or wine-growing did not have to compete with officials who were likewise large landowners. The burghers and farmers at the Cape were assured of a reasonably adequate home market for their products, even if they could not get the prices which they wanted for their wheat, wine and wool, and even if they could not always export their surplus production of those commodities.

Once the pioneering days of Van Riebeeck and his immediate successors were over, white society at the Cape could be divided into three main groups: the bureaucrats, or the Company's officials; the urban free-burghers of Cape Town; and the country free-burghers or the Boers. The eight senior Company officials formed a 'Council of Polity' under the chairmanship of the Governor, and this body (less the Governor) also functioned two or three times a week in its capacity of Council of Justice. From 1685 onwards, two (later, three) burgher representatives sat on this last body, and they were sometimes allowed to represent their fellow citizens in the Council of Polity as well. Some of the senior officials, who were nearly always European-born Netherlanders, were conscious of their real or alleged cultural superiority over the burghers, many of whom were of humble Dutch, French, German or local origin. But it is equally certain that social relations between bureaucrats and burghers were much less strained and formal than they were at Batavia. Mentzel, who noticed the underlying tension between the European-born Dutchmen and the Afrikaner, also noted: 'On public occasions, such as weddings, and the like, I have often seen Under-Merchants, or even officers, dancing with shoemakers' daughters, while their own daughters danced with the sons of trades-people. Pre-eminence is conceded to the Upper-Merchants, since they are members of the government and the heads of the state, but except for them, no man at the Cape regards himself as better than his neighbours.' The penchant of the wealthy widows at Batavia for marrying *predikanten* had its counterpart at the Cape, where, Mentzel tells us: 'Since the *predikanten* rank higher than the ordinary merchants and receive such high salaries, allowances and perquisites they can always make the best matches.' [12]

The wealthier burghers of Cape Town turned their homes into boarding-houses for the officers and passengers of the Indiamen calling at the Cape, while the 'common man' did the same for the sailors and soldiers. Most visitors to Cape Town in the 18th century contrasted the female of the burgher species advantageously with the male, alleging that the former were more lively and intelligent, at any rate while they were still unmarried. Stavorinus was not alone in denouncing the laziness and ignorance of the wealthier male burghers, who led a lethargic life resembling that of their counterparts at Batavia. 'The men who are freemen of the Town are seldom seen abroad : they are generally at home, in an undress, and spend their time in smoking tobacco, and in loitering up and down the house. After dinner, they take a nap, according to the Indian fashion, and in the evening they play a game at cards. They are not addicted to reading, and are, consequently, very ignorant, and even know little of what is doing in other parts of the globe, except from what they may hear by the strangers who visit them from time to time.' Some of the richest burghers sent their sons to be educated at Dutch or German universities, and these returned with a better fund of knowledge than could be acquired at the elementary schools at the Cape, or from the German soldiers and non-com-

12. O. F. Mentzel, *Life at the Cape in the mid-18th Century* (Cape Town, 1919); ibid., *Description of the Cape*, Vol. II (1924), pp. 100–23, for a full description of social life at the Cape. The system of government is fully described in ibid., *Description of the Cape*, Vol. I (1921), pp. 137–60.

missioned officers who were sometimes employed as tutors by the more substantial burghers and farmers.[13]

Stavorinus's strictures did not apply so much to the poorer free-burghers, who, in addition to boarding sailors and soldiers from Indiamen in their homes, also practised a regular craft, 'such as that of the blacksmith, joiner, shoemaker, tailor and so forth'. Their wives, as Mentzel noted, usually made more money by indulging in smuggling trade with their paying-guests and with visiting farmers from up-country. For that matter, all the burghers, rich or poor, engaged in private trade on the side, either directly or (more usually) through their wives. There was a large speculative element in this contraband trade, dependent as it was on the arrival and departure of ships whose cargoes could not be exactly forecast, and the black market was prone to alternate between glut and scarcity. Generally speaking, those provisions which were grown locally were very cheap at the Cape, but imported manufactured goods were very expensive. Passengers and crews of homeward-bound Indiamen brought tea, coffee, Chinese porcelain, silks, cotton textiles and other Oriental goods for private sale, whereas those on outward-bound ships offered European goods and delicatessen. Even Dutch beer and cheese found a ready sale at the Cape, as the local varieties were so inferior. Luckily for the hosts of the 'Tavern of Two Seas', the visiting sailors and soldiers were notoriously free spenders and often squandered their hard-earned gains of years in a few days' stay at the Cape.

Visitors who spent any length of time at the Cape never failed to contrast and compare the burghers of Cape Town with those of the rural hinterland, or Boers (*Boeren*) as they were more often termed. The word 'Boer' originally had a derogatory connotation, as evidenced by the 17th-century translations of 'Boor' and 'Clown'. Van Reede tot Drakenstyn suggested in 1685 that the term 'free-burghers' should be officially changed into that of

13. J. S. Stavorinus, *Voyages, 1768–1778*, Vol. I, pp. 563–7; Vol. III, pp. 435–42; O. F. Mentzel, *Description of the Cape*, Vol. I, pp. 127–8; Vol. II, pp. 75–99; Vol. III, pp. 100–23; P. S. Du Toit, *Onderwys aan die Kaap onder die Kompanjie, 1652–1795* (Cape Town, 1937).

'peasants and farm-hands' (*Boeren en bouwlieden*), presumably to emphasize that they ought to engage in agricultural rather than in commercial pursuits. As time went on, the Boers became divided into two categories. There were those who lived within relatively easy reach of Cape Town, and who could engage in wine-growing and arable farming as well as raising cattle and sheep. Then there were those in the 'moving frontier' districts, who were virtually limited to stock-raising by the nature of the soil, by lack of labour, by the distance from Cape Town and want of roads and by their own desire for freedom from the irksome restrictions imposed by the urban bureaucrats.

Most of the land within a radius of about fifty miles from Cape Town had been parcelled out in freehold farms, each one situated at about an hour's ride from the next. In the remoter districts, the land was originally given out in 'loan places', where the occupier leased the 'land and soil' from the Company during his lifetime, but had no guarantee that the government would confirm the grant to his heirs. Such buildings as the owner erected were, however, his own property and could be sold by him, or by his heirs if the latter were evicted from the land. As the farmer's family grew, a cow or a ewe-lamb were usually set aside with the birth of each child, and all the animals which descended from the original one became that child's property. In this way, each child usually had the nucleus of a respectable herd or flock by the time that he or she became an adult. Every young man, therefore, had an inducement to leave his father's farm and set up on his own in another 'loan-place' farther off. Under the revised land regulations of 1743, sixty *morgen* of each 'loan place' could be converted into freehold, the rest of the farm being held on the old basis of leasehold revocable at the Company's pleasure.

Droughts, floods, disease and natural disasters of one kind or another often decimated the original herds; but Nature usually stages a quick recovery in such circumstances, and most of the Boers were much better off than their namesakes in Europe, as Mentzel duly noted: 'Many of the Boers possess 200 or 300 oxen, 100, 150 or more cows, 2,000 to 3,000 sheep, 40 or 50 horses, 20, 30 or more bond slaves, and a large estate. Many an African Boer, therefore, would think twice about changing places with a German nobleman.' [14] Many others, of course, and particularly those on the edge of the moving frontier, were not so well off as were those nearer Cape Town. They might, and usually did, have plenty of cattle and sheep, but they seldom had more than half a dozen slaves and Hottentots to serve them, and sometimes only one or two. Some of the Cape Town burghers and officials also had small country estates, and the attractive houses in which they lived are well illustrated in the books of Alice Trotter and Dorothea Fairbridge. None of these farmers or landowners became excessively rich, since the conditions for accumulating or spending great wealth did not exist at the Cape, apart from the recurrent periods of economic depression which occurred during the Company's rule.

As was only natural, the farther the distance from Cape Town the more primitive did living conditions become. In the mid-18th century, the last plastered houses were to be found in the neighbourhood of Mossel Bay. The graziers and hunters who were pressing on into the Karroo lived in flimsy shacks or shelters and corralled their cattle at night. The Boers of the frontier districts were often accused of living like Hottentots by their urban compatriots as well as by foreign visitors. Stavorinus, for example, after staying the night at a farm near the Cape, rhapsodized about his hosts in his journal next day in a tone befitting an admirer of Rousseau and Raynal. 'Happy, thrice happy mortals, who, situated at the extremity of the globe, amidst the wilds of Africa formerly so barren and desolate, can lead a life of content and innocence!' He was not nearly so complimentary about the Boers on the remote frontier, who, he was told, 'both in their manners and appearance more resembled Hottentots than Christians'.[15]

Thunberg, who went much further into the interior than did Stavorinus, wrote of the Boers: 'The country people have provisions in abundance, but are frequently in want of furniture.

---

14. O. F. Mentzel, *Life at the Cape in the mid-18th Century*, pp. 39, 129–30; Cf. also ibid., *Description of the Cape*, Vol. III, pp. 98–121; J. C. de Haan & P. J. Van Winter, *Nederlanders over de Zeeën*, pp. 325–6.

15. J. S. Stavorinus, *Voyages, 1768–1778*, Vol. II, pp. 71–2.

One frequently sees chairs and tables made by the farmer himself, which he covers with calf-skin, or makes of platted leather straps. The floors in the houses are formed of earth, beaten down hard and smooth. In order to make them hard and firm, they are overlaid either with a mixture of water and cow-dung, or with bullocks' blood, which renders them at the same time rather slippery.' Glass windows were great rarities, and there were no lofts, garrets or plank ceilings, the beams resting on the walls. Houses, or rather cottages, of this kind, 'built of unbaked clay, formed into bricks, and dried a little in the air', were more typical of the way in which the average Boer farmer lived than were the stately homes of Groot Constantia and Groote Schuur, which the tourist admires today.[16] The paucity of roads rendered the haulage of heavy goods impracticable from (or to) most farms, save in the summer months when the rivers were low and easily fordable by the farmers' ox-drawn wagons. Wood was so scarce in many districts that even charcoal had to be imported from Europe for the use of blacksmiths.

The landward boundary of the colony, which was only thought of in the vaguest terms, was always creeping northwards and eastwards from Van Riebeeck's day onwards, and the tempo of the advance increased rapidly after about 1730. The farmers' sons from early youth were accustomed to a strenuous outdoor life passed in guarding their fathers' flocks, in hunting and in (illegal) trading for cattle with the Hottentots. Successive generations of these frontiersmen felt an increasing urge to push across the Little Karroo and farther into the interior. In this way, Boer graziers and hunters edged the Hottentots out of their best

16. C. P. Thunberg, *Travels, 1770–1779*, Vol. I, p. 256. Cf. O. F. Mentzel, *Description of the Cape*, Vol. III, p. 41. For the stately country homes of Dutch South Africa cf. Alice Trotter, *Old Cape Colony. A chronicle of her men and houses, 1652–1806* (Cape Town, 1903); Dorothea Fairbridge, *Historic Farms of South Africa. The wool, the wheat, and the wine of the 17th and 18th centuries* (London, 1931); ibid., *Historic Houses of South Africa* (London, 1922); G. E. Pearse, *Eighteenth-century architecture in South Africa* (Cape Town, 1937); ibid., *The Cape of Good Hope, 1652–1833. An account of its buildings and the life of its people* (Pretoria, 1956).

pastures and then out of their less desirable lands; and eventually
they came into contact with the southward-moving Bantu tribes
in the 1770s. The Bantu, like the frontier Boers, were pastoral
cattle-owners first and foremost. Armed clashes arising out of
disputes over grazing lands and stolen cattle were therefore
inevitable, despite the Cape government's half-hearted attempts
to stabilize the boundary line between Black and White along the
Great Fish River.

The Company's officials sometimes blamed the frontier Boers
for provoking these clashes, and they declined to sanction aggressive action against the Bantu. Disgusted by this attitude, the
strongly Calvinist Boers of Graaf-Reinet, followed by those of
Swellendam, threw off their nominal allegiance to the expiring
East India Company in 1795, and declared themselves loyal subjects of the States-General but entitled to full regional autonomy.
This profession of allegiance to the States-General need not be
taken too seriously, for many visitors to the Cape in the late 18th
century noticed that the Boers regarded South Africa as their
fatherland rather than the Low Lands by the North Sea which
they had never set eyes on. The ease with which the English
effected their two occupations of the Cape (1795, 1806) is also
indicative of the relative weakness of the Afrikaners' pro-Dutch
feeling. Lieutenant James Prior, RN, was guilty of only mild
exaggeration when he observed a few years later: 'From what I
can learn, the boors, so long as they can sell their cattle to advantage, and remain exempted from strict legal restraints, care
little whether the English or the Chinese possess Cape Town.'
It should be added that some of the frontier communities were
conscious of their cultural isolation, and periodically petitioned
the authorities to send them resident Calvinist ministers and
schoolmasters, but there were very few volunteers for such posts
in the wilds, even when the Company was willing to bear the
expense.[17]

17. J. Prior, R.N., *Voyage Along the Eastern Coast of Africa in the
Nisus Frigate* (London, 1819), p. 11. This remark overlooked the fact
that the trek-Boers soon developed anti-English sentiments owing
to the tendency of British officials to sympathize with the Bantu
rather than with them in the frontier disputes.

In addition to the bureaucrats, burghers and Boers, there was another class of white men at the Cape, who deserve a brief mention. These were the *knechts* or indentured servants, most of whom were recruited from the garrison. Whenever a farmer could not manage his farm(s) by himself, he applied to the authorities at Cape Town for the services of a soldier from the Castle, or (more rarely) a sailor from the hospital. If a suitable man volunteered and came to terms with the farmer, he was then released from military service – though still liable to be called up in an emergency – and 'loaned' to the farmer for the period of a year, his contract being renewable annually. The usual rate of pay for a *knecht* employed as the overseer or supervisor of a farm was Fl. 16 monthly, with board and lodging. Those who were hired as tutor to the farmer's children started with Fl. 14 monthly but got annual rises. Mentzel, who had himself served as a *knecht*, noted: 'This form of employment was a stepping-stone to wealth for competent men. Such men frequently married their master's daughter or widow. In fact, I have known cases where widows engaged *knechts* with a view to matrimony.' Of course, not all *knechts* made good in this way; and those who did not sank to the level of 'poor whites' who earned less than skilled coloured freemen or even slave-labourers.[18]

The employment of ex-soldiers as overseers did not solve the farmers' labour problem. This was done to some extent by the importation and employment of slaves. Since the *Heeren* XVII strictly forbade the enslavement of Hottentots and Bushmen, the authorities at Cape Town were compelled to get their slaves from farther afield. Moçambique and Madagascar became two of their principal slave-markets, and they also imported many slaves from the region of the Bay of Bengal and from Indonesia. The numbers were small at first. There were only about 800 adult slaves at the Cape at the beginning of the 18th century, but they amounted to some 4,000 fifty years later, and to nearly 10,000 in 1780. During the 17th century the white colonists had increased more rapidly in numbers than the slaves, but the position was reversed during the first half of the 18th century. Many of

18. For the operation of the *Knecht* system at the Cape, cf. O. F. Mentzel, *Description of the Cape*, Vol. I, pp. 164–6; Vol. II, p. 114.

the Indian and Indonesian slaves were skilled artists or craftsmen, and some of the latter, under the generic term of 'Slameiers' have kept themselves apart from the general mass of the Cape coloured people to this day. They have little negroid admixture and have preserved some old Dutch folk-songs and turns of expression which are no longer found among the Afrikaans-speaking whites.

The question whether free white or else coloured slave-labour was more economical was discussed by the governor in council in 1716, and all the councillors save the garrison commander plumped unhesitatingly for slave-labour. One of the councillors claimed that an examination of the Company's account-books disclosed that the upkeep of a slave cost about Fl. 40 yearly, whereas that of a white *knecht* was about Fl. 175. It was also argued that slaves were more obedient and worked harder in the hope of eventually being freed, whereas white labourers were apt to take to drink and to become unemployable destitutes. The garrison commander disputed the accuracy of these statements and argued strongly that free white labour would be cheaper in the long run, and more advantageous for the healthy development of the colony. Slaves would always be an expensive nuisance, he stated, owing to the high cost of the slaving voyages, their high death-rate, their tendency to desert, and the number of people required to discipline and look after them. The governor sided with the majority, adding that anybody who doubted that slave-labour was essential should 'take a look at how all the work is done throughout Asia, and in all the colonies in the West Indies, Surinam, etc.' This decision was of vital importance, since the *Heeren* XVII agreed with it, and no further efforts were made to encourage the immigration of European peasants on any considerable scale. The slave population steadily increased, and arable farming became mainly dependent on slave labour for the rest of the century.[19]

Slaves at the Cape were of two main categories: those belong-

19. V. de Kock, *Those in Bondage. An account of the life of the slave at the Cape in the days of the Dutch East India Company* (Cape Town, 1950); A. J. Boeseken, *Die Nederlandse Kommissarisse* (1944), pp. 59–72, for the above and what follows.

ing to the Company, and those belonging to individual officials, burghers and Boers. The number of the Company's slaves was theoretically limited to 450, but in practice there were usually between 600 and 800 in its employ. The Company not only employed them as stevedores, bricklayers, builders, millers, potters, dairymen, grooms, hospital-nurses, bookbinders, gardeners, thatchers, etc., etc., on its own behalf, but lent or hired them out to various officials, who, incidentally, often abused this privilege by employing more of them than they were entitled to do. Many of the residents of Cape Town depended for their livelihood to a large extent on those of their slaves who were trained in various callings and hired out by the day or by the month. Indonesian male slaves made excellent masons, house-painters, confectioners, cooks and fishermen, and many of the women were skilled sempstresses. Negro slaves were used for hard work in loading and unloading shipping, and in the vineyards, farms and vegetable gardens of the colonists.

One feature of Cape life which impressed many visitors was the musical talent of the 'Malay' slaves and the skill with which

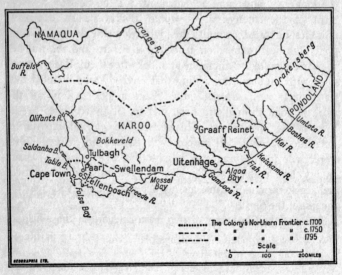

8   Cape of Good Hope and hinterland, 1652–1795

they played entirely by ear. 'I know of many great houses,' wrote Lichtenstein in 1803, 'in which there is not one of the slaves that cannot play upon some instrument, and where an orchestra is immediately collected together, if the young people of the house, when they are visited in the afternoon by their acquaintances, like to amuse themselves with dancing for an hour or two. At a nod, the cook exchanges his saucepan for a flute, the groom quits his curry-comb and takes his violin, and the gardener, throwing aside his spade, sits down to the violoncello.' William Hickey, who prided himself on being a connoisseur of music as well as of wine and of women, averred that the slave flute-players who accompanied his party in their ascent of Table Mountain provided 'the sweetest harmony I ever heard'.[20]

The treatment of slaves by their owners at the Cape favourably impressed most foreign visitors – the splenetic John Barrow always excepted. Captain James Cook, RN, who had seen more of the world than most of his contemporaries, and whose opinions are always deserving of respect, wrote in 1772 : 'The principal inhabitants at the Cape have sometimes from 20 to 30 slaves, which are in general treated with great lenity, and sometimes become favourites with their masters, who give them very good clothing, but oblige them to wear neither shoes nor stockings' – bare feet being the badge of servitude. Of course there were exceptions, and cruel masters may have been relatively more numerous among the up-country Boers than among the burghers of Cape Town, although the evidence on this point is conflicting. But the slaves were not entirely without legal means of redress, and they were entitled to petition for relief if they were atrociously handled or inadequately fed. No doubt they did not

20. Lichtenstein's and Hickey's accounts *apud* V. de Kock, *Those in Bondage*, pp. 94–5. White Netherlanders, burghers and coloured slaves all shared a passion for music. Cf. Jan Bouws, 'De musickbeofening aan die Kaap in die Hollandse Kompanijestijd', in the *Quarterly Bulletin of the South African Library*, Vol. XVI (March 1962), pp. 104–18. Slave orchestras were also a feature of life at Batavia (p. 270), and even on Deshima according to Japanese paintings of the Dutch factory there, one of which is reproduced in plate XI.

always dare to do so, but there are some recorded instances when they did. In 1672, for example, the Company's slaves complained to the visiting Commissioner-General, Arnold van Overbeke, about the insufficiency of their rations and clothing. The complaint was investigated, found to be justified, and orders were issued that they should be better clothed and fed in future.

Private owners who made themselves notorious through the ill-treatment of their slaves were usually – though not invariably – punished; in a few extreme cases, slaves were removed from the control of sadistic owners. In general, the feeding and clothing of the Cape slaves seem to have been fairly adequate throughout the 18th century, and some provision was made for the education of their children. The company maintained an elementary school for teaching some of its child slaves the 'three Rs' and the Dutch language. Private owners sometimes had their slaves' children educated alongside their own, either at an elementary school or in their houses. It was not uncommon for both the Company and private owners to manumit their respective slaves under certain circumstances and with safeguards to ensure that they would not become a charge on the community. Slaves taken to the United Provinces automatically obtained their freedom on arrival, in accordance with a ruling made by the *Heeren* XVII in 1713, nearly sixty years before Lord Mansfield's better publicized judgement that the moment a slave's foot touched the soil of England he was free.[21]

Although slaves were probably better treated at the Cape than elsewhere, the fact remains that their crimes were punished with savage severity as a matter of deliberate policy. Mentzel relates how an unpopular Fiscal was restrained by his colleagues in the Council of Justice from abusing his judicial powers too much, so far as European offenders were concerned, adding signific-

21. Same sources as in note 1 above. In some places in the Netherlands, slaves had already been regarded as automatically and legally enfranchised on their arrival there, and employers who tried to keep them as slaves could be prosecuted. This had long been so in Amsterdam. Cf. G. Rooseboom, *Recueil van verscheyde Keuren en costumen mitsgaders maniere van procederen binnen de stadt Amsterdam* (Amsterdam, 1656), p. 193.

antly: 'He was allowed, however, to have his own way, more or less, with runaway slaves and other malefactors of that race, for if the natives were not deterred from ill doing by the infliction of severe punishments, such as hanging, breaking on the wheel, and impaling, no one's life would be safe. A European, on the other hand, must have committed a very serious crime before he has been punished by death. In the eight years that I was at the Cape [1732-40] only six Europeans were put to death, and they had thoroughly deserved it.' The accuracy of this observation has been disputed, and torture was a legal commonplace under Roman-Dutch Law and was sometimes applied to whites. But Mentzel's testimony is confirmed by that of Stavorinus, writing some forty years later, and by a perusal of the edicts and sentences published in the *Kaapse Plakaatboek*, 1652-1795. It was inevitable in any slave-owning society that slaves would normally be more severely punished than freemen for identical offences – occasional instances to the contrary notwithstanding.[22]

The death-rate among slaves was often high, especially in the 17th century, when new arrivals barely kept pace with the natural wastage. During the 18th century the birth-rate among the slave population increased considerably, 'to which the promiscuous intercourse between soldiers, sailors and female slaves adds its quota', as Mentzel noted. Soldiers and sailors queued up every evening for this purpose outside the Company's Slave Lodge before the gates closed at 9 p.m. Some modern Afrikaner historians maintain that the 'Cape Coloured' population was fathered exclusively by these transient and rowdy elements, and further allege that neither the burghers nor the Boers indulged in miscegenation with coloured women, whether bond or free. These claims are quite untenable in the face of much well-documented evidence to the contrary. Successive governmental edicts promulgated at Cape Town deplored that 'irresponsible people, both among the Company's servants in the garrison of their fortress, as also free settlers or inhabitants of this place', were living in open concubinage with coloured and slave women, procreating illegitimate children, 'who fill both the Company's

22. O. F. Mentzel, *Life at the Cape*, p. 94; J. S. Stavorinus, *Voyages,* *1768-1778*, Vol. I, p. 571; V. de Kock, *Those in Bondage*, pp. 146-97.

and the private owners' slave-quarters'. Some of these miscreants, including several burghers of Cape Town, 'did not scruple to acknowledge in writing that they were the fathers of children conceived in this way'. Worse still, in 1681, the authorities discovered that some soldiers and burghers had been indulging in weekly sexual orgies with female slaves in the Company's Slave Lodge on Sunday mornings, 'stripping themselves mother-naked and dancing together in the sight of other onlookers'. Offenders were threatened with severe penalties such as flogging and branding, but it is clear that miscegenation continued throughout the 18th century, if rather more discreetly.[23]

Mentzel relates that the burghers' teen-age sons often got the good-looking slave girls in their households with child, and though the paternity of these bastards was rarely acknowledged in his day, 'these affairs are not regarded as very serious. The girl is sternly rebuked for her wantonness, and threatened with dire punishments if she dares to disclose who was responsible for her condition; nay, she is bribed to put the blame on some other man. True enough, these tactics are of no avail; her fellow slaves know what really happened, and the story leaks out. Nothing matters, however; it is nobody's business to take the matter further. It would be extremely difficult to prove it; besides the offence is venial in the public's estimation. It does not hurt the boy's prospects; his escapade is a source of amusement, and he is dubbed a young fellow who has shown the stuff he is made of.'

The same thing happened on the farms, and if Thunberg is to be credited (and he is usually a reliable witness), the daughters of the Boers sometimes became pregnant by their father's black slaves. 'In this case, in consideration of a round sum of money, a husband is generally provided for the girl, but the slave is sent away from that part of the country.' It was quite common in Cape Town for a slave-owner to allow one of his female slaves to cohabit with a European as man and wife. Some of the children of these unions were baptized and manumitted, but with the majority 'the fruit followed the womb'. Many of the children born to the female slaves in the Company's Slave Lodge had

23. *Kaapse Plakaatboek*, I, 1652–1707, pp. 151–2, 179–80; *Kaapse Plakaatboek*, II, 1707–1753, pp. 73, 171, 246.

white fathers, 'to whom they frequently bear a most striking resemblance', as Mentzel testified. The Cape-born offspring of a white father and a slave mother was the class of slave most preferred by burghers and Boers in the second half of the 18th century.[24] As in other slave-owning societies, such as those in Brazil and Surinam, the race pattern on a farm was often white owner, half-caste overseer, black slaves.

In addition to miscegenation with household female slaves, who were usually of Asian origins, there was a considerable amount between Boer men and Hottentot women, chiefly in the remote frontier districts where the comely 'Malay' slave-girls of Cape Town were never seen. Sparrman averred that, even when the Boer farmers of these regions had 'quite tolerable' white wives, they were still prone to sleep with Hottentot women, by whom they had children who usually resembled the father more than the mother. This miscegenation is the more surprising, as the Hottentots were usually regarded by the Dutch as the lowest form of human life, with the exception of the Bushmen. It was some considerable time before the Europeans could distinguish properly between the Hottentots and the Bushmen; but the latter eventually fared equally ill at the hands of the Hottentots, Boers and Bantu who successively usurped their lands, being often exterminated like rats. The celebrated Hottentot, Eva, of Van Riebeeck's day, who served as official interpreter and married a Dutch husband, was the equivalent of the solitary swallow that does not make a summer. But if the Boers never married Hottentot women, they mixed with them often enough in the frontier districts to produce whole communities like the Griquas. These were the offspring of miscegenation between the *trekboers* and Hottentot women, and they had such a strong

24. O. F. Mentzel, *Description of the Cape*, Vol. II, pp. 109, 130–33, ibid., op. cit., Vol. III, pp. 113 ff.; C. P. Thunberg, *Travels*, 1770–1779, Vol. I, pp. 137–8, 303. On the problem of miscegenation in colonial South Africa, cf. V. de Kock, *Those in Bondage, passim*; J. E. S. Marais, *The Cape Coloured People, 1652–1937* (London, 1939), pp. 1–31; L. M. Thompson, 'Afrikaner Nationalist historiography and the policy of Apartheid' (*Journal of African History*, Vol. III, 1962, pp. 125–41).

infusion of white blood that they were termed 'Bastards' for the best part of a century. Their few remaining descendants and the numerous other Cape Coloured peoples are at once an embarrassment and a reproach to the present-day advocates of Apartheid.

If there was always tension in South Africa between white and coloured, not many generations elapsed before men and women born of white parents at the Cape began to feel that they were in some ways different from the European born and bred officials and burghers. The word *Afrikaner* was apparently first used in 1707, at a time when the white sons of the soil, whether of Dutch, German or Huguenot origin, had combined to defend what they felt to be their patrimonial rights against the powerful Van der Stel official clique. Although the *Heeren* XVII dismissed W. A. van der Stel and backed the free-burghers on this occasion, rivalry between the South African-born and the European-born was not extinguished thereby but rather the contrary. Mentzel is very enlightening on this problem, and it is amusing to note how this obscure Prussian soldier denounced the first South African-born governor, Hendrik Swellengrebel, for favouring his Afrikaner friends and relations over Europeans. It was an article of faith with Mentzel that the Afrikaner was culturally and intellectually inferior to the European, and there is no doubt that this belief was shared by some of the Dutch officials. Indeed, if Mentzel is to be credited on this point, it was likewise shared by many Afrikaner women of Cape Town; for after noting that many common soldiers of good character married the daughters of burghers, he adds: 'every girl without exception prefers as her husband a man who has been born in Europe to one who is of colonial birth'. Even if this was so in Mentzel's day, I doubt if it lasted much longer. In any event, as Mentzel admitted, the European-born officials' dislike of the uncouth frontier-Boers was reciprocated by the latter, who 'display a kind of secret hatred towards the Europeans'.[25]

Ignorant and unmannerly the frontier Boers undoubtedly were, but they also had a tough Calvinist self-reliance and a sturdily

25. O. F. Mentzel, *Life at the Cape*, pp. 106–17, 128; ibid., *Description of the Cape*, Vol. III, pp. 110–16.

independent spirit fostered by their hard life. From about 1750 onwards their speech diverged increasingly from pure Dutch, and the beginnings of Afrikaans as a spoken language are discernible in the second half of the 18th century. The Cape burghers also began to use a corruptly simplified form of Dutch, partly as a result of daily conversation with their slaves. The exact origins of Afrikaans are still in dispute; but it has been plausibly argued that it originated as a Creole language from the interaction between the Dutch of the white settlers, whether Boers or burghers, and the languages spoken by the Hottentots and slaves, the latter of which certainly contained a strong admixture of Creole Portuguese. Be that as it may, Afrikaans was adopted by the Cape Coloured peoples as their mother tongue, which it remains to this day. In this respect, likewise, South Africa was a colony *sui generis*. Whereas the Dutch failed to implant their language firmly among the peoples of the East and West Indies, they succeeded in doing so among the peoples of South Africa; nor did the period of British rule in the 19th–20th century – 'the century of wrong' – prevent the consolidation and growth of Afrikaans, first as a spoken and then as a written language.[26]

26. T. J. Haarhoff & C. M. Van den Heever, *The Achievement of Afrikaans* (Johannesburg, n.d.). Pending the appearance of Professor M. Valkhoff's forthcoming work, *Studies in Creole Portuguese with special reference to Cape Colony*, attention is directed to his article, 'An historic language: Creole Portuguese', in *African Studies*, Vol. XIX, nr. 3, Johannesburg, 1960.

10

The 'Golden Century' and the 'Periwig Period'

J. C. Van Leur, whose death in the battle of the Java Sea (January 1942) was such a grievous loss to Indonesian historical studies, more than once protested against the common tendency of Dutch historians – and of others in their wake – to contrast the 'Golden Age' of the 17th century with the 'Periwig Period' (*Pruikentijd*) of the 18th, invariably to the disparagement and disadvantage of the latter. He argued that this contrast was the result of a legend spun by the 'revolutionary Patriots' of 1795 to use politically against the *ancien régime* in the Dutch Republic, and fostered by the 19th century 'national romantics' in the literature they wrote about the Golden Age. That the northern Netherlands produced no painters like Rembrandt or poets like Vondel during the Periwig Period did not alter the fact that this despised era 'performed the great work of laying the foundations of modern *bourgeois* culture', in the Netherlands as elsewhere in Europe, Van Leur affirmed.[1]

With all due deference to so distinguished an authority, it seems to me that in some respects at any rate the traditional contrast between the achievements of the Golden Century and the relative stagnation of the Periwig Period is a valid one. It does not date from the times of the 'revolutionary Patriots' and 'national romantics', but was already being discussed and deplored in the mid-18th century, both in the Dutch Republic and in the domain of the East India Company. 'We are living, thank God, in a flourishing century at Batavia,' wrote the Governor-General and his council in 1649, but there is no trace of such confident satisfaction in the correspondence of their successors a hundred years later.[2] The Dutch periodical press during the

1. J. C. Van Leur, *Indonesian Trade and Society*, pp. 266, 271, 288.
2. Compare the reports of the Governor-General and council dated

second half of the 18th century is full of complaints about the real or alleged decline of the national character and energy as compared with a century earlier. Admittedly, some dissenting voices were raised against this widely held belief. One of these critics pointed out (in 1769) that people who compared the past with the present always selected the best in former generations for comparison with the worst in the actual one. He argued that drunkenness, gluttony and disorderly brawling had considerably declined in the 18th century as compared with the 17th, and concluded : 'We dissemble more, but quarrel less.' In taking this line he anticipated by nearly two centuries a modern Dutch historian who wrote : 'We admire Erasmus who, in a turbulent period, described the conversation of friends in a beautiful garden as the height of civilized entertainment; yet we are disgusted with his 18th-century followers who put his theory into practice. We are anti-militarist but loathe the least military society in all Netherland history. There is something purely sentimental and irrational in the attitude of most Netherlanders towards this period.' [3] True enough, perhaps; but the pessimists of the Periwig Period and those who agree with them nowadays had – and have – some good and sufficient reasons for thinking that the glory had departed with the end of the Golden Century.

Rightly or wrongly, a declining population is often regarded as a symptom of national decay, and there were plenty of people in the United Provinces in 1780, including the Prince of Orange, who thought that the population was smaller than it had been a century previously. Unfortunately we have no reliable figures for the Dutch population as a whole in the 17th and 18th centuries, and we have to depend on a few contemporary and conflicting estimates. Pieter de la Court, in his *Interest van Holland* of 1662, calculated the population of the United Provinces at a maximum of 2,400,000, but he admitted that this figure was only

---

8 January and 31 December 1649 (De Jonge, *Opkomst*, Vol. VI, pp. 8–13) with those of 1750 (De Jonge, *Opkomst*, Vol. X, pp. 164–5).

3. B. M. Vlekke, *Evolution of the Dutch Nation*, p. 241; J. de Vries, *De economische achteruitgang der Republick in de achttiende eeuw* (Amsterdam, 1958), p. 173, for the quotation of 1769.

a very rough guess. A more common estimate was just about two million inhabitants, and this figure is accepted by most modern writers. I have not been able to find the source for it, nor any explanation of why this figure seems to have remained unchanged down to the end of the Dutch Republic; for nearly all authorities agree that this was the total in 1795. Yet in Western Europe as a whole there was a rapid rise in the population after the mid-18th century. Why should the northern Netherlands have afforded an exception to this rule, particularly as they were not ravaged by disastrous wars nor decimated by outbreaks of plague during the Periwig Period?

One reason given for the rapid population growth in Western Europe during the second half of the 18th century is that a decline in infant mortality was accompanied by couples marrying earlier in life and so having (other things being equal) more children. We do not know how far these two factors applied in the United Provinces, though an Englishman long resident in Holland referred in 1743 to 'the remarkable barrenness of the Dutch women', as if this was a well-known and uncontested fact.[4] More significant, perhaps, is the fact that the average yearly marriage-rate in Amsterdam during the period 1670–79 was almost exactly the same as that for the years 1794–1803, that is, 2,078 and 2,082, respectively. It is true that the average rate for the intervening years was sometimes higher, but it never exceeded 3,204 in any one year (1746), and the annual marriage-rate fluctuated between 2,100 and 2,500. In any event, it is clear that the population of Amsterdam, always the Republic's most populous and thriving city, increased rapidly between 1580 and 1660, but very slowly between 1662 (some 200,100 or 210,000 souls) and 1795 (some 217,000 or 221,000 souls). The number of houses in Amsterdam remained virtually the same between 1740 and 1795, which likewise indicates that there was no substantial

---

4. *A Description of Holland, or the present state of the United Provinces* (London, 1743), p. 97. The writer adds, with obvious exaggeration: 'In consequence, if this State had not constant and annual supplies of foreigners it would be impossible for it to subsist, and it would be dissolved in a very few years.'

increase in the population during this period, despite Van der Oudermeulen's allegation to the contrary in 1795.[5]

In 1780 Amsterdam was still a thriving port with a great deal of overseas trade, and conditions in some other parts of the United Provinces were much worse in the second half of the 18th century. James Boswell wrote from Utrecht in 1764: 'Most of their principal towns are sadly decayed, and instead of finding every mortal employed, you meet with multitudes of poor creatures who are starving in idleness. Utrecht is remarkably ruined. There are whole lanes of wretches who have no other subsistence than potatoes, gin and stuff which they call tea and coffee; and what is worst of all, I believe they are so habituated to this life that they would not take work if it should be offered to them ... you see, then, that things are very different here from what most people in England imagine. Were Sir William Temple to revisit these Provinces, he would scarcely believe the amazing alteration which they have undergone.' Boswell's testimony was echoed fourteen years later by the Dutch newspaper, De Borger, which stated (19 October 1778) that the economic decline of the nation had reached such a pitch that it seemed as if 'the body of the Commonwealth would shortly consist of little more than rentiers and beggars – the two kinds of people who are the least useful to the country'.[6]

Both Boswell and De Borger may have been laying on the dark colours a bit thick, but there is plenty of other contemporary evidence to suggest that the population of many provincial towns declined at this period, and that houses and streets were demolished to make room for gardens and meadows. This decline was by no means universal, and it seems to have been most

5. Cf. J. de Bosch Kemper, Armoede (ed. 1851), statistical tables XI(c)–XI(f); H. Brugmans, Opkomst en bloei van Amsterdam (ed. 1944), pp. 88–9; Van der Oudermeulen's Memorandum of 1785 apud D. Van Hogendorp, Stukken raakende de tegenwoordigen toestand der Bataafsche bezittingen in Oost-Indië (The Hague and Delft, 1801), especially pp. 80–81, 290–91.

6. F. A. Pottle (ed.), Boswell in Holland, 1763–1764 (London, 1952), pp. 280–81; De Borger, 19 October 1778, apud J. de Bosch Kemper, Armoede (ed. 1851), p. 357.

marked in the small sea-towns of North Holland and of Zeeland, and in several of the inland towns such as Utrecht, Haarlem, Leiden and Delft. What we do not know is where the surplus urban population (if there was one) went. It has been suggested that they may have gone to the peat moors of the north-eastern provinces, which were being developed at this time, and where new villages were being formed. It is significant that the population of the eastern province of Overijssel increased by nearly 90 per cent between 1675 and 1795; but this spectacular increase was almost certainly not reflected in any of the other provinces, and in most of them the population seems either to have stagnated or, perhaps, even to have decreased in some instances. It is unfortunate that Overijssel, one of the smallest and poorest of all the seven provinces, is the only one for which we have accurate population figures in the time of the Republic. Until further research is done in the demographic history of the other provinces, we cannot say whether the total population of the Dutch Republic increased or decreased between 1600 and 1800, in view of the conflicting and piecemeal nature of the available evidence.[7]

If there is considerable uncertainty concerning the total population of the United Provinces in the Periwig Period as compared with the Golden Century, there is less room for doubt that the second half of the 18th century revealed an unmistakable decline in industry in general, and in the fishing industry in particular, as compared with conditions a century earlier. The herring fishery, which was commonly termed a gold-mine of the United Provinces in the first half of the 17th century, still presented an impressive appearance in 1728, when a well-informed English resident in the Netherlands estimated that an average total of about 800 busses were employed in this fishery, making

7. J. de Vries, *Economische achteruitgang*, pp. 167–8, thinks that the population of the Netherlands as a whole, and not merely that of the province of Overijssel, increased between 1700 and 1795; but it seems to me that the weight of contemporary evidence indicates a stagnation or a decline for many places. The figures for Overijssel are derived from Slicher van Bath. Cf. also C. Wilson and Van der Woude's observations in *BMHGU*, Vol. 77, pp. 21, 22, 26.

three voyages a year. Though this total was less than it had been a century earlier, the tonnage of the 18th-century vessels ranged from 30 to 50 tons, whereas they were only 20 to 30 in the earlier period. A modern Dutch authority estimates that the province of Holland alone provided a yearly maximum of about 500 herring busses in 1630, which had shrunk to 219 in 1730 – though here again allowance must be made for the increased tonnage. The same author states that with the exception of Vlaardingen, the number of ships maintained by all the fishing towns decreased during the 18th century, the decline being particularly noticeable in Enkhuizen, which equipped between 200 and 400 busses in the closing years of the 17th century, but only 75 in 1731, and 56 in 1750. The decline was accelerated after 1756, and only about 150–180 busses were engaged in the annual Dutch herring fisheries on the eve of the Fourth English War (1780).

It was a similar story with the cod-fishery and even worse with the whale-fishery. The Dogger Bank cod-fishery still employed 200–300 vessels of 40–60 tons each in the year 1728, according to Onslow Burrish, but this total was apparently considerably less than it had been in the second half of the 17th century. The decline in the cod-fishery was more marked in the last thirty years of the 18th century, and when the Republic collapsed in 1795, only 125 vessels were engaged in this occupation. The decline in the Arctic whale-fishery was equally marked, and although some good catches were occasionally made in the 18th century, the halcyon years of 1675–90 never returned. 'This trade, however,' wrote Onslow Burrish in 1728, 'is thought to be a kind of lottery, and is therefore undertaken by persons of over-grown fortunes, who if they fail this year, expect better luck the next, and do not feel the disappointment; but it is of undoubted and universal benefit to the State in general, as it promotes the increase of navigation, and the consumption of everything that depends on it.' [8]

8. Onslow Burrish, *Batavia Illustrata, or a view of the policy and commerce of the United Provinces, particularly of Holland* (London, 1728), pp. 265–73. The other figures are taken from the section on

The reasons for the decline of the Dutch deep-sea and coastal fisheries during the second half of the 18th century are not far to seek. The chief cause was increasing competition by the fishermen of neighbouring countries, principally England and Scotland, but also Denmark and Norway, not to mention the Flemish fishers from the Austrian Netherlands (Belgium). Hamburg became increasingly important as a staple market for the herring consumed in north Germany and Scandinavia. Most of these countries also adopted protectionist measures to foster their own fishing industries at the expense of the Dutch, the British government in particular making use of subsidies and premiums. The French government placed an embargo on the importation of Dutch herring in 1751, and the Austrian Netherlands, Denmark and Prussia followed this example in 1766, 1774 and 1775 respectively. There was also less demand for herring in 18th century Europe, owing to a change in dietary habits, and by the end of this period the demand could be satisfied by a total of 300 European herring-busses, whereas at one time 500 Dutch busses had barely sufficed. But the quality and technical excellence of the Dutch herring fisheries and packers retained their primacy down to the end, and in 1780 about half of the total European demand for cured herring was still supplied by the Dutch. The reasons for the parallel decline in the Dutch cod-fishery are less clear, although increasing competition by English and French fishers off the Newfoundland Banks and by Flemings nearer home from Ostend and Nieuwpoort obviously had a good deal to do with it.

The decline in the Dutch fisheries inevitably affected to a greater or lesser extent the numerous ancillary trades and occupations with which they were closely connected. These included the timber trade with the Baltic, which provided the wood for building and repairing the busses; the salt trade with Portugal and France, which provided the salt for curing the herring; 'the carpenters, caulkers, smiths, ropemakers and sailmakers, with the

the fisheries in J. de Vries, *Economische achteruitgang*, pp. 137–49, and the sources there quoted.

coopers, who make the prodigious number of casks used for package of the herrings; the net-makers, and all other little trades who furnish the several instruments necessary in the manufactory', as Onslow Burrish noted in 1728. He calculated that in this way the herring fisheries alone gave 'employment and subsistence to thirty thousand families at least, not including that vast number of people, who get their living by the necessary consumption of all kinds of clothing and provision that they occasion'. When the whaling, cod, coastal and inland fisheries are added to the herring industry, we can see that a substantial proportion of Dutch labour was directly or indirectly concerned with the prosperity of these fisheries as a whole, even if we regard Pieter de la Court's estimate of 450,000 people as directly dependent on them in 1662 as somewhat exaggerated. The fisheries were doubly valued as a nursery of seamen and a source of employment for labour ashore; and this was why the winter cod-fishery in the North Sea was still maintained in the 18th century, although it gave little or no commercial profit, owing to the high cost of maintaining the ships and equipment in the stormy winter weather.

Another noticeable factor in the decline of the Dutch fisheries was the increasing shortage of deep-sea fishermen, of whom there had been no lack in the 17th century, by the unanimous testimony of Netherlanders and foreigners. The fisheries suffered grievously in the major wars in which the Republic was involved – from the ravages of the Dunkirkers between 1600 and 1645, from English attacks in the Anglo–Dutch wars, and, above all, from French corsairs in the War of 1701–13, when the herring fishery was virtually destroyed. But the intervening years of peace enabled a greater or lesser recovery to be made after each war, though it is probable that some fishing families did not return to the sea as their means of livelihood. The foreign fishing companies which tried to compete with the Dutch in the 18th century endeavoured to tempt experienced Dutch fishers into their employment, at any rate in their earlier years. It is uncertain how many succumbed to these temptations, but in 1756 the majority of skippers in the service of the recently founded

Society of the Free British Fishery (1750–72) were mostly Dutch-men or Danes.[9]

The States-General periodically promulgated edicts forbidding Dutch merchant-seamen and fishers from taking service with foreign nations, but the frequent reiteration of such edicts implies that they were not well observed. We have no means of calculating how many Dutch fishers served abroad in defiance of these edicts, nor whether their absence was temporary or permanent. What is certain is that the manning of the Dutch fishing fleets became – and remained – a problem in the 18th century, which it had never been in the 17th. It has been reliably calculated that at the end of the 18th century the Dutch deep-sea and coastal fisheries together employed only two-thirds of the number which had been necessary for the herring-fishery alone in 1600. It is likewise certain that increasing numbers of Norwegians, Danes and North Germans helped to man Dutch fishing-vessels in the 18th century, just as they did in the States Navy, in the East Indiamen and in the merchant marine. It has been suggested that these (mostly raw) hands took the place of more experienced Dutch seamen who entered the foreign navies and merchant-ships, but we have no proof that this happened on any note-worthy scale. They certainly did not serve in any great numbers in English merchant-ships, which, save in war-time, seldom employed more than a few hundred foreigners all told.

Whatever the reasons, it is indisputable that the Dutch fisheries, though still nurseries of seamen, were not nearly so important in this respect in 1780 as they had been a century earlier. During the Nine Years War of 1689–97, the Dutch were able to send about 100 warships to sea every year manned with about 24,000 men, apart from the numerous privateers they fitted out and the thousands of sailors in the Indiamen and merchant-ships which sailed the Seven Seas with or without convoy. In August 1781, at a time when the whole of their seaborne trade and fisheries were virtually paralysed and thus many seamen should have been available for enlistment in the navy, it was only with great difficulty that the Dutch were able to send to sea the

9. J. de Vries, *Economische achteruitgang*, pp. 137–49, for most of the above and what follows.

modest fleet of seventeen sail manned with 3,000 men, which fought so stoutly at Dogger Bank under Rear-Admiral Zoutman. By the end of this disastrous war they were barely able to secure 19,176 men out of the 30,046 they required for manning forty-six ships of the line and thirty-eight frigates. Only one conclusion can be drawn from this state of affairs, which is likewise reflected in the other evidence: the seafaring communities of Holland and Zeeland must have decreased considerably between 1680 and 1780.[10]

This decline in the Dutch fisheries and in the numbers of the men employed therein was not regarded with indifference by those contemporaries who were aware of it, and who were in a position to attempt some remedial measures, even if these achieved no lasting results. Several protectionist measures, designed to help the Dutch herring-fishers, packers and dealers against the foreign competitors, were taken by the States of Holland in the second half of the 18th century, including the award of premiums and subsidies after the English example. The States of Zeeland went even further, and in 1759 awarded a cash premium to all fishing-vessels in that province. The results were disappointing if one may judge from the example of Zierickzee, which was one of the principal maritime Zeeland towns. This place maintained a fishing fleet of some forty sail in 1745, which had shrunk to seventeen or eighteen in 1785. This decline was paralleled in the number of merchant ships registered in the same port, which decreased from about sixty or seventy sail in 1760 to a mere fifteen, 'large and small', twenty-five years later. Corresponding figures for the other Zeeland sea-towns, such as Veere, Vlissingen and Middelburg, are lacking, though the last two ports still had an important share in the shipping trading to the East and West Indies, as well as Western Europe. But many of the smaller ports probably declined in the same way as Zierickzee. The 'dead

10. Cf. C. R. Boxer, 'Sedentary workers and seafaring folk in the Dutch Republic', in J. Bromley & Kossmann (eds.) *Britain and the Netherlands*, Vol. II, pp. 148–68. For the paucity of foreign hands in English merchant-ships in the 17th and 18th centuries see R. Davis, *The Rise of the English Shipping Industry in the 17th and 18th centuries* (1962), p. 136.

towns' of Zeeland and North Holland, which have long formed one of the main tourist attractions in the Netherlands, date not from the 19th century but from the second half of the 18th.

As stated above, the Dutch herring-fishers, curers and packers maintained their technical superiority over their foreign competitors down to the end, even though they inevitably lost ground numerically, but the Dutch whaling industry declined both quantitatively and qualitatively. Whereas in the second half of the 17th century the Dutch had been the undisputed leaders in the whale fisheries, a century later they were overhauled and displaced by the English. The latter improved their catches by making longer voyages and using heavier ships, which could follow the whales deeper among the drifting ice-floes. They also introduced new and improved techniques, such as experimenting with mechanical harpoons which eventually displaced the hand-thrown variety. The Dutch owners and whalers did not adopt these newfangled methods, or did so only belatedly; and they did not participate in the seal-hunting which the English and Germans exploited in conjunction with their whaling voyages.

This conservative and unenterprising mentality was also reflected in other and more important branches of Dutch trade and industry during the Periwig Period, contrasting with the enterprise and dynamism of the Dutch merchants and mariners in the Golden Century. We have had occasion to observe (pp. 120–22) that the Dutch lost their 17th-century lead in maritime cartography and navigational techniques to their English and French rivals, and they were equally slow to adopt new and improved methods in shipbuilding. Stavorinus and Dirk van Hogendorp both criticized the directors of the Amsterdam chamber of the East India Company in the last quarter of the 18th century for their reluctance to build flush-decked instead of deep-waisted ships, although, as Stavorinus noted in 1774: 'It is incontrovertible that a flush-decked ship is much more able to withstand the force of the waves than a deep-waisted one.' There is also a remarkable contrast between the attitude of the directors and servants of the Dutch East India Company towards their English counterparts and rivals in the 17th as compared with the 18th centuries. Down to about 1670 the Dutch considered themselves as superior in energy and ability, as well as in capital and in material resources, to the English. Moreover, the English frequently admitted their relative inferiority. In the last quarter of the 17th century the relative attitudes of the two rivals begin to change. We find the English growing more aggressive and self-confident, and the Dutch becoming doubtful of their ability to compete on level terms with the English in places like the coast of Coromandel, where the VOC did not enjoy unchallenged control of the sea as it did in Indonesian waters. The shift became still more noticeable in the 18th century, particularly in the second half, when the official correspondence of the VOC is full of lamentations about the superiority of the English and the threat they posed to the Dutch, even in Indonesia.

It is difficult to avoid the conclusion that the English had become in fact more enterprising and able than the Dutch in the East. Admittedly their progress was mainly due to their now greatly superior capital resources and to the economic advantages they derived from their possession of Bengal and their domination of the China Trade. But there was evidently some truth in Dirk van Hogendorp's allegation that the employees of John Company were as a rule more able than those of Jan Companie, and this was just the opposite of the relative position of the two Companies in the first half of the 17th century. The reasons for this change require further investigation and research, but one contributory cause may have been the increasing tendency of the VOC to rely on uneducated 'louts from the heart of Germany', who had no particular incentive to work hard for Dutch directors and shareholders. Complaints of the real or alleged inferior calibre of the Company's servants always existed, but these allegations seem to have been more justified in the second half of the 18th century, as reflected in the reports of Nicholas Hartingh, the outstandingly capable Resident and Governor of North-east Java in the years 1746–61.[11]

11. For Hartingh's reports see J. de Jonge, *Opkomst*, Vol. X. Cf. also the previously quoted works of Van der Oudermeulen (1785), Dirk van Hogendorp (1801) and J. de Vries (1959), for relevant statistics and discussion of Dutch merchant shipping and fishing fleets in the 18th century and the decay of some of the maritime towns.

The decline of the Dutch East India Company in the second half of the 18th century was, however, in some respects more apparent than real, for the volume of this trade in relation to the seaborne trade of the Republic as a whole actually increased in this period. This increase is reflected in the numbers of outward-bound East Indiamen, which are tabulated below.

Professor Brugmans has argued from these figures that the volume of VOC shipping virtually doubled between 1631 and 1780, but it seems to me that this deduction is not altogether warranted. It is obvious that the number of Indiamen sailing between the Netherlands and Java was doubled in this period, but the number of those engaged in the interport trade of Asia may have declined by just about as much. Whereas in the second half of the 17th century, from five to ten Indiamen, many of them of the largest size, sailed annually from Batavia to Nagasaki, in the second half of the 18th century they averaged only one or two. Similarly, the number of Dutch Indiamen engaged in the trade with India dwindled into relative insignificance in the period 1750–80, compared with a century earlier, while the trade

THE OUTWARD-BOUND EAST INDIA FLEETS, 1611–1781

Period	Ships
1611–12–1620–21	117
1621–2 –1630–31	148
1631–2 –1640–41	151
1641–2 –1650–51	162
1651–2 –1660–61	226
1661–2 –1670–71	257
1671–2 –1680–81	219
1681–2 –1690–91	209
1691–2 –1700–1701	241
1701–2 –1710–11	271
1711–12–1720–21	327
1721–2 –1730–31	379
1731–2 –1740–41	365
1741–2 –1750–51	315
1751–2 –1760–61	276
1761–2 –1770–71	303
1771–2 –1780–81	294

to some regions, such as the Red Sea and the Persian Gulf, was abandoned altogether. Admittedly there were slight increases in other regions, such as the trade with Canton, and perhaps with Ceylon: but these did not compensate for the marked decline in the numbers of Dutch ships engaged in the interport trade of Asia from the Moluccas to Malabar as a whole. In 1640, for example, there were eighty-five Dutch Indiamen in Asian seas, exclusive of those on the point of sailing to or arriving from Europe. In 1743 this total had shrunk to forty-eight ships, nor was the decrease in numbers offset by any great increase in individual tonnage.[12]

During the Golden Century and in the Periwig Period, Dutchmen and their jealous trade rivals were both apt to claim that the Dutch East and West India Companies – more especially the former – were the chief pillar, prop and stay of the commercial prosperity of the United Provinces. This impression is not confirmed by such relevant figures as we have on this point, including those given by Van der Oudermeulen in 1785, who was one of the *Heeren* XVII, and one of those who advanced this claim. He gives the following figures for the value of Dutch seaborne trade on the eve of the Fourth English War:

Region	millions of guilders
Trade with the East Indies	35
Trade with the West Indies and America	28
Trade with European countries	200

Of the European countries, he estimated the value of Dutch trade:

With England	42–4
With France	36–8
With the Baltic Region	55

12. I. J. Brugmans, 'De Oost-Indische Compagnie en de welvaart in de Republiek', (*Tijdschrift voor Geschiedenis*, Vol. 61, Groningen 1948), pp. 225–31; J. de Jonge, *Geschiedenis van het Nederlandsche Zeewezen*, Vol. I, pp. 799–805; Feenstra Kuiper, *Japan en de buitenwereld in de achttiende eeuw*, p. 23 n; J. S. Stavorinus, *Voyages to the East Indies*, Vol. III, p. 413, gives a total of thirty-seven Dutch ships in Eastern seas in 1768, exclusive of outward- or homeward-bound Indiamen.

On the other hand, we must remember that most of the goods imported by the Dutch from the East and West Indies were not consumed in the United Provinces but were re-exported to other European countries. The anonymous author of *A Description of Holland*, published in 1743, may have been exaggerating somewhat, but not much, when he wrote: 'At this day, for two or three millions of guilders in specie, which the Dutch Company sends to the East Indies, they bring home fifteen or sixteen millions in goods, of which the twelfth or fourteenth part is consumed amongst themselves; the rest is re-exported to the other countries of Europe, for which they are paid in money.' Van der Oudermeulen claimed in 1783 that 'three-quarters and seven-eighths' of the cargoes imported from East India were re-exported from the Netherlands, tea and coffee excepted, of which great amounts were consumed in Friesland and Groningen; 'so that one can certainly claim that our nation drives most of its East India trade with foreigners, to its own great advantage.' Unfortunately we cannot tell what was the proportion of colonial products in relation to the Dutch export trade with other European countries as a whole, but it must have been very considerable. Van der Oudermeulen was obviously guilty of special pleading when he argued that the collapse of the VOC would not merely be disastrous for the state but would adversely affect every individual Dutchman. The course of events in 1802–14, when the Netherlands were virtually without any trade with their former colonies, showed that this was not true. But it is likely that the Dutch East India Company contributed more to the general welfare of the United Provinces in the 17th and 18th centuries than Professor Brugmans is willing to allow. Apart from the thousands of men to whom the Company gave direct employment, it helped indirectly to maintain the 30,000 sailors who manned the Dutch merchant-ships engaged in the Baltic, Mediterranean and European Atlantic trades, in which the re-export of colonial goods such as spices, tea, coffee, tobacco and textiles played such a prominent part.[13]

13. Cf. Van de Spiegel's 'Schets tot een vertoog over de intrinsique en relative magt der Republijk' of 1782 (ed. J. de Vries in the *Economisch Historisch Jaarboek*, Vol. XXVII, The Hague, 1958, pp.

There is another aspect of Dutch seaborne trade which we must glance at before briefly considering the developments in agriculture, industry and finance. This is the smuggling trade – above all, that with England. It is obviously impossible to ascertain the extent of this contraband trade, but it is certain that it helped to provide for the livelihood of thousands, particularly in the coastal towns of south Holland and Zeeland. For nearly the whole of the 18th century England was the best market for the sale of tea, and the heavy duties levied by the English government on this commodity inevitably encouraged smuggling on both sides of the North Sea. The war of 1780–4, and the passage of Pitt's Commutation Act in the last year, dealt a severe blow to the Zeeland maritime communities in this respect, as Van der Oudermeulen admitted in 1785. Dutch whalers long carried on a contraband trade with Iceland and other places, and the cod-fishers in the North Sea likewise indulged in smuggling nearer home. The burdensome network of excise duties which bore so heavily on the poorer classes in the United Provinces was, of course, a reason why many Dutch mariners were prepared to smuggle goods into Dutch ports as well as out of them; but humble sailors and fishermen were not the only or even the principal offenders in evading import and export duties. Merchants and shipowners did so on a considerable scale, and this was one of the reasons why the provincial admiralties were so often 'in the red', since their incomes depended largely on this uncertain and fluctuating source. Critics of these duties and of the excise network alleged that they not only kept up the cost of provisions, and thus the cost of living at home, but likewise encouraged foreigners to trade directly with each other instead of using the Dutch as middlemen, as they had done in the 17th century. A typical instance was afforded by the export of sugar, coffee and indigo from Bordeaux to Germany and the Baltic. Whereas at one time three-quarters of these commodities had been consigned via Amster-

81–100), and Van der Oudermeulen's Memorandum of 1785 in D. Van Hogendorp, *Stukken* (1801), pp. 37–400 especially pp. 127–275, 315–19.

dam and one-quarter via Hamburg, by 1750–51 these proportions were exactly reversed.[14]

One of the numerous writers who deplored the decline of Dutch seaborne trade in 1780 alleged that the real trouble was that shipowning had become increasingly separated from sea-faring. In the 17th century many merchant-skippers had been owners or part-owners of their ships, and they had placed their sons and relatives aboard and furthered their prospects of promotion. They had also been actively concerned in the sale of the cargoes, and directly interested in the profits to be gained by advantageously disposing of the same for the owners or co-owners. 'Nowadays', this critic claimed, 'the shipowners are mostly merely in the business for carrying freight, and their cargoes belong mainly to foreigners, and they receive no profits for the transportation thereof, save only what they are paid for the freight.' He further alleged that the foreign correspondents or associates of these shipping firms or partnerships (*rederijen*) often got their own nationals placed as deck-officers and skippers of such ships. These men, in their turn, enlisted, favoured and promoted their compatriots in preference to native-born Netherlanders. The latter, becoming discouraged at being passed over for promotion, either took to drink and debauchery or else left the sea-service in disgust.[15]

This writer, like most pamphleteers, was obviously overstating his case. It is evident that shipowning gradually became a full-time occupation in the northern Netherlands from the second half of the 17th century onwards, but this process was very far from completion in 1780. Several branches of the maritime trade, such as the timber and grain trade with the Baltic, were still largely conducted on the old footing, and skippers were still the merchants and factors of their cargoes. But it is equally evident – or so it seems to me – that foreign participation in ships sailing

14. A. Kluit, *Iets over den laatsten Engelschen oorlog met de Republiek, en over Nederlands koophandel, dezelfs bloei, verval, en middelen van herstel* (Amsterdam, 1794), pp. 302–39, especially pp. 306–7.

15. Anon, *Aanmerkingen op de bedenkingen van Mr G. Titsingh*, Amsterdam, 1780 (Pamphlet-Knuttel nr. 19466).

under the Dutch flag became much more noticeable at this time. Whereas during the Eighty Years War Dutch shipowners and skippers had often traded in the Iberian Peninsula and elsewhere by masquerading as Hansa and Scandinavians, by 1780 the position was reversed. This malpractice was of long standing, and we find De Ruyter complaining about it in 1663, when he informed the Amsterdam Admiralty that he had found at Malaga several Hamburg ships provided with Dutch papers. Their skippers had openly boasted that for a few guilders they could easily bribe some burgher at Amsterdam who would swear on oath that the vessel was Amsterdam-owned, 'whereas in reality all the owners live in Hamburg'. De Ruyter urged the admiralty to stop this abuse, but it was even more prevalent over a century later. Kluit complained in 1794 that any Dutch burgher could claim he was the owner of a ship, and he did not have to produce proof of such a declaration. The inevitable result was that many foreign merchantmen sailed under Dutch flags and with Dutch ships'-papers.[16]

When due allowance is made for exaggeration by interested parties, it must, I think, be admitted that the sinews of Dutch maritime strength had weakened considerably during the 18th century. The best contemporary authorities – Van de Spiegel and Van der Oudermeulen – were agreed that in 1780 the Dutch merchant-fleet (including the East and West India Companies) still gave employment to some 30,000 or 40,000 mariners. At first glance this does not seem to indicate such a very great change from 1588, when the Vice-Admiral of the province of Holland boasted that he could mobilize 30,000 fighting sailors within a fortnight, or from 1688 when William III sailed from Hellevoetsluis to inaugurate the 'Glorious Revolution' in England. But in 1588 and 1688 the seafaring population of Zeeland and North Holland was undoubtedly greater than in 1780, and the Dutch Republic in its prime can hardly have disposed of much fewer

16. G. Brandt, *Het leven en bedryf van den heere Michiel de Ruiter* (Amsterdam, 1687), pp. 263–4; A. Kluit, *Iets over den laatsten Engelschen oorlog* (1794), pp. 336–9. For the evolution of shipowning as an occupation in its own right in 18th-century England see R. Davis, *The Rise of the English Shipping Industry in the 17th and 18th centuries* (1962), pp. 81–109.

than 80,000 qualified seamen – and the total may well have been more. Moreover, although these totals presumably included the foreign-born seamen then available in the Netherlands, we have reason to believe that their relative proportion was even higher in 1780 than it had been either one hundred or two hundred years previously.

If we turn from the sea to the soil of the northern Netherlands, we find that Dutch agriculture made a better showing than Dutch shipping in the 18th as compared with the 17th century. Although the commercial and financial interests of the Dutch Republic did more to shape its economic structure than did the agricultural sector, yet agriculture perhaps employed more hands than did either trade or industry. This was certainly true of the five land provinces (counting Friesland as one) in both the Golden Age and the Periwig Period, and it was probably true of Zeeland and south Holland as well in the second half of the 18th century. Dairy produce was the outstanding aspect of Dutch farming. It was calculated in 1740 that the North Quarter region of the province of Holland alone produced about 20 million pounds of cheese in an averagely good year. The year 1740, incidentally, was a disastrous one for Dutch agriculture, for an exceptionally severe winter in 1739-40 was followed by a wretched summer. The suffering among the working classes was intense, and though its catastrophic effects cannot have been permanent, other people besides Stavorinus who were writing forty or fifty years later dated the decline of the United Provinces from then. Butter was another important Dutch dairy export, though this had to meet severe competition from Irish butter between 1666 and 1757 when the English government banned the importation of the latter, thus compelling the Irish farmers to expand their markets in Flanders, France and the Iberian Peninsula.

The raising of beef-cattle, horses, sheep and pigs was of much less importance than dairy farming, and there were widespread ravages by cattle-plague in 1713-23, 1744-56, and 1766-86, as well as localized outbreaks in the intervening years. The origin and cure of this disease were not scientifically understood, but the provincial States promulgated edicts enjoining various remedial or preventive measures. These injunctions were usually ignored by the peasants, partly from a distrust of the 'gentlemen' who promulgated them, and partly because they regarded the disease as a visitation of the wrath of God which it was impious to resist. In the last two decades of the 18th century a more reasonable attitude began to prevail as the result of efforts by a few progressive private farmers and by agricultural societies to encourage the inoculation of cattle against disease. Despite the ravages of cattle-plague, the losses were often more than made good after a few years by importation from abroad and by home breeding. Even in the poor and backward province of Overijssel, cattle raising increased between 1750 and 1800. On the other hand, the prevalence of cattle-plague did induce many farmers to turn wholly or partly from stock-raising to arable farming. In Groningen the switch was mainly to growing grain, in Holland to market gardening, and in Friesland to planting potatoes. In some districts sheep-folds increased for the same reason, and there were about 20,000 sheep on the island of Texel in the mid-18th century.

The oppressive incidence of provincial taxation and the burden of the excise network were two reasons why a considerable number of farmers in north Holland left the land for other occupations in the first half of the 18th century. In the second half of this century there was a general rise in agricultural prices over most of Western Europe. This probably helped to offset the burden of taxation for the farmers and peasants in some of the United Provinces and thus made life a bit easier for them. It certainly did so in Overijssel – the only province for which adequate statistics are available – where the rise in agrarian prices reduced the tax burden by about half. But this was not general, and elsewhere the increase in agricultural prices may have been more than offset by marked increases in provincial and municipal taxes and imports from about 1690 onwards.

Technical improvements in Dutch agriculture during the 18th century were introduced only tardily and incompletely, as compared with developments in contemporary France and England. The average Dutch farmer and peasant clung obstinately to the techniques employed by his 17th-century ancestors and regarded all innovations with suspicion. Peasants the world over were –

and are – inherently conservative in their ideas, and the 18th-century Dutch peasant was no exception. The spreading of new ideas and techniques among the rural population was largely dependent on the interest and co-operation of the village school-master and the local *predikant*, neither of whom were usually of an inquiring turn of mind. Some of the larger landowners experimented with new agricultural instruments, such as Tull's sowing-machine, and between 1750 and 1784 a number of the more enterprising farmers and landowners formed societies for the improvement of agriculture after the French and English models. But the results of their propaganda, their experiments and their efforts only began to bear fruit in the closing years of the Republic. On balance, however, it is clear that agriculture in general, and market gardening and arable farming in particular, were relatively flourishing in the second half of the 18th century and more particularly in its last two decades, thus contrasting with the noticeable decline in fishing and industry. More land was reclaimed from sea and swamp during this period, but the greatest single cause for the relative prosperity in agriculture was the increase in prices for agrarian products.[17]

The undeniable decline in Dutch industry as a whole during the 18th century was not common to all branches, nor was the chronological sequence always the same. The textile industry was one of the first to suffer, being one of the most exposed to sharper foreign competition. Its decline can be dated from about 1730, although some sections of this industry were supported by the export requirements of the East India Company down to 1795. The cloth industry of Leiden, which had reached its highest point in 1671 with an annual production of 139,000 pieces, thereafter declined disastrously. In 1700 it produced only 85,000 pieces; in 1725, 72,000; in 1750, 54,000; in 1775, 41,000 and in 1795 a mere 29,000 pieces. Not surprisingly this decline in Leiden's greatest industry was reflected in a parallel shrinkage of the working-class population (p. 306). Breweries, brandy-distilleries, sugar-refineries, salt- and soap-processing firms, dye-works, tobacco factories, oil-mills and diamond-cutting, all of which had

17. J. de Vries, *Economische acheruitgang*, pp. 150–66, and the sources there quoted, chief among whom is Slicher van Bath.

flourished in the Golden Century, did not all decline in the Periwig Period, though some of them did, especially in the second half of the 18th century. The diamond-cutting industry maintained itself down to the last days of the Republic, as did the paper-making industry, largely owing to the high quality of these two products. The same applies to the high-quality velvets manufactured at Utrecht. Brandy-distilleries were still flourishing in 1771, when 85 per cent of this one-time 'national drink' was being exported to markets which included North America as well as the domains of the Dutch East and West India Companies. The dyeing and tobacco industries also held their own for most of the 18th century, although they declined in some localities. The famous Delft potteries, which reached their apogee in 1685–1725, declined thereafter, though not disastrously so. Brick- and tile-kilns continued to flourish, and their products were exported in ballast to the Baltic regions after the domestic demand had been satisfied. On the other hand, the train-oil industry inevitably declined with the decrease of the whale-fisheries.

Nowhere was the overall decline of Dutch industry in the years 1750–95 more clearly reflected than in shipbuilding. In the 17th century the Dutch shipwrights were kept fully employed in building, repairing and replacing ships for the fisheries, the navy, the European seaborne carrying trade and the two India Companies, apart from the vessels they built for sale or charter abroad. It has been calculated that there were then about 500 sea-going ships built yearly in the Republic, excluding those built on foreign account and the small craft used on inland waterways. Despite inevitable ups and downs, the shipbuilding industry remained a flourishing one for the first quarter of the 18th century, but it then began to taper off. Its decline became more noticeable after about 1750 and rapidly increased in the last quarter of the century. The Zaan region near Amsterdam, which was the 17th-century equivalent of what the Clyde became in Queen Victoria's reign, still had in 1707 over sixty yards where a total of 306 big and small vessels were under construction. In 1770 there were only twenty-five or thirty ships being built there; between 1790 and 1793 an average of only five yearly; and after 1793 only one. Rotterdam possessed twenty-three shipbuilding yards in 1650, and though these had shrunk to five by the end of the century, the position had improved again a hundred years later; but this recovery did not compensate for the catastrophic decline of the Zaan. Friesland actually recorded a marked increase in the number of ships during the 18th century, since 2,000 vessels were registered in that province in 1779, which was the largest number in any of the Seven Provinces. But the great majority of these craft were small coasters of under 80 tons, which were of little or no significance in the seaborne-trade of Europe.[18]

The reasons for the general decline of Dutch industries during the 18th century are fairly obvious. In comparison with their most dangerous competitors, France and England, the northern Netherlands were very poor in raw materials and their internal market was much smaller than in those two countries. During their period of prosperity in the Golden Century many Dutch industries besides the cloth industry of Leiden had expanded far beyond the demands of the home market and were primarily dependent on the export trade. When the protectionist measures adopted by neighbouring countries from the time of Colbert onwards effectively stimulated the consumption of their own manufactured goods at the expense of Dutch exporters, the Dutch industrialists could not fall back on an increased internal demand, nor was it possible greatly to increase their sales in the tropical dependencies. Moreover, the Dutch industries had originally been primarily finishing industries for the products of other countries, such as linen and woollen goods from England, but in course of time these countries made sufficient technical progress to undertake these finishing processes themselves. When the Industrial Revolution got under way in the second half of the 18th century, the Dutch were at a further disadvantage owing to their almost total want of coal and iron. The most important Dutch industry was

18. 'Dit blijkt te klarer, wanneer men overweegt, dat er in ons Land geen Provincie is, die meer reederijen heeft van smakken, koffen, galjooten en diergelijke vaartuigen dan Vriesland, zonder daarom commercie te hebben' (A. Kluit, op. cit., pp. 322-3). For the other facts and figures cf. J. de Vries, Economische achteruitgang, pp. 83-98.

the textile industry, and it was inevitably this which suffered most. With the exception of the Dutch Republic, it has been justly observed: 'Textiles were at the very heart of mercantile policy in all countries'.[19] The prohibitive duties placed on Dutch finished and manufactured cloth by England and France in the second half of the 17th century were successively followed by similar protectionist legislation in Russia, Prussia, Denmark, Norway and Spain in the first quarter of the 18th century. The resulting decline in the Dutch textile industry was unavoidable.

Apart from protectionist- and mercantilist-inspired legislation, one reason why foreign countries had been able to improve their industries at the expense of those of the Dutch was that they had enticed skilled labourers from the Netherlands in the early stages of developing their industries. In fact, the emigration of skilled labourers continued even after the foreign industries were functioning satisfactorily, because industrial unemployment in the northern Netherlands during the 18th century induced many workers to emigrate. We have no means of calculating how many, but in 1751 the States-General promulgated an edict forbidding the emigration of certain categories of skilled workmen, especially textile operatives, ropemakers and saw-mill workers. This was by no means the only example of such legislation, but there is no reason to suppose that these edicts were anything but futile and easily evaded by those people who wished to depart. Still less could the authorities prevent foreign workmen from taking service in Dutch trades or factories to learn their respective techniques and then returning home to exploit their qualifications.

Another reason given by many contemporaries for the decline of Dutch industry in the second half of the 18th century was that the wages in the Seven Provinces, and more particularly in Holland, were higher than in most countries. For instance, the weekly wage for calico-printers in Switzerland was the equivalent of Fl. 3.50 in 1766, of Fl. 3 at Augsburg in 1760 and Fl. 9–10 in Holland. On the other hand, there were wide variations between wage-rates in different regions of the Seven Provinces. In some

19. E. F. Herkscher & E. F. Söderlund, *The Rise of Industry* (1953), *apud* J. de Vries, *Economische achteruitgang*, p. 101.

places higher wages were paid in the country districts than in the towns. In other places the situation was reversed, and some Dutch industrialists shifted their factories from Holland to north Brabant and Overijssel, where local conditions permitted ruthless exploitation of the poor. 'People who know the peasants of Brabant', wrote an eyewitness in 1785, 'must acknowledge that they are deprived of all the comforts in life that are properly the part of human beings. They drink sour buttermilk or water, they eat potatoes and bread without butter or cheese, they are miserably clothed, they sleep on straw. A prisoner in Holland lives better than a peasant in Brabant.'[20]

It is difficult to say how far the allegedly 'high' wages of some Dutch skilled labourers formed a factor in the decline of Dutch industry. Just as farmers always complained about the weather, and merchants about crippling taxation or unfair foreign competition, so industrialists were apt to think that their own adequately paid labour force was being undercut by the sweated labour of foreign competitors. As late as the year 1740, an Englishman long resident in Holland, after noting that both the Dutch and the English had brought the arts of the gunsmith and the gun-founder to a high degree of perfection, added : 'As we have a considerable advantage over the Dutch in our Mediterranean and Levant passes, it were to be wished that our taxes were reduced, or that in the meantime our workmen would contrive to live lower, and work as cheap as the Dutch', in which event, he argued, the whole of the arms-trade with the Ottoman Empire and the Barbary States would fall into English hands.[21]

Whether workers in the Dutch arms-industry subsequently maintained their technical ability on a level with that of their English competitors, I do not know; but it is worth noting that it was just in the 1740s that British economic growth started

20. B. M. Vlekke, *Evolution of the Dutch Nation*, pp. 259–60; J. de Vries, *Economische achteruitgang*, p. 107, for the differing wage-rates. The problem is examined more closely in C. Wilson, 'Taxation and the decline of empires', in BMHGU, Vol. 77, pp. 10–26.

21. *A Description of Holland* (1743), pp. 236–7.

accelerating and the first phase of the Industrial Revolution got under way. Forty years later the general decline of Dutch industry was lamented by a Netherlands industrialist in the following terms: 'One cannot refrain from observing that there are very few industries or trades here which are not in need of improvement; both as regards the form as also the means of their respective processes. Copper-smiths, brass-founders, workers in iron and steel and workmen of that kind, are all found to be rather unskilful, and, when their products are carefully compared with those of foreign workmen, they are found to be inferior. The workmanship here is clumsier, and the piece is usually much less well finished, than that made elsewhere; and one can presume that it comes more expensive because the foremen here have not been properly trained.' In the same year (1779) a leading Leiden cloth-manufacturer deplored the general lack of initiative among Dutch industrialists and employers, and their deep-rooted aversion to experimenting with new techniques and new methods.[22] What was good enough for their ancestors was good enough for them, and this seems to have been a marked trait of Dutch society in the closing decades of the Periwig Period, whether in the towns and fields of the northern Netherlands or in the hinterland of the Cape of Good Hope.

This lack of initiative and enterprise in so many Dutch industries, and to some extent in Dutch agriculture, afforded a striking contrast to the state of affairs a hundred years previously, when Dutch entrepreneurs, industrialists and technicians were in the van of commercial and technical progress in the Western World. As Charles Wilson has rightly observed: 'The Dutch technician was to the 17th century what the Scotch engineer was to the 19th century, but in even wider fields of economic activity. He was to be found wherever profitable occupation offered and he was in demand wherever government or private enterprise was in need of technical or managerial skill.' A century later he was nothing of the kind, as a contributor to De Koopman ruefully acknowledged in 1776: 'We are no longer innate inventors, and originality is becoming increasingly rare with us here. Nowadays we only make copies, whereas formerly

22. J. de Vries, *Economische achteruitgang*, pp. 108–12.

we only made originals.'[23] No doubt some allowance must be made for exaggeration in these and many other similar jeremiads published in Dutch periodicals during the second half of the 18th century; and we may recall here Captain James Cook's tribute to the skill and efficiency of the Batavian shipwrights in 1770. But I venture to suggest that contrary to what some recent writers have claimed, the Periwig Period in the United Provinces *was* a time of stagnation rather than of consolidation, when compared with the achievements of the Golden Century in most, though admittedly not in all, respects.

The contemporaries who bemoaned the economic decay of the Dutch Republic in the last half – more especially in the last quarter – of the 18th century were inclined to place the principal blame on the allegedly self-satisfied and short-sighted rentiers and capitalists, who preferred to invest their money abroad rather than in fostering industry and shipping at home and thus relieving unemployment. There was undoubtedly an attitude of '*je m'en fiche*'-ism in the Netherlands and its tropical possessions during the last quarter of the 18th century, which, if it existed at all a century earlier was not then nearly so marked. The periodical *De Borger* wrote of the prosperous rentiers of 1778: 'Each one says, "It will last my time and after me the deluge!" as our [French] neighbours' proverb has it, which we have taken over in deeds if not in words.' A few years later, Dirk van Hogendorp wrote from Java that the most popular maxim among his compatriots there was 'the going will be good as long as I live, and what happens after my death won't worry me then'.[24]

23. C. Wilson, *Holland and Britain* (London, 1945), pp. 14–18. The quotation from *De Koopman* of 1776 is *apud* J. de Vries, *Economische achteruitgang*, p. 63 of the notes and note (300).

24. *De Borger* of 19 October 1778, *apud* J. de Bosch Kemper, *Armoede* (ed. 1851), p. 354–8, where the comparison between the energetic entrepreneurs of the 17th century and the slothful rentiers of the 18th is drawn at great if not altogether convincing length; E. de Perron-de Roos, 'Correspondentie van Dirk van Hogendorp', pp. 140–41, 144, 264–8. Cf. also Anon, *Nederlandsch India in haar tegenwoordig staat* (c. 1780), pp. 17–18, 48; *Nederlandsch–Indisch Plakaatboek*, Vol. XI, pp. 55–6, 226; F. de Haan, *Oud Batavia*, Vol.

We have seen that some of these complaints were exaggerated (p. 303), and in any event the increase in unearned income from Dutch investment capital during the 18th century – Van de Spiegel estimated this surplus profit at a yearly total of 27 million florins in 1782 – offset to a great extent, or possibly even more than offset, the decline in other sectors of the national income. But it did not compensate for the rise in proletarian poverty and unemployment. Recent historical research on the reasons for the economic decline of the northern Netherlands in the second half of the 18th century has established that economic factors – many of them unavoidable, such as the development of industry and shipping in neighbouring countries – were primarily responsible for this. There were, however, some other subsidiary causes, which might, perhaps, have been mitigated or avoided altogether if the social structure of the Republic had been other than it actually was.

In the first place (as Johan de Vries has pointed out) there was the preponderantly commercial tradition inherited from the Golden Century, when the Dutch merchants dominated the sea-borne trade of so much of the world, and almost came to believe that they had a God-given right to do so. The social prestige of the merchant was always much higher than that of the industrialist, or of most other people outside the ruling oligarchic circle; and this commercial tradition, prestige and inclination was not favourable for the development of an industrial mentality. People who made a fortune, or even a comfortable living, from industry or craftsmanship were apt to change over to a merchant's calling as soon as they had enough capital to do so, and to bring up their sons as merchants. The decentralized structure of the government of the Republic and the interprovincial jealousies of the self-styled 'United Provinces', which had not greatly hindered their economic growth in the Golden Century, became greater obstacles in the changed circumstances

---

II, pp. 9–17, for some typical examples of the prevailing corruption and cynicism in the Dutch East India Company at this period, which it would be very easy to multiply, and which are much more convincing than the denunciations of the rentiers in the fatherland.

of the 18th century, when foreign competition was more effective. The financial contributions of the various provinces to the 'generality', which had been fixed during the period 1609-21, remained unaltered down to the end of the Republic, despite the abortive efforts of some statesmen to revise them in accordance with the changing circumstances. Political divisions and mutual mistrust between the pro- and anti-Orange factions in the second half of the 18th century also meant that sensible suggestions for reform put up by one side were automatically rejected or sidetracked by the other. Inter-provincial jealousies sometimes prevented agreement from being reached on the improvement of roads or canals crossing provincial (or even municipal) boundaries. Corruption and nepotism among the regent-oligarchs had certainly existed in the 17th century, but did not impair their efficiency to the same extent as occurred with their descendants in the Periwig Period, when 'contracts of correspondence' became the rule rather than the exception.

The common late-18th-century allegation that Dutch capitalists and rentiers who invested part of their capital in English and French funds were thereby helping the Republic's most dangerous competitors was probably unjustified. These countries would have developed their trade and industry even without the aid of Dutch capital. England was also an exporter of capital, though admittedly not on the same scale as the Dutch. Johan de Vries has pointed out that England was able to bear the financial burden of the War of American Independence without undue difficulty, even at a time when the Dutch recalled part of their capital from London. He argues that the real adverse repercussion of the practice of investing in foreign countries, which Dutch capitalists developed in the 18th century, was that it continued longer into the 18th century than was economically justifiable.[25]

Whether some forms of the economic decline of the Dutch Republic could have been prevented or not, by 1780 the process had gone far enough for all to see. The merchant-bankers and the wealthy rentiers might never have 'had it so good', but the condition of the poor seems to have been even worse than it was a century previously, particularly in the inland towns. Boswell's

25. J. de Vries, *Economische achteruitgang*, pp. 172-80.

description of Utrecht in 1763 (p. 305) anticipated an observation by Luzac twenty years later: 'Nobody who has any feeling, and some love for his fatherland, can walk through the inland towns with dry eyes.' In 1792 another eyewitness deposed: 'Everywhere we look attentively around us we find the sad truth confirmed that the well-being of that class of people who lead a working life is steadily declining.' The general rise in the cost of living during the second half of the 18th century was certainly one reason for this, as the Zeeland blue-stocking, Betje Wolff, noted in 1778. Increasing poverty was evident not only among the declining working-class population of towns such as Leiden, Delft and Zaandam, but in the rural province of Overijssel, where the growth in population between 1675 and 1767 was accompanied by a speedier increase in poverty. The result was not only a greater gulf between rich and poor but also a greater gulf between the upper and lower middle classes in the towns.[26]

Despite the increasing religious tolerance and the declining religious bigotry; despite the efforts of such bodies as the Economic Branch of the Holland Society of Sciences to improve social and economic conditions by precept and example; despite the efforts of Betje Wolff and her sympathizers to educate and uplift the masses; despite the decrease in drinking gin and brandy and the increase in drinking coffee and tea – despite all these and other improving aspects of the Enlightenment which might be mentioned, I have no doubt that the land of Rembrandt, Vondel and De Ruyter was a better as well as a more stimulating place in which to live than was the land of Cornelis Troost, Bilderdijk and Zoutman.

26. J. de Vries, *Economische achteruitgang*, pp. 170–72.

Appendix I
Chronology 1568-1795

Since this is not a factual, narrative history except in so far as it illustrates the ten themes which I have chosen for discussion, the following outline chronology may help the reader to establish the sequence of events.

1568   Abortive revolt in the Netherlands crushed by Alva. Execution of Egmont and Hoorn at Brussels (June)

1572   The sea-beggars' capture of Den Briel (April) followed by a new surge of revolt in Holland and Zeeland. Massacre of St Bartholomew (August)

1579   Union of Utrecht (January) between the seven northern and self-styled United Provinces of Holland, Zeeland, Utrecht, Guelderland, Overijssel, Groningen and Friesland. The regions subsequently captured formed the 'Lands of the States-General' or 'The Generality'

1580   Union of the Crowns of Spain and Portugal in the person of Philip II

1581   Prince William I of Orange, Stadtholder of Holland, Zeeland and Utrecht, and the States-General of the Seven Provinces, formally renounce their allegiance to Philip II of Spain

1584   Assassination of William I (July). Rise of the Muslim empire of Mataram in central Java begins, 1582–1613

1585-6   Parma's capture of Antwerp followed by accelerated emigration of Calvinists and capital from the southern Provinces to the northern. Leicester's abortive governor-generalship in the Seven Provinces. First Iberian embargo on Dutch shipping (May 1585)

1588   Prince Maurice appointed Stadtholder. Anglo-Dutch defeat of the Spanish Armada

1590-1600   Great expansion of Dutch seaborne trade to the Mediterranean, West Africa and Indonesia

1600   Foundation of the English East India Company. The first Dutch ship reaches Japan. Unification of Japan under the *de facto* rule of the Tokugawa Shogunate after the battle of Sekigahara, 1600–1863

1602   Foundation of the Dutch East India Company

1605   Dutch capture Amboina and drive the Portuguese from the Moluccas

1606   Dutch fleet blockades the Tagus. A Spanish expedition from the Philippines recaptures part of the Moluccas. Unsuccessful Dutch attacks on Moçambique and Malacca

1607   Heemskerk destroys a Spanish fleet off Gibraltar

1609   Inauguration of the Twelve Year Truce with Spain. Dutch factory at Hirado in Japan

1610–12   Dutch settlements founded in Guiana and the Amazon region, these last being subsequently destroyed by the Portuguese. Fort Mouree founded on the Guinea Coast (1612)

1614   Dutch fur-traders active on the Hudson River

1618–19   Synod of Dordrecht. Execution of Oldenbarneveldt. Outbreak of the Thirty Years War. Dutch found Batavia on the ruins of Jakarta. Anglo-Dutch rivalry in the East Indies temporarily changed into an Alliance in 1619–23. Mataram reaches the height of its power under Sultan Agung (1613–45). Achin reaches the height of its power under Sultan Iskander Muda (1615–36). Islamization of Macassar

1621   Expiration of the Twelve Years Truce. Establishment of the Dutch West India Company

1624–5   Dutch take and lose Bahia. Spinola captures Breda. New Amsterdam founded on Manhattan Island. Dutch repulsed at Puerto Rico and Elmina. Death of Maurice, who is succeeded by his brother, Frederick Henry, as Stadtholder

1628–9   Piet Heyn captures the Silver Fleet (September 1628). Dutch capture Hertogenbosch. Spaniards unsuccessfully besiege Bergen-op-Zoom. Mataram unsuccessfully besieges Batavia. Death of Jan Pietersz Coen

1630   Dutch begin the conquest of Pernambuco (N.E. Brazil)

1637   Frederick Henry recaptures Breda. John Maurice completes conquest of Pernambuco. Van Diemen makes an alliance with Raja Sinha of Kandy against the Portuguese in Ceylon

1638 Dutch capture Elmina in Guinea and begin conquest of coastal Ceylon

1639 M. H. Tromp destroys a Spanish Armada in The Downs (21 October)

1640 Catalonia and Portugal revolt from Spain, which subdues the former in 1656 and recognizes the independence of the latter in 1668. Dutch defeat a Portuguese armada off Pernambuco

1641 Dutch capture Malacca (January), the Maranhão and Luanda (August) from the Portuguese, with whom they also conclude a Ten Year Truce at The Hague (June). The Dutch are now the only Europeans allowed in Japan (Deshima at Nagasaki) till 1853

1644–5 Dutch naval expeditions force the passage of the Sound and protect Dutch trade in the Baltic. John Maurice's departure from Pernambuco, followed by rebellion in N.E. Brazil against the Dutch. Manchus inaugurate their conquest of China

1647 Death of Frederick Henry, who is succeeded by his son, William II, as Stadtholder

1648 Spain recognizes Dutch independence by the Treaty of Münster (January). Portuguese recapture Luanda and Benguela (August)

1650–51 Premature death of William II after an abortive *coup-de-main* against Amsterdam. Abolition of the office of Stadtholder (save in Friesland and Groningen), and inauguration of the period of the so-called 'True Freedom'. Passage of the English Navigation Act discriminating against Dutch seaborne trade

1652–4 First Anglo-Dutch War, ending in a decisive Dutch defeat in the North Sea and regional Dutch victories in the East Indies and the Mediterranean. Van Riebeeck founds the settlement at Cape Town. Johan de Witt becomes Grand Pensionary of the Province of Holland and the effective leader of the Republic until 1672. Portuguese expel the Dutch from N.E. Brazil. Arnold de Vlaming completes the conquest of the Amboina group (1650–56)

1658–9 Dutch intervene in the Baltic and relieve the pressure of the Swedish attack on Denmark. Dutch complete the conquest of coastal Ceylon (1654–8)

1661–3   Dutch make peace with Portugal and complete the conquest of Malabar from the Portuguese. Coxinga captures Formosa from the Dutch, and the Spaniards evacuate the Moluccas. First Dutch attack on Macassar

1664   English take some Dutch forts on the Gold Coast and the North American colony of New Netherlands in time of peace

1665–7   Second Anglo-Dutch war, culminating in the Dutch raid on the Medway and the Treaty of Breda. Final subjugation of Macassar by Speelman and Aru Palakka

1668   Triple alliance between Dutch Republic, England and Sweden

1672–4   Third Anglo-Dutch War and invasion of the Republic by the French. Murder of the brothers De Witt (August 1672) and re-establishment of the Stadtholdership in favour of Prince William III. Revolt of Trunajaya inaugurates the decline of Mataram which recognizes Dutch suzerainty by Treaty of 1677

1677–8   Further Dutch naval intervention in the Baltic. William III marries Mary, daughter of James Duke of York. Treaty of Nymegen (August 1678)

1679   Death of John Maurice of Nassau-Siegen and Joost van den Vondel

1682–4   Subjugation of Bantam by the Dutch. Manchu conquest of Formosa

1685   Revocation of the Edict of Nantes followed by influx of Huguenot refugees into the Republic

1688–97   War of the League of Augsberg. William III becomes King of England (1689). Sino-Russian Treaty of Nertchinsk (1689). Treaty of Ryswijk (1697). Coffee tree introduced into Java from Arabia

1702   Death of the King-Stadtholder, William III, and inauguration of the second Stadtholderless period in the Republic

1702–13   War of the Spanish Succession. Treaty of Utrecht. Civil war in Mataram and first Javanese War of Succession

1717–23   Second Javanese War of Succession

1740–43   Massacre of Chinese at Batavia followed by extension of fighting into the interior of Java and a new war in Mataram, ending with further cession of territory by the Susuhunan

1747–8 Republic involved in the War of the Austrian Succession and its territory invaded by the French. Abortive middle- and working-class movements against oligarchic misrule. William IV made Stadtholder of all seven Provinces, and the office is made hereditary in the House of Orange

1751 Death of William IV, and practical resumption of regent-oligarchic rule during minority of his son

1749–55 Third Javanese Succession War ending with the division of Mataram into the states of Jogjakarta and Surakarta

1756–63 Seven Years War, during which the Dutch profit as neutrals but suffer from considerable English interference with their seaborne trade. A Dutch expedition to restore their position in Bengal miscarries completely and is annihilated by the English (1759)

1766 William V assumes the functions of the Stadtholdership. Rivalry between the pro- and anti-Orange factions in the Netherlands grows steadily worse from now onwards

1780–84 Fourth Anglo-Dutch War with catastrophic effects on Dutch seaborne trade and colonial power. Growth of anti-Orangist feeling among the self-styled 'Patriotten' (Patriots)

1787 Armed Prussian intervention restores full power to the Stadtholder. Thousands of the 'Patriotten' seek refuge in France

1793 Republic involved in the French Revolutionary War. French invasion, at first successful, checked at Neerwinden (18 March)

1794–5 Another French invasion, facilitated by a severe frost, is virtually unopposed (December–January). The Stadtholder flees to England (18 January 1795), and the old régime collapses ignominiously. First English occupation of the Cape of Good Hope

1795 Dutch East India Company formally dissolved (31 December), and its debts and possessions taken over by the Batavian Republic

Appendix II: Some salary scales of seafaring and overseas personnel 1645-1700

(a) *Monthly rates of pay for the Dutch Navy, October 1652*

Captain	Fl. 30
Lieutenant	Fl. 25
Schipper (master)	Fl. 24
Opper-Stuurman (Pilot, or chief mate)	Fl. 30
Surgeon, with his medicine-chest	Fl. 30
Sailors	Fl. 10–11

(all the above exclusive of ration and subsistence allowances)

(b) *Basic rates of pay for overseas employees of the East India Company in the second half of the 17th century*

Rank and status	Monthly pay in florins
(i) MERCANTILE	
Opper-koopman (senior merchant)	80–100
Koopman (merchant)	40–60
Onder-Koopman (junior merchant)	36–40
Boek-houder (writer, book-keeper)	18–24
Assistant (clerk)	16–24
(ii) MARITIME	
Schipper (master)	60–80
Opper-Stuurman (first mate)	36–50
Onder-Stuurman (second mate)	24–36
Hoogh-Bootsman (boatswain)	22–26
Schieman (boatswain's-mate)	20–24
Steward	20–24
Cook	20–24
Steward's-mate, cook's-mate	14 each
Quartermaster	14
Sailmaker	18
Sailmaker's-mate	14
Surgeon	36–50

Rank and status	Monthly pay in florins
Surgeon's-mate	24–28
Cooper	16
Cooper's-mate	13
Ship's-carpenter	30–48
Carpenter's-mate	24–28
Master-gunner	20–24
Gunner's-mate	14
Quarter-gunner	12
Provost (master-at-arms)	14–15
Ship's-corporal	14–16
Able Seamen	10–11
Ordinary Seamen	7–10
Hooploopers (apprentice seamen)	7
Ship's-boys under 16 years old	4–6

(iii) MILITARY

Captain	80
Lieutenant	50–60
Ensign	36–40
Sergeant	20
Corporal	14
Landspassaat (Lance-Corporal)	12
Adelborst (cadet)	10
Private soldier	9
Raw recruit	7–8
Drummer	6–10

(iv) ECCLESIASTICAL

Predikant (Qualified Preacher)	80–100
Krank-bezoeker and Ziekentrooster (sick-visitor, catechist)	30–36

(v) CRAFTSMEN AND ARTISANS

House-carpenter	15–16
Mason	15–16
Gunsmith	12–14
Smith	12–14
Locksmith	12–14
Sword-cutler	14
Furniture-maker	14

Other craftsmen and technicians, ranking as fully qualified 'block-makers, blacksmiths, copper-smiths, tin-smiths', etc, were engaged by the Company (in 1695) for service in the East at the rate of as many guilders a month as they were earning stuivers a day in the United Provinces.

The foregoing salary-scales are deduced from a comparison of those given in the printed *Reglement op't aanneemen en gagieren van't volk na Oost-Indien, te weten Zeevaarende en Militaren*, dated 1 November 1692; Nicolaus de Graaff's *Oost-Indie Spiegel* of 1703 (pp. 56–7 of the LV edition of 1930); P. Van Dam (ed. Stapel), *Beschryvinge*, Book I, pp. 557–60. The variations are chiefly due to conduct and place and length of service, those who re-enlisted after their first term usually being paid at a higher rate. For comparison with the wage-scales prevailing in the second half of the 18th century, see the very detailed scale promulgated in July–August 1753, printed in Van der Chijs, *Nederlandsch-Indisch Plakaatboek*, Vol. VI (1889), pp. 456–93. Cf. also O. F. Mentzel, *Life at the Cape in mid-18th Century* (Cape Town, 1919), pp. 164–6, and ibid., *Description of the Cape* (ed. 1921), pp. 153–60. These give not only the basic salaries but also the monthly emoluments and allowances. It may be noted that many of the more senior posts were substantially better paid in the second half of the 18th century, but the basic monthly wage of the common sailor and soldier remained exactly the same – 9 Florins.

(c) *Basic rates of pay for the employees of the Dutch West India Company on the Gold Coast, 1645–7*

Rank and status	Monthly pay in florins
(i) MERCANTILE	
Opper-Koopman (Senior merchant)	60–90
Commies (merchant)	24–50
Onder-Commies (junior merchant)	20–24
Assistant (clerk)	8–14
(ii) MARITIME	
Schipper (master)	40
Stuurman (mate)	20–25
Boatswain	13–17
Boatswain's-mate	16
Master-gunner	15

Rank and status	Monthly pay in florins
Gunner	9–10
Sailmaker	13
Steward	11
Cooper	14–16
Carpenter	16–24
Sailors	9–14 according to length of service

(iii) MILITARY

Ensign	39
Sergeant	18
Corporal	12
Lance-Corporal	11
Cadet	10
Soldier	8
Drummer	9–10

(iv) ECCLESIASTICAL

Lay-Reader, Catechist, or Sick-Visitor	30–36

(v) CRAFTSMEN AND ARTISANS

Smith	28
Locksmith	15
Coppersmith	14
Mason	10–12

The surgeon on the Gold Coast was paid a basic wage of Fl. 25–30 a month, and had to maintain his medicine-chest and instruments out of his own pocket, as was the case with his colleagues of the Navy and the VOC.

The above rates are all exclusive of emoluments and ration-allowances, etc., and are taken from K. Ratelband, *Vijf Daghregisters van het Kasteel São Jorge de Mina, 1645–1647* (The Hague, 1953), pp. lviii–lxiii. For comparison with the scales prevailing on the Gold Coast about fifty years later see W. Bosman, *Nauwkeurige Beschryving van Guinese Goud-Tand-en Slave-Kust* (Utrecht, 1704), pp. 91–100.

As with the VOC, the basic rates of pay in the WIC service varied widely in accordance with the capability, experience, length and place of service of the recipients in the same grade or category.

Appendix III: A note on the principal coins, weights and measures mentioned in the text

The Dutch guilder or florin (represented by the sign Fl.) contained 20 stuivers, and may be regarded as the equivalent of the English florin. It was not generally current in the East, but the Dutch East India Company's accounts were kept in guilders and stuivers, local currencies being converted at conventional rates which varied widely. The expression 'a ton of gold', which often occurs in the Dutch records, merely means 100,000 guilders' worth of anything For the first half of the 17th century the Spanish-American rial-of-eight was widely used in the East by the Dutch both as real money and as a unit of account, being usually converted at about 48 stuivers, and considered as the (slightly overvalued) equivalent of the rix-dollar (2½ florins). A series of monetary reforms in the Netherlands and Batavia in 1656–8 resulted in the rial and the rix-dollar both being fixed at 60 stuivers, but *payments* in the East India Company's service being adjusted in such a way that there were henceforth two kinds of stuivers, 'light' and 'heavy', the former corresponding to four-fifths of the silver stuiver. The matter was complicated by the fact that the guilder or florin of account still remained at 20 stuivers, though these were reckoned as being 'heavy' in the Netherlands and 'light' from the Cape of Good Hope to Nagasaki. Thus, in effect, as Mentzel pointed out, salaries were calculated in the books at the rate of 20 stuivers per florin but paid out locally at the rate of 15 stuivers per florin. In the new Batavian monetary system, the rix-dollar at 3 florins (or 60 stuivers) now replaced the rial-of-eight as money of account, while guilders also continued to be used as such. For the complicated conversion rates and the fluctuating values of the numerous coins used by the Dutch in the East cf. *Uytrekening van de goude en silvere munten, inhout der matten en swaarte der gewigten in de respective gewesten van Indiën* (Middelburg, 1691); C. Scholten, *The Coins of the Dutch Overseas Territories, 1601–1948* (Amsterdam, 1953); K. Glamann, *Dutch-Asiatic Trade, 1620–1740* (Copenhagen, 1958), pp. 50–72; W. H. Moreland, *From Akbar to Aurangzeb. A study in Indian economic history* (London, 1923), pp. 329–43.

The Dutch pound weight most commonly used was the Amsterdam pound, the weight of which was 0·494 kg. or practically 1·09 lb. avdp.

The Dutch *last*, or ton of shipping space, is usually taken as the equivalent of 120 cubic feet or 2 tons (measurement). The *last* was also equated with 2 dead-weight tons = 2 metric tons burden; or 2,000 Amsterdam lb. = 4,356 lb. avdp. = 1,976 kg. (F. C. Lane in *Economic History Review*, Vol. XVII, p. 229).

The Dutch mile was very variable but usually taken as the equivalent of the English league (3 miles) in the 17th century.

Select bibliography

This bibliography is limited to a list of the fuller titles of the principal works cited in the footnotes, with the addition of a few exceptionally important monographs and articles. The omission of certain recent works such as Enno van Gelder's *The Two Reformations in the 17th Century* (The Hague, 1964) is explained by the fact that they only came to the author's notice after his manuscript was in the press.

I. Gosses & J. Japikse, *Handboek tot de Staatkundige Geschiedenis van Nederland* (3rd edition, The Hague, 1947), gives detailed bibliographies after each chapter. These bibliographies can be brought virtually up to date by consulting those published in the *Algemene Geschiedenis der Nederlanden*, listed below. Periodical articles published before 1954 are listed in the 10-volume work edited successively by L. D. Petit, H. Ruys, Aleida Gast & J. Brok-Ten Broek, *Repertorium der verhandelingen en bijdragen betreffende de geschiedenis des Vaderlands* (Leiden, 1907–59), which is still in progress. The excellent colonial bibliography by W. P. Coolhaas, *A Critical Survey of Studies on Dutch Colonial History* (The Hague, 1960), includes all but the most recent works in this field. These, as well as those dealing with the Netherlands, are equally well surveyed and evaluated by E. & J. Kossmann in their serial 'Bulletin critique de l'historiographie néerlandaise', which has been published annually in the *Revue du Nord. Revue historique trimestrielle. Nord de France-Belgique-Pays Bas* (Lille, 1954 to date), and long may this invaluable guide continue to appear.

Aitzema, Lieuwe van, *Saken van staet en oorlogh, in ende omtrent de Vereenigde Nederlanden, 1621–1668* (6 vols., The Hague, 1669–72).

Algemene Geschiedenis der Nederlanden (12 vols., Utrecht, 1949–1958). Vols. 5–8 are the relevant ones for the period 1567–1795.

Anon, *A Description of Holland: or, the present state of the United Provinces. Wherein is contained a particular account of the Hague, and all the principal cities and towns of the Republick ... of the manner and customs of the Dutch, their constitution, etc., etc.* (London, 1743).

Select bibliography

Arasaratnam, Sinappah, *Dutch Power in Ceylon, 1658–1687* (Amsterdam, 1958).

Barbour, Violet, *Capitalism in Amsterdam in the Seventeenth Century* (Baltimore, 1950).

Barlow's Journal of his Life at Sea in King's Ships, East and West Indiamen and other Merchantmen from 1659 to 1703 (ed. Basil Lubbock, 2 vols., London, 1934).

Bell, A. E., *Christian Huygens and the Development of Science in the Seventeenth Century* (London, 1947).

Bijdragen en Mededelingen van het Historisch Genootschap gevestigd te Utrecht (Utrecht, 1878 to date). In progress. Prior to 1878, the title began with the word Kroniek.

Bijdragen voor de Geschiedenis der Nederlanden (The Hague and Antwerp, 1946 to date). In progress.

Böeseken, Anna J., *Nederlandsche Commissarissen aan de Kaap, 1657–1700* (The Hague, 1938).

Böeseken, Anna J., *Die Nederlandse Kommissarisse en die 18de eeuse samelewing aan die Kaap* (Cape Town, 1944).

Bosch Kemper, Jeronimo de, *Geschiedkundig onderzoek naar de armoede in ons vaderland, haare oorzaken en de middelen, die tot hare vermindering zouden kunnen worden aangewend* (Haarlem, 1851). An abridged version was published in 1860.

Bosman, Willem, *Nauwkeurige Beschryving van de Guinese goud-, tand-, en slave-kust, nevens alle desselfs landen, koningryken en gemenebesten* (Utrecht, 1704). The English translation, *A New and Accurate Description of the Coast of Guinea*, was published at London, 1705, reprinted, 1721.

Boxer, C. R. (trans. and ed.), *The Journal of Maarten Harpertszoon Tromp, Anno 1639* (Cambridge, 1930).

Boxer, C. R., *Jan Compagnie in Japan, 1600–1850. An essay on the cultural, artistic and scientific influence exercised by the Hollanders in Japan from the 17th to the 19th centuries* (The Hague, 1950). Revised edition of a work first published in 1936.

Boxer, C. R,. *The Dutch in Brazil, 1624–1654* (Oxford, 1957).

Britain and the Netherlands. Papers delivered to the Oxford–Netherlands Historical Congress, 1959 (London, 1960). Edited by J. S. Bromley & E. H. Kossmann. Vol. II, *Papers Delivered to the Anglo–Dutch Historical Conference 1962* (Groningen, 1964), appeared after the present work had gone to press.

Brugmans, H., *Opkomst en bloei van Amsterdam* (Amsterdam, 1944). Posthumous edition of A. Le Cosquino de Bussy & N. W. Posthumus.

Busken Huet, Conrad, *Het Land van Rembrand. Studien over de Noord Nederlandsche Beschaving in de zeventiende eeuw* (3 vols., Haarlem, 1886).

Carr, William, *An Accurate Description of the United Netherlands* (London, 1691). First published at Amsterdam under a different title in 1688, this work continued to be reprinted under varying titles and in slightly differing editions, mostly with the omission of Carr's name, down to 1744 at least.

Carter, Alice, 'The Dutch and the English public debt in 1777' (*Economica*, May 1953, pp. 159–61).

Carter, Alice, 'Dutch foreign investment, 1738–1800' (*Economica*, November 1953, pp. 322–40).

Carter, Alice, 'The Dutch as neutrals in the Seven Years War' (*The International and Comparative Law Quarterly*, July 1963, pp. 818–34).

Chijs, J. A. van der, *Nederlandsch–Indisch Plakaatboek, 1602–1799* (12 vols., Batavia, 1885–94).

Colenbrander, H. T., *Jan Pieterszoon Coen. Levensbeschrijving* (The Hague, 1934).

Court, Pieter de la, *Interest van Holland ofte gronden van Hollands welvaren* (Amsterdam, 1662). First published under the pseudonym of V.D.H., this work was reprinted in a revised and enlarged edition in 1669 entitled *Aanwysing der heilsame politieke gronden en maximen van de Republike van Holland en West–Vriesland*, and translated into English under the title of *The True Interest and Political Maxims of the Republick of Holland and West-Friesland* (London, 1702), wrongly ascribed to Johan de Witt.

Dagh-Register gehouden int Casteel Batavia vant passerende daer ter plaetse als over geheel Nederlandts India, 1624–1682 (23 vols., Batavia, 1896–1931).

Dam, Pieter van, *Beschryvinge van de Oostindische Compagnie* (4 books in 6 vols., The Hague, 1927–54). First 5 vols. edited by F. W. Stapel, the sixth by Baron van Boetzelaer van Asperen en Dubbeldam.

Davies, David W., *The World of the Elseviers, 1580–1712* (The Hague, 1954).

Dillen, J. G. van, *Het oudste aandeelhoudersregister van de Kamer Amsterdam der Oost-Indische Compagnie* (The Hague, 1958).

Du Perron, E., *De Muze van Jan Companjie. Overzichtelike verzameling van Nederlands-Oostindiese belletrie uit de Companjiestijd, 1600–1780* (Bandoeng, 1948).

Du Perron, E. & D. Roos, E., 'Correspondentie van Dirk van Hogendorp met zijn broeder Gijsbert Karel, 1783–1797' (in BTLVNI, Vol. 102, pp. 125–273, The Hague, 1943).

Eekhof, A., *De Hervormde Kerk in Noord-Amerika, 1624–1664* (2 vols., The Hague, 1913).

Eekhof, A., *De Negerpredikant Jacobus Elisa Joannes Capitein, 1717–1747* (The Hague, 1917).

Elias, Johan E., *Het voorspel van den eersten Engelschen oorlog* (2 vols. in one, The Hague, 1920).

Elias, Johan E., *Geschiedenis van het Amsterdamsche Regentpatriciaat* (The Hague, 1923).

Elias, Johan E., *Schetsen uit de geschiedenis van ons zeewezen, 1568–1654* (6 vols., The Hague, 1916–30).

Feenstra Kuiper, J., *Japan en de buitenwereld in de achttiende eeuw* (The Hague, 1921).

Fockema Andrae, S. J., *De Nederlandse staat onder de Republiek* (Amsterdam, 1962).

Geer, W. Van, *De Opkomst van het Nederlandsch gezag over Ceilon* (Leiden, 1895).

Geyl, Pieter, *The Revolt of the Netherlands, 1555–1609* (London, 1962).

Geyl, Pieter, *The Netherlands in the Seventeenth Century,* Part I, 1609–1648 (London, 1961). Part II, 1648–1715 (London, 1964).

Geyl, Pieter, *Geschiedenis van de Nederlandse Stam* (3 vols., 1958–9). In progress. The three volumes published so far cover the period down to 1798.

Geyl, Pieter, *Studies en Strijdschriften* (Groningen, 1958).

Glamann, Kristof, *Dutch–Asiatic Trade, 1620–1740* (Copenhagen and The Hague, 1958).

Gonsalves de Mello, José Antonio, *Tempo dos Flamengos. Influência da Occupção Holandesa na vida e cultura do Norte do Brasil* (Rio de Janeiro, 1947).

Graaff, Nicolaus de, *Reysen van Nicolaus de Graaff na Asia, Africa, America en Europa, mitsgaders zijn Oost Indische Spiegel* (Hoorn, 1701 and 1703). Cf. also under Warnsinck, J. C. M. *infra.*

Groeneveldt, W. P., *De Nederlanders in China. De eerste bemoeiingen om den handel in China en de vestiging in de Pescadores, 1601–1624* (The Hague, 1898).

Haan, F. de, *Priangan. De Preanger–Regentschappen onder het Nederlandsch bestuur tot 1811* (4 vols., Batavia, 1910–12). Covers far more ground than is indicated by the title.

Haan, F. de, *Oud Batavia. Gedenkboek uitgegeven door het Bataviaasch Genootschap van Kunsten en Wetenschappen naar aaleiding van het driehonderdjarig bestaan der stad in 1919* (2 vols., and album of plates, Batavia, 1922).

Haan, J. C. de & Winter, P. J. van (eds.), *Nederlanders over de zeeën. 350 jaar Nederlandsche Koloniale Geschiedenis* (Utrecht, 1940).

Hannay, David, *The Great Chartered Companies* (London, 1926).

Havart, Daniel, *Op-en Ondergang van Cormandel, in zijn binnenste geheel open, en ten toon gesteld* (Amsterdam, 1693).

Hickey, William, *Memoirs of William Hickey, 1749–1809* (ed. A. Spencer, 4 vols., London, 1919).

Hogendorp, Dirk van, *Stukken raakende de tegenwoordigen toestand der Bataafsche bezittingen in Oost Indië en de handel op dezelve* (The Hague and Delft, 1801). See also under Du Perron & De Roos, above.

Hollandtse Mercurius, 1650–1690 (41 vols. in 8, Haarlem, 1651–91). First word of title variously spelt *Hollandtze, Hollandsche,* etc.

Huizinga, J., *Nederland's beschaving in de zeventiende eeuw. Een schets* (Haarlem, 1941).

Hullu, J. de, 'Ziekten en Doktors op de schepen der Oost-Indische Compagnie' (in *BTLVNI*, Vol. 67, 1913, pp. 245–72).

Hullu, J. de, 'De handhaving der orde en tucht op de schepen der Oost-Indische Compagnie' (in *BTLVNI*, Vol. 67, 1913, pp. 516–40).

Hullu, J. de, 'De voeding op de schepen der Oost-Indische Compagnie' (in *BTLVNI*, Vol. 67, 1913, pp. 541–62).

Hullu, J. de, 'De Matrozen en soldaten op de schepen der Oost-Indische Compagnie' (in *BTLVNI*, Vol. 69, 1914, pp. 318–65).

Jameson, J. F., *Willem Usselincx, Founder of the Dutch and Swedish West-India Companies* (New York, 1887).

Jameson, J. F. (ed. and trans.), *Narratives of New Netherland, 1609–1664* (New York, 1909, reprinted 1959).

Japikse, N., *De verwikkelingen tusschen de Republiek en Engeland, 1660–1665* (Leiden, 1900).

Japikse, N., *Johan de Witt* (Amsterdam, 1928).

Jonge, J. C. de, *Geschiedenis van het Nederlandsche Zeewezen* (5 vols., Haarlem, 1858–62).

Jonge, J. K. J. de, *De opkomst van het Nederlandsch gezag in Oost-Indië. Verzameling van onuitgegeven stukken uit het oud-koloniaal archeif* (11 vols., The Hague and Amsterdam, 1862–83).

Kaapse Argiefstukke. Kaapse Plakaatboek, 1652–1806 (6 vols., Cape Town, 1944–51). Edited by M. K. Jeffreys & S. D. Naudé.

Kernkamp, J. H., *Johan van der Verken en zijn tijd* (The Hague, 1952).

Select bibliography

Keuning, J., 'Ambonnezen, Portugezen en Nederlanders. Ambon's geschiedenis tot het einde van de zeventiende eeuw' (reprinted from *Indonesië*, Vol. IX, 1956, pp. 135–68).

Knuttel, W. P. C., *Catalogus van de pamfletten-verzameling berustende in de Koninklijke Bibliotheek* (8 vols. in 10, The Hague, 1889–1926).

Kock, Victor de, *Those in Bondage. An account of the life of the slave at the Cape in the days of the Dutch East India Company* (London, 1950).

Laet, Johannes de, *Iaerlyck Verhael van de verrichtinghen der Geoctroyeerde West-Indische Compagnie in derthien boecken* (Leiden, 1644). Quotations are taken from the 5-vol. Linschoten Vereeniging edition by S. P. L'Honoré-Naber & J. C. M. Warnsinck (The Hague, 1931–7).

Leuftink, A., *De Geneeskunde bij's Lands oorlogsvloot in de 17e eeuw* (Assen, 1953).

Leur, J. C. van, *Indonesian Trade and Society. Essays in Asian social and economic history* (The Hague, 1955).

Meilink-Roelofsz, M. A. P., *Asian Trade and European Influence in the Indonesian Archipelago between 1500 and about 1630* (The Hague, 1962).

Mentzel, O. F., *Life at the Cape in the mid-Eighteenth Century; being the biography of Rudolf Siegfried Alleman, Captain of the military forces at the Cape of Good Hope* (Cape Town, 1919).

Mentzel, O. F., *A Geographical-Topographical Description of the Cape of Good Hope* (3 vols., Cape Town, 1921–44). Publications of the Van Riebeeck Society, Vols. 2, 4, 6 and 25.

Onslow Burrish, *Batavia Illustrata: Or, a view of the policy and commerce of the United Provinces: particularly of Holland, with an enquiry into the alliances of the States General with the Emperor, France, Spain, and Great Britain* (London, 1728).

Oost-Indisch-praetjen, voorgevallen in Batavia tusschen vier Nederlanders. Den eenen een Koopman, d'ander een Krijghs-Officier, den derden een stuyrman, en den vierden of den laetsten een Kranckebesoecker (n.p., 1663). Knuttel nr. 8756.

Parival, Jean de, *Les Delices de la Hollande ... ouvrage revue, corrigé, changé et fort augmenté* (Leiden, 1662).

Perron, see Du Perron.

Poelhekke, Jan, *De Vrede van Munster* (The Hague, 1948).

Ratelband, K., *Vijf Dagregisters van het Kasteel São Jorge da Mina (Elmina) aan de Goudkust, 1645–1647* (The Hague, 1953).

Raychaudhuri, Tapan, *Jan Company in Coromandel, 1605–1690. A* study in the interrelations of European commerce and traditional economies (The Hague, 1962).

Rees, O. van, *Geschiedenis der Staathuishoudkunde in Nederland tot het einde der achttiende eeuw* (2 vols., Utrecht, 1865–8).

Renier, G. J., *The Dutch Nation. An historical study* (London, 1944).

Schoute, D., *De Geneeskunde in den dienst der Oost-Indische Compagnie in Nederlandsch-Indië* (Amsterdam, 1929).

Schrieke, Bertram, *Indonesian Sociological Studies* (2 vols., The Hague, 1955).

Slicher van Bath, B. S., *De agrarische geschiedenis van West Europa, 500–1850* (Utrecht, 1960). An English translation of this book was published after the present work had gone to press in 1963.

Snapper, Frits, *Oorlogs invloeden op de overzeese handel van Holland, 1551–1719* (Amsterdam, 1959).

Sousa Coutinho, Francisco de, *Correspondência diplomática de F. de S. C. durante a sua embaixada em Holanda, 1643–1650* (ed. E. Prestage *et al.*, 3 vols., Coimbra and Lisboa, 1920–55).

Stavorinus, Johan Splinter, *Voyages to the East Indies; by the late John Splinter Stavorinus, Esq., Rear-Admiral in the service of the States-General. Translated from the original Dutch by Samuel Hull Wilcocke, with notes and additions by the translator, the whole comprising a full and accurate account of all the present and late possessions of the Dutch in India, and at the Cape of Good Hope* (3 vols., London, 1798).

Temple, William, *Observations upon the Provinces of the United Netherlands. By Sir William Temple of Shene, in the County of Surrey, Baronet, Ambassador at the Hague, and at Aix la Chappelle in the year 1668. The third edition, corrected and augmented* (London, 1676).

Terpstra, H., *Jan van Neck, Amsterdam's admiraal en regent* (Amsterdam, 1960).

Thunberg, Carl Pieter, *Travels in Europe, Africa and Asia. Performed between the years 1770 and 1779* (4 vols., London, 1795).

Tijdschrift voor Geschiedenis (44 vols., Groningen, 1920–64). In progress.

Toit, P. S. du, *Onderwys aan die Kaap onder die Kompanjie, 1652–1795. 'N Kultur – historiese studie* (Cape Town, 1937).

Troostenburgh de Bruyn, C. A. van, *De Hervormde Kerk in Nederlandsch Oost-Indië onder de Oost-Indische Compagnie, 1602–1795* (Arnhem, 1884).

Trotter, Alice, *Old Cape Colony. A chronicle of her men and houses from 1652 to 1806* (Cape Town, 1903).

Select bibliography

Udemans, Godfried, 'T Geestelyck Roer van't Coopmans schip. Dat is: Trouw bericht hoe dat een coopman en coopvaerder, hem selven dragen moet in syne handelinge in pays ende in oorloge, voor Godt, ende de menschen, te water en te lande, insonderheyt onder de heydenen in Oost-ende West-Indien. Den derden druck, verbetert ende vermeerdert by den Autheur (Dordrecht, 1655).

Unger, W. S., 'Bijdragen tot de geschiedenis van de Nederlandse slavenhandel', articles reprinted from the Economisch-Historisch Jaarboek, Bijdragen tot de Economische Geschiedenis van Nederland, vols. 26–8 (The Hague, 1956–61).

Valentyn, François, Oud en Nieuw Oost-Indien, vervattende een naukeurige en uitvoerige verhandelinge van Nederlands mogentheyd in die gewesten (5 vols. in 8, Dordrecht & Amsterdam, 1724–6).

Vlekke, B. H. M., Evolution of the Dutch Nation (New York, 1945).

Vlekke, B. H. M., Nusantara. A History of the East Indian Archipelago (Cambridge, Mass., 1945).

Vries, Johan de, De economische achteruitgang der Republiek in de achttiende eeuw (Amsterdam, 1959).

Warnsinck, J. C. M. (ed.), Reisen van Nicolaus de Graaff gedaan naar alle gewesten des Werelds, 1637–1687 (The Hague, 1930).

Wilson, Charles, Anglo–Dutch Commerce and Finance in the Eighteenth Century (London, 1941).

Wilson, Charles, Holland and Britain (London, 1945).

Wilson, Charles, Profit and Power. A study of England and the Dutch Wars (Cambridge, 1957).

'Taxation and the decline of empires, an unfashionable theme' (BMHGU, Vol. 77, Utrecht, 1963, pp. 10–26).

Zumthor, Paul, Daily Life in Rembrandt's Holland (London, 1961).

Index

Index

FOR THE BEST IN PAPERBACKS, LOOK FOR THE

In every corner of the world, on every subject under the sun, Penguin represents quality and variety – the very best in publishing today.

For complete information about books available from Penguin – including Puffins, Penguin Classics and Arkana – and how to order them, write to us at the appropriate address below. Please note that for copyright reasons the selection of books varies from country to country.

In the United Kingdom: Please write to *Dept E.P., Penguin Books Ltd, Harmondsworth, Middlesex, UB7 0DA.*

If you have any difficulty in obtaining a title, please send your order with the correct money, plus ten per cent for postage and packaging, to *PO Box No 11, West Drayton, Middlesex*

In the United States: Please write to *Dept BA, Penguin, 299 Murray Hill Parkway, East Rutherford, New Jersey 07073*

In Canada: Please write to *Penguin Books Canada Ltd, 2801 John Street, Markham, Ontario L3R 1B4*

In Australia: Please write to the *Marketing Department, Penguin Books Australia Ltd, P.O. Box 257, Ringwood, Victoria 3134*

In New Zealand: Please write to the *Marketing Department, Penguin Books (NZ) Ltd, Private Bag, Takapuna, Auckland 9*

In India: Please write to *Penguin Overseas Ltd, 706 Eros Apartments, 56 Nehru Place, New Delhi, 110019*

In the Netherlands: Please write to *Penguin Books Netherlands B.V., Postbus 195, NL–1380AD Weesp*

In West Germany: Please write to *Penguin Books Ltd, Friedrichstrasse 10–12, D–6000 Frankfurt/Main 1*

In Spain: Please write to *Alhambra Longman S.A., Fernandez de la Hoz 9, E–28010 Madrid*

In Italy: Please write to *Penguin Italia s.r.l., Via Como 4, I-20096 Pioltello (Milano)*

In France: Please write to *Penguin Books Ltd, 39 Rue de Montmorency, F-75003 Paris*

In Japan: Please write to *Longman Penguin Japan Co Ltd, Yamaguchi Building, 2–12–9 Kanda Jimbocho, Chiyoda-Ku, Tokyo 101*

PENGUIN POLITICS AND SOCIAL SCIENCES

Political Ideas David Thomson (ed.)

From Machiavelli to Marx – a stimulating and informative introduction to the last 500 years of European political thinkers and political thought.

On Revolution Hannah Arendt

Arendt's classic analysis of a relatively recent political phenomenon examines the underlying principles common to all revolutions, and the evolution of revolutionary theory and practice. 'Never dull, enormously erudite, always imaginative' – *Sunday Times*

Ill Fares the Land Susan George

These twelve essays expand on one of the major themes of Susan George's work: the role of power in perpetuating world hunger. With characteristic commitment and conviction, the author of *A Fate Worse than Debt* and *How the Other Half Dies* demonstrates that just as poverty lies behind hunger, so injustice and inequality lie behind poverty.

The Social Construction of Reality Peter Berger and Thomas Luckmann

Concerned with the sociology of 'everything that passes for knowledge in society' and particularly with that which passes for common sense, this is 'a serious, open-minded book, upon a serious subject' – *Listener*

The Care of the Self Michel Foucault
The History of Sexuality Vol 3

Foucault examines the transformation of sexual discourse from the Hellenistic to the Roman world in an inquiry which 'bristles with provocative insights into the tangled liaison of sex and self' – *The Times Higher Education Supplement*

Silent Spring Rachel Carson

'What we have to face is not an occasional dose of poison which has accidentally got into some article of food, but a persistent and continuous poisoning of the whole human environment.' First published in 1962, *Silent Spring* remains the classic environmental statement which founded an entire movement.

Adam, Eve and the Serpent   Elaine Pagels

How is it that the early Church, advocate of individual free will, came to preach the doctrine of original sin and to regard sexual desire as the inherent and shameful enslavement of humanity? This paradox is explored by the author of *The Gnostic Gospels*.

Islam in the World   Malise Ruthven

This informed and informative book places the contemporary Islamic revival in context, providing a fascinating introduction – the first of its kind – to Islamic origins, beliefs, history, geography, politics and society.

The Orthodox Church   Timothy Ware

In response to increasing interest among western Christians, and believing that a thorough understanding of Orthodoxy is necessary if the Roman Catholic and Protestant Churches are to be reunited, Timothy Ware explains Orthodox views on a vast range of matters from Free Will to the Papacy.

Judaism   Isidore Epstein

The comprehensive account of Judaism as a religion and as a distinctive way of life, presented against a background of 4,000 years of Jewish history.

Mysticism   F. C. Happold

What is mysticism? This simple and illuminating book combines a study of mysticism with an illustrative anthology of mystical writings, ranging from Plato and Plotinus to Dante.

The Penguin History of the Church: 4   Gerald R. Cragg
The Church and the Age of Reason

Gerald Cragg's elegant and stimulating assessment of the era from the Peace of Westphalia to the French Revolution – a formative period in the Church's history – ranges from the Church life of France under Louis XIV to the high noon of rationalism and beyond.

Archaeology and Language The Puzzle of Indo-European Origins
Colin Renfrew

'His most important and far-reaching book: the pace is exhilarating, the issues are momentous ... *Archaeology and Language* breaks new ground by bringing the findings of the two sciences back into relationship more successfully than any other scholar in this century ... We have come a long step closer towards understanding human origins' – Peter Levi in the *Independent*

The Dead Sea Scrolls in English G. Vermes

This established and authoritative English translation of the non-biblical Qumran scrolls – offering a revolutionary insight into Palestinian Jewish life and ideology at a crucial period in the development of Jewish and Christian religious thought – now includes the Temple Scroll, the most voluminous scroll of them all.

Hadrian's Wall David J. Breeze and Brian Dobson

A penetrating history of the best-known, best-preserved and most spectacular monument to the Roman Empire in Britain. 'A masterpiece of the controlled use of archaeological and epigraphical evidence in a fluent narrative that will satisfy any level of interest' – *The Times Educational Supplement*

Before Civilization The Radiocarbon Revolution and Prehistoric Europe
Colin Renfrew

'I have little doubt that this is one of the most important archaeological books for a very long time' – Barry Cunliffe in the *New Scientist*. 'Pure stimulation from beginning to end ... a book which provokes thought, aids understanding, and above all is immensely enjoyable' – *Scotsman*

The Ancient Civilizations of Peru J. Alden Mason

The archaeological, historical, artistic, geographical and ethnographical discoveries that have resurrected the rich variety of Inca and pre-Inca culture and civilization – wiped out by the Spanish Conquest – are surveyed in this now classic work.

FOR THE BEST IN PAPERBACKS, LOOK FOR THE

PENGUIN HISTORY

The Victorian Underworld Kellow Chesney

A superbly evocative survey of the vast substratum of vice that lay below the respectable surface of Victorian England – the showmen, religious fakes, pickpockets and prostitutes – and of the penal methods of that 'most enlightened age'. 'Charged with nightmare detail' – *Sunday Times*

Citizens Simon Schama

The award-winning chronicle of the French Revolution. 'The most marvellous book I have read about the French Revolution in the last fifty years' – Richard Cobb in *The Times*. 'He has chronicled the vicissitudes of that world with matchless understanding, wisdom, pity and truth, in the pages of this huge and marvellous book' – *Sunday Times*

Stalin Isaac Deutscher

'The Greatest Genius in History' and the 'Life-Giving Force of Socialism'? Or a tyrant more ruthless than Ivan the Terrible whose policies facilitated the rise of Nazism? An outstanding biographical study of a revolutionary despot by a great historian.

Jasmin's Witch Emmanuel Le Roy Ladurie

An investigation into witchcraft and magic in south-west France during the seventeenth century – a masterpiece of historical detective work by the bestselling author of *Montaillou*.

The Second World War A J P Taylor

A brilliant and detailed illustrated history, enlivened by all Professor Taylor's customary iconoclasm and wit.

Industry and Empire E. J. Hobsbawm

Volume 3 of the *Penguin Economic History of Britain* covers the period of the Industrial Revolution: 'the most fundamental transformation in the history of the world recorded in written documents.' 'A book that attracts and deserves attention ... by far the most gifted historian now writing' – John Vaizey in the *Listener*